# GERRY ADAMS

# Hope and History

## MAKING PEACE IN IRELAND

BRANDON

First published in Britain and Ireland in 2003
by
Brandon
an imprint of Mount Eagle Publications
Unit 3 Olympia Trading Estate, Coburg Road, London N22 6TZ, England
and Dingle, Co. Kerry, Ireland

ISBN 0 86322 317 6

10 9 8 7 6 5 4 3 2 1

The lines from *The Cure at Troy* by Seamus Heaney are reproduced by kind permission of the author.

Cover design by id communications, Tralee
Cover photograph: AP/RN
Typesetting by Red Barn Publishing, Skeagh, Skibbereen
Printed and bound in the United Kingdom

# Contents

Acknowledgements ix

Introduction 1

The Hunger Strikes 4

The Sagart 13

First, Tentative Steps 26

The Anglo-Irish Agreement 34

Searching for a Breakthrough 41

The Battle of the Funerals 49

Murder on the Rock 57

John Hume Plays His Part 75

The Killing of Pat Finucane 84

The End of the Thatcher Era 92

Early Ceasefires 100

British Pre-conditions 115

President Robinson Comes to Belfast 125

The Downing Street Declaration 136

Americans for a New Irish Agenda 151

Party Conferences 162

A Space for Hope 174

America Again 184

Seizing the Moment 196

Major Mistakes 203

My Hero, Nelson Mandela 213

President Clinton on the Falls Road 230

Towards All-Party Talks 240

"Putting It Up to a Bully" 254

Talks at Last 265

Barred from the Mother of Parliaments 279

"Nothing But the Same Old Story"                    290
A New Ceasefire                                      295
To Castle Buildings                                  302
Meeting Tony Blair                                   312
Progress – and Setbacks                              327
The Good Friday Agreement                            343
Unfinished Business                                  369
Epilogue                                             377
Glossary                                             389
Biographies                                          391
Index                                                394

Human beings suffer.
They torture one another.
They get hurt and get hard.
No poem or play or song
Can fully right a wrong
Inflicted and endured.

History says, Don't hope
On this side of the grave,
But then, once in a lifetime
The longed-for tidal wave
Of justice can rise up
And hope and history rhyme.

So hope for a great sea-change
On the far side of revenge.
Believe that a farther shore
Is reachable from here.
Believe in miracles
And cures and healing wells.

From "The Cure at Troy"
by Seamus Heaney

*Do Dhrithle le grá*

# *Acknowledgements*

This book would not have been written without the help of Richard McAuley, who read reams of records of meetings, minutes, letters and other documents, and gave up a huge amount of his time to dredge up texts, check dates and research other information. I am grateful to him and to Chrissie who tolerated it all. Siobhán O'Hanlon is the keeper of the records who diligently collected and filed every possible piece of documentation in the period following the opening of Sinn Féin's dialogue with the British government until recent times. *Tá mé buíoch díot, a Shiobhán.*

Others shared their memories of the time. Without Fr Alec Reid and Fr Des Wilson there would not have been an Irish peace process at this time. Martin McGuinness, Pádraig Wilson, Dawn Doyle read my first draft; I am still waiting on responses from them. Rita O'Hare had her say; so did Mitchell and Ted and Pat Doherty. Any mistakes which may have slipped through are entirely their fault. Through Rita's good offices Niall O'Dowd, and Eric and Mark in *An Phoblacht* supplied me with bits and pieces.

Steve MacDonogh first published my writing in 1982; I am grateful for his editorial guidance and for his patience with this tome as it grew in size and missed a few deadlines in the process. My thanks to Steve, Máire, Siobhán, Terry and everyone at Brandon.

My thanks also to my friends and comrades and to everyone else who tolerated me at a very busy time in our lives as I got this story out of my system. A special word of thanks to the Sinn Féin negotiating team and to everyone who helped us; to Big Eamonn who looked after me since after I was shot through many miles of struggle. Thanks also to all the republicans and nationalists who had faith in us and in themselves, and to our allies throughout the world.

Special thanks to that generation of republicans in Ireland, the United States, Britain, Australia and elsewhere, who laboured in the lean years and kept faith through dark days. These men and women are personified by Joe Cahill. There are many people of my generation whose names I do not mention. Every one of them contributed to this story, and they have their own place in it and their own version of it. To have named everyone who contributed would require a telephone book. I thank them all.

Many discussions occurred in the homes of citizens, republicans who gave our team the use of their bedrooms or back kitchens. Not the most conducive conditions for Sinn Féin's decision-making process but better than our electronically monitored offices or other facilities. I thank them also.

In the course of the period relived in these pages many comrades and friends were killed. I regret that I cannot mention them all. They have been with us in all of our dealings with the British government. I extend solidarity to all their families.

Others have died since, some of natural causes. Again, these are too numerous to mention, but Mary Hughes, Tom Cahill and Terence "Cleaky" Clarke were big influences in our struggle and in my life.

Finally, to Colette who continues to put up with me and to Gearóid and Róisín and Drithle for much happiness and even more dirty dishes. *Míle buíochas agus grá daoibh.*

Gerry Adams,
Belfast, Ireland
August 2003

# Introduction

Sometimes I go to the edge of the world: to the north-west of Ireland, where on dark, clear nights the skyscape stretches for ever. I'm there now, trying to figure out how to tell the story of the Irish peace process. Here on the edge of Europe, a huge expanse of ocean stretches in front of me to New York and the Americas. Inland, at my back, across rugged mountain ranges lies the road to Belfast. Beyond, separated from Ireland by a narrow sound of water, is Britain.

Sitting here now, reflecting on all that has passed, my mind is crowded with memories, with different and conflicting emotions. How do I make sense of all of this so that it becomes your sense? It's difficult to absorb all that has happened. The reader may think that people close to these events have a sense of what's happening, but that's not always the case.

For example, an image has remained with me of a friend of mine, Jim Gibney, in the days after he was released from prison after serving a six-year prison sentence. This was around March 1988 – the month three unarmed IRA volunteers were shot dead by undercover British troops in Gibraltar. When they were being buried some days later in Belfast's Milltown Cemetery, there was a loyalist attack on the mourners at the gravesides. Three people were killed and scores were injured. A day or two later, at one of these funerals, two armed undercover British soldiers who drove into the cortège were seized by the crowd and shot dead by the IRA.

This maelstrom of events – from the killings at Gibraltar, through the long journey home of the remains, the Milltown Cemetery killings and the subsequent killings of the two British soldiers – were among the most frightening, dramatic, tragic episodes of the recent past.

In the course of the attacks, of the panic, the fear, the noise, the screams, the colour, the scariness of it all, Gib's presence sticks out. Days before, he had the exhilaration of release from prison. To be pitched into this madness from the relative sanctuary of a prison cell – that was his reality. Those who died during those days died in a different reality, and those who killed them had their own reality as well.

1

All around us – skirting the pandemonium, the killing, the dying – buses and cars whizzed by, people got on with their lives. If you could have lifted yourself high above the scene, you could have witnessed the whole picture. In the eye of it, you could see only what was immediate to you.

So why with all else that was happening is it the image of Gib that stays in my mind? Maybe because I thought it was worse for him than for the rest of us. But was it?

In telling the story of the Irish peace process, I can only tell my experience of it, my understanding of it, my role in it. It is not my business to offer an objective account of events or to see through someone else's eyes. Nor is it my responsibility to document these events. My intention is to tell a story. It is my story. My truth. My reality.

My task is to connect this small-picture perspective to a big-picture screen. In trying to write a personal narrative from inside the process, I want also to make sense to the reader standing outside of it.

I say it is my story, but, of course, it's only my version, *my truth*. I don't say it will be the full story. Here at the beginning it is impossible to see how this tale will unfold. Even as I pen these words, the story is still unfolding, still sensitive, still fragile. A happy ending – finally, eventually – is, it seems to me, more important than a tell-all story now.

The story involved is specific: it is personal, it is individual. It is a personal journey, but it is also communal. It is the story of a process which affects not only those who are directly involved.

The process affects all who live on the islands of Ireland and Britain. Looking back on the changes involved, it is worth noting that they occurred and were influenced by a world that was also in transition. The road to the end of apartheid in South Africa; the re-unification of Germany; the attempt to modernise and the eventual collapse of the USSR; the end of the cold war; the beginning and the end more recently of a peace process in the Middle East.

Getting to an agreement was difficult enough. Getting that agreement implemented and resolving the consequences of an unprecedented phase of conflict involving the IRA, British forces and their allies within Irish loyalism is a mighty task indeed. Can a peace process deal with all of this? Clearly that is the hope of those who want it to succeed. Or will the peace process collapse? That is the intention of those who are against the changes that are required.

But what of the story which has evolved thus far? Where do I start to recount that? Where do I begin to tell my tale?

Perhaps by introducing myself. My name is Gerry Adams. My life began in 1948 in the city called Belfast on the island called Ireland. Belfast is the second city of this island, but it holds less than half a million souls. I have lived here all my life. Belfast is a fine city. Its greatest asset is its people. But for all our fine points, we Belfast people are divided in our loyalties and subjected on this account to great difficulties. The last thirty years or so have been very cruel years. I have survived them. So far. Many others have not. Friends. Enemies. People I knew well. Others I did not know. It is a wonder to me that we have come through it all.

# Chapter One

## *The Hunger Strikes*

Belfast is where this story begins. I returned there from Long Kesh after completing two prison sentences, which had kicked in when internment ended in 1975. My prison sentences arose from my failure to escape from internment. Poetic justice. When the rest of the internees were released, a handful of us wannabe Steve McQueens were kept behind at Her Majesty's pleasure. Who says the British establishment doesn't have a sense of humour? It is enough to make you cry. I cried all the way from the no-jury Diplock court. When all the rest of the internees were back home with their friends and families, me and the rest of our motley crew were transported back to Long Kesh, all trussed up like individually wrapped turkeys in the tiny claustrophobic compartments of a heavily armoured paddy wagon. Internment was dead. Long live internment.

My next few years were spent in Cage Eleven. When I was released from there in 1977, the Belfast I returned to was a different place from the one I had been scooped – arrested – in. For one thing I was "free". But I had decided not to live in our home. It was too dangerous. I also wanted to continue with the work which internment had interrupted. But I had a wife and a young son waiting for me. Colette had prepared a good home for us in my absence. Gearóid, who had been born months after my arrest in 1972, was now over four years old. Our time together so far had been limited to the prison visits. We had a lot of catching up to do.

Many of our friends were working. One dear comrade offered me night shift work in the local bakery. That way, he reasoned, I could continue with my republican work during the day and earn a few pounds for my family during the night. A baker by night, a revolutionary by day. And the dough was good, he said. It is a testament to Colette's steadiness that she put up with me during this period.

I plunged back into politics. I also renewed my relationship with my

4

cousin Kevin Hannaway, with whom I was very close prior to my imprisonment. The Hannaways were one of Belfast's spinal republican families, particularly in the Clonard area. Kevin was a republican activist, arrested and tortured by the British army following the introduction of internment. He and a handful of others – known as the guinea pigs – were subjected to inhuman and degrading treatment, sensory deprivation and ill-treatment over a protracted period. Following his release from Long Kesh, Kevin and his wife and family lived in Clonard, also home to the monastery where the Redemptorist Order was based in West Belfast. It was where Fr Alec Reid lived.

I met him on the first Easter Sunday after my release when, at my request, he intervened to negotiate an end to the inter-republican feuds in Belfast. Our friendship grew from then. Fr Des Wilson worked with Fr Reid on that initiative. I have known Fr Des since 1969. Both these men were deeply committed to living the gospel message and to making it relevant to the particular circumstances in which they ministered.

They had different relationships with the institutional Church. Fr Des was a Belfast man, from the Ormeau Road. Ordained in 1949, before becoming a priest in my home parish of St John's in 1966 he had been a staff member and the spiritual director for a decade and a half in St Malachy's College, one of Belfast's main Catholic grammar schools. The move from comfortable middle-class academia to disadvantaged, deprived working-class reality was to have a profound effect on him. It soon brought him into dispute with the Church authorities over the use of Church resources. He resigned from clerical positions and founded Springhill Community House Education Development Project in 1972. He went on from there to be involved in a range of progressive community, educational, economic and anti-sectarian projects. Fr Des was now more or less his own man.

Fr Alec Reid also had more freedom than most priests because he belonged to an order – the Congregation of the Most Holy Redeemer, popularly known as the Redemptorists – which fully supported the work he was doing. The Redemptorists' mission is to "preach the values and the blessings of the Christian Gospel to people everywhere but particularly to the poor, the marginalised and the downtrodden". He was ordained in 1962 and three years later was appointed to Clonard Monastery.

From 1969 and throughout the intervening years of conflict, the Sagart (the Irish word for priest), as Fr Reid came to be called by all of us, was constantly involved in peace-making ministries. The objective of these was

5

to give comfort and support to the people living at the coalface of the violence; helping prisoners and their families; and promoting understanding and reconciliation between the people of Belfast. Another ministry was to foster dialogue and friendship between the separated Christians of Belfast, a cause he took especially to heart, working tirelessly to move the conflict off the streets and on to the conference table.

In the wake of the 1977 inter-republican feuding, Fr Reid and Fr Des succeeded in establishing an arbitration and mediation process between different republican organisations. The two also spent an enormous amount of time in seeking to engage with others in the Churches, in the British and Irish political establishments, and among loyalists, in efforts to find a way to end the violence.

Fr Alec came to public attention in 1988 when he administered the last rites to two armed undercover British soldiers, Derek Wood and David Howes, who were killed by the IRA after being seized by mourners when they drove into the funeral of IRA volunteer Caoimhín MacBradaigh. This quiet, unassuming pastor's photograph was flashed worldwide as he knelt by the almost naked, bloody body of one of the dying soldiers spread-eagled on waste ground in West Belfast.

Republicans' affinity with the Church at a time when all Catholics were deemed to be legitimate targets by loyalist death squads is entirely understandable. But during the civil rights struggle in the 1960s, there was no Archbishop Tutu or Bishop Romero to publicly campaign for people's rights, and in a changing Ireland the relationship between people and the Church changed. Strictures and denunciations from Church leaders were not only disregarded but were contested, particularly by younger people. The failure of the hierarchy to meet the challenges of that period may be excusable, but the elitist and judgmental attitude taken against members of their own flock at a time of great upheaval and trauma – following, for example, the pogroms of 1969 or the curfews and state killings by British state forces – was deeply hurtful and disturbing for some people. It radicalised many of them.

I tended to see the failings of the institutionalised Church as human failings. Spirituality or fundamental Christianity, or indeed any of the great religions, have at their core a belief in human dignity and human rights. Christians have no monopoly on that. Neither does any particular Christian denomination. Sometimes that simple observation is lost among all the man-made rules and regulations which bind up human institutions like the Catholic Church.

Priests are only human too, of course. Many of them were ill-equipped or unready for the upheavals that took place in Ireland – particularly in the North of Ireland – from the late 1960s onwards. The tendency of the Church was to control people, not to liberate them.

In the late 1970s, the Sagart and Fr Des were heavily involved in prison work. The conditions in the women's prison at Armagh, where at that time around thirty-two women were incarcerated, were dreadful. The prison conditions in the H-Blocks of Long Kesh were even worse. Five hundred men were on a blanket protest. They had been refused the right to wear their own clothes, unlike other republican prisoners in another part of Long Kesh. The removal of political status by the British government was part of their strategy to criminalise the overall political struggle.

The prison element of this strategy commenced in 1976. Prisoners convicted of offences after March 1976 were denied political status. They refused to accept that they were criminals and refused to wear the prison uniform. This led to their being denied routine facilities and the right to exercise, to reading material, to association and so on. With only a blanket to cover them, the bulk of these prisoners, known as the blanket men, were held in solitary confinement. As more and more were convicted in the special non-jury courts, the prison administration put two men to a cell. The blanket men were subject to constant harassment and beatings, and eventually their toilet facilities were withdrawn from them. The contents of chamber pots were thrown on to prisoners' beds by prison warders. The prisoners responded by refusing to shave, wash or empty chamber pots. All furniture was then removed from the cells by the Long Kesh administration.

In February 1978, I was back in prison again. After a particularly horrific IRA bombing at the La Mon Hotel in which twelve people were killed, there was a round-up of Belfast republicans. I was among them. I wasn't questioned at all about the La Mon bombing. All my interrogation was about Sinn Féin activities. After seven days' detention, I was charged with IRA membership. I was held for seven months and then, after a fiasco of a trial, the charges were dismissed. My solicitor P.J. McGrory's submission that I had no case to answer won the day, setting an important legal precedent.

I spent part of my imprisonment in the H-Blocks of Long Kesh, where I joined the protestors on the remand wing. I also met with some of the blanket men whom I knew from Cage 11. I was shocked by the conditions they were living under and the extent of the brutality by the

7

administration. I came out of prison determined to change that. We reorganised the Sinn Féin POW department and formed a small committee to concentrate on the prisoners' issues.

We moved to provide a more effective lobbying support for the prisoners. They were persuaded to adopt five demands, which expressed in a humanitarian way the substance of the conditions they required. Our objective was, on the one hand, to try and make it easier for the British government to move, while at the same time opening the prison issue up for support from a broader range of people. It was from these initiatives that the prisoners' campaign, organised mainly by family members in the Relatives' Action Committees, moved into a broad front phase with the establishment of the H-Block/Armagh Committee.

At that time, Cardinal Ó Fiaich was the head of the Catholic Church in Ireland. He was a popular Church leader, scholarly but down-to-earth and close to his native South Armagh roots. It was Fr Reid who suggested that we meet with Cardinal Ó Fiaich on the prison issue, and myself, Fr Des, Danny Morrison and Kevin Hannaway travelled regularly to Ara Coeli – the Primate's residence in Armagh – to discuss the situation. The Cardinal informed the British Secretary of State Humphrey Atkins of these meetings and tried to mediate a resolution of the prison protest.

In August 1978, Cardinal Ó Fiaich visited the H-Blocks at our request. After the visit he said: "One could hardly allow an animal to remain in such conditions, let alone a human being. The nearest approach to it that I have ever seen was the spectacle of hundreds of homeless people living in the sewer pipes of the slums of Calcutta. The stench and the filth in some of the cells with the remains of rotten food and human excreta scattered around the walls was almost unbearable. The authorities refused to admit that these prisoners are in a different category from the ordinary, yet everything about their trials and family background indicates that they are different . . . The problem of these prisoners is one of the great obstacles to peace in our community. As long as it continues it will be a potent cause of resentment in the prisoners themselves, breeding frustration among their relatives and friends and leading to bitterness between the prisoners and prison staff. It is only sowing the seeds of future conflict."

The Cardinal's public intervention was the first major breakthrough on the prisoners issue. It occurred against the background of ongoing conflict and at a time during which the British government was pushing ahead with its other counter-insurgency strategies.

Sinn Féin was also being radically overhauled by the leadership at that time, led by Ruairí Ó Brádaigh. We were reviewing our attitude to a wide range of issues, debating and discussing ways to make political advances. Speaking at the annual Bodenstown commemoration at the graveside of republican Wolfe Tone, I acknowledged that "Our most glaring weakness to date lies in our failure to develop revolutionary politics and to build a strong political alternative to so-called constitutional politics."

The revamped prisoners' campaign intensified its outreach, publicity and street campaigning. Despite all the efforts, public and private, the British government remained unmoved. In October 1980, the first hunger strike commenced. The prisoners had canvassed the possibility of such a departure for some time. It was mainly pushed by some of the older or more experienced men, like Bobby Sands and Brendan Hughes. The Sagart was close to both of them and was visiting them in their cells very often. Brendan Hughes was the Officer Commanding (OC) of the prisoners at that time. He became the leader of the first hunger strike and Bobby Sands replaced him as OC.

Fr Reid was devastated by the commencement of the first hunger strike. He had lobbied ferociously for an end to the dispute. He wrote reams of letters, including a number of appeals to the British authorities. Not long after the beginning of the first hunger strike, he took seriously ill. The stress of trying and failing to get a resolution to this issue took its toll, and the Sagart was moved by his superiors out of Belfast. I used to visit Fr Reid in a Drogheda hospital. On one occasion Colette and I found him in a very distressed state as the health of the hunger strikers deteriorated. Paradoxically, while the plight of the prisoners and their families and the ongoing conflict continued to wear him down, he took great comfort from the messages of support that the imprisoned men smuggled out to him.

The Sagart was almost a year out of commission – an awful year for all of us. The first hunger strike ended just before Christmas. By then three women prisoners in Armagh and the seven men in the H-Blocks had been joined by thirty more H-Block prisoners. The condition of one of the original seven, Sean McKenna, deteriorated quickly.

With the commencement of the hunger strike, the British government opened up contact with republicans. Through a contact in the British Foreign Office – code-named "Mountain Climber" – a channel of communication that had been used during the 1974 IRA/British government truce was reactivated. Fr Reid's role had been filled by another Redemptorist priest, Fr Brendan Meagher. The British said they wanted

9

a settlement of the issues underpinning the protest and committed to setting out the details in a document to be presented to all of the prisoners formally and publicly after they came off hunger strike.

"Mountain Climber" brought the document to Fr Meagher, who delivered it to Clonard Monastery where I and a few people who were assisting the prisoners were waiting for him. As he was briefing us, Tom Hartley, the head of our POW department, burst into the room where we were meeting to tell us that the hunger strike was over in the Blocks.

Sean McKenna's condition had continued to deteriorate. As the leader of the hunger strike and knowing that a document was on its way, Brendan Hughes had intervened in order to save Sean's life. The women in Armagh ended their fast later when they got news of the H-Blocks' decision.

In this new situation, without the pressure of a hunger strike to focus them, the British moved away from their commitments and from the document. The channel of communication was once more closed down. The prisoners were furious. Bobby Sands had wanted to recommence the fast almost immediately after there was evidence of British duplicity. We persuaded him to hang on. He manfully tried to work with the prison administration to find a way through the difficulties.

But someone somehow somewhere within the British system had decided that the prisoners were defeated. This was best illustrated by Prime Minister Margaret Thatcher on a visit to Belfast on 28 May when she declared that the hunger strike "may well be their [the IRA's] last card". A sensible, more strategic administration would have kept to its commitments and defused the prison issue by building a settlement. But the stakes were very high. This had never been solely a prison dispute.

Criminalisation was but one element in an integrated British strategy. The prison was the battlefield because the British system was intent on making it the breaker's yard for the republican struggle. They were intent on defeating that struggle, not on finding a political and peaceful settlement.

So despite all our efforts, despite the Herculean efforts of Bobby Sands and his comrades, the die was cast. In March of 1981, the second hunger strike commenced. It was led by Bobby. When it ended eight months later, on 3 October, ten hunger strikers were dead. Bobby Sands had been the first to die on 5 May. He was followed over the following four summer months up to August by Francis Hughes, Raymond McCreesh, Patsy O'Hara, Joe McDonnell, Martin Hurson, Kevin Lynch, Kieran Doherty, Thomas McElwee and Micky Devine.

Almost fifty others were killed on the streets, including seven killed by plastic bullets. Three of these were children: Paul Whitters, aged fifteen, Julie Livingstone, aged fourteen and Carol Anne Kelly, aged twelve; one was a thirty-year mother, Nora McCabe. They and Henry Duffy, aged forty-five, Peter Doherty, aged thirty-one and Peter Magennis, aged forty-one, all died in controversial circumstances in which their killers in the RUC and British army clearly breached the guidelines for the use of these lethal weapons.

The plastic bullet was a weapon of control and intimidation. In an effort to frighten the tens of the thousands who were marching that summer in support of the hunger strikers, the British Crown forces used these weapons indiscriminately and in huge numbers. Hundreds were seriously wounded, many crippled and scarred for life. May 1981 saw more plastic bullets fired – 16,656 – than in the previous eight years. Altogether almost 30,000 plastic bullets were used in 1981.

Another among those to die was fourteen-year-old Desmond Guiney, a Protestant teenager who died with his father Eric on 7 May, in the street rioting that took place after Bobby Sands died. The youngster was helping his father deliver milk when their lorry was stoned by rioters on the New Lodge Road in North Belfast and went out of control, crashing into a lamp-post.

The events of that awful summer of 1981 polarised Irish society, North and South.

The prisoners were perceived to be the soft underbelly of the republican struggle. The British thought they could be isolated, beaten, intimidated and coerced into accepting the label of criminal. But republican prisoners are political prisoners – men and women of conviction, commitment and determination. The H-Block and Armagh prisoners resisted. They endured horrendous conditions and bore great physical cruelty with fortitude and courage. At the end, when no other course of action was open to them, they went on hunger strike in defence of their integrity as republican political prisoners, in defence of this republican struggle, in defence of their comrades in the prison and to assert their humanity.

None of this was part of any clever republican plan or strategy. It was at its core a very individual response by prisoners in Armagh women's prison and in the H-Blocks of Long Kesh. When Kieran Nugent, the first republican to be sentenced after March 1976, refused to wear prison clothing, he was soon joined by other republicans. Of course, they were

11

responding to a British strategy, authorised at the highest level of the British establishment. But on a personal and individual basis, whether in the blocks or in Armagh prison, the prisoners were instinctively following Kieran's defiant assertion, "If they want me to wear a criminal uniform, they will have to nail it to my back." And that is exactly what the prison authorities tried to do.

In the course of the hunger strike, Bobby Sands was elected as MP for Fermanagh and South Tyrone in the North. In the South of Ireland other hunger strikers were elected. The hunger strike had a particular impact there. It raised a fundamental moral question about the role of the South in Britain's war in Ireland. It made a political impact that shook the system to its foundations. It was not just the fact that one hunger striker, Kieran Doherty, was elected TD for Cavan/Monaghan. Or that another prisoner, Paddy Agnew, was elected TD for Louth, and other prisoners, including Joe McDonnell and Mairéad Farrell, attracted substantial electoral support. It was the fact that the hunger strike unmasked the unwillingness of the South's political establishment to do anything for the hunger strikers, or indeed do anything to challenge British rule in a part of Ireland.

The stories of the hunger strikes have been told elsewhere. For those of us who were part of that period, it is hard to imagine that it was over twenty years ago. It is as if it were yesterday. How do you explain the hunger strikes? You can't. How do you come to terms with what happened? It is impossible. It can be understood only if we appreciate the incorruptibility and unselfishness and generosity of the human spirit when that spirit is motivated by an ideal or an objective greater than itself.

People are not born as heroes. The hunger strikers were ordinary men who in extraordinary circumstances brought the struggle to a moral platform which became a battle between them and the entire might of the British state. In the course of their protest, the hunger strikers smashed the British policy of criminalisation. Today, years later, it is clear to me that their legacy is still unfolding. The idealism of the hunger strikers and the other prisoners in the Blocks and Armagh remains an example to republicans, even those who were only children during that terrible time.

# Chapter Two

# *The Sagart*

The Sagart was out of circulation during the period of the hunger strike. Throughout those dreadful months he slowly got better, first in the South of Ireland, then in Rome where he went for a break. The Sagart enjoyed Rome, delighted in wandering through the city and eventually finding his way back to the Redemptorist House at nightfall. One day he was wandering blissfully across St Peter's Square, reflecting on how different this was from Belfast with its daily bombing attacks and intermittent gun battles. As he tried to get closer to where the Holy Father John Paul II's procession was passing, an armed man dashed forward close to the Sagart and shot the Pope.

The poor Sagart went to Rome for a break from the war in Belfast, only to walk into an ambush on his boss, in St Peter's Square of all places. In a state of some understandable shock and concern for the Pope's well-being, he then made the mistake of recounting his experiences to friends back home. It was a story that was to be told and retold with suitable irreverence in typical black Belfast style for years after that.

It wasn't until July of the following year that the Sagart was allowed to return to Ireland, but on condition that he didn't come North. His superiors were afraid that his fragile health could be undermined if he was allowed to become re-involved in his previous activities.

The Sagart, like everyone else closely involved, took the hunger strikes personally. He knew all or most of the hunger strikers. He knew their families. He felt strongly that the prison dispute should have been settled long before it ever got to a protest. He felt even more strongly now that the Church had a responsibility to use its influence to resolve the causes of the conflict. He was determined to persuade his superiors to allow him to return to his work at Clonard. Eventually they relented.

He and I resumed our discussions. There were lots of issues. The war was continuing with intensity. The British system, despite the defeat of the criminalisation policy, continued to push ahead with the strategies it had developed in the 1970s.

The IRA was back with a vengeance also. The tolerance and support for armed actions among sections of nationalist opinion were considerably widened and deepened by the hunger strikes. Armed activity intensified after this watershed period.

The propaganda battle also intensified – especially from the Irish establishment, including the Catholic Church. I publicly challenged this. I felt that no one in a position of power had the right to criticise physical force republicans without criticising British militarism as well. More importantly, they had to face up to the need to develop an alternative means or method of struggle.

Fr Reid and Fr Wilson continued to argue strongly that a way out of conflict could be found if the Catholic Church would take the lead in developing a conflict-resolution process. It was they, and particularly Fr Reid, who encouraged me to privately develop the ideas which I had been debating publicly with the bishops. I was mindful of the Sagart's recent illness, but his deep-rooted desire to see beyond the violent morass into which the conflict had fallen was apparent.

I became engaged in a public debate with the Catholic hierarchy, in particular with Bishop Cahal Daly, over the Church's failure to play a leadership role in issues of justice. I had not great confidence that the bishops could be brought to the position advocated by my two friends. Unlike Churches elsewhere – for example, in South Africa or Latin America – the Church leaders in Ireland, not least the Catholic hierarchy, were conservative and, in some cases, detached from the most disadvantaged sections of the people. But I felt that they had no special right to preach on these matters in a one-sided way – especially when they were not engaged in finding another way forward. I was also politically driven to challenge those who I thought were pursuing by accident or design an anti-republican agenda.

Discussions within Sinn Féin involved all of these issues. The hunger strikes – particularly the popular mobilisations in support of the prisoners and the electoral interventions North and South – accelerated the process of political strategising within the party. This was further boosted when Owen Carron, Bobby Sands's election agent, was elected for Sinn Féin to the Fermanagh/South Tyrone seat with an increased majority.

The hunger strikes had radicalised Irish society in the South, as well as in the North, and at popular level throughout nationalist Ireland British policy was being criticised and scrutinised. The national question was again centre stage. Republicanism was finding a new popularity, which was crucially important for the development and growth of Sinn Féin. As we searched for the ideas and policies to guide the direction we should take, one thing quickly became apparent: we needed to engage with our opponents in debate on these matters. As I continued my dialogue with the Sagart, I realised that this was especially the case on the issue of peace. Our opponents had hijacked the word peace. Republicans needed to reclaim it. For too long, others had used the word peace in a narrow political way to attack republicans. What was peace: was it merely the absence of war? What caused peace? How could it be achieved? What was justice? Could there be peace without justice? Could we find common ground with our opponents? Was there an alternative?

I was prepared therefore to work with the Sagart and Fr Des and to contribute to their endeavours. This was as much to challenge the Church leaders as anything else. Although I would have been happy to be wrong, I was sceptical that they could fulfil the role that Fr Reid and Fr Des expected or hoped for them.

Other useful and challenging initiatives were later to come out of the Clonard community in parallel with the Sagart's work. Fr Gerry Reynolds was engaged in ecumenical outreach, and this led to myself and other Sinn Féin people meeting with a range of people from unionist backgrounds.

I found these engagements energising and thought-provoking. The people we met were sincere religious types from mainly middle-class backgrounds. Few if any of them were involved in party politics. All were unionists, mainly with a small u. They had never been subjected to republican arguments. Few if any of us had been subjected to unionist arguments, and as we developed our peace strategy these discussions informed our deliberations. They also generated differences of opinion and approach among republicans.

In October 1982, the British held elections to an Assembly in the North. Sinn Féin decided for the first time to contest elections. To the annoyance of our political enemies and the chagrin of the BBC – who had predicted the party's winning a derisory 3 per cent – Sinn Féin took over 10 per cent of the vote and five seats. I was one of those elected. The others were Danny Morrison, Martin McGuinness, Jim McAllister and Owen Carron. These elections were a big breakthrough for us.

Not all republicans were enamoured by the electoral strategy which emerged out of the hunger strike experience. There were those who felt that taking such a course risked turning Sinn Féin into just another Irish constitutional party and disempowering the republican struggle, in particular the armed struggle.

In the same month, the Sagart's determination to move beyond our discussions and to bring an end to conflict was given renewed focus when Thomas Cochrane, a part-time sergeant in the Ulster Defence Regiment (UDR) – a locally recruited predominantly unionist paramilitary force – was captured by the IRA as he travelled to work from his home outside Bessbrook in South Armagh.

Two days later a Catholic man, Joseph Donegan, was kidnapped in Belfast by a UVF gang led by Lenny Murphy. The UVF gang – known as the Shankill Butchers – had a fearsome reputation. Many of their randomly picked Catholic victims were killed using cleavers, axes and butcher's knives, from which the gang earned its name.

The Sagart was moved by these events to go beyond the letter writing and discussion stage. He contacted a senior republican whom he had known since the early 1970s. The two of them travelled to South Armagh to try and secure the release of Sergeant Cochrane. This republican, a close friend of mine, was later to become an important IRA conduit for the Sagart and a good ally. On this occasion, their intervention was too late. The UDR soldier was already dead.

In the meantime, Joseph Donegan was taken to a house in the Shankill area and beaten with a spade until he died.

The deaths of the two men touched Fr Reid deeply. In a letter several years later the Sagart recalled these events and wrote: "My only aim is to help those who, if the present situation continues, will be killed, injured or imprisoned over the next few weeks and months and whose personal tragedies will blight, not only their own lives, but also the lives of those to whom they are near and dear."

Joseph Donegan was the 2468th victim of a conflict which, in its current manifestation, had begun in 1969. Thousands of explosions had occurred, tens of thousands of people had been injured, many of them scarred mentally and physically for life, many more had been forced to flee their homes, and a whole generation had been lost to conflict.

Just over two weeks later, Lenny Murphy, leader of the Shankill Butchers – who, it is alleged, was personally responsible for eighteen killings, including that of Joseph Donegan – was himself shot dead by the IRA.

Several weeks later, on 11 November, three IRA volunteers were killed on the outskirts of Lurgan in North Armagh when a special unit of the

RUC, its Headquarters Mobile Support Unit (HMSU), fired over 100 rounds into their Ford Escort car. This was the first in a series of incidents in that area which within four weeks saw six men die at the hands of the RUC in incidents which became dubbed as "shoot-to-kill". Another of those to die was a seventeen-year-old who was shot dead at a hayshed outside of Lurgan. It later emerged that the shed had been bugged by MI5.

Two weeks after that killing, the INLA (Irish National Liberation Army, a small republican splinter-group) bombed the Dropping Well public house at Ballykelly in County Derry. Seventeen people – including eleven British soldiers – were killed when a bomb exploded in a crowded dance hall.

The Sagart's concern was being sorely tested. But it was strengthened, not weakened, by these and other events.

Danny Morrison and I were to visit London at the invitation of Ken Livingstone – Labour leader of the Greater London Council – to meet Labour MPs and councillors, and visit the British parliament. This was too much for the unionists and the Conservatives, as well as sections of the right-wing press, and on 8 December British Home Secretary William Whitelaw banned our visit under the Prevention of Terrorism Act (PTA); for good measure he also banned Martin McGuinness. This was the same Willie Whitelaw who had flown Martin and me, and other republican leaders, to secret talks in London in 1972.

Ken Livingstone and two party colleagues, Councillors Steve and Kathy Bundred, visited Belfast the following February for two days. They found themselves at the centre of a media firestorm of criticism but refused to be cowed by fierce condemnation from the Conservatives, the media and their own party leadership. They were welcomed warmly in republican Belfast, but later back home again Ken had a visit from the police to warn him that unionist paramilitaries were trying to kill him.

Many others in the British Labour Party, including Jeremy Corbyn MP and Tony Benn, also refused to be silenced by their party leadership and – individually and through groups like the Labour Committee on Ireland – fought to raise the issue of British policy in Ireland. Other Sinn Féin representatives went to Britain in the following years; in an effort to frustrate such efforts at dialogue, some of them were also later banned under the PTA's exclusion orders.

In June 1983, I was elected as the MP for West Belfast, defeating a range of other candidates, including Gerry Fitt, the long-time holder of that seat and former leader of the SDLP. A strong supporter of the British government during the hunger strikes, Fitt was supported in the election by a range of establishment figures. The fact that the people of West Belfast chose me to represent them was seen as – and was in reality – another significant breakthrough for Sinn Féin.

It was also very gratifying for me. A few years before, I would never have considered standing for election. When we did decide on an electoral strategy of sorts, I had been naively surprised when my name was proposed for the Assembly election the previous year. Now, a short time later, I was to be the Right Honourable Member for West Belfast. Sinn Féin was and remains an abstentionist party, so the question of attendance in the chamber of the British House of Commons did not arise. However, I was resolved that our interpretation of abstentionism would be for active abstentionism.

We would utilise our mandate in an active way to promote our position nationally and internationally. We would also champion the cause of West Belfast, not only the most disadvantaged and deprived area of the North but also a victim of ongoing unionist and British aggression.

Sinn Féin had been getting its act together. Alex Maskey was the first Sinn Féin member elected to Belfast City Council, to be joined later by Sean McKnight. A reorganised party structure, still ad hoc and underdeveloped, was strengthened by some of the prisoners coming out of the cages of Long Kesh, the H-Blocks and Armagh women's prison. Some of the ideas we had theorised about while incarcerated could now be put to the test.

Since my election to the Assembly, and particularly during the Westminster contest, I visited all nationalist parts of the constituency – including some that I had not been in since 1971. The housing conditions were appalling. I cancelled an election canvas in Moyard where raw sewage was seeping on to the streets. I couldn't ask people for their votes in those circumstances, but I promised to be back after the election. Sinn Féin activists initiated campaigns in support of social and economic justice for our constituents or we supported already established efforts. Housing was to be a huge issue for us. It was also to be one of our most successful efforts, culminating in the mass demolition of slums like Moyard, Divis Flats, Springhill, Unity Flats, Beechmount and the T-Blocks in Turf Lodge. The credit goes mainly to the local residents and community activists, but Sinn Féin involvement was significant, not only in winning the demands for demolition but in community involvement in planning and developing new housing projects.

I enjoyed the local work. The ability to improve in a real way the conditions in which people lived energised me. This is where I cut my political teeth. The issues were those which first grounded me in the need for equality and social justice. I was invigorated and uplifted by the efforts of people working in the community and voluntary sector to tackle poverty and deprivation. We launched a series of campaigns, and I consciously tried to ensure that my status as MP could be used by local campaigners to get access to the agencies and institutions which generally locked them out.

I was also genuinely shocked at the neglect of the constituency by other representatives, and I was surprised that a lot of what they undertook as constituency work was really the stuff of clientelism. I didn't doubt that some of this was well intended. It was an easy trap to fall into. But it wasn't about achieving real change or challenging the system. After a decade and a half on the run, underground or in prison, the mandate to be of service to the people of West Belfast and to challenge the system and build radical politics openly was hugely uplifting.

Internal developments within the party were creating their own stresses and strains. The electoral strategy had already caused some tensions, but these increased around a prolonged debate on the party's federalist policy. In 1972, Sinn Féin had adopted the Éire Nua – New Ireland – policy. This policy proposed the establishment of a federal structure of government in which there would be a central government and four provincial parliaments based on the four ancient provinces of Ireland: Ulster, Munster, Leinster and Connacht. This meant in effect that the six Northern counties would – after British withdrawal – become part of a provincial parliament within a new federal all-Ireland arrangement. The island of Ireland would be a single, independent state.

Over several of our Ard Fheiseanna – annual conferences – the New Ireland debate became quite bitter and heated at times. Eventually, over two-thirds of the delegates at the November 1982 Ard Fheis voted to remove federalism from the Sinn Féin constitution. I was one of those leading the debate in favour of that position; I wanted to see federalism retained as a policy option rather than a constitutional imperative.

Ruairí Ó Brádaigh, who was deeply disappointed by these changes, held on to the leadership for another year. However, in November 1983, he resigned, citing in his resignation speech the rejection of Éire Nua and the commitment to an electoral strategy as the principal reasons for his leaving.

I was elected in his place as president of Sinn Féin, a job I did not want. I felt inadequate for the position. I also didn't know how I could fit everything in between elected responsibilities, efforts to build the party, the ongoing tensions of the conflict, my own life and family, as well as my own political view that Sinn Féin – as an all-Ireland party – should have a Southern-based leader. Others could have done the job, particularly Martin McGuinness. He and I are about the same age, and over the years we have become close. As a young man in Derry, he witnessed the early attacks on the civil rights marches and in 1969 took part when the people of Derry repulsed an RUC invasion of that area. In 1972, he and I were both part of the republican delegation that flew to London to meet the British government and negotiate a truce. That was when we met. He also served several terms of imprisonment in the South for IRA membership. Martin was now a senior Sinn Féin leader. One of those who helped develop and promote our peace strategy, he had prevailed on me to become Sinn Féin Vice-President some five years earlier. Because of this, I was probably now seen as the more natural successor to Ruairí Ó Brádaigh.

A personal and painful postscript to my election as MP occurred almost a year later. During an election canvas, the RUC had attempted to take a tricolour from some election workers. In the North, the flying of the tricolour (the Irish national flag) was illegal, and the RUC took every opportunity to remove it or threaten those who flew or carried it. An ugly situation developed. When I tried to calm the angry mêlée, I was arrested. Several others and I were charged with obstruction as a result of the confrontation. I was summonsed to appear in the magistrates' court in Belfast on Wednesday, 14 March 1984.

I hadn't been in Belfast city centre in ages. Years of living underground, on the run, targeted by both loyalist and state forces, provided an incentive to stay on home ground in the republican heartland of West Belfast. However, I could not avoid going to the court or a bench warrant would have been issued for my arrest. It would also have given some validity to the RUC's trumped-up charge. I was resolved to face them down on this.

There was some risk in going to the court. In those days, Sinn Féin had no security back-up. Three of us – Bob Murray, Sean Keenan and I – had been summonsed. The best way to proceed, we concluded, was to be dropped directly at the front of the court building and then picked up there later. So casual was our approach that we simply asked a friend to drop us down. Because he was not able to pick us up again, we asked him to get someone else to do that. Joe Keenan, no relation to Sean, who happened to be in the Sinn Féin office at the time, decided to come along with us for the *craic*. Our journey to the courthouse was uneventful. When we went inside the busy building, everything seemed normal.

I was unsettled. It was a familiar feeling, an old friend, coming back to warn me of impending danger. I scanned the benches in the public gallery. The scattering of people there stared blankly back, gazed into space or chatted in low tones to their neighbours.

Here in Belfast city centre, in the enemy territory of the court building, surrounded and hemmed in, I was bound to be nervous. But this was more than that. My antenna had never let me down before. It was practically screaming "Danger, danger" at me. And yet there was no obvious sign of danger in sight.

I checked my watch. It was 12 o'clock. P.J. McGrory, my solicitor, approached our group. "We won't get heard until after lunch," he said.

"Can we stay here?" I asked.

"As far as I know, the court closes for lunch. Maybe you could wait in one of the offices? I'll check."

"No," he said on his return. "Everyone has to leave. Security. I'll give you a lift back."

"No, P.J. Thanks a million. We have a lift arranged. Kevin Rooney is waiting for a phone call. It's not the lift that's worrying me. It's coming in and out of here."

P.J. could see I was concerned. "Is there anything you want me to do?"

"No," I said, seeking to reassure him, "we'll be all right."

Minutes later, the court went into recess for lunch. Sean had phoned for our lift. P.J. waited with us in the big hall of the court building. As we chatted, I continued to scan the diminishing throngs of people who swept by us on their way out of the building. Soon our group and a few court officials and RUC men were the only ones left. We made our way to the entrance.

Kevin Rooney's car arrived at the pavement just as we did. We clambered noisily inside – me into the front passenger seat, Bob, Joe and Sean into the back seat – and Kevin drove slowly off into the heavy rush-hour traffic.

"We're going for a fish and chip out of Long's," Joe Keenan announced.

"OK," we agreed.

"Long's it is, then," Kevin assented, edging the car into the main traffic flow.

Soon we were into the one-way traffic system. My antenna was still on full alert, but I settled back into my seat and reassured myself that we were anonymous in the lanes of slow-moving vehicles.

"How's the case going?" Kevin Rooney asked me.

"It hasn't even started yet," I told him.

We drove past the back of the City Hall.

"Who's paying for the grub?" Sean Keenan slagged.

"I'll pay," said Kevin.

Then the car window came in around me. I felt the thumps and thuds as bullets struck home. The crack of the gunfire came after. Everything was in slow motion.

"Hit the deck!" Bob Murray yelled. Joe Keenan was screaming at the top of his voice.

"Jesus, Mary and Joseph, I give you my heart and my soul. Jesus, Mary and Joseph, assist me in my last agony. Jesus, Mary and Joseph, may I bring forth my soul in peace with you. Amen." I mouthed the prayers we had been taught since childhood while the car windows and upholstery splintered and exploded around me. "So this is what it is like," I thought.

I was hit. As our car slowed to a crawl, I could see that Kevin Rooney was hit as well. The shooting had stopped after what seemed an eternity.

"Keep driving!" I screamed at Kevin. As he did so I asked, "Are you OK?"

"Yes," he said.

"Go straight to the Royal."

The Royal Hospital was a few minutes' drive away in West Belfast. Kevin drove there, car horn blaring as he cut his way through traffic, jumping traffic lights and heading up the Grosvenor Road.

Clumped together in a heap on the back seat, Bob Murray was trying to comfort Sean and Joe Keenan. Bob had escaped unscathed. Sean was badly shot up. Hit in the face, he stared up at me silently, his big eyes wide open as I whispered an Act of Contrition towards him. Joe Keenan was shot in the arm in what was to prove a very painful wound. The bullet had hit bone.

I was shot a number of times – it later transpired that I had been hit by five of the twelve bullets fired at us – but I knew I was still alive, a big plus. I congratulated myself. Within minutes, due to Kevin Rooney's bravery, we were in the safety and care of the hospital. I was able to walk in but was immediately ordered on to a trolley. One of the first people I saw was my Aunt Ena, a hospital worker.

I asked Ena to get word to my wife Colette and our son Gearóid. I didn't want them to get news of the shooting through media reports. Gearóid was at school anyway and safe enough. My brothers Paddy and Sean arrived and walked into a confrontation with the RUC. It wasn't long until Colette arrived and, as word of the incident spread, scores of republicans descended on the Royal. The RUC numbers increased also. When I arrived out of the operating theatre, I found myself almost a prisoner in a small side ward. Visitors were harassed. The RUC behaviour was outrageous. They attempted to search visitors, and there were a number of altercations between them and Colette before some modicum of sense was established.

I couldn't wait to see Gearóid, and he seemed to take all this in his stride. I was glad children are so resilient, though I knew despite his age that it was bound to affect him. However, another tragedy soon affected us all.

As a child I stayed regularly with my Granny Adams, a seminal influence. One of my favourite people, my Uncle Paddy, used to visit regularly. He loved dogs, gardening, walking and was a self-taught and well-read scholar. He was a strong republican, a prisoner and escapee in the 1930s. To his delight, he was interned for a short period in the 1970s while in his sixties. He felt liberated by his incarceration, amused in a quietly proud and understated way that the British government considered him a threat.

Later in 1981, when his namesake, my brother Paddy, was shot and almost killed by the British army in an incident at the funeral of H-Block hunger striker Joe McDonnell, Uncle Paddy intervened. He saw Paddy's semi-conscious body being kicked and beaten with rifle butts as he was dragged into a British army vehicle. As the vehicle moved off with his nephew inside, Uncle Paddy lay down in its path, trying in vain to block its way.

When I was growing up he took an interest in all my youthful sporting exploits, modest though they were. Now he was part of the hospital vigil – except on Saint Patrick's Day. Paddy's Day, with the wearing of the green and the drowning of the shamrock, was one of his favourite traditions. That morning, he and my Auntie Annie visited me and left a few quid. They went off for a walk, Annie to the shops and Paddy to the Felons Club for a jar. An hour later he was admitted to the Royal with a head injury he received as a result of a fall. Colette saw him being brought into the emergency room. She came to tell me the sad news.

Uncle Paddy's death was a huge blow to our family. Not long after, I left the hospital. My colleagues feared that I was vulnerable and open to another attack. The RUC presence added to, rather than reduced, that concern. I myself was convinced that there had been involvement by British agencies in the murder bid. It was all too convenient: a well-publicised court case, the three wannabe assassins free to hang around the court and then outside in its precincts as we delayed inside.

Apparently, they had given up – or so they said later – and came on us in the one-way traffic flow in the city centre. In the shooting, one of the hitmen was accidentally wounded. Then, their job done, botched though it was, they were arrested by two off-duty members of the Royal Military Police and an off-duty soldier in the UDR, who just happened to be close at hand. The British army press office vehemently denied any collusion in the attack.

Our suspicions were later confirmed when it emerged that the hit squad from the UDA was in fact captured by soldiers belonging to the Special Air Service (SAS), who were then working under the British army's Intelligence and Security Group. This was acknowledged some years later by a British intelligence source to a BBC journalist, who was told by the British source that an agent working within the UDA had "tipped them off about a plan to assassinate" me. I was not told of the threat to my life, nor was any effort made by the SAS team, who followed us from the courthouse, to intercept the loyalists before the attack.

So I could understand the concerns of my friends and comrades. By now Belfast republicans had organised a round-the-clock vigil at the hospital. I was well treated there, but signed myself out after five days, though I was in a lot of pain. Danny Morrison persuaded me that we shouldn't allow the loyalists to think we had been rattled by their attack, so that afternoon we held a press conference in West Belfast. It was also politically important to highlight our belief that the British had set this whole operation up.

I don't remember much of it now. I recall accusing British intelligence of complicity in the attack and pointing to the different stories they had told in the twenty-four hours after I was shot. After that, I went off to a friend's house where Colette and Gearóid and I stayed together.

Some time after, I spoke to P.J. McGrory, who advised me to submit a claim for compensation under the criminal injuries scheme. The Northern Ireland Office (NIO) had included a provision to make life easier for those classed as victims of terrorism by allowing for the issuing of a certificate by the Chief Constable of the RUC to that effect. This was intended to relieve the applicant of the burden of proving that the injuries were terrorist-related and to speed up the process of receiving compensation. It all sounds straightforward, but in my case the Chief Constable issued a certificate that a shooting incident had occurred, but which neglected to mention the fact that I had been shot! This despite the fact that those arrested and charged with my attempted murder were convicted.

P.J. had to take separate proceedings in the High Court to force the Chief Constable to issue a new certificate confirming that I had been the victim of an attack. The NIO then sought a ruling that, by virtue of my membership of Sinn Féin and its perceived support for the IRA, I was ineligible for compensation. Fearful that one consequence of this was that other republican families seeking compensation would be blocked, I withdrew my claim.

Apart from the to-be-expected aches and pains associated with bullet wounds, all of us went on to recover to one degree or other from our injuries. Even at the time I had no sense of personal animosity towards the men who tried to kill me. While feeling great appreciation for their incompetence, I had no great regard for them, but I did understand that they did what they did because of the political conditions in which we lived.

I did feel a sense of outrage that they were probably – or at least some or one of them was almost certainly – being handled by a British government agent. Those who tried to kill us were being presented to the world as loyalist terrorists or even counter-terrorists acting on their own account. While loyalists or unionist paramilitaries have their own agenda and not all of them acted as dupes, they are in effect an arm of British military operations.

So among the grey-suited politicians or officials who governed our affairs, who tried to demonise and defeat our struggle, who cosied up to prelates and Irish political leaders and enlisted their support or acquiescence, were some who subverted – by terrorism – the right of people on our islands to live in peace and harmony together. They did so with the authority of the British government.

# Chapter Three

## *First, Tentative Steps*

The Inis Eoghain peninsula lies in north-west County Donegal, across the border and a few short miles from Derry city. That was where I went to recuperate from my injuries. A republican family in Derry, friends of Martin McGuinness, very kindly gave Colette and me the use of their mobile home not far from Buncrana. A local republican not long out of prison in England, Raymond McLaughlin, and his wife Mary made sure we were not lacking in any home comforts. Eddie Fullerton, the local Sinn Féin councillor, and his friend Jim Ferry looked in on us as well.

Our Gearóid, who was ten, came to stay with us until he had to return to Belfast for school and, more importantly from his view, to compete in a school handball championship. I was well on the mend by then and delighted when his side emerged as champions. Although I was dragged off occasionally for meetings, the month or so we stayed in Inis Eoghain – in those pre-mobile phone days – was an idyllic period for Colette and me. It was also the longest uninterrupted space we had had on our own together since we were married.

Inis Eoghain is a beautiful part of the world, sprinkled with scatterings of little villages, deserted beaches, high cliffs, rapid rivers and rugged mountain ranges. We explored them all and moved on to neighbouring peninsulas with zeal. It was great to be alive and on our own, with nothing to do except to do nothing.

But time passed quickly. I was soon myself again, except for a nagging pain in my upper left arm. This was to get worse in the next few months. When I eventually went back to the Royal Hospital, half-mad with pain, it was to discover that they had left a bullet in me by accident. It was a heavy calibre pistol round, and the copper jacket had infected my arm. The senior surgeon, Mr William Odling-Smee, quickly sliced a scalpel into what had become a sizeable swollen lump in the fleshy part of my arm and removed the offending bullet. As he did so, we were both almost overcome by the odious smell which immediately arose from the poisoned wound. For weeks later, threads of the tweed coat and the shirt I was wearing when I was shot emerged from the wound as it slowly healed. Somewhere or other, I still have the bullet which Odling-Smee presented me with that day.

Our sojourn in Inis Eoghain was over. Belfast beckoned. There was a lot to be done. This included the ongoing work with the Sagart. Since I had become party president, our conversations at the monastery now had a slightly different status. I had more authority and, in theory at least, room to manoeuvre.

I mainly met with the priests on my own; sometimes Kevin Hannaway was there. Fr Reid, as I said earlier, retained his own contact with the IRA. I continued to work with a small core group which included Martin McGuinness, Mitchel McLaughlin, Tom Hartley, Danny Morrison and Jim Gibney. Pat Doherty from Donegal was another part of our leadership team, and Rita O'Hare, who was exiled, and Lucilita Bhreatnach were among those who were to emerge from within Sinn Féin ranks in Dublin to play significant roles nationally within the party.

Dialogue is crucial to any effort to find a solution to conflict. The anti-republican campaign by the establishment, including the Catholic hierarchy, was in full flow. Right across the spectrum – from covert military operations, outright and open police aggression, a range of coercive "laws", a daily diet of propaganda – the nationalist and republican base was subjected to full frontal attack from all sides.

By now there was a culture of resistance throughout the nationalist and particularly the republican working-class heartlands in both urban and rural regions in the North. There was also a resilient network of support throughout the South. Nothing would shift this core support, of that you could be certain. That is not to say that the people who made up this base were immune to pressure or incapable of being affected by downturns in the struggle. On the contrary, they were generally thoughtful, committed individuals or families.

For everyone who might become disillusioned, someone else would take his or her place. Opposition to British rule provided the engine for armed republicanism in the absence of any concrete efforts to undo the evil of partition or the British connection. Resistance to injustice or perceived injustice is as old as humanity itself. So the republican core support in the South, like that in the North, regenerated itself again and again through all the twists and turns of the 1970s and in the awful summer of the H-Block hunger strikes.

Important as the spirit of endurance was, we needed to move from a culture of resistance to a culture of change. The challenge would be to discover how to make that move, how to even get the space to think about it amidst all the other priorities and stresses. The most underdeveloped aspects of our struggle were its politics. The politics of resistance were adequate for armed struggle, but our cause had to be about more than that.

For our part, while we held up dialogue as a central tenet, we were not taking initiatives to bring it about. Some tentative steps had been taken to build politically during the 1972 IRA truce, but they had not been sustained – not surprising, given that I and others like me found ourselves back on the run and back in jail after the truce broke down. But in the late 1970s, internal discussion and political planning resumed, despite the practical priority of the continuing war and the prison protests. In fact, these protests – and more particularly the hunger strikes – accelerated this process of political development as the 1980s opened.

By that time the changes within Sinn Féin were profound, although they may not have penetrated very deeply into the party. There was still a decided failure to develop the struggle on an all-Ireland, thirty-two county basis. While the party membership was from all over Ireland, the focus was on what was happening in the North.

The Assembly and Westminster elections had proved there was support for our position. There was also support for armed struggle. I myself felt that it was a necessary form of struggle, and I defended this position without being dogmatic about it. It was also my view that there could be no military solution. The conflict did not arise from a military problem. It was a political conflict which required a political solution. But the military, or as they would put it, the security imperative, was at the core of all aspects of British policy. This policy was publicly endorsed by the Irish government – at least until the hunger strikes.

Within republicanism, armed struggle was the dominating tendency. There was a belief that only the IRA could move the British government. While Sinn Féin's policies for a New Ireland were progressive on social, economic, political, cultural and gender issues, there was little connection between this vision of the future and the hard realities of the present. The hunger strikes had opened up all these issues for re-examination for those of us who wanted to re-examine them.

The war had its own dynamic. It was difficult to see how the cycle of state violence, including loyalist and institutionalised violence, and republican violence could be broken. Or even if anyone in positions of power and influence wanted to break it. There had been three IRA ceasefires in the 1970s. All had collapsed because of British duplicity and bad faith.

The ceasefires also failed because others – the Irish government, the political parties and all of the Churches – failed to build on the opportunity for peace that these ceasefires created. The Irish government in particular (through Section 31 of the Offences against the State Act) imposed media censorship, excluding the voices of republicans. The Dublin establishment colluded in the lie that the conflict in the North was a criminal conspiracy.

I explained to Fr Reid that a consequence of these experiences was that the IRA had rejected any notion of ever again having a ceasefire, short of the British government declaring its intention to withdraw. However, I put to him my view that armed struggle occurs in the absence of an alternative way to bring about conditions of justice and equality. The focus, therefore, of those wishing to see an end to armed struggle had to be on building this alternative. Those who could make the most impact were in positions of power. That meant the Irish establishment, the Irish government and the other political parties. The Churches, too, had to be part of building an alternative. Those within the Churches serious about ending the conflict could best do so, not through the politics of denunciation, but through developing objectives and support for strategies which tackled the root causes of conflict.

The Catholic hierarchy was nowhere near such possibilities. For some considerable time, my discussions with the Sagart centred around the failure of the hierarchy to defend its flock, to stand up for justice and to protect it from injustice. The public position of the hierarchy, in the main, was selective and aimed at republicans. Moral arguments against violence were only directed against the "men of violence", never at the British agencies, only occasionally at loyalists.

For many republicans who were also Catholics, this moral doublespeak was a source of enormous annoyance. It led to an increasing loss of influence by the Church among nationalists living in the real world of discrimination, inequality and conflict in the North. The political establishment's position of refusing to meet with republicans was – with the exception of Cardinal Ó Fiaich, who met with us privately – the line followed also by the Catholic hierarchy.

This made a nonsense of the Christian philosophy. On more than one occasion, I made the point to the Sagart that if the leadership of a Christian Church refuses to speak to people because it regards them as sinners, it is contradicting the clear example and teaching of Jesus.

Fr Des once remarked, "By the time the bishops get around to talking to people, there'll be nobody who will see any point in talking to them."

Specifically, I drew attention to remarks made by the Pope on his visit to Ireland in September 1979. Then, our political opponents had made much of his appeal "in language of passionate pleading. On my knees I beg you to turn away from the paths of violence and to return to the ways of peace."

What had been overlooked were his equally telling remarks on the responsibilities of political leaders. Speaking at Drogheda, Pope John Paul II had said: "To all who bear political responsibility for the affairs of Ireland, I want to speak with the same urgency and intensity with which I have spoken to the men of violence . . . I urge you who are called to the noble vocation of politics to have the courage to face up to your responsibility, to be leaders in the cause of peace, reconciliation and justice."

This protracted phase of our discussions was less about how the Church should tackle the issue of conflict resolution than it was about how the Church faced up to the issue of conflict and its underlying causes. In other words, it was about what side the Church should be on. In my public challenge to Bishop Cahal Daly, I concentrated on the issue of the Church's selective condemnation of violence. Because the bishop's position on the IRA was often argued on moral grounds, I also asked what was the moral position on the British partition of Ireland, or the right of the Irish people to national self-determination. I queried why Catholic members of the British Crown forces did not have their moral obligations spelt out to them in the same way as Catholic members of the IRA. On one occasion Dr Daly called on people not to vote for Sinn Féin and raised the possibility that those who did could be committing a sin.

Dialogue was a two-way street. It wasn't just republicans talking to others. It meant Irish republicans being prepared to listen carefully and to take into account what would be said to us, at the same time expecting others to give equal consideration to what we had to say.

Looking back now at this time, it strikes me that this emphasis on dialogue may seem strange, but Sinn Féin were being treated as pariahs. In the South, we were censored. Our successes in the Assembly elections brought these issues into sharp relief. We now had a mandate, but it was being set at naught.

This needed to be challenged. Those who had for so long preached democracy at us were now ignoring our democratic rights. They were also denying the fact that republicans had as much right to peace as anyone else. Peace didn't just mean an absence of conflict; it also meant the presence of justice, democratic rights, including national rights and equality. Sinn Féin needed to challenge our opponents on these issues and to find out if there were amongst them those who were prepared to develop common positions.

I told Fr Reid, therefore, that I was prepared to go on my own and in the strictest confidence to initiate the dialogue with the Church, with the SDLP, with the Irish government, with whoever I could talk to, if it would make a difference. I did so with the express support and involvement of the small cadre of leadership activists that I was associated with. We may not have been fully aware of the import of our initiative, but we were taking the first tentative steps in the development of a peace strategy.

Those I wanted to talk to had priorities of their own. Following the hunger strikes and the popular support for Sinn Féin's first modern efforts to build electorally, the Irish establishment had sought ways to counter the emerging radicalisation of Northern politics. Since its establishment, the SDLP had never been challenged electorally by Sinn Féin.

The Irish government set about throwing the SDLP a lifeline. Dealing with the cause of nationalist alienation in the North became its widely published focus when it established the New Ireland Forum. But in a stupid, counter-productive and short-sighted contradiction of its stated intention, it banned Sinn Féin from attending the Forum. It went ahead without us, and published a report in May 1984.

This report was produced by the three main political parties in the Irish parliament – Fianna Fáil, Fine Gael and the Irish Labour Party – and by the SDLP in the North. Its purpose was to achieve an agreed approach to the North. The report produced three options – a unitary thirty-two county state, a federal arrangement or joint authority of the North exercised by London and Dublin equally.

In the meantime, the British establishment was rocked to its very core when the IRA exploded a bomb in October at the Conservative Party conference in Brighton. The Grand Hotel – where many of the Conservative Party's most senior leaders were staying, including Prime Minister Margaret Thatcher – was devastated when a bomb exploded at 2.54 a.m. in room 629.

Thatcher had just finished work on her keynote conference speech, which she was to deliver the following day. She was in the sitting room of her first floor suite when the force of the blast blew out the front wall of the hotel. Several of the floors and part of the roof crashed down. Thatcher survived, but five others were killed and over thirty were injured, several severely.

In a statement later that day claiming responsibility, the legacy of Thatcher's attitude to the hunger strikers resonated in the IRA's words: "Mrs Thatcher will now realise that Britain cannot occupy our country and torture our prisoners and shoot our people in their own streets and get away with it. Today we were unlucky, but remember we only have to be lucky once – you will have to be lucky always. Give Ireland peace and there will be no war."

I was sorry for the loss of life and injury caused by the bombing, but it was obvious that the attack was related directly to the horror of the H-Blocks and the tragedy of the hunger strikes. Given the consequences of Margaret Thatcher's policy in Ireland, the Brighton operation was enormously popular among Irish nationalists and republicans.

Several weeks later I described as totally hypocritical the description by British critics of the bombing as an attack on democracy. I pointed out that, "The British connection, the partition of this country, and the resultant suffering and grief is far from democratic."

I am not a violent person. I have often been accused, particularly by my opponents, of being in, or having been in, the IRA. It is a charge I have always rejected. Then and now, my primary objective has been to get the British government to face up to its responsibilities in respect of Ireland. The people of Ireland have a right to be free of the British connection. The British government has no right to be in Ireland. In the absence of any alternative, armed actions represent a necessary form of struggle against the British administration and in pursuance of national independence. There are considerable moral problems in relation to armed struggle, of course; but for those who want an end to armed actions, tackling injustice and the underlying causes of conflict, and building an alternative to armed struggle, is the only way to proceed with any possibility of success. For me, as an Irish republican, this means working to bring about a new beginning and building a new political dispensation. I have also argued that a successful peace process means bringing an end to physical force republicanism.

I believe this is achievable. Our peace strategy is a personal and political priority for me. It is the central plank of Sinn Féin policy and our main function as a political party. Contrary to the propaganda of our enemies and the perception of others, Sinn Féin is not the "political wing" of the IRA, nor do we advocate violence.

If that were the case, it would be much easier to manage republican responsibilities and obligations to a conflict-resolution process. It has never been easy. However, in all of my dealings with the British and Irish governments, with the United States government and with other political parties and political representatives, I have worked on two simple rules of thumb. Firstly, I will not deceive them about the IRA. Secondly, I will not deceive the IRA.

There would not be a peace process without the IRA. Others have countered, "Well, if it wasn't for the IRA there wouldn't be any need for a peace process." As reasonable as that may sound, it evades the point. At the time I am writing about, the IRA had no intention of suing for peace. But as the work of the small group interacting with Fr Reid continued, as he kept his IRA contact informed of developments and as the networking built into a process, and as I or Martin McGuinness started to engage more and more with the IRA leadership on the question of a peace process and the potential for Sinn Féin to play a pivotal role in this, then the IRA showed that its courage wasn't just about making war. It was prepared to help to create the conditions for making peace.

Only a strong, undefeated group could have taken the risky path to peace that was to emerge from the Sinn Féin peace strategy. But back in 1984 no one could know where that strategy would take us all. Back then there was no such strategy. There was only war.

# Chapter Four

# *The Anglo-Irish Agreement*

A month after the Brighton bombing, the British and Irish governments were locked in discussions. Margaret Thatcher wanted greater security co-operation, specifically a joint security zone that would allow British troops to operate on the Southern side of the border. The Irish Taoiseach, Garrett Fitzgerald, proposed joint authority over the North – a concept Thatcher had once likened to "burglary". There was no meeting of minds. The summit ended and each politician went off to their respective press conferences. When asked what had emerged from the meeting, Thatcher brusquely dismissed the proposals contained in the Forum report. "I have made it quite clear that a unified Ireland, that is out. A confederation of two states, that is out. Joint authority, that is out."

Fitzgerald began his press conference unaware of Thatcher's remarks. He was immediately tackled by an Irish media angered by her tone. Thatcher's arrogant rejection of the Forum report, her "Out, out, out" public dismissal of the Taoiseach's propositions and his totally inadequate response when asked about it by the press outraged nationalist opinion in Ireland. Despite his efforts to make the most of a bad summit, the Taoiseach was clearly surprised by her comments. He floundered, his face dropped, and he looked weak and inept.

Fr Reid seized upon the Forum report as a positive development within nationalism and wrote to the Bishop of Down and Connor, Dr Daly, and Cardinal Ó Fiaich, arguing for the need for dialogue between republicans and those responsible for the Forum report. He also advanced this as a topic for dialogue between republicans and the Church.

While this private dialogue was taking place, a "battle for ideas" was being waged in a series of public letters and articles that passed to and fro between myself and Bishop Daly. This public debate with the Bishop went on for over a decade.

Cahal Daly was recognised as the Church's leading theologian and was publicly very critical of the IRA and of republicans. He frequently described the armed struggle of the IRA as "immoral and evil". His moral denunciations were reserved primarily for republicans, generally ignoring the role and responsibility of the British government and its security agencies. Specifically, when he called on republicans to renounce violence and join the peaceful struggle for the rights of nationalists, I asked, "What peaceful struggle?"

I posed the challenge: "Those republicans who engage in armed struggle, or who defend the legitimacy of armed struggle in pursuance of Irish independence, do so, not through any fixation with physical force, but through a necessity. Those who voice moral condemnation of this tactic have a responsibility to spell out an alternative course by which Irish independence can be secured. I for one would be pleased to consider such an alternative."

The following year, 1985, was to be a busy one. In May, Sinn Féin won fifty-nine seats and 11.8 per cent of the vote in local councils across the North.

The Sagart and Fr Des were now coming to terms with the reality that we weren't getting far in our efforts to engage with the Catholic hierarchy, with the exception of Cardinal Ó Fiaich. The Church structures were not amenable to getting responses to the questions we were putting.

So my two friends were trying to work their way through all this, with Fr Des showing slightly less patience than Fr Reid. Cardinal Ó Fiaich was advising the Sagart privately on the best way to proceed and who would be the best people to contact. Out of this came a suggestion that there should be an effort to get questions tabled at the Bishops' Conference – that is, the formal meeting of the Irish bishops. I wrote to the conference, asking the hierarchy to facilitate dialogue between Sinn Féin and the SDLP, and Sinn Féin and the Irish government. At a subsequent meeting with Fr Reid – which also included Fr Des and Fr Gerry Reynolds – we came up with the idea that the Bishops' Conference should consider setting up a working group to examine the issues raised in my letter and report on how the Church might respond.

It was felt that this group could try to define the role of the Church in the search for peace. There was also a suggestion that such a working group should look at defining and creating "alternative methods" for achieving political aims and defining and creating the conditions for cessations.

It was still my view that the Church was not making full use of the resources available to it and I said so. As it turned out, none of these ideas from the Sagart or his friends were taken up by the hierarchy.

By this time, at Cardinal Ó Fiaich's suggestion, the Sagart was also speaking and writing to Dr James Lennon, Auxiliary Bishop of Armagh, and Dr James Kavanagh, Auxiliary Bishop of Dublin. These were his points of contact into the Bishops' Conference.

The Sagart met with SDLP deputy leader Seamus Mallon, potentially the most important of his contacts so far. If Mallon agreed to discussions with us, we could explore the potential for building an alternative to armed actions. Seamus Mallon was one of the old school of older SDLP leaders. A party man through and through, he was a vigorous and articulate promoter of SDLP policy.

The Irish government was busy as well. Officials had been in protracted negotiations with Downing Street. Notwithstanding Thatcher's rejection of the Forum report, there was a serious ongoing effort by the two governments to regroup in the changing political situation in the North caused by the hunger strikes. As always, the emphasis of the Thatcher government was on security. It sought more co-operation from Dublin and an ability, for example, for British forces to cross the border and penetrate into the South. Dublin, for its part, while it was later to make concessions on these matters, argued for a more political approach.

In July the Sagart wrote a paper which sought to identify the military and political conditions in which those who were engaged in armed struggle might agree to consider a ceasefire. He drew up a detailed list of proposed conditions and asked for an initial response from republicans. At its core, the sine qua non condition for an "alternative method" was an agreement between the nationalist parties around a united policy of aims and methods for solving the conflict and for bringing about a just peace.

He sent his paper to the IRA leadership through his own contact and was told that if these proposals were put into effect, republicans would seriously consider them to see if they constituted an alternative method.

The Sagart then met the senior unionist lawyer Desmond Boal in the early part of the summer. He told him that, from his conversations with republicans, he felt that the only credible alternative approach which might interest the IRA was a "political coalition between the main nationalist parties – especially between the SDLP and Sinn Féin". Together they might "create a political force sufficiently powerful to persuade the IRA to desist from the 'armed struggle' and to give their backing to it as 'the alternative method'."

To the Sagart's surprise, Boal's response was "one of positive, wholehearted enthusiasm". He spoke of his ability in that new situation to persuade the leaders on the unionist side to sit down and talk to Sinn Féin and the SDLP.

Fr Reid told Seamus Mallon of this conversation and of my broad support for this approach. Arrangements were made – through Dr James Lennon, Auxiliary Bishop of Armagh – for me to hold a meeting with Seamus Mallon in August, which Dr Lennon would facilitate. This was, however, cancelled following the death of a Catholic building contractor killed by the IRA because it claimed he supplied building materials to the British forces.

The SDLP deputy leader suggested to the Sagart that he should come back to him two or three weeks later to talk about another arrangement for a meeting. Concerned that Mallon might feel exposed by attending such a meeting, the Sagart had reminded him that he would be there at the invitation of "responsible Church leaders" and that he could bring someone with him.

Fr Reid also hinted that if Mr Mallon felt incapable of having the meeting, he was thinking of approaching the SDLP leader, John Hume. Mallon told him not to do that and to come back in several weeks. It was agreed that a meeting between myself and Mallon should occur on 10 October. However, when the Sagart tried to speak to Mallon and confirm the arrangements, he found it difficult to pin him down. A September meeting was cancelled at the last minute because of party business. Eventually, in a phone conversation on 5 October, the SDLP deputy pulled out of the planned meeting. He felt that the discussions then taking place between the British and Irish governments needed to be allowed to conclude. Mr Mallon suggested that the Sagart come back to him in another two or three weeks. I felt that private, personal discussions with Mallon could be worthwhile. However, I told Fr Reid that if Mallon preferred a party-to-party meeting, Sinn Féin would appoint three or four people to discuss how to work out the detail of a common policy with three or four people similarly appointed by the SDLP.

At the end of October, the Sagart again contacted Seamus Mallon, repeating the suggestion, already discussed with him, that Sinn Féin and the SDLP should "hammer out a common political policy for achieving a just and lasting solution".

Around this time, Dr Lennon contacted me to say that he, too, felt that discussions between Sinn Féin and the SDLP needed to wait until the outcome of the Anglo-Irish negotiations then taking place.

The negotiations between London and Dublin culminated on 15 November 1985 with the signing of the Anglo-Irish Agreement. Presented by both governments as a landmark agreement, it was widely seen as an effort to bolster the SDLP in its electoral battle with Sinn Féin.

The essence of the treaty was that Britain formally agreed to give the Dublin government a limited say in the Six Counties, which were to remain as part of the United Kingdom. It aimed to force a realignment within unionism so that there could be a new internal arrangement in the North which would isolate republicans. In the event, the Anglo-Irish Agreement antagonised the unionists without either isolating republicans or accommodating the SDLP. The unionists united and vigorously protested against the "Diktat", as they described the agreement. Their deep sense of betrayal was made all the more acute by the fact that their champion, Margaret Thatcher, had signed the treaty. The Dublin government claimed the Anglo-Irish Agreement as a great success, promoting the line that "the nationalist nightmare was over". Tragically, it was not.

Despite the hype which attended the Anglo-Irish Agreement, we were satisfied that it would not undermine Sinn Féin electorally. Our electoral base was solid and resilient. At the same time, the IRA could not be militarily defeated even by the use of tactics which would clearly have been politically counter-productive for the London government. British policy instead aimed more and more towards containment, though this strategy was clearly inadequate. There was a military and political stalemate. While Irish republicans could prevent a settlement on British government terms, we lacked the political strength to bring the struggle to a decisive conclusion. Military solutions were not an option for either side; this had consistently been the Sinn Féin position.

In these circumstances, the side which broke the stalemate would have the initiative. Republicans could block British strategy, could survive a long stalemate, but the political goals of republicanism meant we needed to do much more than either of these things if our struggle was to be successful.

Sinn Féin needed to go on a political offensive. This would require us taking political initiatives, but our ability to do so was quite limited. There was no real possibility of involving the IRA in such initiatives; in fact, there was no real consideration given to the IRA's role. The thought processes within the two organisations, that is Sinn Féin and the IRA, were quite independent and jealously guarded, particularly by the army. Contrary to popular opinion, there was no integrated strategy. Separate development at all levels meant that while Sinn Féin was coming to contemplate political initiatives as part of a greater political offensive by us, the army continued, almost in a separate sphere, with its armed offensives. In truth, while there may have been misgivings about particular operations, there was no real dissent from the need for armed struggle. It was taken for granted that that was the way of things.

The Anglo-Irish Agreement was part of a British offensive, an initiative underwritten by both the London and Dublin governments. We felt that we needed our own initiatives, to be on the political offensive. We needed to challenge our opponents. Struggles are essentially won in the first place in people's minds. It was a matter of having a vision, of setting objectives and devising plans and programmes to achieve those objectives and to make the vision a reality. A struggle could not stand still. Politics had to govern everything we did and it had to be about empowering people, about changing the way we lived and the society in which we lived. If we were to get equality, we needed to take risks and concede no ground to our opponents. We had to take ground. This was the new context within which Sinn Féin had to develop and evolve our political strategy.

The Sagart's efforts to arrange a meeting with Seamus Mallon ran into the ground. Mr Mallon had given Fr Reid questions for Sinn Féin, which the Sagart and his colleagues felt should not be passed on because they believed them unreasonable and unfair. The questions would set conditions on the discussions before the discussions had begun.

The basis for Sinn Féin's involvement in discussions with the Church and SDLP had been spelt out some months earlier. We were being invited by Church representatives to take part in discussions with other political representatives. Republicans were not in favour of conducting discussions through intermediaries, as this method was unsatisfactory. But we were willing to co-operate fully with the Church representatives, not least because we understood that the SDLP might have required some cover for meeting with us. This had been one of the points that the Sagart had made. Those who broke the "no meeting with Sinn Féin" approach of the governments and other parties would need protection from media and political criticism. I agreed that the discussions could take place under the auspices of the Church, with a Church representative in the chair. Sinn Féin would give these discussions the highest priority. We would devote the necessary time, energy and resources to make them successful.

However, Seamus Mallon's apparent refusal to agree a definite arrangement was leading to mounting frustration. The Sagart and his colleagues were increasingly of a view that there was a need for a more formal approach to the SDLP, probably through John Hume.

At the same time, the first tentative contact was opened up with Charlie Haughey, leader of Fianna Fáil, then the opposition party in the Dáil.

Shortly after the New Year, fifteen by-elections took place in the North to the Westminster parliament. They had been precipitated by the resignation of all fifteen of the sitting Unionist MPs in the House of Commons in protest at the signing of the Anglo-Irish Agreement. The tactic backfired on the Unionists when the SDLP's Seamus Mallon snatched the Newry and Mourne seat away from the UUP's Jim Nicholson.

Further efforts were made by the Sagart to engage Mallon in talks with Sinn Féin but all to no avail. Perhaps the Anglo-Irish Agreement had encouraged Mallon to think that the SDLP now had the measure of Sinn Féin. Perhaps he was too busy building on the advantage the Agreement appeared to offer his party. Whatever the truth, around the middle of March 1986 Seamus Mallon told Dr Lennon that he would not meet Sinn Féin.

The way was now clear for a direct approach to the leader of the SDLP, John Hume.

# Chapter Five

# *Searching for a Breakthrough*

By now Fr Reid had moved with others to create a Clonard Church Ministry, a special peace-making ministry within the Redemptorist Order. The ministry, based on the historic tradition of the Church's providing sanctuary, made a clear distinction between political dialogue and political matters. It had no role to play in politics except to insist on "Godlike compassion for people" because that is the supreme value of human affairs "and the first principle of all human relationships, including those of politics".

"Translated into practice this means that the only Christian and human way to conduct political affairs and to resolve the conflicts that arise from them is the way of communication and dialogue, practised by each participant with the respect and compassion that are due in justice and charity to every other participant."

In the absence of such dialogue, the ministry argued for the Church to fulfil its pastoral responsibility to use all resources to promote dialogue.

The Sagart had developed his thinking, partly in response to the failure of the institutional Church to participate in any peace-making imperative. His role was institutionalised, supported by his own order with the active support of Cardinal Ó Fiaich. But the hierarchy did not sign on.

The Sagart now focused on his own order. It was Fr Stephen Mahoney, a Redemptorist provincial, who first wrote to John Hume asking if he would meet some priests from Clonard Monastery. Fr Mahoney also thanked the SDLP leader for his help in trying to secure the release of a Redemptorist priest – Fr Rudy Romero – who had been kidnapped by the military in the Philippines.

When Mr Hume wrote back, he gave the Redemptorist provincial the latest news on Fr Rudy but made no mention of the requested meeting. While some of his colleagues thought this a sign that John Hume wasn't interested in meeting, the Sagart thought there had been some sort of mistake and decided to write himself.

In a letter sent on 19 May 1986, the Sagart set out his pastoral and moral reasons for writing and the background to efforts in recent years to achieve a lasting peace. He spoke of our commitment to finding an alternative. "The essence of this proposal is that the nationalist parties, North and South, would agree, through dialogue between themselves, to formulate and then to co-operate in a common nationalist policy of aims and methods for resolving the conflict and establishing a just and lasting peace. This would mean that while retaining their own separate identities the nationalist parties would make an ad hoc agreement to combine their political forces and to act in unison in a common campaign for reconciliation and peace." The Sagart set out three broad proposals to the SDLP leader and asked for his advice and comments on them.

John Hume phoned the monastery the next day. He and the Sagart, along with Fr Seamus Enright and Fr Reynolds, met on 21 May. The meeting could not have been friendlier. Mr Hume told them that he agreed in principle with their efforts, but he expressed concern about some restraints placed on him because of the Anglo–Irish Agreement.

I met the Sagart a short time later and he reported his conversation to me. I explained Sinn Féin's position on the Anglo–Irish Agreement and said we would need a great deal of persuasion to change our attitude. While I appreciated that the Agreement might place constraints on Mr Hume, it couldn't be so weak that it would be seriously endangered by a dialogue between us. I was prepared to co-operate with any arrangements Mr Hume might wish to make and with any conditions he might want to lay down for confidentiality. In this respect Fr Reid offered the use of various locations belonging to the Redemptorists as places where safe and confidential meetings could take place.

The Sagart went to and fro between us for a short time, and eventually we arranged to meet. This was a big departure for John Hume. In an earlier effort to commence dialogue in January 1985, during a BBC radio debate, I told John that Sinn Féin would be issuing an invitation to the SDLP for talks. The SDLP's leader's response was to rubbish this invitation. He claimed that it was the leadership of the IRA which made the important decisions, and he insisted that he would only talk to the "organ grinders".

Shortly afterwards, the IRA took up this challenge, issuing an invitation to Hume for talks. He refused a further invitation to talks from Sinn Féin, labelling the party "mere surrogates". The idea of a meeting between the SDLP leader and the IRA was attacked by a section of the political elite in Dublin. Taoiseach Garrett Fitzgerald went live on the state radio, RTÉ, to read a prepared statement in which he said that any meeting between Hume and the IRA should be broken up, and he warned that members of the Army Council, if identified, would be arrested. So much for it being good to talk.

As it turned out, these talks collapsed before they could begin when John Hume objected to an IRA proposal to video record the opening and closing statements. The IRA felt a true record of the meeting would guarantee no misrepresentation and would allow the IRA some balance of media coverage. Hume refused.

Afterwards the IRA rebuked Mr Hume. For his part he said, "Since the IRA has now confirmed beyond any shadow of doubt that they believe that only an 'armed struggle' can solve the problems of this community there is no point whatsoever in discussing politics with their political wing."

This was part of the backdrop to our first meeting, which occurred in September. It was friendly and constructive. I put it to John that the nationalist parties needed to co-operate to press the British into setting aside the 1920 Government of Ireland Act. John agreed to look at the provisions of the act, but he outlined his reservations. His preference was to stick with the Anglo-Irish Agreement in which the British implied that they had no interest in staying in Ireland. I said that it wasn't possible to make progress on *implied* attitudes. It would be helpful if the British explicitly stated their attitude on this matter. John asked me what response the IRA would make if the British were to make such a statement. I didn't know. I couldn't speak for the army. Still, I believed the only way to deal with the issue of armed republicanism was to develop an alternative. That required the two governments working together, but it especially meant, on the Irish nationalist side, all of us working towards common objectives. We also discussed the need to heal the divisions between us and the unionists.

In the course of these discussions, John told me that my redoubtable friend and long-time solicitor, P.J. McGrory, had written to him, advising him to keep an eye on what was happening within Sinn Féin. This letter, along with Fr Reid's detailed briefing, had persuaded John to meet with me. We had a good first meeting. John Hume was down-to-earth and easy to talk to. I agreed to relay our discussions back to the IRA, and he said he would try to establish whether the British government would be prepared to say the sort of things I had suggested would be helpful.

Looking back on these discussions now, it strikes me that it took a very long time before they began to bear fruit. There are many reasons for this. For example, the policy of refusing to talk to Sinn Féin was deeply embedded in the political systems in Ireland and Britain. It was a big step for anyone to go against the two governments and breach this policy.

In reality dialogue is what happens every day and in all our lives. Once the first step was taken, it was obvious that this was the common sense thing to do. For example, some of John Hume's neighbours were Sinn Féin members. They met in the course of travelling to and from their homes. Martin McGuinness lived only a few streets from the Hume home. So did Mitchel McLaughlin. Mr Hume's home city, Derry, is a close community. There was extreme polarisation between the SDLP and some republicans, but John Hume was close enough to the pulse of that community to know that the republicans could not be ostracised out of existence. He also knew that allegations of criminality or gangsterism were untrue. As he has since said many times, republicans believed in what they were doing.

John Hume's stature as the leader of nationalists in the North should have insulated him against any criticism for talking to Sinn Féin. It is arguable that his leadership was best suited for such ground-breaking moves. But, in fact, it took real courage for him to engage in dialogue and to rise above all of the strictures, especially given the invective poured on him when our discussions became public.

There was also a high level of armed activity during this period. The IRA and the British forces were dug in. Shooting or bombing incidents were occurring almost on a daily basis. The loyalists also were busy, many of their operations occurring at the behest of British military and police agencies.

The two governments were trying to manage the fall-out and the implementation of the Anglo-Irish Agreement. The main unionist parties – the Ulster Unionist Party and the DUP – united in opposition to "the Thatcher sell-out", and unionism went into convulsions. James Molyneaux, the UUP leader at that time, and Ian Paisley, leader of the DUP, organised a protracted series of street agitation.

John Hume and I were both facing party-political difficulties at the time, albeit of very different kinds.

Throughout all of our engagements, from the very first meeting, I found John to be extremely tense. His way of working was different from mine: I had a core of people with whom I worked. John did not appear to confide in anyone within his own party. At the beginning this may not have been such a big drawback because confidentiality was crucial, but I came to realise that his way of keeping things to himself was due to more than the sensitive nature of our work. It was down also to the lack of any real relationship between him and his deputy leader, Seamus Mallon. This was to cause problems later, especially within John's own party leadership.

For our part, Sinn Féin was moving through a crisis. There had been broad support among activists for our electoral strategy, not least because this was seen to be successful. Ruairí Ó Brádaigh had been president of the party from 1970 until 1983. Under his leadership, a younger, mainly Northern element had come to play a greater role in developing party strategy.

The main resistance to the direction we were pursuing came when we argued for the development of an electoral strategy in the South. Ruairí was quite logically concerned that this would lead to an end to abstentionism – an important constitutional issue for the party. Abstentionism prohibited republicans from taking up any seats we might win in the Irish or British parliaments and in any assembly or parliament within the North. I didn't appreciate and understand Ruairí's concerns then because abstentionism was not an issue in the North. Active abstentionism worked there. In the South, it was different. And so Ruairí Ó Brádaigh resisted the development of an electoral strategy for the Irish parliament which involved attendance.

By 1986, our leadership put a proposal to the annual Ard Fheis for an end to abstentionism in the South. This was a fundamental political departure, and with it came threats of a split in our party. In the year preceding the debate, the letter columns of *An Phoblacht*, our party newspaper, were filled with those arguing for and against this change to the party's constitution.

It was a deeply emotional issue. Words and accusations like "traitors", "betrayed", "collaborators" and "sell-out" began to be thrown at those of us arguing for a change. Abstentionism had been part of the internal debate that split republicanism in 1969. It had then resulted on a number of occasions in republicans shooting and killing each other.

Now, as party president, I had to confront this issue. I came to be convinced that abstentionism towards the Irish parliament – the Dáil – had to go. I argued that it was a tactical matter. Could we advance our republican objectives better by taking seats in the Irish parliament or not? If we could, we had a responsibility to take that leap of imagination. As it turned out, the IRA was the first to take the plunge. Its constitution also barred IRA volunteers from taking seats in or supporting republicans who were prepared to take seats in the Dáil.

Suddenly and unexpectedly, a statement on 14 October revealed that an IRA convention had been held "after much careful planning". The IRA statement revealed that, "several sections of the Constitution of Óglaigh na hÉireann were amended, and by more than the required two-thirds majority, the delegates passed two particular resolutions. The first removed the ban on volunteers discussing or advocating the taking of parliamentary seats. The second removed the ban on supporting successful republican candidates who take their seats in Leinster House [the Irish parliament]."

Just over two weeks later, Sinn Féin's Ard Fheis was held in the Mansion House in Dublin. It was probably the best attended Ard Fheis in decades. It was also tense. Rumours of splits and walkouts abounded. In my presidential speech on the Saturday, I told the conference that, as the political conditions change, so must republican strategy. As a group, we were often successful when we had a flexible approach and at our weakest when we were forced into a static political position. The removal of abstentionism would not provide a magic-wand solution to our problems. In the South of Ireland, it would only clear the decks. Delegates and visitors to our Ard Fheis had to cease being spectators of a struggle in the Six Counties and become pioneers of republicanism in the Twenty-six Counties. We had to change our strategies, but not our objectives.

The main debate on abstentionism took place the following day, Sunday, 2 November. Pat Doherty, our national organiser, put Motion 162 from the Ard Chomhairle. It called for an end to abstentionism toward the Irish parliament and stipulated that successful candidates would not draw their salaries for personal use. The debate lasted five hours. Fifty-four delegates rose and spoke to the motion. One delegate claimed that to go into the Irish parliament would be "betraying the Republic", while another described Leinster House as a "sewer of filth created by the British". Another said, "When you lie down with the dogs you get up with the fleas."

Veteran republican John Joe McGirl, vice-president of the party and a close friend and a former abstentionist member of the Dáil in the 1950s, seconded the motion and told the hushed hall that after a lifetime working to promote abstentionism he had changed his mind. He believed that we had to make changes if we "were not going to hand down this struggle to another generation".

During the lunchtime break I met with Ruairí, Dáithí Ó Conaill and others who were against changing the constitution. I appealed to them to stay within the party, and not to walk out. After thirty minutes, it was clear that if they lost the vote they would leave.

Though very frustrated, I contained myself until that meeting was over. Then I sneaked out the back of the Mansion House with Colette on to Stephen's Green. I walked with her around the lawns and ponds at a furious pace, railing against the stubbornness of Ruairí and his friends. I had a lot of respect for them and I could see their point about abstentionism, but now that I had a national responsibility to create and promote strategy, I could see no strategic merit in their position. All of this I conveyed to Colette with great feeling. I could understand people leaving the party because they disagreed with its direction. But to divide our already meagre forces and to spend time and energy on such a pointless enterprise seemed futile to me. Surely there was more to unite us than to divide us?

When the vote was called in the late afternoon, 429 delegates voted for the change, 161 against. This ensured the necessary two-thirds majority. Immediately after the vote was announced, Ruairí and about forty of his colleagues stood and left the hall. Most of those who had voted against the change to the constitution stayed at the Ard Fheis. Those who left went to the West County Hotel where they established a new party, "Republican Sinn Féin".

While all of this turmoil was happening, the Sagart continued to plot a resolute course forward. He wrote to Charlie Haughey, then leader of the Fianna Fáil party. Fianna Fáil is the largest political party on the island and the dominant one in Southern politics. It was founded as a breakaway from Sinn Féin by Eamon de Valera in 1926. It describes itself as "the Republican Party", and up until the early 1970s it wrapped itself in the verbal rhetoric of Irish republicanism, laying claim to the United Irish movement of the late eighteenth century and the legacy of the executed leaders of the 1916 Rebellion.

In 1970, Irish politics was rocked by allegations that Irish government ministers – including Charlie Haughey and others – conspired to smuggle guns into the North for the defence of beleaguered nationalists there. Some of those accused claimed that they had been acting with the authority of the government. That indeed is my understanding of what occurred.

The Taoiseach Jack Lynch sacked Haughey, and he was later charged with conspiracy to import arms and ammunition illegally. Mr Haughey and three others were acquitted. He subsequently succeeded Lynch as leader of Fianna Fáil in December 1979. He was Taoiseach during the hunger strikes, when his role was less than edifying, the cause of considerable criticism by republicans. In more recent times Mr Haughey had been critical of the Anglo-Irish Agreement and of British demands to scrap Articles 2 and 3 of the Irish constitution – perceived by unionists to be offensive because they claimed jurisdiction over the whole of the island.

The Sagart sought to engage Haughey in a dialogue with Sinn Féin. Two months later, in January 1987, Charlie Haughey again became the Taoiseach. Contact between the Sagart and Mr Haughey remained intermittent after that. The two of them met on a number of occasions, and the Sagart also recruited well-known writer and historian Tim Pat Coogan to lobby Mr Haughey about our project. It wasn't until 1988 that these endeavours produced a result, but even then Mr Haughey held back from authorising government contact with us. Instead he authorised a Fianna Fáil party delegation to meet with Sinn Féin representatives.

This effort to develop an alternative was painfully slow. The Sagart and his colleagues continued to do their best, but we were being met with rejection – either of the outright variety or a less forthright but nonetheless negative, long-fingering kind that was debilitating and corrosive.

But it is obvious now that the real breakthrough had already occurred. In the midst of all the let-downs, procrastination, death and destruction, the relationship which was to slowly build between John Hume and myself was to be the springboard for leaps of imagination in the time ahead.

# Chapter Six

# *The Battle of the Funerals*

A cadre of senior party members was beginning to gel in an effort to build Sinn Féin as a relevant political organisation. A huge number of people came into Sinn Féin in the wake of the hunger strikes. We were not developed sufficiently to utilise the talents and energies of all these people in a programmatic way. Perhaps some were disappointed at the organisation they joined. That was our fault, not theirs.

But out of the prison struggle came a revitalised Sinn Féin, conscious perhaps for the first time of our ability to galvanise public support and to marshal support through elections. The hunger strikes were the beginning of the end of spectatorism in republican politics.

There was no questioning of the option of armed struggle. While there has never been any uniformity of republican opinion on aspects of armed struggle, armed struggle was accepted as the context in which we had to build politically.

We focused on a number of essentials: structured popular support; the need to develop an international outreach; propaganda and publicity; the development of relevant radical republican politics.

Our discussions broke some of these elements down. For example, structured popular support involved building a political party – Sinn Féin. An important internal dimension to this was the establishment of a Six County body responsible for the Sinn Féin organisation in the North. This was a hotly debated departure away from the old nine-county Ulster Cuige. It was seen by some as partitionist, but for us it was a practical step to deal with the political reality of two separate states on the island. Released prisoners, mainly from the North, with ideas and energy, including Richard McAuley and Denis Donaldson, joined with Mitchel McLaughlin and Gerry Ó hEara from Derry, Jim McAllister from South Armagh, Mary Hughes from North Belfast, Marie Moore,

Tom Cahill and Joe Austin, also from Belfast, and Francie Molloy from Tyrone.

We learned that building popular support meant making alliances with others of like mind – even on short-term issues. It meant breaking out of isolation. It meant getting an end to censorship. It meant working in tandem with people. Campaigning issues had to be prioritised dependent upon the importance of the issue and our ability to advance on that front.

Another important aspect – the international dimension – led us to contemplating where our best potential lay. We could draw from experience from other struggles – whether the Palestinian struggle or the anti-apartheid struggle in South Africa. We needed to affect public opinion within Britain itself about what was being done in its name, by its government and forces in our country. The European Union (or the EEC, as it was at this time) was also an important theatre. But the area with the greatest untapped potential for us, we decided, was Irish American opinion in the USA. This judgement was to have profound implications in the time ahead.

As we developed an ability to advance on all of these matters, even though it was only theoretical at this stage, our increasing willingness to compete with, to challenge, to debate, to discuss, issues of conflict or issues of peace with our opponents saw the beginning of a change in the relationship between the republican struggle and British strategy. From this point on, British strategy in Ireland was reactive to the growing strength of republicans. From 1981 on, Irish republicans became the engine for change, pushing and shoving the British government into positions they would have preferred to avoid.

All of this took place against a background of intensive military activity by both the IRA and British forces, as well as intense efforts to politically marginalise Sinn Féin.

I was very keen that we engage with unionists. Unionist antipathy toward us was such that there was little contact. As part of its pastoral mission, Clonard Monastery worked closely with a number of Protestant clergymen, and in September we started holding meetings in the monastery with Ken Newell of Fitzroy Presbyterian Church in South Belfast, the Revd Sam Burch and another senior Presbyterian minister from North Belfast. In time, others were to join these discussions, held sometimes three times a month. Fr Gerry Reynolds chaired the meetings.

The people we met were mostly middle-class unionists, without party affiliations, and with little comprehension of the dismal conditions in nationalist ghettos. I told them the story of South African Steve Biko, the radical black anti-apartheid activist who challenged white middle-class liberal Donald Woods to understand what motivated him.

"We know how you live," Biko said. "We clean your homes and mind your children and tend to your gardens. You don't know how we live. Don't judge us until you see what we put up with."

Those we met also had a message. It was about how we were viewed by those they ministered to. It was about how they viewed the armed struggle, how they attended funerals of IRA victims, how all this affected them and their congregations.

The first couple of our discussions were no-holds-barred encounters. But despite the gap of understanding, there was a willingness by everyone involved to listen.

On 1 May 1987, Sinn Féin produced and published *Scenario for Peace*, a document which marked the public launch of our developing peace strategy. We called for an end to British rule and argued that an enduring peace would only come about as a result of a process which won the support of a wide representation of Irish, British and international opinion. Such a peace process would have to contain the necessary mechanics of a settlement: the framework, timescale and the dynamic necessary to bring about an inclusive, negotiated and democratic settlement. Specifically, we spelt out the centrality of the "right of the Irish people, as a whole, to self-determination and their freedom to exercise that right". We also called for the establishment of an all-Ireland Constitutional Conference that would seek to negotiate a new constitution and system of government.

The publication of *Scenario for Peace* was an important initiative. We circulated it widely, nationally and internationally. While many of the ideas were already part of Sinn Féin proposals going back to 1972, we now dealt with the future of unionism and its relationship with the rest of the people of this island. We also argued, as part of a process for decolonisation, for the British government to repeal the Government of Ireland Act of 1920.

We subjected *Scenario for Peace* to a very critical review, led internally by Mitchel McLaughlin, an innovative thinker who was described as being able to get to parts of unionism other republicans couldn't reach. A formidable leader, he became one of the main builders of the Sinn Féin organisation.

Internal strategising, networking with the Sagart and talking to John Hume, as well as reorganising Sinn Féin, were not the only matters to be dealt with. There were issues of life and death on the streets.

A month before we launched *Scenario for Peace*, prominent North Belfast republican Larry Marley was shot dead at his front door by loyalists acting on information supplied by British sources. I had met Larry Marley in prison, where he had spent fourteen years. He and I had a common interest in escapes, though he was much more successful than me. Before his release, Larry was one of the main innovators of the great escape out of the H-Blocks. At the time that Larry was killed, the British government had instigated a strategy of attacking republican funerals. This arose from their policy of presenting the republican struggle as a criminal enterprise – hardly borne out by the presence of large crowds of mourners following coffins, usually flanked by guards of honour, sometimes accompanied by a firing party. The British objective was to drive mourners off the streets, to depoliticise the funerals of people who, generally speaking, had been killed by them or their surrogates.

Between December 1983 and May 1987, over twenty-five republican funerals were systematically attacked by the RUC and British troops. This controversial tactic caused widespread anger. It was exacerbated by the double standards of the Catholic hierarchy, which forbade the draping of the coffin in church with the Irish national flag, the tricolour. British Crown forces dead, however, were buried in Catholic churches with full military honours, including the Union flag on coffins.

At a time of great trauma, the role of the Church should have been to give solace, comfort and hope. Despite the efforts of decent priests, the bishops' ban on the Irish national flag alienated many, especially young republicans.

This period – which became known as the "Battle of the Funerals" – was an especially traumatic time. Most of those being buried were young men, the majority killed violently by assassins or in ambushes by British troops or the RUC. Their homes were then sealed off by huge numbers of heavily armoured Crown forces. In many cases, I witnessed mourners being abused. I was abused myself on more than one occasion. It was also difficult to get to a funeral. Even though I was an MP, I was often delayed at roadblocks or detained on the side of the road for hours on my way to a burial. Others suffered similar treatment. Irish wakes sometimes last a few days, during which friends, family and neighbours gather to comfort the bereaved. I witnessed RUC officers taunting mourners outside wake-houses. On two or three occasions, I saw riot police urinating in the gardens of wake-houses.

Bereaved families were told that no flag or any other emblem could be placed on the coffin and no guards of honour would be tolerated. The IRA responded quickly to this tactic by firing its volley of shots in honour of the dead person at a time and in a location that suited itself. It also scaled back any uniformed guards of honour. But from the British viewpoint, the battle of the funerals was more about breaking the spirit of the families and the communities involved than in dealing with the IRA.

Conflict erupted at funerals; plastic bullets were fired; there was hand-to-hand fighting and tense stand-offs. The stand-off at Larry Marley's funeral lasted days. His wife Kathleen was determined that her husband would be buried as he would have wanted, and as she thought he deserved. The heavy police presence was particularly oppressive. Fr Reid was among those who tried to negotiate a way for the funeral to proceed, but the RUC wouldn't budge. Eventually, the size of the crowd which gathered and the huge international media presence forced the RUC back. The funeral went ahead. It was led by thirty-five armoured RUC Land-Rovers and took over seven hours of determined resistance – including sporadic fierce fighting as the RUC attempted to close in around the hearse – before Larry was laid to rest in the republican plot at Milltown Cemetery. By the time the cortège reached West Belfast, it was joined by thousands of republicans who had been unable to get into the north of the city.

Larry's funeral was the biggest display of republican support since the hunger strikes. In scenes reminiscent of the mid-1970s, old women shook their fists at British soldiers. Patients at the Royal Victoria Hospital came out into the streets in their dressing gowns and slippers to show their support.

The day after we published *Scenario for Peace*, another IRA volunteer, Finbar McKenna, was killed when the bomb he was using on an attack on the Springfield Road barracks in West Belfast exploded prematurely. Once again, the family was hemmed in at their home. Thousands of mourners turned out. There was a bloody confrontation when they were attacked by baton-wielding and plastic-bullet-firing RUC men. Fr Reid was caught up in the press of people as we battled our way down the narrow streets of West Belfast.

During the three years of the battle of the funerals, the burials become massive intimidating displays of British military might, with hundreds of heavily armed, riot-clad RUC officers and British troops, scores of armoured vehicles and military helicopters in the skies overhead. During the burial of three IRA volunteers in Strabane, a journalist counted at least 130 armoured Land-Rovers on duty that day.

By far the biggest single loss to the IRA occurred at Loughgall in County Armagh exactly one week after *Scenario for Peace* was launched. Eight IRA volunteers and one civilian were killed when they were ambushed during an attack on an RUC barracks at Loughgall. The IRA unit, mostly in a Toyota van, approached the barracks along with a hijacked JCB digger carrying a 200-pound bomb. The SAS were lying in wait for them. Outnumbering the IRA by three to one, they were split into six groups, five in positions around the barracks, one inside. They had twenty-nine weapons, including two general-purpose machine-guns, Heckler and Koch G3 rifles and Browning 9mm pistols. When two of the IRA volunteers got out of the van and began shooting at the barracks, the SAS opened fire, firing over 600 shots. All of the IRA men had multiple bullet wounds. All of them also had single shot head wounds.

Danny Morrison and I were returning from a meeting in the South when we heard the news on his car radio. The first report was unclear, but it was obvious that there had been a large number of fatalities. It soon emerged through the media and the republican grapevine that those killed were volunteers. Later, it transpired that a civilian had been killed by the SAS also.

I spent that awful week on a sad, pitiable tour of wake-houses where I and Martin McGuinness and others in the Sinn Féin leadership were welcomed with great dignity by bereaved families. Then followed the funerals. The RUC were again present in large numbers but, for the most part, they kept their distance. They made no attempt to intervene when IRA guards of honour carried each tricolour-draped coffin a short distance. But there was harassment of people travelling to the funerals. I was detained on the road to one of the funerals of one of the Loughgall dead, Jim Lynagh. Our car was stopped by the RUC on the Armagh–Monaghan border. I got out of the vehicle and walked off, thwarting the RUC's intention to delay me. They angrily released the driver after a few minutes, and we made it on time to join the huge crowd at Jim's funeral. Martin McGuinness, Danny Morrison and I were among those who gave the funeral orations.

I spoke at Jim Lynagh's funeral. Jim was aged thirty-one and from County Monaghan in the South. He had been imprisoned in the 1970s and was a former Sinn Féin councillor on a local urban council. I told the mourners that Jim would not have complained about the enemy action: "He probably would have thought that they did not have to shoot some of the younger volunteers, but he would not have complained. Loughgall will become a tombstone for British policy in Ireland and a bloody milestone in the struggle for freedom, justice and peace."

The Loughgall funerals were demonstrations of support for the families of the dead volunteers. As I marched along through beautiful lush green early Irish summer countryside, part of the throng behind the coffins of these young men, I could feel a deepening sense of republican determination and defiance among the mourners. Here in County Tyrone – which had lost so many young patriots, not just at Loughgall but in other incidents – I felt a special affinity with the people around me. Republican Tyrone had lost many of its bravest and best and was facing up to its losses with determined, dignified defiance. The SAS had killed eight IRA volunteers. I instinctively knew that, all around me, other Tyrone republicans were making the decision to step forward and take their places. That was the nature of struggle.

Republicans weren't the only ones to suffer mass killings that year. In Enniskillen in November, eleven civilians were killed by the IRA. Those killed had gathered in the Fermanagh town for the annual Remembrance Day service. While the attack had been targeted on the guard of honour provided by the locally recruited Ulster Defence Regiment of the British army and not against the civilians taking part in the ceremony, the operation was wrong in its conception as well as in its execution. It was a disaster.

A bomb hidden in a community centre exploded without warning, bringing the building down on those who had gathered at the ceremony.

The impact of this was enormous. My response was that what the IRA did was wrong. The people who had gathered there were victims of an IRA action which should not have happened.

There was anger among our core group. Some people couldn't understand how such an action had been contemplated by the army. Our local councillors were in shock. Paul Corrigan was chairman of Fermanagh District Council. He and the rest of the Sinn Féin representatives, who were the largest group on the council, behaved in an exemplary manner, but they were in an impossible situation. When the SDLP moved a motion of no confidence in Paul they were supported by the unionists. Paul refused to resign. He believed the SDLP were being politically opportunistic. He had done nothing wrong as chair and had our support.

Only six years after Bobby Sands died on hunger strike and brought the republican struggle to a high moral platform, the Enniskillen bomb not only robbed eleven civilians of their lives, but it left the IRA open to accusations of callousness and indifference. This was particularly so because the occasion was a service of remembrance of British war dead.

Enniskillen came at the end of a turbulent week. Seven days earlier a trawler shipping IRA weapons into Ireland was captured off the coast of France. When the *Eksund* was searched it contained 150 tons of assorted weaponry. Five Irishmen were captured. The captain of the boat told how the weapons had been brought from Libya. He also claimed that four previous shipments had got through to Ireland.

The end of 1987 was marked by a turmoil of reaction across the island of Ireland. The Irish government moved to deal with what it described as a renewed threat from subversives. Throughout the state 50,000 homes were raided. Nothing of any significance was discovered except for a number of empty underground bunkers. In defence of this unprecedented activity, the Irish Minister for Justice Gerry Collins in a television broadcast said: "No state can tolerate a situation where arms of the value and power we are talking about are held by any group other than the lawful security forces."

# Chapter Seven

## *Murder on the Rock*

The Enniskillen catastrophe was seized upon by the British establishment. While 1987 had been a particularly vicious year, the capture of the *Eksund* and the claim that other shipments of arms had been landed now sent alarm signals through the corridors of power in the Irish capital, as well as London.

It was also the year in which Sinn Féin consolidated our electoral support in the British Westminster elections of June, the fifth major election campaign fought by us in the North since 1982. Coming almost two years after the Anglo-Irish Agreement and three and a half years after the publication of the Forum report, it was a crucially important contest. There was a huge onslaught on the Sinn Féin electorate with the British and Irish establishments, the Catholic hierarchy and a generally compliant media attempting to persuade Sinn Féin voters to stop supporting our party. Despite this our vote remained solid at 11.4 per cent, and I was returned as the MP for West Belfast. The overall unionist vote went down, and the SDLP increased by 3.2 per cent.

Amid the death and destruction, John Hume and I continued with our dialogue and the Sagart persisted with his networking. At the end of 1987, we decided that John and I would begin party-to-party meetings. The Sagart formally wrote to both of us as "an interested third party", inviting Sinn Féin and the SDLP to "explore whether there could be agreement on an overall nationalist strategy for justice and peace".

I brought the invitation to our Ard Chomhairle and received a positive response. We set up a sub-committee to handle the details of the talks.

John and I met on Monday, 11 January, for several hours. For the first time, our meeting was publicised. There was an immediate and generally hostile response from the governments, the other political parties and sections of the media. The British Secretary of State Tom King condemned the meeting and questioned John's judgement. The unionist response was unanimously hostile, the leader of the Ulster Unionist Party describing it as "sinister" and a "fatal step for democracy". Invariably, there was speculation about an IRA ceasefire. We quickly moved to categorically state that there was "no military agenda" to the talks. John Hume dismissed speculation of "ceasefire talks", but he found himself increasingly and uncharacteristically barracked during interviews.

He and I continued to meet separately. Little did we know that our discussions were to be pushed into the background when the wider community, but especially republicans, were plunged into an unimaginable series of bloody events.

It began on 6 March 1988. It was a Sunday, and a woman otherwise totally unconnected to our story was gazing out her apartment window in Gibraltar. She said she had been watching two people – a man and a woman – making their leisurely way down the road and was then distracted. She did not know that the couple were Irish. The man was Dan McCann, the woman Mairéad Farrell.

The woman's attention was next drawn by a series of loud bangs. When she looked toward the petrol station, the couple were now lying on the pavement, the women slightly over the man. Another man was standing near the pavement about two feet from the couple. She heard five or six more bangs. "I couldn't believe what I was seeing." The man appeared to be firing straight at the couple.

She saw the gunman get into a police car. He was driven away. Another local woman at her kitchen window had a direct view over the forecourt. She says a police siren drew her attention. She then saw a police car travelling from the direction of the Spanish border. It screeched to a halt and three men with guns leapt out. The driver wore a Gibraltarian police uniform. As the three men leapt the barrier on the central reservation she heard a shot. In a media interview later she said the couple immediately "put up their hands . . . like giving themselves up". The gunmen separated: two in the front, one to the side and the rear. Immediately, there was a series of shots, which she believed was delivered by all three. She is adamant that the couple had their hands in the air and that they made no movement towards their clothing. She believes Dan McCann tried to protect Mairéad Farrell. She also related how a blond-haired gunman "went into a crouched position and took deliberate aim at them". He "bent down and carried on shooting at their heads". She could see blood spurt out. "It was something I will never forget. It was horrible. It made me feel bad. I keep thinking I will wake up and this will all be a dream."

She also recalled the blond-haired gunman picking up discarded shells.

At the same time, another Irishman, Sean Savage, was hotly pursued by yet another gunman who opened fire without warning. Savage was shot in the back, and the gunman continued to fire shots into him as he lay on the ground.

A witness sitting in a car about ten yards away said: "I saw a man lying prostrate on his back under a tree. Another man was standing over him with his foot on his chest. I was horrified by what I saw. There were children and girls near by. They were upset and screaming. The man then showed an identity card to the girls. Shouting, 'Stop, this is the Police.' With his other hand he then bent down and fired his gun two or three times into Savage's chest."

Almost immediately after the executions of Mairéad Farrell, Dan McCann and Sean Savage, the British Ministry of Defence briefed the media that armed terrorists had been shot dead after a shoot-out. They also said that a bomb had been discovered outside the Governor's residence.

Republican West Belfast had been awash with rumour since the news reports about the killings early that evening. Dan McCann and Mairéad Farrell were well-known republicans of long standing. Sean Savage, though from a republican background, would not have been as well known. Very few people would have been aware of the trio's presence in Gibraltar, though friends or family may have known that they were not in Belfast. Families would not have linked the absence of their loved ones with the deaths now being reported. But within hours of the killings, rumours of who was involved were circulating.

I knew Dan McCann and Mairéad Farrell. I did not know Sean Savage. Mairéad Farrell had turned thirty-one three days before her death. She was probably the best known publicly of the three. In 1976, she had been convicted of participating in a bomb attack on a hotel, in which a colleague, Sean McDermott, was shot dead. She was sentenced to fourteen years in prison at the time when the British had just ended political status for prisoners and had embarked on a brutal campaign to treat political prisoners as criminals.

As OC of the republican women prisoners in Armagh prison, Mairéad was in the front line of the prisoner's battle against British penal policy. In 1980 she and two other women spent nineteen days on hunger strike as part of an effort to force the British to end the criminalisation policy. The following year, as the prisoners and their supporters sought to escalate the pressure on the British, Mairéad stood as a prisoner candidate in the 1981 general election in the South of Ireland.

She was released in September 1986 after ten and a half years in prison and became a public spokesperson for women prisoners, particularly against strip-searching. She also reported back to the IRA.

Dan McCann was thirty when he died. His wife Margaret and he had two small children, Daniel, aged four, and Meabh, aged two. Dan's parents owned a small butcher's shop, which had been a family business on the Falls Road since 1905. They were well known and liked. Dan joined the IRA when he was seventeen and was subsequently arrested several times over the following years. A frequent target of harassment, of death threats from British troops, on one occasion he narrowly escaped an abortive assassination attempt by a loyalist death squad. The last time he was imprisoned was on the word of an informer who subsequently retracted his evidence. Dan was released with three others who had been held on the same charges. One of these was Sean Savage.

I didn't know Sean. The youngest of the three killed that day, he was twenty-three. Sean was an Irish language enthusiast whose family had lived in the Kashmir Road in West Belfast, not far from Dan McCann's family. Sean was just four when in August 1969 the pogrom against Catholics – which is often taken as the start of the "Troubles" – saw many of the small houses in the streets around his home burned to the ground and several people, including a fifteen-year-old schoolboy, killed by loyalist mobs.

Like Dan McCann, he joined the IRA when he was seventeen. He spent one brief period in prison. He was well known in the Downfine area where his family had moved, and he was often to be found in the company of his younger brother Robert, a Down's syndrome boy.

In common with everyone else I was shocked by the killings. As the names of the dead emerged, I was upset to find that they were people I knew from families I knew. Danny Morrison, then Sinn Féin's National Director of Publicity, was the first republican I saw after the news broke. He had heard the first newsflash while listening to a programme on Radio Wales. By the time he contacted me, rumours were already circulating. Not long after, we were contacted by family friends of those killed. The IRA had contacted the McCann and Farrell families confirming the sad news that Dan and Mairéad were dead. Later we got the news about Sean Savage. A group of us pulled together to see what we could do about this unfolding tragedy. As we met in a house in Lenadoon in West Belfast, the first IRA response was broadcast.

"Three Irish Republican Army volunteers are believed to have been shot dead whilst on active service in Gibraltar. All three come from West Belfast and were attached to an active service unit of General Headquarters staff. Their families have been notified, but their names are being withheld until all relatives have been informed. Contrary to British army reports, none of the volunteers were armed when they were shot, so there could have been no gun battle."

The fact that the IRA dead were attached to General Headquarters meant that it was very difficult to get any information locally, and anyway our little group resolved very quickly that our first task was to help the families. In the first instance, this meant getting legal assistance. So while some of us went off to meet with the families, Joe Austin, a senior member of Sinn Féin, and I travelled to North Belfast, to the home of my friend and lawyer, P.J. McGrory. He knew Mairéad and Big Dan and Sean personally, having acted for all three of them at various times. Phyllis, his wife, and he were shocked as we told them the news in the sitting room of their home. He readily agreed to meet any of the families who wanted him to represent them. The first task was to secure the return of the remains. There was nothing that could be done about that at such a late hour and we agreed to meet early the next morning.

That meeting started in P.J.'s home at 9 o'clock on the Monday morning. It was the first time the families had met. They shared their grief and pain as myself, Danny Morrison, P.J. and Joe Austin awkwardly offered our condolences.

On P.J.'s advice, it was agreed that someone from Sinn Féin would travel to Gibraltar to claim the remains and bring them home. The families were asked to nominate someone to accompany the republican official. P.J. also advised that the Sinn Féin representative should have power of attorney to claim the bodies on behalf of all of the families.

As we left P.J.'s home, it was clear from his initial enquiries that there were going to be difficulties in getting the remains of the dead volunteers back to Ireland. The next forty-eight hours or so were stressful ones for all of us, but particularly for the families. The media was on overdrive. All eleven British national newspapers reported the story that a bomb had been found at the scene of the Gibraltar killings. Many gave detailed information about the size, purpose and type of bomb, as well as how it was defused. *The Times* even went as far as to print a map of where the bomb was allegedly planted. According to the *Daily Telegraph*, the three were challenged and killed after planting a 500-pound car bomb.

The British Foreign Secretary Sir Geoffrey Howe announced his approval of the killings in the British House of Commons. He claimed that the three were challenged and killed because "they made movements which led security personnel to believe their lives were in danger". British government officials later maintained that Mairéad Farrell seemed to reach into her purse for either a gun or to detonate a car bomb. Howe's statement, the *Independent* noted, was given with such conviction that the British Labour Party's Foreign Affairs spokesperson George Robertson felt moved to add his congratulations to the security services.

Howe also admitted that the three had been unarmed and that no trace of a bomb or bomb-making materials had been found anywhere in Gibraltar. Robertson clearly didn't listen to the detail of Howe's statement. Nonetheless the Labour spokesperson said, "The very fact that this enormous potential bomb was placed opposite an old folks home and a school underlined the cynical hypocrisy of the IRA."

There was no bomb. In fact, there was no shoot-out. There were no verbal challenges. There was no attempt to effect an arrest. The three people gunned down were unarmed.

Eyewitnesses said that Farrell, McCann and Savage offered no resistance and made no threatening movements. But the British government sought to create a climate in which the killings could be viewed as justified. Many of the international media carried the first British spins as fact.

Meanwhile Joe Austin and Mairéad's brother Terry travelled to Gibraltar. The two left on Wednesday, 9 March. They went to the morgue in the British Naval Hospital where they identified Mairéad, and Joe confirmed the identities of Sean and Dan.

Our endeavours to bring the bodies back met obstacle after obstacle. Spanish Customs refused to accommodate the removal. Airport handlers at Gatwick and Heathrow in London announced they wouldn't handle the bodies. Anyway, the families didn't want them going through any British airport. We were in a quandary. Initial investigations about transporting the remains to Tunisia or Morocco to ease travelling arrangements back to Ireland proved impossible. The only apparent solution was to charter an airplane. We had no money but, as always in times of crisis, good people covered the cost. Getting a plane was another problem. Suddenly all of the Irish carriers were either solidly booked, their planes were being serviced or they simply said no!

The families were transfixed in their grief. Their homes were inundated with friends, relatives and neighbours. Republican Belfast came together as a caring community in support of the bereaved clanns. And in England, too, there were signs of independent thinking. On Thursday Eric Heffer, the Labour Party MP and former party chairperson, denounced the Gibraltar killings as an "act of terrorism" and as "tantamount to capital punishment without trial". He was supported by over sixty Labour MPs.

At Queens University in Belfast, where Mairéad had been a first-year student, there was a sit-in at the Vice-Chancellor's office by students when the university refused to lower its flag to half-mast in accordance with tradition when a student or faculty member died.

By the end of the week the RUC were warning the mourning families that they would take action against the funerals. In an "open letter" they demanded that the families publicly state that "without qualification" the funerals would take place "within the law" and without "paramilitary trappings".

On Monday, over a week after the killings, Joe Austin arrived back in Ireland on a BAC 111 chartered from Luton in Britain with the bodies of the three volunteers. Joe sat in the empty plane on its sole seat beside the three strapped down coffins for the sad journey from Gibraltar to Dublin. Shortly after 4 o'clock on a rainy, dull afternoon, the plane arrived at Dublin airport.

As the plane landed in Dublin and Mairéad, Dan and Sean were again back on Irish soil, IRA volunteers in Belfast fired volleys of shots over a little memorial display which included three photographs of the Gibraltar dead.

I, Martin McGuinness and a few others from the Sinn Féin leadership had travelled to the airport along with representatives of the three families. In order to protect the families from the media, we waited in the restaurant of the Coachman's Inn on the Dublin Road close to the airport. I was touched by the sympathetic way the staff there responded to the families, as well as the presence of thousands of people who had gathered on the approach road to the airport.

A small group of us along with the families were taken to a maintenance hangar where the coffins were unloaded. As the three coffins were wheeled on trolleys through the hangar, workers stopped what they were doing and stood in silent groups. Many blessed themselves and some said prayers out loud. Mairéad came first, followed by Sean, then Dan. Veteran republican Joe Cahill reached out to touch Mairéad's coffin. Unbeknown to any of us, including Joe, he was suffering from colon cancer. The effect of this, allied to the emotion of the occasion, saw him falter for a split second. I thought he was going to collapse and I moved forward instinctively, but Joe gathered himself and stood united with the rest of us as we received our dead friends.

The three were first taken to the mortuary, then into a small chapel. Fr Piaras O'Duill offered prayers as the three coffins were draped in the Irish national flag, flanked by guards of honour. After the prayers, we began the 100-mile trek back to Belfast.

When I reflect on the killings at Gibraltar, the journey from Dublin airport to Belfast comes immediately to mind. Indeed, when I travel the main Belfast to Dublin Road at evening time, which I do regularly, I remember that long journey home.

The first leg from the airport to the border was uneventful, except for the remarkable numbers of people gathered along the roadside or who thronged into the towns and villages we passed through. It was 10.30 p.m. when the three hearses – with their tricolour-draped coffins – and accompanying cars with relatives and friends reached the border. So huge was the crowd in Dundalk that the cortège took one and a half hours to make its way through the thousands and thousands of people gathered on that dark March night. At the border, the main road was blocked by a large force of RUC and British army. The RUC wanted the flags removed from the coffins. There was a stand-off, which finally ended when I suggested that the flags would remain on the coffins but could be covered with wreaths.

An interesting insight into the times we lived in was provided by the Irish state broadcasting service, RTÉ. One of its journalists, Jenny McGeever, filed a report from the border, which included remarks from Martin McGuinness. Under the censorship law – Section 31 – broadcasting his voice was forbidden. When the report was broadcast early the next morning, it was terminated before it finished by a producer who heard Martin's voice. Jenny McGeever was subsequently sacked.

Meantime, the cortège, with its four-mile-long convoy of cars, was brought to a standstill by sympathetic crowds gathered in Newry. We could make our way forward only at walking pace. A number of times during this stretch of the journey the RUC tried to separate the hearses from the rest of the cortège. While they succeeded in forcing armoured Land-Rovers into the convoy, we prevented them from isolating the three hearses by putting our cars between them. It was after 1.30 in the morning before we left Newry.

On the outskirts of the County Down town, a small crowd of loyalists standing beside members of the RUC threw stones at the hearses and the mourners' cars. A brick smashed a side window in the car carrying Dan McCann's father Gerry. This car was driven by Paddy Clarke, a well-known Irish language activist who was later shot and killed by the UDA in front of his wife and son, in February 1992. The brick hit Sean Murray on the shoulder, bouncing off and striking Dan's brother-in-law on the head, cutting him badly.

There was still a forty-mile journey to Belfast, mostly along stretches of dual carriageway and motorway. Our convoy travelled fairly quickly. There was a sense of real danger as we sped our way through dark countryside on a road which skirted various villages and towns. These are mostly unionist and loyalist dominated, and we were attacked a number of times by stone or bottle throwing mobs as we passed through them. In quieter stretches in between – at crossroads and intersections – smaller groups of nationalists had gathered. They must have been waiting there for hours. Sometimes just two or three people, sometimes a score or more stood in silence as we sped past.

Otherwise the road itself was deserted. In Belfast, where the M1 meets Kennedy Way on the fringe of West Belfast, a large crowd had gathered awaiting the arrival of the remains. It had been a long wait: eight days since the killings at Gibraltar and almost nine hours since our cortège had left Dublin airport. We had radio contact with Belfast, and when we arrived on to the M1 motorway at Sprucefield, I spoke to my friend Terence "Cleaky" Clarke. He was in a house on the Andersonstown Road, a short distance from the waiting crowd. He wanted to leave there to inform others that we would arrive shortly. Closing down the radio link, I was satisfied the rest of the journey would be uneventful. I remember vividly saying as much to Cleaky. "OK, *chara*," he said. "We'll see you in a few minutes."

The radio went silent. At around 2.30 a.m. we swept around a bend on the M1 into the dark shadow of the trees which line the back of Lady Dixon Park. There was no other traffic on the motorway. I suspect this part of the motorway was sealed off. Our convoy was now flanked by scores of heavily armoured RUC Land-Rovers which commenced to hedge us in. Suddenly the hearse in front of us braked sharply. We skidded to a halt. The Land-Rovers pressed so closely around the cars that we couldn't open the doors. I rolled down my window. The night was loud with the sound of revving engines, the thud of armoured vehicles and the clamour of shouted commands.

"They're trying to separate us from the hearses," Big Eamon, our driver, said.

"Don't let them," I hissed.

The grey-armoured Land-Rovers were within inches. None of the RUC officers spoke, but our car was in the middle of a huge phalanx of armoured vehicles. It took up the entire breadth of the motorway. We remained stationary for what seemed an age. Then the loud mechanical intimidating noise of the vehicles changed. There was the clanging of doors as RUC officers clambered back on board.

"They're starting to move again," I shouted. "Don't let them separate us. Stay up his arse!"

The convoy moved off again.

"They've the rest of the cars boxed in," Eamon exclaimed.

We now drove at high speed. The RUC had succeeded more or less in hijacking the hearses. The family members and other mourner's cars were far behind. The original intention was to leave the M1 at Kennedy Way where sympathisers, other family members, friends and neighbours of the three dead volunteers were keeping a silent vigil. As we approached the sliproad, Eamon swore grimly.

"They're forcing me off the motorway," he exclaimed.

So they were. Inch by inch, in a nerve-wracking high-speed manoeuvre, a number of Land-Rovers were pushing between us and the hearses in an effort to slow us down and edge us out. Nothing was said. Their intention was clear. There was little we could do about it. We were being squeezed out by the sheer weight and intimidating speed, noise and bulk of the armoured vehicles. As we careened into the sliproad and off the motorway, Eamon braked on to the hard shoulder. We were infuriated at the ability of the RUC to hijack the remains, amazed to see the sheer size of the operation as the convoy of heavily armoured vehicles sped past.

Disappointed, frustrated and bone-tired, we drove the short distance to Kennedy Way. A huge crowd still patiently waited. It was after 3 a.m. I told the crowd what had happened and asked them to go home.

At the Sinn Féin head office on the Falls Road, other colleagues had been waiting for our return. We speculated among ourselves about where the RUC were bringing the remains. "They may have to do other autopsies."

"Maybe they're trying to stop the families from having republican funerals."

To our surprise, within minutes we got news that all the remains had been escorted by the RUC directly to their respective family homes.

66

"The bastards!" someone exclaimed. "All of that was about showing they are in charge."

We were exhausted after this long day. We had also heard a news report a few hours earlier that a man had been shot dead by the British army in Turf Lodge. Now we learned that he was an IRA volunteer called Kevin McCracken. Kevin lived not far from Sean Savage's home, which was ringed by British troops. He was preparing to launch an attack on the British army. It was subsequently revealed at the inquest that when he was shot, his rifle was unloaded.

Martin McGuinness and I visited all the family homes – including Kevin McCracken's – and spoke to the families. The Gibraltar families wanted the coffins of Mairéad, Sean and Dan opened. Some of us opened Big Dan's coffin and later Mairéad's. When we took off the coffin lids there was a thin lead lining across the inside of each coffin, which had to be cut open. Myself and Kevin Hannaway used car snips to remove the lead from Mairéad's coffin.

After Mairéad had been released from prison, Tom Hartley and I went to see her at her parents' home. She was in great form. I rarely saw her after that, though she did canvas with us during the election. A team of us including Mairéad ended up at our house for soup and sandwiches. A few nights before she was killed, I saw her in Ballymurphy at a presentation to the families of the volunteers killed at Loughgall. Mairéad made the presentation to Jim Lynagh's mother. Now, as we peeled back the lead lining from her coffin, I couldn't recognise the bright, alert, engaging young woman as the corpse that gazed up at us. Poor Mairéad.

The same morning a twenty-five-year-old Catholic, Charles McGrillen from the Ormeau Road in South Belfast, was the victim of a sectarian assassination by a loyalist death squad belonging to the largest loyalist organisation, the Ulster Defence Association (UDA). As he was working in the yard of Dunne's Stores on Annadale embankment, a lone gunman shot him.

The following day, Wednesday, 16 March, Kevin Mulligan, a twenty-seven-year-old Catholic from East Belfast, died from injuries he had received eight months earlier in another sectarian attack by the UDA.

That morning in West Belfast – as the bereaved families of the Gibraltar shootings prepared for their funerals – it appeared that the RUC had departed from their normal confrontationist strategy toward republican funerals. Instead of the usual blockade of the wake-houses and the saturation of the neighbourhood and funeral route, there was little more than the routine British army and RUC presence visible in West Belfast. In their statement of 11 March the RUC had said that if there was any IRA presence at the funerals, "the RUC will have no choice but to do its duty, distasteful as it is in such circumstances". The IRA for its part had made its position clear: "IRA volunteers of the Belfast Brigade have fired a three-volley rifle salute to coincide with the arrival on Irish soil of comrades Mairéad Farrell, Dan McCann and Sean Savage. The Irish Republican Army has now paid its honour to its fallen volunteers. We wish the bereaved families of Mairéad, Sean and Dan peaceful and dignified funerals."

The battle of the funerals had become a battle about legitimacy. But each day of the ten days since Dan, Sean and Mairéad had been killed at Gibraltar had seen controversy. There were appeals and calls from local community leaders and Church leaders and a lot of private pressure on the families not to have republican funerals. There was also a certain amount of pressure on the RUC, whose aggressive tactics at republican funerals were unpopular with nationalists. Internationally, the images of riot police or British troops attacking mourners told their own story.

As we left Dan McCann's parents' home, many people were relieved that the family were not to endure the gauntlet that other funerals had to run. Dan's funeral walked part of the way up the Falls Road and then drove to St Agnes's chapel where it was to be joined for a joint requiem Mass with Sean Savage's funeral. Mairéad's Mass had been celebrated the night before, and her funeral was to join the other two outside the chapel after Mass was over. In due course the enormous funeral cortège made its way down the Andersonstown Road to Milltown Cemetery. Belfast had not seen a funeral like this since those of Bobby Sands, Joe McDonnell and Kieran Doherty – the Belfast hunger strikers – in 1981.

Along the route and in Milltown Cemetery there were no British soldiers or RUC present on the ground, but an omnipresent helicopter kept watch from the skies. The cemetery itself is under continuous surveillance from the RUC barracks at its front gate, from British army posts on a nearby high-rise building and a British army base across the motorway which runs along the bottom of the cemetery.

Despite the grief and anger caused by the killings and the anguish of the ten days wait for the return of the remains, the absence of trouble and of the RUC meant that by the time we got to the cemetery, mourners had relaxed. The three volunteers were to be buried in the Republican Plot, and because there were three coffins and three large family groups, a larger than usual section around the plot had been cordoned off.

I was to be the main speaker at the graveside ceremony – delayed slightly because the graves had to be widened to accommodate the slightly larger coffins. I noticed a white van parked below us on the hard shoulder of the motorway at the edge of the cemetery. I presumed that it was the British army or the RUC and paid it little attention as the funeral ceremony began with prayers by Fr Alec Reid and Fr Raymond Murray. Fr Murray was the prison chaplain to Armagh women's prison where Mairéad had served her sentence. When they finished the prayers, Mairéad and Sean's coffins were lowered into the grave. I was helping to lower Big Dan's coffin in on top of the other two when there was a loud explosion behind me.

At first, confusion. No one knew what had happened. There was a second thump, another grenade blast, followed by shouts and screams as people took cover behind headstones and cars. I responded instinctively, seizing the microphone and trying to restore calm. All around me, people were crouching or lying behind headstones. Out of the corner of my eye I could see Cleaky pulling a man, who later turned out to be a journalist, into cover. The injured from the first grenade blast were lying on the ground being comforted by other mourners. A section of the crowd was chasing a man later identified as Michael Stone. For some reason, I thought there were two attackers. To this day I don't know if I was mistaken or not, but from the vantage point of the Republican Plot it was possible to see the panorama of confusion unfolding all around me. Below, the white van was still stationary on the motorway.

Grenade blasts and gunshots continued as the attacker, Stone, retreated towards the motorway. Armed with two handguns, he fired at the mourners who gave chase. He would turn and run, then stop to fire again at his pursuers or throw another hand grenade. His grenades exploded in the midst of the hundreds of mainly young people in pursuit. Closer at hand, people were comforting the scores of people injured by shrapnel. Cars were filled to overflowing as the injured were rushed to hospital.

I continued to appeal for calm over the microphone. Thinking back on it now, I have no recollection of anything I said. The bulk of the mourners remained around the plot and we restored some sense of order. It was now obvious that Stone's grenades, which he had aimed at the families and leadership group on the plot, had fallen short because of the size of the roped-off area.

We needed to continue with the burial ceremony. Dodie McGuinness from Derry was to chair the proceedings. I handed the microphone back to her and she proceeded with her remarks. As we buried our dead and paid homage to them, gunshots could still be heard above the dull thumps of grenades as they exploded in the soft earth of the cemetery.

The gunman – Michael Stone – eventually reached the perimeter of the graveyard. He was chased on to the motorway where he tried to stop cars while firing at his pursuers. Eventually the young people closed in on him and he was hit on the head with a wheelbrace. At this point the RUC arrived on the scene. Stone was dragged away and driven off in an RUC vehicle.

Stone had killed three young men. Thomas McErlean, aged twenty, was a married man with two young children and his wife expecting their third. I knew Thomas's mother Sally well. She was a prominent community activist. John Murray, aged twenty-six, married with two children, was killed also. He was from South Belfast and a promising soccer player. Caoimhín MacBradaigh, aged thirty, an IRA volunteer, had also been shot and killed. Over sixty others had been injured. Among them was a pregnant mother of four children, a seventy-two-year-old grandmother who received stomach wounds, and a ten-year-old boy, who was hit in the back.

I believe the attack on the funeral was conducted with the knowledge or co-operation of elements of the British intelligence agencies. I made this clear at a hastily convened press conference not long after we left Milltown. Collusion with loyalist paramilitaries has long been an important part of British strategy. Stone was a member of the UDA, an organisation largely run by the RUC Special Branch and British military intelligence. Stone subsequently was convicted of these three killings and he also admitted to three others: Paddy Brady, a Sinn Féin member shot dead in November 1984; a Catholic workman, Kevin McPolin, killed in Lisburn in November 1985; and a Catholic van driver, Dermot Hackett, in County Tyrone in May 1987.

The following morning we were back in Milltown again. We made our slow way from Kevin McCracken's home in Turf Lodge to the local church, and from there to the cemetery. We were joined by about 10,000 other republicans in a sad, silent, determined procession. The air of tension was palpable. Scores of hastily assembled stewards marshalled the proceedings. Some people were bandaged, and many commented that they had to steel themselves to return to Milltown.

Kevin was buried on Saint Patrick's Day. Later that afternoon I addressed a rally in Casement Park. The rally was in support of the Birmingham Six – the Irish men wrongfully imprisoned in Britain for allegedly carrying out bomb attacks in Birmingham in November 1974 in which nineteen people had been killed.

Over the next day or so I visited the homes of the young men killed in the Milltown attack. At the burial of Thomas McErlean, I expressed solidarity with the families of all the victims. I said a few words of thanks for the courage he and the others had shown in defence of the mourners.

Neither Thomas nor John Murray was politically active. Caoimhín MacBradaigh was. He was a volunteer and the IRA had acknowledged that in a statement. His funeral was on Saturday. There was a real danger that someone else would try to emulate Michael Stone. The funerals that week were all high-profile events. The television footage of Stone shooting and throwing hand grenades as he retreated from the cemetery had been broadcast internationally and repeatedly shown locally. There were media reports that Martin McGuinness, Danny Morrison and I were his main targets. Such was the speed of events and the volume of activity that there was no chance to put together any specific security around our leadership people.

The killings continued with the shooting dead on the Friday evening by the IRA of a young woman near Belleek, in County Fermanagh.

Caoimhin was buried on Saturday. His interment would bring an end to a long, sad, frenzied week of funerals. I think that was in all our minds as the large cortège made its weary, reflective way along the Andersonstown Road. The RUC had continued with the stay-away approach, which had first emerged at the funerals of Dan, Mairéad and Sean. Ahead of us, there were stewards and a row of black taxis slowing down oncoming traffic. Then, suddenly, there were shouts and the sound of a car accelerating towards us. I caught sight of it as it hurtled at breakneck speed into the slip road parallel to the funeral procession and in front of a row of shops.

Unable to drive forward because of the press of mourners walking on the side road as well as the footpath, the car's panicked driver crashed through the gears, then reversed at speed out in front of the shops and alongside us. People were shouting, screaming. The funeral came to a confused, uncertain halt. I will always remember Jim Gibney standing slightly apart from the throng up on the pavement, looking in understandable anxiety towards the commotion at the head of the procession where the car had been blocked in by a black taxi. None of us knew what was happening.

Just out of prison and into two weeks of mayhem, Gib, like the rest of us, was unable to see beyond the press of people. It was more than anyone should be expected to bear. People were dashing past him on all sides. Or instinctively closing ranks. Gib stood in bewilderment, part of it all but apart from it all. Like the rest of us, he was trying to see beyond the funeral throng to the seething, confused and smaller mass of people who appeared to have surrounded the car.

Suddenly the crowd fell back a little. Someone screamed, "He's got a gun!"

One of the two gunmen in the trapped car fired a shot.

The crowd closed in again. I remember saying that we should keep the funeral moving. We had been in risky situations at other funerals. Many times during the battle of the funerals, the RUC and British army attacked us, especially with plastic bullets. A few hundred yards from where we now stood my brother Paddy had been shot, seriously wounded by the RUC when they attacked the funeral of H-Block hunger striker Joe McDonnell. The best thing for us to do now was to stay calm and to stay together.

"Keep everyone together and keep going."

That is what we did. A smaller, uncertain cortège, we kept going nonetheless. Minutes later, word came that there were two gunmen in the car which had careened into the funeral. Then a whisper that they were Brits – undercover SAS men. Seconds later we passed the Kennedy Way roundabout where a lifetime ago, or so it seemed, thousands had gathered to meet the bodies of the Gibraltar dead. Now – just as we passed that spot – a number of single shots rang out. I instinctively knew that whoever had been in the car was now dead.

The British army helicopter, which had been the only visible sign of Crown forces, was now behind us, back where the funeral had been attacked. That is probably the one thing that everyone was clear about: we had been attacked. So it was a subdued but defiant journey once again into Milltown Cemetery where thousands gathered around the Republican Plot. There, Caoimhín's mother Bríd made a passionate appeal in Irish to those gathered when she said, "Jesus, Mary and Joseph, we pray to you today to remove the British from our country so that we may have peace." She led a number of other prayers in Irish and ended with the words, "May the Lord have mercy on the soul of my son and of all the dead no matter who they are."

I was moved by Mrs MacBradaigh's words. It had been a bewildering few weeks in which people were stunned, frightened, angered, shocked and frustrated by the Gibraltar killings, and then the deaths at the funerals. Other people died also. Caoimhín's mother's compassion for all the dead "no matter who they are" was for me a sign of hope amidst the mayhem.

Others were not so balanced. It emerged that the two gunmen apprehended by mourners were executed on the spot by the IRA. They were undercover British army officers Derek Wood and David Howes.

The Sagart was photographed giving the last rites to the two dying soldiers, who had been beaten and stripped by a section of the crowd. He later told a local community paper, "My first thought was that the funeral had been attacked again and I went in the direction of the gunfire." The pictures of him kneeling beside the soldiers' outstretched bodies were broadcast and published worldwide. There was a crescendo of outrage from establishment spokespersons. Seamus Mallon, deputy leader of the SDLP, said that the people of West Belfast "have turned into savages". Others said we were "animals".

While the killing of the two soldiers was undeniably brutal, to demonise the people of West Belfast was both counter-productive and wrong. Those who described us as savages were either feeding off their own ignorance or cynically fuelling a propaganda campaign to criminalise our community. What happened at Caoimhin's funeral was terrible, but it was a spontaneous, instinctive response of people trying to prevent a reoccurrence of Wednesday's Milltown massacre. Everyone at the funeral – mourners, journalists, priests and stewards – thought this and acted accordingly. The British army's explanation for the presence and behaviour of their two armed undercover operatives remains totally unsatisfactory.

The short period from the killing of the three IRA volunteers at Gibraltar to the killing of the two British soldiers in Belfast was a tragic, terrible cameo of the conflict. Twelve people were killed in the space of thirteen days. The majority of them died in very public circumstances and in the presence of thousands of other people.

As eyewitnesses to the Gibraltar killings came forward, the truth started to emerge. Even then, the eyewitnesses were subjected to a campaign of black propaganda and vilification. When the BBC and the Independent Broadcasting Authority scheduled two programmes about these killings, British Prime Minister Margaret Thatcher tried to force them not to screen their programmes. Thatcher was "outraged" when the programmes were aired over a month after the Gibraltar killings. She later accused the television companies of undermining democratic freedom and the rule of law. She also complained that "trial by television or guilt by accusation is the day that freedom dies".

The programmes claimed that two of the three IRA members, Mairéad Farrell and Dan McCann, had their hands up when they were shot, and that the third victim, Sean Savage, was shot in the back and then in the chest and head at point blank range.

In fact, Sean Savage had been shot sixteen times: five times in the head, five in the back, five in the front and one to the hand. Mairéad Farrell was shot three times in the back at about three feet. Dan McCann had been shot twice in the back and three times in the head.

# Chapter Eight

# *John Hume Plays His Part*

Within days of Caoimhín MacBradaigh's funeral, delegations from Sinn Féin and the SDLP met for our first formal discussion. John Hume and I had met on 3 March to agree an agenda for talks and to arrange an exchange of papers. That meeting was three days before the Gibraltar killings. Two weeks later, on St Patrick's Day, we presented the SDLP with a written summary of our position on an overall political strategy for justice and peace.

The history of engagement between us and the SDLP up to this point was not a happy one. Now with the Sagart's careful advance work, the private meetings between John Hume and myself, and the preparatory work done by the two of us away from the media spotlight, there was the opportunity for some actual progress.

On 23 March, the Sinn Féin and SDLP delegations met for the first time. It was a beautiful spring morning. Tom Hartley, Danny Morrison, Mitchel McLaughlin and I arrived in an old battered black taxi. It was an armoured vehicle – one of a number purchased by Sinn Féin to protect members against attacks.

St Gerard's is run by Fr Reid's Redemptorist Order, and it and Clonard Monastery, Liguori House in Dublin and the monastery in Dundalk were to play a central role over the years as a neutral environment for private dialogue. The venue for the meeting was kept secret.

The SDLP delegation, led by John Hume, included the party's deputy leader Seamus Mallon, Sean Farren, who had served as party chairperson for five years, and Austin Currie, who had been a member of the old Nationalist Party before founding the SDLP with Hume and others.

It was an awkward first meeting as we sat opposite each other at the table in the large room set aside for us. Most of us had never met each other before, but had actively been political adversaries for almost two decades.

The situation was tense on the streets outside. Each side had its own pressures. Before he left, Fr Reid prayed for the success of our efforts and urged us to find common ground. We then had coffee and began.

It had been a long road. Mallon's rejection in early 1986 of meetings between us had appeared to kill off the possibility of Sinn Féin and the SDLP getting together for discussions. The Anglo-Irish Agreement had just been signed the previous November between London and Dublin. The SDLP's star was in the ascendancy and its future seemed secure.

Two years later the Agreement had failed to win over nationalists or to isolate republicans as its authors had hoped. On the contrary Garret Fitzgerald's famous remark after the Agreement was signed, that the "nationalist nightmare is now over" was now haunting all its nationalist proponents. Calls by the SDLP for the disbandment of the locally recruited and predominantly unionist Ulster Defence Regiment had failed to achieve anything. Talk of reforming the RUC had come to naught. The treaty had failed to halt the shoot-to-kill operations of the British forces. Indeed, some twenty nationalists and republicans had been murdered in such actions since November 1985. In addition the Stalker-Sampson report into the first shoot-to-kill actions in 1982 had been suppressed; none of the RUC involved in the subsequent cover-up were to be prosecuted; and Britain had rejected Amnesty International's call for a full and independent inquiry into shoot-to-kill. Moreover, the release, and reinstatement into the British army, of British soldier Private Ian Thain after serving less than four years of a life sentence for the murder of a young nationalist, Thomas "Kidso" Reilly, in West Belfast, caused outrage among nationalists.

The Agreement was a potent counter-insurgency weapon for the British because constitutional nationalism had bought into it. Its failure to deliver real and meaningful change would cause problems for the SDLP and the Irish government, but it was still the only show in town and they weren't for walking away from it.

The two delegations were to meet twice more and I was to have one more separate meeting with John before the talks ended in September. The papers we exchanged – all eventually published by Sinn Féin at the end of the process – and the discussions we held centred around a number of key issues. These were: the role of the British government; the future of unionism and of the unionist veto over change and progress; the international dimension and improvements in conditions for nationalists living within the Six Counties.

The SDLP view was that the British government was neutral and that the conflict derived from the attitudes held by nationalists and unionists. They rejected a proposal by us – in a paper entitled "Persuading the British – a Joint Call" – for the Irish government, Sinn Féin and the SDLP to seek to persuade the British government to adopt a strategy to end the union.

The core of Sinn Féin's position was spelt out in our first document, *Towards a Strategy for Peace*. We criticised the SDLP claim of British neutrality. This claim ignored all the historic evidence of British domination in Ireland and was wholly contradicted by the events of the past twenty years.

We argued that justice and peace can best be established when the Irish nation can exercise its right to national self-determination. Any strategy to achieve this must secure maximum political unity in Ireland. I proposed that we launch a concerted political campaign nationally and internationally to win support for Irish demands and to mobilise support in Britain.

The Sinn Féin delegates also sought to address unionist concerns. We called on Irish nationalists to assure them of our full commitment to their civil and religious rights. We argued the need to persuade unionists of the benefits of an Irish society based on equality and national reconciliation. This required a democratic structure. There had to be national and international action to defend democratic rights and improve the social and economic rights and conditions of the population in the Six Counties.

We pointed to our concerns that the British were about to introduce new anti-discrimination legislation, which would fail to give legal status to affirmative action measures. In proposals for joint action, we proposed that the two parties should launch a broad-based campaign around the issues of discrimination and equality of opportunity in employment. The SDLP refused to support a campaign of this kind.

But while it would have been a foolhardy person who would have predicted that our two parties would reach agreement, much was achieved.

Crucially, we shared the political view that the Irish people have the right to national self-determination and that there would be no internal – that is, no Six County based – solution. Our parties agreed that a peaceful solution must involve Northern unionists and that every effort must be made to get their agreement to any change. We also acknowledged that the real question was how to end the British presence in Ireland in a manner which leaves behind a stable and peaceful situation.

However, the discussions also sharpened our understanding of the differences between us. The SDLP held an aspiration for a United Ireland, but that was all. It had no strategy and identified no actual methodology by which that aspiration could be achieved. However, Irish unity and the end of the British political connection was our hard-headed, absolute objective – not a vague aspiration. We were determined to achieve it in the here and now, not at some unforeseen point up a very long road. Armed republicanism had an armed strategy to achieve this. Sinn Féin and all other thinking republicans knew that the type of Ireland we wanted required much more than armed actions. But persuading physical force republicans to end these actions meant providing an alternative strategy that could effect real and substantial change. This would mean serious commitment from others to the goal of unity.

The SDLP delegation was not even in the ballpark. Apart from John Hume, they were hostile, confrontational, on occasion arrogant. They seemed intent on getting all of their anti-republican angst off their chests. The SDLP delegation produced papers that were in fact the basis of speeches and statements which were publicly used during our discussions to attack us. Not that I am complaining. To build a political offensive was to encourage public debate.

Inevitably, the rumours about an IRA ceasefire persisted through the eight months of intermittent meetings. There is some evidence to suggest that this arose partly as a result of some off-the-record briefings by SDLP sources, probably seeking to strengthen and justify their participation in the discussions. The discussions themselves were made more difficult by tensions within the SDLP. Occasionally, these tensions spilled into the media. In June Eamon Hanna, a former party secretary, said that the talks were being used by Sinn Féin to "upstage the SDLP". Hanna claimed there was pressure on to end the talks, and he complained about Hume's "authoritarian" manner. Later, in a sharp rebuke of his party leader, Eddie McGrady, the SDLP MP for South Down, remarked: "Terrorism will not be defeated by giving Sinn Féin a leg-up from the gutter."

The republicans had a strong feeling that the SDLP delegation seemed to be in these discussions under sufferance. Some clearly saw us as a political threat. Since the founding of their party, they had been the unchallenged representatives of nationalist opinion in the North in all discussions with London, Dublin and the USA. They were not used to others who shared their constituency challenging their stance and the efficacy of their position. So some parts of our discussions became an exercise in putting Sinn Féin in our place – second to them.

None of this came as any great surprise. The SDLP had long been a willing partner in the policy of isolating and marginalising Sinn Féin. We were more the "enemy" than the British and the unionists for some of the SDLP leadership. We were the upstarts, and right up to the end of the discussions, Seamus Mallon, Austin Currie and Sean Farren lectured and hectored us.

John Hume came at it differently. He realised that we were serious about discussing how our objectives could be achieved in a non-violent and non-threatening manner. John had come to appreciate that what was required was a new political process with a viable and effective political strategy to achieve Irish unity.

The inter-party discussions had become what one colleague described to me as "the dialogue of the deaf". By August, we knew the process had run its course, but it had been an enormously productive learning experience for our team. Despite the attitude of some of the SDLP leadership, of the two governments, the unionists and elements within the media, it was my view at the end of eight months of detailed debate that these exchanges had been important.

Our leadership group reviewed these talks in what was to become a standard way of working for us. Preview, consensus and review became normal working practice for the small focus groups we put together to deal with this developing process. Answerable to wider discussion or working groups and then back to the Ard Chomhairle of the party, we were fast developing an efficient focus and a collective approach to problem-solving and developing strategy and tactics.

Our review of the dialogue with the SDLP concluded that these talks, as well as all experience to date, showed that what was required was an alliance of Irish political parties and opinion, informal or otherwise. This alliance had to pursue objectives which looked at the interests and well-being of the people of this island with the aim of normalising relations between the people of the island and also between us and Britain.

We concluded that our efforts should be focused on working with John Hume. He had shown a greater interest than his colleagues. The discussions between him and me were constructive. Our developing relationship and our one-to-one talks pointed the way to the future.

Looking back on that period, it is possible to see the shape of Sinn Féin's peace strategy which was to emerge in the 1990s. In a situation in which the British government is clearly the strongest participant, any alternative to armed struggle, or any strategy to achieve justice and peace in Ireland, had to involve the maximum consensus on the Irish nationalist side.

Crucially, the end of delegation meetings did not mean the end of my private discussions with John Hume or the work of the Sagart. We had a sense of a real potential to bring about change if only we could create the right conditions. Our talks were popular among nationalists. I had a sense of growing nationalist confidence.

Moreover, Sinn Féin's involvement in discussions with the SDLP leadership was not limited to the objective set by Fr Reid. We were also interested in examining aspects of SDLP policy and in opening up a debate which would put democratic options on a public agenda. That is why we published the SDLP papers along with our own at the end of the talks.

During our lengthy discussions I came to know John Hume well. At his best he has an instinctive affinity for people, a generous, down-to-earth, common touch. At his worst he can be stressed out and very tense. While he looked to his party interests as well as any party leader would, he also looked at the bigger picture. At all times, his motivation was to bring an end to the killing.

Some commentators say that John was not a good political or party manager. In my view he was a good leader, in the fullest meaning of that word. Others disagreed with his approach and, in fairness, maybe not all of them were fully informed of developments. And perhaps with good reason. It is difficult to keep issues confidential if too many people know. But these were matters for John's judgement, not mine, except when rumblings within the SDLP frustrated our efforts.

I got the distinct impression at different times that there were efforts from within his party hierarchy to restrict John's room to manoeuvre. He never said anything directly to me, but after some of his executive meetings he was extremely unhappy, and at different junctures of our dialogue – particularly if we were releasing joint statements – he would be quite troubled about how his colleagues would react.

I also got to know John's wife, Pat. A wonderfully warm and down-to-earth person, she was always pleasant. I travelled quite often to meet with John, usually in their home in Derry or at Greencastle in Donegal. No matter what else was happening, Pat was always friendly and welcoming.

But no matter what progress John and I made, we needed Dublin on board. I had been encouraging the Sagart to pursue this. The public discussions between Sinn Féin and the SDLP, which Taoiseach Charlie Haughey had privately backed when informed of them by John Hume, provided the public cover for meetings between Irish government representatives and our representatives. However, when he finally authorised contact, Charlie Haughey decided that it would be party-to-party meetings (Sinn Féin and Fianna Fáil) rather than meetings with Irish government representatives.

He asked Dermot Ahern, a Dundalk-based solicitor and a TD, to head up the discussions. With him, Haughey sent Martin Mansergh, his principal advisor on Anglo-Irish affairs. Mansergh played a unique role in our ongoing efforts because he retained this position with Haughey's two successors. He sustained a continuity in the Irish government's approach. He is a historian who began his career as a diplomat in the Irish Department of Foreign Affairs before being recruited as a Fianna Fáil adviser by Haughey.

The two meetings that occurred in May and June 1988 – during the time we were also meeting the SDLP – were held in the Redemptorist monastery in Dundalk. Mitchel McLaughlin and party Vice-President Pat Doherty and myself attended. Both Dermot Ahern and Martin Mansergh were nervous about the meetings. They were blunt in their assertion that Charlie Haughey could go no further than private party-to-party discussions with us. The core of our dialogue centred on the issue of self-determination. The Irish government and certainly Fianna Fáil had – like the SDLP – an aspiration towards Irish unity, but had never done anything to advance it. We had the same discussion with the Fianna Fáil delegation that we were having with the SDLP.

We explained to them that nationalists in the North felt alienated from Dublin because of its failure to energetically pursue unity. I told them that the benefits to nationalists of the Anglo-Irish Agreement – and we had yet to be convinced that there were any – were not worth the provocative impact it was having on unionism. If unionism was to be put through a crisis, it should be over something that was advancing the objective of Irish unity.

The mood of the meetings was different from those with the SDLP, perhaps because Fianna Fáil did not feel threatened by Sinn Féin electorally at this time. Maybe it was because they couldn't really find fault with our analysis of the national question. Maybe it was because we were from the North and brought first-hand experience of the issues addressed. At any rate, the Dundalk dialogue was a good start. Significantly, it brought Martin Mansergh into discussions with Sinn Féin. This continuity on the Fianna Fáil side was to be useful later in developing the peace process within the Irish government.

Irish government involvement was crucial to any efforts to develop the basis for a peace strategy. The two different political realities, the effects of seventy years of partitionism, and the sometimes servile attitude which Irish governments affected towards their British counterparts made the relationship between the two governments an unhealthy one. Britain was a powerful nation, a former colonial power. Ireland is a small nation, colonised by the English. All of this made thinking outside the frame difficult for Dublin.

Some of the governing parties in the South, unlike Fianna Fáil, didn't even pretend to be republican or nationally minded. The SDLP was more or less Dublin's political wing in the North. Before the SDLP, the old Nationalist Party performed a similar role. And while there may have been tensions between what are referred to as Northern nationalists and the Irish government, this was generally kept in the private domain.

There is nationalist and republican sentiment in all the political parties in Ireland, North and South, with the obvious exception of the unionists. However, the Irish establishment do not want to see a national republic on the island. They will not work for a New Ireland if they feel that their class interests will be threatened. So they were bound to be cautious or hostile to other ideas. Popular opinion, therefore, was the key. Where the people decided to go, politicians would follow. Especially in the South. Especially on the national question. Especially in Fianna Fáil. No party knew the people better or had the same organisation and resources to stay close to them.

There were all sorts of political difficulties to be resolved. But in politics, too often expediency rules. The ongoing conflict should have been an incentive for peace-making efforts, but it wasn't. Charlie Haughey was overly cautious, probably reflecting mainstream Dublin opinion at that time. He certainly was reflecting the views of both governments.

The Tory government policy towards Ireland continued to be little more than a war policy. All their strategies were aimed at defeating republicanism. Margaret Thatcher was obviously a huge influence in all of this. It is my view that she authorised the killings at Gibraltar as a lesson to armed republicanism. There was also a huge number of nationalists and republicans arrested following the killing of the two British soldiers at Caoimhín MacBradaigh's funeral. They included Cleaky. With other mourners, he was subjected to a show trial and sent back to Long Kesh. Others received life sentences. There was huge and justifiable indignation within republican Belfast about this.

But 1988 wasn't just the year of the Gibraltar killings and the other deaths which followed at the funerals. During that summer, six British soldiers were killed in an IRA operation in Lisburn. Three months later in County Tyrone, eight British soldiers were killed in a landmine attack.

The issue of killings by the state had also come to the attention of Amnesty International. These disputed killings – referred to usually as shoot-to-kill – were the subject of an Amnesty report, which sought a judicial inquiry.

After the IRA killing of the eight British soldiers in Tyrone, Thatcher moved to introduce a media ban on Sinn Féin spokespersons. She also removed the right to silence for detainees. I liked the contrariness of this coercion. Republicans could not talk on the media. Republicans were compelled to talk in the interrogation centres.

London defended its censorship by drawing attention to Section 31 of the Broadcasting Act in the South of Ireland. This censorship act had been in place for fifteen years, completely banning republican spokespersons from the airwaves. The British law was different. The voices of Sinn Féin spokespersons could not be broadcast, but the onus was on journalists to police the censorship. Some later enlisted actors to mimic our words. The ban was to be lifted for elections. This led Eddie McGrady, the SDLP chief whip, to query why wasn't Sinn Féin also banned during elections.

That same month I celebrated my fortieth birthday at a surprise party with family and friends. I didn't feel forty. It didn't seem so long since 1968 when, on the eve of my twentieth birthday, the RUC attack on a civil rights demonstration brought the apartheid nature of the British state in Ireland to international attention.

Twenty years of struggle later, 1988 ended with the European Court of Human Rights at Strasbourg finding against the British government over the period of time it could hold detainees under its Prevention of Terrorism Act. The British Home Secretary Douglas Hurd – who had just weeks earlier introduced the censorship restrictions – was now forced to announce that Britain intended to derogate from the European decision. This was the eighth occasion that Britain had derogated. It now held the distinction of having been brought before the European Court more often than any other signatory to the European Convention. Britain now had the worst human rights record of any state in western Europe.

# Chapter Nine

# *The Killing of Pat Finucane*

Derogating from the European Convention on Human Rights wasn't the only public manifestation of Britain's secret and often dirty war in Ireland. Collusion – the recruiting, training and arming of unionist paramilitaries as a counter-insurgency tool against the IRA – was a central strategy of British policy. The attempt on my life in 1984 is one example of this. There are many others.

Their tactics were drawn from decades of British experience in fighting colonial wars elsewhere. Collusion between British forces based in Ireland and the various loyalist paramilitary groups was not new. The old Ulster Volunteer Force, a quasi-military group established by unionist political leaders prior to partition eighty years earlier, worked closely with the British army. Subsequently its membership came to form the basis of the police force, the paramilitary RUC, after the Northern state was established. But between then and 1969, the world had changed. Britain had fought and lost some fifty colonial conflicts across the globe. The empire was no more, unless you count us. In any case, in the spring of 1970 Brigadier (later General Sir) Frank Kitson took command of the 39th Brigade, which covered the Belfast area. Kitson was the British army's foremost expert on counter-insurgency.

The previous year he had published a book, *Low Intensity Operations: Subversion, Insurgency and Counter-Insurgency*. It became the textbook for British counter-insurgency strategy in Ireland. Kitson argued that to win against a guerrilla enemy which had the support of its community or at the very least a significant proportion of its community, one needed to reshape the government, the judiciary, the law, the police and the media. All government policies – social, economic, cultural, infrastructural – had to be moulded to suit the aim of defeating the enemy. He wrote: "The fundamental concept is the working of the triumvirate, civil, military and police, as a joint and integrated organisation from the highest to the lowest level of policy making, planning and administration."

Perhaps more significantly, in light of the relationship between the British state and unionist paramilitaries, Kitson rationalised the use of death squads and the corruption of justice: "Everything done by a government and its agents in combating insurgency must be legitimate. But this does not mean that the government must work within exactly the same set of laws during an emergency as existed beforehand. The law should be used as just another weapon in the government's arsenal, in which case it becomes little more than a propaganda cover for the disposal of unwanted members of the public."

The British initiated Kitson's counter-insurgency approach. The Military Reconnaissance Force – sometimes referred to as the Military Reaction Force or MRF – was set up. They killed Catholics and Protestants and carried out actions, including bombings, which sought to discredit the IRA. British intelligence agencies, working with the RUC and its Special Branch, began infiltrating the myriad loyalist paramilitary groups that had emerged in 1969 and 1970. Of course, not all loyalists are dupes. They have their own agenda – much of it anti-Catholic and based upon sectarian hatred or fears. But by and large the war aims of extreme unionism were the same as those of the British counter-insurgency strategists.

It was British intelligence agencies that helped establish the Ulster Defence Association, which became the largest and deadliest of the loyalist counter-gangs. The UDA, which remained a legal organisation for almost twenty years, and the UVF carried out an indiscriminate campaign of killings against Catholics. They were frequently supplied with information on republican activists by the British intelligence agencies, the RUC or Special Branch, including files, photographs and details of cars and movements.

In 1982 the Force Research Unit (FRU) was established as a unit within the British army Intelligence Corps. According to its senior commander, "The secret role of the FRU is to obtain intelligence from secretly penetrating terrorist organisations in Northern Ireland by recruiting and running agents and informers."

One of the first people to be recruited by the FRU was loyalist Brian Nelson. A former British soldier, he had joined the UDA in 1972 and was convicted in 1974 of the kidnapping of a partially sighted Catholic man, Gerald Higgins. Higgins was taken to a UDA club where he was tortured, including being subjected to electric shocks. He wasn't killed by his kidnappers but died shortly after as a result of his ordeal. Nelson served only slightly more than three years in prison for this. He was recruited by the FRU in 1983 and was told to rejoin the UDA. Two years later, he was appointed the UDA's Intelligence Officer in its West Belfast Brigade. Essentially his job was to gather intelligence on potential republican targets for the Ulster Freedom Fighters – the cover name used by the UDA to carry out its attacks. Then, and later in 1987 when he became the UDA Senior Intelligence Officer for the entire organisation, his associates in the FRU helped him update his intelligence files.

Nelson handed over to the FRU photographs of various targets in the South of Ireland, as well as the bulk of the UDA's targeting file. According to Nelson, the FRU removed out of date information and gave him back a more efficient target list. Nelson then rented a flat, and the FRU gave instructions to the RUC that it was not to be raided. Throughout his time as Senior Intelligence Officer, Nelson kept the FRU abreast of any new information on targets he himself gathered.

In the summer of 1985, the UDA leader Andy Tyrie sent Brian Nelson to South Africa. The UDA had been approached by Dick Wright, an agent for the South African arms manufacturer Armscor, formerly from the North of Ireland. He offered weapons in return for missile parts or plans obtained from the huge military production plant at Shorts in East Belfast. Nelson's job was to decide how serious this proposition was. He informed the FRU.

Nelson spent two more weeks in South Africa, having been told by the FRU that his trip had been cleared at the highest political level. There he met Charles Simpson, another British agent, also a member of the South African Defence Forces. On offer were assault rifles, machine-guns, Browning pistols, RPG launchers, hand grenades and explosives.

Nelson returned to the North and informed the FRU of the offer. In a journal he later wrote in prison, Nelson recorded that the first shipment into the country had been successfully smuggled through untouched. Subsequently, the UDA, UVF and Ulster Resistance carried out a bank robbery in Portadown, which netted £325,000, part of which was then used to purchase a shipment of arms. It consisted of 200 AK47 automatic rifles, 90 Browning pistols, 500 fragmentation grenades, ammunition and 12 RPG rocket launchers. The shipment arrived in the North in late 1987 or early 1988 and was divided up between the three loyalist groups. The UDA almost immediately lost its share when two cars were stopped at a checkpoint and the car boots were found to be full of rifles, handguns and grenades.

The impact of this weapons shipment (which the British knew about from Nelson, from other agents in the North, as well as in South Africa) is to be found in the statistics of murder which now emerge. In the three years prior to receiving this weapons shipment, loyalist death squads had killed thirty-four people. In the three years after, they killed 224, wounding scores more.

The dramatic rise in the number of Sinn Féin activists and family members being killed can be traced directly to this fact and to the information the FRU and the Special Branch were passing on to their agents within the loyalist death squads.

As the UDA's Senior Intelligence Officer from 1987, Nelson provided its death squads, and it is believed the UVF also, with scores of files, primarily based on information provided to him by the FRU. His handlers provided him with a taxi to conduct his surveillance activities and a hollowed out spirit level to hide incriminating documents. Nelson wasn't the only British agent working within the loyalist organisations. All were receiving and providing information to their death squads on potential targets.

In February 1989, Pat Finucane, a human rights lawyer whom I had come to know fairly well through his work representing the hunger strikers in 1981, was shot dead at his home. Pat was a good, conscientious solicitor who worked long, difficult hours under trying conditions. He came from a working-class background. In fact, he and I went to the same school on the Falls Road. He was also a husband to Geraldine and a father to three young children.

His devotion to human rights, his diligence in pursuit of his calling, and his success even when up against a judicial structure as biased as that which existed in the North of Ireland, had brought him to the attention of others. Within the RUC, he was a figure of hate. British intelligence agencies were plotting against him. Loyalist death squads, heavily infiltrated by agents and informers, were pointed at him as someone to be "took out".

As he and his family sat down for their Sunday evening meal on 12 February 1989, two masked gunmen forced their way into the family home in North Belfast. Pat was shot two or three times in the chest and stomach. As he lay on the floor, he was shot another eleven times. Geraldine was wounded in the attack.

The leader of the UDA group which carried out the killing was a Special Branch agent: Tommy Lyttle. The man who subsequently confessed to being the UDA gunman who killed Pat Finucane was Ken Barrett, also a Special Branch agent. The UDA man who supplied the gun was William Stobie, a Special Branch agent – later killed in 2001 by the UDA when he threatened to lift the lid on the Finucane case. And, of course, the man who provided the intelligence for the killing was Brian Nelson, a British army agent.

Two days after Pat's killing, Sinn Féin Councillor John Davey was shot dead a short distance from his home. John was a big gentle farmer, who had been interned during the 1950s. A year before, he had escaped death in a similar gun attack by Michael Stone – the man involved in the attack on mourners in Milltown Cemetery. Over the next six years, two more Sinn Féin councillors, eleven party activists, and seven family members, including brothers, sons, spouses and partners, were to be killed. Many others were seriously wounded. Republican homes and Sinn Féin offices became frequent targets of attack by loyalist death squads.

Almost one year after the murder of Pat Finucane, Brian Nelson, Tommy Lyttle and other UDA members were arrested by a team of detectives under the command of a senior British police officer John Stevens. The Stevens Inquiry had been established in September 1989 following the killing of Loughlin Maginn, a man loyalists claimed was a member of the IRA. They produced British army or RUC intelligence files in support of this contention. By the end of September, lists containing over 250 names, photographs and addresses of "suspects" belonging to the RUC and British army had been released to the media by loyalist groups intent on proving that they acted on accurate information. Within months, over two and a half thousand British army and RUC files were released by loyalists to the media.

Embarrassed by mounting evidence of collusion, the British had ordered an inquiry. The terms of reference were set by the Chief Constable of the RUC, who insisted on being consulted if the inquiry moved beyond a very narrow remit around leaks relating to Loughlin Maginn.

British Intelligence was worried that Brian Nelson might be arrested. He was given instructions not to say anything and told that they would ensure his release. Nelson ignored this advice when he was arrested. He talked to the Stevens team at length about his role. In the meantime, British Intelligence moved to lift all of Nelson's intelligence material, and the Chief Constable ordered that the Stevens Inquiry be given no access to it unless authorised by Special Branch.

A few months later, a summary of the Stevens Report was published.

The full report has remained secret. As a result of the inquiry, 2,600 documents came to light; forty-seven people were prosecuted with collusion-related offences; thirty-two were members of the UDA and fourteen were members of the Ulster Defence Regiment, including two members of the UDR who were convicted in relation to the killing of Loughlin Maginn. No member of the RUC or British army or its intelligence services were charged or convicted of their collusion in any of the many acts of violence carried out by their agents within the loyalist death squads. Of the loyalists arrested, only Brian Nelson faced serious charges because of his statements to the inquiry.

As his trial opened, he faced thirty-four charges, including two of murder. According to an extensive report by British Irish Watch, FRU files and Nelson's own journal reveal his involvement in at least fifteen murders, fifteen attempted murders and sixty-two conspiracies to murder. When the trial opened on 22 January 1992, the most serious charges against Nelson, including those for the murder of Terence McDaid and Gerard Sloan, were dropped.

A week before the trial, the judge, Lord Justice Basil Kelly, met with British Prime Minister John Major and the Lord Chief Justice Brian Hutton. A deal was struck between Nelson and the British Attorney General Sir Patrick Mayhew. It meant that little evidence was produced against Nelson and the least possible information was presented. The court also received a letter of support from British Defence Secretary Tom King.

Nelson pleaded guilty to a range of lesser charges, and his former boss – only referred to in court as Colonel "J" – gave evidence praising his work as an agent, claiming that Nelson had saved hundreds of lives. This included an absurd claim that Nelson had saved my life by supplying information of a plot to attach a bomb to the roof of my car while I was conducting constituency business at a downtown Housing Executive offices. Nelson was sentenced to ten years in prison and released after five. The Force Research Unit received at least seventy-four honours and awards for its work.

Amnesty International in its report *Political Killings in Northern Ireland* concluded: "The trial of UDA intelligence chief Brian Nelson revealed that a very high level of information on both loyalist personnel and operations was held by the army and the RUC. The trial also obliquely highlighted that little was done to disrupt these operations, to save lives, to dismantle loyalist groups and to take severe measures to deter collusion.

Brian Nelson's military handlers who allegedly provided information which assisted in targeting some individuals for murder, were not charged with any offence."

Even now, getting to the truth of all of this remains difficult. In December 2002, Martin McGuinness and I met at their request with police officers involved in the third Stevens Inquiry into collusion, the role of Brian Nelson and the killing of Pat Finucane. Both of us had been targeted by Nelson and his friends in the late 1980s, and it appears that the RUC Special Branch knew this. The Stevens Inquiry team wanted to know whether the RUC had ever warned us of the threats to our lives. Of course, the answer was no. In fact, this meeting, years later, was the first time we had been approached by any police officer about attempts to kill us. On the contrary, police officers actually directed and colluded in these attempts.

I knew many of those killed and injured during this period of intensification in the attacks by unionist paramilitaries. It was a very difficult time attending the wakes of party colleagues or their family members. Trying to give comfort, but more often finding myself being comforted by the strength and determination and resilience of the grieving families.

Life for me was an endless series of "safe" houses. Friends, relatives and often strangers opened up their homes to provide me with a bed and a place to rest. Like hundreds of others, my existence was not exceptional. It had become for many people a way of life made bearable by the love and support of our families and the kindness of other families who were prepared to put up with the risks involved in sheltering a political dissident.

Colette and Gearóid moved into the house of our good friend Kathleen Thompson. Kathleen had first given us shelter in the early 1970s, when we were not long married and I was on the run. She and Eamonn Largey, her first husband, used to vacate their home at weekends to give us the place to ourselves. Tragically, Eamonn was killed in a car accident. Through all these trials and tribulations and all the other twists and turns of our lives, Colette and Kathleen remained close. Indeed, our Gearóid and Kathleen's two daughters, Áine and Máire, were practically reared together. Years later, Kathleen remarried. Her new husband, Harry, was a friend of ours. When Kathleen fell ill with cancer, Colette moved in to help rear the girls and to nurse Kathleen as she slipped into terminal illness. Her death was a great blow for us all.

After I was shot, Harry insisted that Colette move from our more vulnerable home back into our old safe house. Harry was concerned about Gearóid and Colette's safety. His fears were well founded.

It was June 1993. It was around midnight. Colette was in bed at the time watching a late film. Gearóid, who was nineteen, was in another room catching up on some late night studying. The front of the house was in darkness and the street deserted. Then a hand grenade – part of the South African shipment – was thrown at the front bedroom window. It bounced off the toughened glass before exploding with a bang – loud enough for me to hear some distance away in another part of the district. The front porch was destroyed, windows in the house and in the home of our neighbours, Maureen and Billy McCulloch, were smashed. There was glass and debris everywhere.

Within minutes, I got news of the attack. By the time I arrived, the RUC and British army were on the scene. Not so difficult for them, as there is a barracks at the bottom of the street – less than 100 yards away, with high-tech surveillance cameras constantly monitoring movement in and out of the area.

On arrival I found an organised and unflappable Colette taking tea into several elderly neighbours who were badly shocked by the attack. Gearóid was firmly telling a large RUC man that his mammy didn't want him in her home. The RUC wasn't greatly interested in collecting evidence or forensics in any case; I found the lever from the grenade in the garden after they left. I have it yet as a key-ring. Mercifully – unquestionably due entirely to the toughened glass – no one was hurt.

The report of the Stevens Inquiry has now been delayed several times. It is expected to be published sometime in 2003. However accurate its contents – and we will make judgements on that when we see it – the full story of collusion has yet to be told.

# Chapter Ten

# *The End of the Thatcher Era*

Peter Brooke was the thoughtful face of British rule in Ireland. On 3 November 1989, on the occasion of his hundredth day as London's Secretary of State with responsibility for the North, he gave an interview that caused consternation among unionists and probably among many within his own system. Asked about the IRA, he acknowledged that it "is difficult to envisage a military defeat of such a force because of the circumstances under which they operate". He also suggested that in changed circumstances the government "would need to be imaginative" if the "terrorists . . . wished to withdraw from their activities". As evidence of this, he recalled the British experience in Cyprus where a British Minister had said "never" and within two years all of that had changed and the British had left.

Almost immediately, Brooke was forced into clarifying, correcting and explaining his remarks to an angry unionism. But his comments had been listened to carefully by republicans. Here was the possibility of a real debate. We re-issued our *Scenario for Peace*.

At that time, the unionists were continuing their boycott of the British government in protest at the Anglo–Irish Agreement. The UUP leader James Molyneaux came from the do-as-little-as-possible tendency of unionism. This seemed to work on the assumption that any attempt by unionists to take initiatives to address the issues underlying the conflict would move them into dangerous, uncharted waters. Very much under the influence of the arch-conservative and English racist Enoch Powell, who represented the UUP in South Down, Mr Molyneaux was by now an avowed integrationist. He had moved away from the idea of devolution, except perhaps of a very limited variety, and saw the best interests of unionists being served by strengthening ties at Westminster, a place where he felt very much at home.

As we have seen, the Anglo-Irish Agreement was in response to the radicalised political situation in Ireland – particularly, the growth of Sinn Féin in the North. A lot of the Agreement was smoke and mirrors. But to the considerable annoyance of unionists, it showed that if they refused to move, then a British government was prepared to move without them. The British government looking – even looking slightly googley-eyed like the Thatcher government – at the bigger picture was prepared to move in its own interests over unionist heads.

By the time Peter Brooke moved here, unionist protests at the Agreement led by Ulster Unionist Party leader William Molyneaux and Democratic Unionist Party leader Ian Paisley had petered out. Their campaign was without any real target to vent their rage against except the RUC or nationalists. Attacks on these embarrassed the unionist leaderships. Peter Brooke came at a time when unionists were ready for some sort of dialogue.

In August, a fifteen-year-old boy from the Oldpark area in North Belfast was killed by a plastic bullet fired by the RUC. He was the seventeenth person to be killed by these lethal weapons. Eight of the seventeen were children. Thousands more had been injured over the years, some scarred and crippled for life.

In September, the IRA bombed the Royal Marines Music School in Deal, killing eleven British soldiers.

Five months later, Brooke initiated a process of talks between the other parties – excluding Sinn Féin. In the following ten months, this process made no progress, and on 31 October 1990, he called a halt to it. Brooke received regular briefings from John Deverell, senior MI5 officer and overall head of intelligence in the North. He was informed by Deverell of a little known line of contact between the British and republicans. The point of contact – three people in the Derry area – had been used in the 1970s and again during the hunger strike period a decade earlier, but not since then. The British government representative, a senior British intelligence agent, Michael Oatley, who was their point of contact with the three Derry people, was about to retire. Deverell wanted permission to put someone else into Oatley's position.

Brooke had also been briefed on the Sinn Féin/SDLP talks. He was aware that John Hume and I were still in touch, still meeting regularly. And like most of his predecessors, he was an avid reader of our weekly paper, *An Phoblacht/Republican News*. It was also said that, on his arrival in Belfast, he had read many of the textbooks and history books about Irish republicanism in an attempt to better understand us. All of this led him to conclude that reactivating the "line" might be useful. His orders were that there should be "deniability" built into any resumption of contact. This meant that because the channel to republicans was through the Derry link, Brooke and the British government could continue to deny that there was "direct contact". Deverell also ensured that the only officials in the Northern Ireland Office – Britain's colonial office in Belfast, through which it ran the Six Counties – who would know of the line would all be British born. London didn't trust the local civil servants and feared, with considerable justification, that the predominant unionist ethos of the civil service would lead to leaks.

The British contacted the Derry link. Oatley said that he would like to meet Martin McGuinness before he left. Martin and I had been aware of the line of communication since the hunger strikes in 1981, although I did not know who was involved or how it worked, and had never asked. Both Martin and myself knew that the line went back to the 1974 IRA truce with the British government. We were both in prison at that time – he in Portlaoise in the South and I in Long Kesh – and we were enormously suspicious about this form of contact, not least because of our experience during the hunger strikes.

We wanted talks with the British, but we did not want to do our business through go-betweens. Apart from the direct discussions with John Hume, and despite the Sagart's endeavours, none of the other contacts were being conducted to our satisfaction.

At this time John Hume and I were persevering in our efforts to work up a common position. Despite our best efforts, this was frustratingly slow. John was also keeping the Irish government up to date on this process, but he was not an intermediary for us with anyone. He knew and understood why we were adamant that we alone would represent ourselves in any negotiations. Still, he had our approval to test the British government on some issues that he and I agreed on. He knew that Sinn Féin did not represent the IRA on any issue, that we did not negotiate for them and that the main thrust of our developing peace strategy was to work up an alternative to armed struggle.

So here we were: being asked to accept an invitation to meet with a British government official through a line of communication whose existence we knew the British government had never acknowledged, and which had not served republicanism well in the past. Martin knew the Derry people involved. There was no problem with their sincerity. But who was using whom in this situation? Why had London waited until Oatley was leaving?

Martin knew the dangers involved, but he was keen to proceed. The Derry contacts were putting forward compelling arguments. Even though we had reservations, if the British government wanted to engage with us, we had a duty to facilitate this, even in a cautious exploratory way. Having sorted out our own heads on this issue, we knew what we had to do next. We had to touch base with the IRA. There was no way to proceed unless they were on board. And there was no point in informally sussing army people out. This was an issue for the Army Council.

The British portrayal of the IRA is of a Mafia-type organisation made up of psychopaths and criminals, of men and women wedded to violence for its own sake. This was and is an entirely propagandistic position. The IRA members Martin McGuinness and I were to meet were capable of carrying on the war against the British for a long time. It had already lasted twenty-five years, several times longer than the longest previous campaign against the British presence in Ireland. For the first time, it had crossed several generations, involving men and women in their sixties and seventies, as well as young people, and all of those in between. The IRA was reputed to be the most effective guerrilla army in the world. It certainly didn't lack tenacity, courage and determination.

The only possible reason London wanted any dialogue with republicans was to achieve an IRA ceasefire. Even if the Sinn Féin leadership could be persuaded to go down this road, to get the IRA leadership to entertain this possibility meant convincing it that the republican cause would be advanced this way, that it was the Army's responsibility to assist such a development and encourage such a process. We were not yet in that position and furthermore we did not know if or when we would be.

At present, all we could possibly hope to achieve was to brief the Army Council fully on the ongoing work with the Sagart and John Hume and to get support for Martin going along to meet with Michael Oatley. Any results from this engagement would have to be judged as they developed. That is, if they developed. We had no great confidence they would.

In a 1990 press interview, an IRA spokesperson had said, "We can state absolutely, on the record, that there will be no ceasefire, no truce, no cessation of violence short of a British withdrawal. That, as blunt as that is, is our position." The Sinn Féin leadership had to persuade the army leadership of the merits of the strategy we were developing. Looking back on it now, it wasn't even a matter of convincing the IRA people to support the Sinn Féin position. Some did, others didn't. But eventually as the Sinn Féin strategy came together, most agreed to give that position a chance.

The difficulty with the Sinn Féin position was that it relied on the efficacy of an alternative, dependent to a large extent on progressive elements within Irish society and abroad. Some of these were tied to the Irish establishment, which had spent most of its energy denouncing and condemning the IRA, or working with the British and the unionists to defeat it. The prospects for success of an alternative would also be dependent on the most progressive elements within unionism and the British government itself.

Secrecy has been an essential part of the peace process. While my preference is that the process should be open, transparent and accountable, the reality is that there have been many times when private meetings have played a pivotal role in resolving difficulties, in reassuring a potential ally or building confidence with an opponent.

The contact with the army leadership – which was to become regular and constant as the process developed – has to remain one of the largely untold parts of the peace process. Those who would come to play perhaps the most important part in initiating the search for peace within armed republicanism will remain, except to their close associates, anonymous figures unknown to the general public, generally quiet and private citizens who shun publicity.

The case we put to them was straightforward. We did not ask anyone to buy into anything. We simply made a detailed presentation of where our discussions with the Sagart and John Hume were and reported on the approach by the British government through the Derry contact. We made the case that Martin should do the meeting as requested, but that we wanted their support for this – or at least their goodwill.

Some of those we met were against this proposition. Not against the meeting itself or against talks or the involvement of our core group and the work we were doing. They were not even in principle against Martin being involved in an exploratory process. If anything that was the least difficulty. His credentials were impeccable. Their big problem was about the nature of the line of communication and what it would all lead to. If Sinn Féin was to have meetings, then those meetings should be with political representatives, not with spooks or spies.

No one we spoke to was enthusiastic about this engagement, but, as they were not being asked to do anything, no one moved to block what we were proposing. The cautious mood was probably best summed up by one of the volunteers at the meeting.

"I think we should do nothing but note that we have been informed that Sinn Féin will be sending Martin McGuinness to do a meeting requested by the British government. Martin will not be representing us at that meeting. We wish him well and we appreciate all the work that is being done with Fr Reid and with John Hume."

And that was that.

Back at the core group, we decided to proceed and agreed that Martin attend the meeting only on a listening brief. The meeting took place in October. The Derry contact was also present. It was a low-key meeting that lasted around three hours. They discussed the political situation in general, the British government's attitude to Irish republicanism, and the current state of British policy and British-Irish relations.

Oatley told Martin that he was to retire from government service. He gave no indication that he would be replaced. Martin listened carefully and reported all of this back. A short time later, Oatley passed to Denis Bradley – one of the three Derry people who made up the line of contact – the text of a speech that Peter Brooke was to make a few days later in London. The speech, delivered on 3 November, addressed the role of the British in Ireland and the issue of British "neutrality". Brooke said: "The British government has no selfish strategic or economic interest in Northern Ireland: our role is to help, enable and encourage. Britain's purpose, as I have sought to describe it, is not to occupy, oppress or exploit, but to ensure democratic debate and free democratic choice. That is our way."

Our daily experience told us a different story from the one Brooke was pushing. But the fact was that he had said it while Margaret Thatcher, the British Prime Minister, was his boss. It was she who had once famously claimed that the North of Ireland was "as British as Finchley".

Brooke's remarks also came against a backdrop of momentous change in the world. The Berlin Wall had come crashing down the previous year, and a month earlier Germany had been reunited. Poland, too, had seen great changes with Lech Walesa elected President. Hungary had elected Vaclav Havel and the Soviet Union was in the process of dissolving. And of course, the previous February, like hundreds of millions around the world, I had sat in front of my television watching Nelson Mandela emerge after twenty-seven years in prison from the Victor Verster prison. That evening he spoke before tens of thousands in Capetown. Republicans in Ireland watched the battle of ideas between the ANC and the South

African government with mounting excitement. We watched. We listened. We learned.

Peter Brooke certainly wasn't telling the truth as we understood and experienced it. His explanation of British strategy in Ireland was not ours. But his remarks did suggest possibilities worth exploring. We were up for trying to persuade the British government to embrace a strategy that would right the wrongs of Britain's long involvement in Ireland, to reach out to unionism and to move British policy to one that ended the union.

Unfolding events on the world stage were evidence that governments, and apparently intractable situations, could change. I publicly wrote a lengthy response to Brooke's remarks, as did Mitchel McLaughlin. Our view was that the onus was on those who believed that there was an alternative to armed struggle to prove it. Still, we acknowledged that Brooke's remarks were interesting and the position he was proposing deserved to be explored.

Privately, the back channel was again open. Over the next few years, it took the form of occasional messages, details of ministerial meetings and confidential reports on the progress of the renewed British government talks initiative between the other parties and the Irish government. It also included a face-to-face meeting involving Martin McGuinness, another Sinn Féin colleague Gerry Kelly, and the new British representative, Colin Ferguson – or "Fred", as he was called by us. We were later told that his real name was Robert McLaren.

The Sagart was a man not given to wanting his name or face in the public arena. Yet he was so encouraged by Brooke's public speech and the republican responses to it that he wrote to *The Irish Times*, appealing to Irish political parties and the Catholic Church to talk to republicans. He was convinced that republicans would only give up the armed strategy for a political strategy if they were satisfied that such a strategy would be organised enough and strong enough to pursue the traditional aims of Irish nationalism.

Two weeks later, Margaret Thatcher was forced to resign from the party she had led through three successful general elections. Her strident approach and right wing policies had become increasingly unpopular in Britain. Her leadership style grated on the suits who ran the Conservative party. More importantly, it was felt she would lose the next election. As news of the coup broke in Ireland and events started to unfold, I watched the demise of the "Iron Maiden" with a sense of interested bemusement. This was one 10 Downing Street tenant who had worked her way deep into the psyche of Irish nationalists and republicans. And English miners and other working people as well. Now on our television screens, and much to her own visible disappointment, she was being evicted from number 10. All the ruthlessness, treachery and warped humanity of a Shakespeare play were there. On the Falls Road in Belfast, you could have sold tickets for the television news.

John Major was installed as Prime Minister at the end of November 1990. Several days later I wrote to him. The idea of writing to a British Prime Minister came to me after reading that Ho Chi Minh persisted in writing to the heads of the various foreign governments involved in his country. He did this for years, in bad times and better times. In light of the recent reopening of the back channel and my very real belief that we were only going to make progress through dialogue, I felt that writing to Major might be one way of engaging with the person who now had responsibility for British policy in Ireland. Then, in one of those lovely wee quirks that endear Sinn Féin to me, the Major letter was sent to 10 Downing Street, Belfast, by one of my geographically challenged colleagues. I am sure Uncle Ho never had that problem. But, eventually, we got it right. The letter landed on John Major's desk in February.

# Chapter Eleven

## *Early Ceasefires*

Despite all the death and destruction, 1990 ended with a surprising initiative from the IRA. That Christmas was the first Christmas in fifteen years that the IRA called a three-day ceasefire. Looking back on it now, this might not seem like such a big deal. At that time, it was. For the IRA leadership to publicly announce even such a short temporary ceasefire was a departure. It caused considerable and understandable argument and rumours within the IRA base. There was also widespread discussion and a general welcome, certainly at popular level, for the IRA announcement. But within armed republicanism, many questions were being asked.

The media, too, was full of questions. It was also full of the answers. Little matter, like a lot of journalistic comment, these had little basis in fact. The speculative stories paraded as exclusives, quoting "sources" and presented as insider information, fed into the republican rumour mill. No one should doubt the difficulties this caused. At a time when the Sinn Féin leadership was trying to develop new ideas on a range of issues, our energies and time were being distracted into scotching, or trying to scotch, a series of conspiracy theories. This was to become a pattern in the process, even up to the time of writing.

All politics, at some level or other or at some time or other, tend towards conspiracies. Some will argue that this is indeed the nature of all politics. I believe totally in politics as a means to empower people. Information in this context is power. But in our situation, as we sought to build the delicate process towards peace, it was impossible to give all activists access to all information. Most of the time there was little information to share. That didn't stop the rumours. It may have actually encouraged them. One of the most important negotiations for any leadership is the negotiation with your own side. Without this, the process will founder on internal difficulties.

This Christmas ceasefire was the initial test of all this. It was a gesture, a message of goodwill, aimed at public opinion – including unionist opinion. Those involved were bound to know that it would also be well received by the Sagart, John Hume and others working with the Sinn Féin leadership. There was an internal dimension concerned with what this unprecedented initiative might lead to. The Christmas ceasefire did not mean that the IRA had come on board with any of this. But it was a sign of things to come, evidence that the IRA leadership was able to think outside the frame when it wanted to.

Six weeks later the British government got a sign of a different kind. The IRA mortar-bombed 10 Downing Street. There is a frequently played television shot, recorded by a television camera, of the front door of 10 Downing Street shaking as the mortar bomb exploded in the back garden.

On the day of the attack, 7 February 1991, the War Cabinet, the body overseeing Britain's involvement in the Gulf War with Iraq, was meeting. The mortar landed just fifteen yards from where the ministers sat at the long table in the Cabinet room. Much of the blast was absorbed by the recently installed reinforced windows. Nonetheless, the explosion was of such force that it smashed these. Government officals and ministers in the Cabinet room, and in other surrounding rooms, were showered with glass. No one was injured. The mortar had been fired from a transit van parked just 200 yards away in Whitehall.

At our annual Ard Fheis in Dublin, I felt it was important to publicly address the issue of civilian deaths and injuries arising out of IRA operations. I wasn't prepared to engage in the sort of semantics that others used to condemn republicans, but then refuse to comment on the actions of the British army or RUC, or those killings carried out by loyalists. I spoke out on incidents in which civilians were killed or injured because that was the correct thing to do. I said, "Our dismay, our regret and our sympathy with the plight of families bereaved by the IRA is genuine." However, I pointed out, "Deprived of any alternative, armed struggle is the response of the oppressed, in any situation, to their oppression." Further, I said I wanted to speak directly to IRA volunteers. "You have a massive responsibility. At times, the fate of this struggle is in your hands. You have to be careful and careful again."

In the North, Brooke was still trying to breathe life into his stalled inter-party talks initiative. In March the Birmingham Six – six Irishmen who had been wrongly convicted of two IRA bomb attacks in Birmingham in 1974 in which twenty-one people were killed – were cleared of any involvement in the attack and released. These, and other miscarriages of justice, cast a spotlight on the criminal behaviour of the British police and on a justice system which turned a blind eye to this behaviour. That same month, the UVF shot dead three young people at a mobile shop on the Drumbeg estate in Craigavon in North Armagh.

A report by the British government's Fair Employment Commission again showed that Catholics in the North were still two-and-a-half times more likely to be unemployed than Protestants. The reality for Catholics was that the old patterns of discrimination remained intact even after almost twenty years of direct rule by the British government. The anti-discrimination laws were ineffective, evidence of the British government's unwillingness to challenge this area of economic domination by unionism.

In April, we were told by the line of communication that the Combined Loyalist Military Command – an umbrella group for all of the main loyalist paramilitary organisations – was about to announce a ceasefire to facilitate the inter-party talks. This announcement came on 22 April, a month after Peter Brooke told the British House of Commons that he had finally invited the unionist parties, the SDLP and the Alliance Party, for talks.

To facilitate the talks, the Irish Taoiseach Mr Haughey announced that the two governments would suspend the inter-governmental element of the Anglo–Irish Agreement. Unionist sensitivities satisfied, the talks commenced. In July, the talks and the ceasefire broke down.

In the meantime, the IRA was waging a relentless war against the British forces. In May alone, it carried out over thirty military attacks. Seven British soldiers and RUC officers were killed. In June, three IRA volunteers – Lawrence McNally, Pete Ryan and Tony Doris – were killed when they were ambushed in Coagh, County Tyrone. In that month and July, three British army helicopters came under attack in Fermanagh.

Over the summer, 1000 additional British troops were sent into South Armagh. They reinforced, rebuilt or constructed new hilltop forts which dominate that landscape to this day. And in Belfast a number of young people from the greater Ballymurphy area of West Belfast were arrested and taken by the RUC to the Castlereagh interrogation centre. The youths, aged between seventeen and twenty-one, were held for up to six days. Four were forcibly coerced, through mental and physical torture, to sign written confessions prepared by their interrogators. They were denied access to lawyers for the first seventy-two hours. Some months later, a further three young men went through the same ordeal and the Ballymurphy Seven campaign began.

Among those arrested was my nephew, Ciaran McAllister. His arrest was to have a significant effect on my mother. She had spent twenty years visiting her husband and sons and sons-in-law and other relatives, family members and friends in prisons throughout Ireland. Ciaran was to be the first of another generation – a third generation. Although she never said so to me, his incarceration added considerably to the stresses in her life.

Also arrested was seventeen-year-old Damien Austin, the son of our friends and comrades Joe and Janice Austin. This was to be his second ordeal in months. The first time he was verbally abused, punched, slapped and spat upon by interrogators. He was burned in the face by a cigarette, his trousers and underpants were repeatedly pulled down and a cigarette lighter was held toward his pubic hair. He was also told loyalists would kill him.

His torturers in Castlereagh frequently punched him in the stomach, the throat, on the arms and the back of the head. He was choked until he almost passed out and death threats were made against him. His doctor was eventually allowed in to see him. In an affidavit to the High Court, the doctor recorded that he "found evidence of severe assaults". On 28 August, Amnesty International took the unprecedented decision to issue an "urgent action" notice on Damien Austin. This was the first time this procedure had ever been used in the North. In these cases, Amnesty has to act rapidly to prevent the ill-treatment or possible execution of prisoners. According to Amnesty: "An appeal is issued when Amnesty International believes it has received reliable and accurate information in such cases."

While the Ballymurphy Seven were eventually to be released, their case highlighted the continuing use of officially sanctioned torture as a means of securing confessions and of intimidating detainees. In keeping with the Frank Kitson strategy of moulding the law to suit the political and counter-insurgency needs of the British government, confession evidence was admissible in the North's special non-jury courts. According to Helsinki Watch, this ensured "that the standard for admissibility of confessions in courts permits the admissions into evidence of unreliable confessions and violates the right of defendants to a fair trial".

Kadar Asmal was the chairperson of the Anti-Apartheid Movement in Ireland and a lecturer in law in Dublin. He subsequently became a minister in the post-apartheid South African government. He concluded that the "whole administration of justice is perverted and the vocabulary of dissent itself is prostituted. The use of special courts, where 10,000 people have been prosecuted and found guilty from 1973 to 1988, the use of supergrasses, the deliberate adoption by the administration of what one judge in Northern Ireland called 'the final court of appeal' – the lethal use of firearms to remove people who are embarrassments to the policies of the administration: all of these measures have been criticised or condemned by a series of governmental or unofficial international enquiries or by the invocation of international standards. My contention is that the United Kingdom is behaving and has behaved in the North in the same way that colonial powers exerted their sovereignty in the old-fashioned empires."

That summer Sinn Féin member and councillor Eddie Fullerton was shot dead in his home in Buncrana in Donegal. Roused from his sleep, he grappled with his killers when they broke into his home in the middle of the night. His killing raised once again the issue of collusion, including whether Garda briefing to the RUC could have aided those who shot him. Eddie was an extremely popular individual. A larger than life character, he starred at Ard Fheiseanna and was a popular local representative. Eddie looked after me and Colette during our sojourn in the caravan not far from where he lived. It was with great sadness that we travelled back to that idyllic spot for the funeral of our friend.

In July 1991, Denis Bradley informed Martin McGuinness that a new British representative (replacing Michael Oatley) had met with the Derry group. He had verified his status by producing a letter signed by Peter Brooke. The letter was read by Bradley and the two others and kept by the British representative. His status was further verified by Michael Oatley.

That was the beginning of a series of periodical meetings and occasional telephone conversations between the Derry group and the Brits. This channel provided us with detailed briefings on British government policy. Meetings took place both in the North and in London. The British representative declared that his objective was to ensure that republicans knew the thinking of his government. We also presumed that he was trying to build up a relationship with the Derry link group, as well as indirectly with us. He assured us that John Major had authorised this contact.

For our part, while persisting with private engagements, Sinn Féin was also continuing with the public debate. I wrote to the two governments, to other party leaders, Church leaders and others in August seeking open-ended discussions on the conflict in the North and arguing for the development of a peace process.

But very few were prepared publicly to stick their necks out to discuss these matters with us. The two governments were secretly talking to us, so we shrugged our shoulders each time we heard a minister from either government attack Sinn Féin and reject discussions with us. For their part, the leaders of the four main Churches regularly reiterated their refusal to talk with us. They did not have the same problem with other political groups or parties, with governments or the armed agencies of the British state. The attitude of the main Churches was entirely selective, expedient and political; all generally supportive of the establishment. If the Christian Churches are to play a meaningful role in almost any situation, they must have a clear commitment to inclusive dialogue.

In my latest letter, I reminded the Church leaders of the recent comments of Archbishop Tutu of South Africa who had visited Ireland a few months earlier: "Let your negotiations be as inclusive as possible. Don't let any feel they've been excluded. Let them be represented by those they regard as their authentic spokespersons. Otherwise talks, as we have discovered at home, become an exercise in futility." Regrettably, though we had Fr Reid and his co-workers, we had no Archbishop Tutu in Ireland.

In September, another Sinn Féin councillor, Bernard O'Hagan, was killed. This killing was in the North. Married with three young children, Bernard was a college lecturer and the second of our councillors in Magherafelt Council to be killed. John Davey had been shot dead two years earlier. Unionist councillors refused to accept a motion of sympathy for Bernard's death.

Earlier that year, the Sagart drew up another paper, similar to those he had produced already, outlining a "Proposal for a Democratic Over All Political and Diplomatic Strategy for Justice, Peace and Reconciliation". This proposal reflected the dialogue and broad agreements reached during the Sinn Féin/SDLP talks. In essence, he was proposing a Peace Convention. John Hume and I incorporated his ideas into our continuing discussions.

Fr Reid was facilitating these discussions in Clonard, writing and talking to each of us separately and together and travelling to Dublin to meet Martin Mansergh. The themes were constant. What could they say to convince republicans that the British were neutral? What was needed to construct the peace process? What role had the Irish government in all of this? It had to defend Irish national interests in the way Britain defended British national interests. What of the unionists? How to unlock the political mindsets on all sides? Out of this debate slowly emerged the idea of a joint declaration between the two governments. It wasn't such a daft proposition. The Anglo-Irish Agreement was essentially a joint declaration.

Taking his cue from the Sagart's paper to our two parties in 1988, John Hume wrote the first draft of a joint declaration for the two Prime Ministers in October. He took his draft to Charlie Haughey, who asked Martin Mansergh to look at it. A number of other Irish officials – Seán Ó hUiginn, a senior diplomat in charge of the Anglo-Irish division of the Department of Foreign Affairs, and Dermot Nally, secretary to the government – were also pulled into the frame. Out of their deliberations, an amended document emerged which John brought back to me. Essentially, it was a rehash of the contemporary position of both the British and Irish governments. It was totally unacceptable to us.

It was useless. The Irish government was giving us a position which it thought the British government would accept. It should have been putting together a position required for peace in Ireland, standing up for the interests of all the people of our island, mobilising Irish diplomatic and political resources in so doing.

As we saw it, a joint agreement was only as important as what it said. A peace strategy did not have to be dependent on a statement from the two governments, not at the beginning anyway. A common Irish nationalist position independent of or in tandem with a joint position of the two governments could be just as important. The argument we had put consistently about the need for an alternative to armed struggle was valid. The problem was that those we were dealing with on the Irish side did not seem capable of producing such an alternative. Increasingly, we would have to spell out to them what was required. We would also have to figure that out for ourselves. Not in terms solely of what would satisfy armed republicanism, although that was important. But more crucially the challenge for us was to establish what would actually provide a vehicle for freedom and justice and a lasting peace on our island.

We were now exploring positions secretly with the British, talking privately to John Hume about a peace initiative around a joint declaration, and also dealing indirectly but separately with the Irish government through the Sagart. We were exploring tentatively with supporters and others in the USA what contribution (if any) could come from that country. John was also talking to the British and to the Irish government. One colleague described our efforts at the time as "keeping balls in the air". As any juggler worth his balls knows, keeping more than two in the air at the same time requires a lot of focus and concentration.

We were to complicate it even more. It wasn't just a matter of getting a joint agreement from London and Dublin as John was trying to do. Unless we applied ourselves, an alternative to armed struggle would never be built. And it required the co-operation of others. It also required a strategy from us: a Sinn Féin peace strategy. The Irish peace process was born out of that discussion.

Our goal seemed simple enough: to get agreement between the Irish government, ourselves and John Hume, on the text of a joint declaration and the mechanisms to give effect to it and then present it to the British government. Allied to this, to put in place a broad consensus on the Irish nationalist side, including Irish America, to pursue a policy towards peace and justice and to engage with the unionists on this.

Our immediate task was to persuade the Irish government and John Hume that this was the right course of action: for them to stand up to the British government on that basis. Trying to influence these disparate elements into moving towards positions that would advance republican and democratic goals was going to be a hard job of work. This was particularly so because all our efforts were taking place against a constantly changing situation. And against an increasingly violent one.

At Christmas 1991, the IRA announced another three-day ceasefire. The line of communication remained active, and, as the year started, some of the messages related to the discussions between myself and John Hume. But the major part of these briefings was taken from reports of the progress, or lack of it, in the inter-party talks. At the same time, as one arm of the British government talked to us, another arm – the British army – leaked hints about the possibility of internment being used against republicans. This theme was taken up by some British, unionist and Dublin-based politicians and commentators. It was the equivalent of using petrol to put out a fire. Political opposition to Sinn Féin had reached such a pitch among other parties in the South that we were refused the use of our usual venue, the Mansion House, in Dublin to hold our annual Ard Fheis. Other public buildings were denied to us as Fianna Fáil, the Labour Party and Fine Gael abused their municipal authority to bar us. Eventually, the Ballyfermot Residents Association, in the working-class community of Ballyfermot – a sprawling Dublin district not unlike its Northern urban cousins in Derry or Belfast – offered us the use of their community centre.

Lucilita Bhreatnach was the Ard Rúnaí, or general secretary of the party. She comes from a well known and radical family who are immersed in the Irish language and cultural movement. Irish is her first language. She has Spanish, English and Italian as well. Lucilita headed up our head office team to get the logistical and other political back-up in place while a voluntary team of painters, carpenters and other construction workers headed up by my old friend from Long Kesh, the mural painter Danny Devenney, transformed the community building. The theme of our 1992 Ard Fheis was "Towards a Lasting Peace in Ireland". The document of the same name was the culmination of almost a year of work. It was described by some outside Sinn Féin as "more analytical, more thoughtful and more realistic".

The paper called on the British government to use its influence to convince the unionist section of our community that their future lay in Ireland. It called on the Irish government to work to persuade the unionists of the benefits of Irish unity and to persuade the international community to support a real process. The document looked at the role of the two governments, the SDLP and how a process of national self-determination had to be an integral part of national reconciliation.

It also acknowledged that armed struggle was recognised by republicans as an option of last resort when all other avenues to pursue freedom have been attempted and suppressed. We argued that constitutional nationalism, as represented by the Irish government and the SDLP, had no strategy to pursue a national democracy. Of course, we weren't simply bystanders in this. Our efforts with the Sagart, John Hume and others were about moving the SDLP and the Irish government towards building that credible Irish nationalist strategy. As part of the debate around "Towards a Lasting Peace in Ireland", I remarked that republicans might have to accept interim phases and interim arrangements while still working for a united Ireland.

*Towards a Lasting Peace in Ireland* marked a major shift in Sinn Féin thinking. Before then republicans had a notional view of a settlement coming from discussions, as in 1972, or in the 1920s, between ourselves and the British government. Now the onus for progress was being put very much on the two governments with sovereign power and authority. This explicit recognition that republicans had not the political strength on our own to effect the scale of change that we wanted went unnoticed by most commentators.

Towards the end of March, I travelled to Downing Street in London to hand in a copy of *Towards a Lasting Peace in Ireland*. There was obviously a publicity element to this trip, but it went beyond newspaper column inches or TV footage. It was about getting our ideas on the public agenda and engaging British public opinion in particular. Failure to do this was one of the big past weaknesses of the Irish struggle. While there is an inherent jingoism within elements of British public opinion, and while people in Britain generally are ignorant of what its governments have done in Ireland, I retain a confidence in the ability of the British people to do the right thing by Ireland, and Britain also, if there is an open and informed debate about the issues involved.

Throughout 1992, the British government representative was active in briefing us. Peter Brooke made a number of keynote speeches at this time, and we were advised of these in advance.

The war also continued unabated. In January 1992, eight workers employed in the refurbishment of an RUC barracks were killed in an IRA landmine attack. Two weeks later, a man presented himself as a journalist at the Sinn Féin office on the Falls Road. The office, housed in a dilapidated end-of-terrace building, contained most of Sinn Féin's national departmental outreach in the North, including our press centre. It was also a pick-up point for minibuses taking prisoners' relatives to various jails. There was always a mass of people, including journalists, coming and going through the security grill to take their place in the small waiting room. There they sat, alongside constituents queuing for attention at my advice centre. That day was no different. Michael O'Dwyer, a twenty-one-year-old who sat with his two-and-a-half-year-old son on his knee in the advice centre reception room, was waiting for help on a housing problem. Paddy Loughran was staffing the reception. Paddy was sixty-one with a large family of eight. Paddy had a habit of addressing everyone as "ye boy ye". He greeted the "journalist" who then used a pump action shotgun to kill him and Pat McBride, another local Sinn Féin worker. Michael O'Dwyer died also. Other Sinn Féin workers were injured.

The gunman, an RUC officer, then left the office and drove off. His body was found later at Ballinderry. He had shot himself with the shotgun.

I was at a meeting with others in the Sinn Féin leadership in Conway Mill a short distance away. We dashed back to the office to a scene of bedlam, arriving at almost the same time as the RUC and the media. There was jostling and scuffling as the families and friends of people who worked in the office arrived there along with other republicans. As the bodies of the dead were removed, there were scenes of high emotion.

The next day, 5 February, two members of the UDA walked into a betting shop on the Ormeau Road in South Belfast and shot dead five

Catholics. Almost exactly two weeks later, four IRA volunteers were ambushed and killed when they attacked the RUC barracks at Coalisland in County Tyrone.

For Irish parliamentary politics, 1992 was also a turbulent year. There was a heave against Charlie Haughey and he fell victim to the long knives. Albert Reynolds took over as Taoiseach in February. Briefed by Charlie Haughey about the ongoing private discussions and later by John Hume, it wasn't long before the Sagart himself was talking to Reynolds about the work which was being done on a possible joint declaration. The new Taoiseach's direct input gave a new impetus to the Irish government's role and to the work of rewriting and redrafting the joint declaration. Much of this relied on Fr Reid who, independently of John Hume, was travelling to and fro between me and the Irish government.

John was also talking to the British, including John Chilcot in the Northern Ireland Office (NIO). In March 1992, Chilcot told the SDLP leader that the Brits accepted that the Stormont talks process with Brooke was not going to meet the needs of the moment and that their real interest lay in a more comprehensive project – something along the lines of this initiative, but not a joint declaration.

I spent a lot of time travelling in the South and with a team of leadership people drawn from our strongest areas. We applied ourselves to the necessary tasks of building party structures throughout the island. This was time-consuming. Pat Doherty did trojan work travelling the country by public transport, providing a fire brigade service of sorts to the weaker areas, while others in the developing national leadership tackled the daunting challenge of building up their own local or regional structures. Despite the repressive ambience, there was a steady stream of people joining the party. Our structures had retained a thirty-two county shape of sorts, but it was hard work trying to point it in the right direction. Getting that direction was a task in itself. Apart from the big issue of the North, the party was consumed with trying to agree the correct mix of social and economic policies, particularly in the South. Internal education was one of our big chores. Breaking out of isolation remained a primary objective.

In April, John Major called an election. We had been preparing for that for some time. I spent most of the campaign canvassing throughout the other constituencies, but I knew when I returned to West Belfast in the last few days of the contest that something was wrong. We had a first class election team, and in the course of the previous few years we really had brought new politics – the politics of empowerment – to one of the most deprived and disadvantaged areas in western Europe. But something was amiss. Our opponents in the SDLP were fighting an aggressively negative campaign. This was doing us no harm in our heartland districts. Our team, as always, was enthusiastic, the response on the doorsteps was positive and the indications of support showed that we were on line to retain the seat. But I had a niggling instinct that something was wrong.

And it was.

The SDLP was represented by long-time Belfast councillor and local doctor, Joe Hendron. They had campaigned vigorously to win the seat back since we won it nine years earlier. This time their strategy was to persuade unionist and loyalist voters to tactically vote for Dr Hendron in order to take the seat from Sinn Féin. This strategy was enhanced by the involvement of a range of very reactionary forces within loyalist and unionist West Belfast. Several thousand unionist votes were marshalled.

We didn't see the unionist vote coming at us in West Belfast. But by the time I was going to the count in Belfast City Hall, our team knew we were in trouble. Siobhán O'Hanlon and Aidan McAteer deduced that as they watched the Shankill Road ballot boxes opening. They phoned me. Poor Fra McCann – one of our stalwarts in struggle, but always a bundle of nerves during election counts – was almost on the Prozac.

When I joined the count, Joe and I were neck and neck, but he was drawing ahead. One count and a recount later he won, with a majority of 589.

John Hume later told me that it was this event that persuaded him that I was serious about our discussions and my desire to build a peace process. Had I leaked that John and I were in secret discussions, the loyalist vote would have stayed at home and I would have won the seat. John Hume told me that my refusal to break confidence and exploit our discussions for party political or personal reasons convinced him of my good faith.

Whatever else was happening, there was no way that I would have jeopardised these discussions. They were more important than party politics and we were making progress. Furthermore, Albert Reynolds was showing more interest in our efforts than his predecessor. I knew there would be republicans all over West Belfast who would be kicking themselves for not voting. The SDLP had fought a clever campaign and Joe Hendron deserved his victory. Our vote went up marginally, but complacency within a section of our base was our downfall. We resolved that that would not happen again.

After the count, we had a motorcade around nationalist West Belfast to thank our voters. People came out in defiant droves to salute us. It was overwhelming. By the time we got to Springhill, the press of people was so strong that we had to abandon our cars. I was presented with a bouquet of flowers, a bottle of champagne and two ounces of pipe tobacco.

Joe Hendron remarked ruefully, "You would think they won the election. They organised a victory cavalcade." We didn't, but we had started fighting the next election even before we left the City Hall.

At this time Siobhán O'Hanlon was working in my constituency office. She was the mainstay of our constituency outreach and managed both my schedule and secretarial work. She also was a former prisoner. As we started to formalise our approach to the communications with the British government, Siobhán came into our group and acted as anchor person.

John Major was returned to Downing Street with a reduced majority. His policy on Ireland remained unchanged. So did the IRA's. The day after Major's election success, a huge bomb was detonated by volunteers in the commercial centre of London. The economic cost to the British government was enormous. Some estimates put the figure as high as £700 million. The human cost, too, was high: three people, including a fifteen-year-old girl, were killed.

Before long Peter Brooke was replaced as British Secretary of State by Patrick Mayhew. As the British government's Attorney General, Mayhew had authorised the Brian Nelson deal to cover-up the British role in the loyalist death squads and the killing of citizens. Mayhew almost immediately recommenced Brooke's inter-party talks initiative. Privately, he authorised the continuation of the back channel.

Separately engaging the Irish government through the Sagart and John Hume was making the difficult process of creating a joint declaration even more problematic than it needed to be. We had given the Irish government a position in June 1992 from John and myself which the IRA indicated support for. But it was now being argued over through this indirect process of negotiation. I wrote to the new Taoiseach, arguing that there was a danger of misunderstandings, that face-to-face meetings would speed the process up. I wrote to him again in September 1992 to assure him that, while there was a political risk for all of us, republicans would not break or breach confidentiality. We were negotiating out a process that would place our entire struggle on the line. It was vital to decisions we might need to make that we had the opportunity through face-to-face contact to make a judgement on the "intent" of the Irish government.

The decision to authorise meetings with us was clearly a crucial decision for Albert Reynolds. Lobbied ferociously by the Sagart and working on his instinct, Albert made the right call. On 14 October and again on 22 October, Martin McGuinness and Aidan McAteer met Martin Mansergh at the Redemptorist Monastery in Dundalk. Further meetings were to take place. These engagements were vital.

According to the Taoiseach, he later told the British Prime Minister about the process of discussions. He also told Major he would only bring a formula to him when he thought it had real potential.

My concentration on our efforts slipped for a time in September when our family suffered a grievous blow. My mother Annie had not been well. Nothing obvious or visible, although when I had recently seen her I had thought she looked a little wan. We had met after a ceremony in Bombay Street where a plaque was unveiled at the house where Tom Williams had lived with his granny. Williams was an IRA volunteer hanged in Belfast prison in 1942. It was as our car was leaving Bombay Street that I saw my mother. As it was a cold, wet and windy evening, we hustled her into taking a lift home.

A short time before this, she had suffered a small stroke. This followed an altercation at her home with the RUC. A grandson, Patrick Mulvenna, was painting the front door of her house. His father, also Patrick, an IRA volunteer, had been killed by the British army in 1973 three months before the birth of his son. On the day my mother suffered the stroke, an RUC armoured Land-Rover passed and then slowed down as its occupants spotted Patrick. Patrick, seeking to avoid harassment, went indoors. My mother was in the kitchen. Seconds later, RUC officers charged into the house shouting and yelling abuse at young Patrick. My mother intervened and ordered them from her home, but it was some minutes and further verbal abuse later before they left. My mother took sick afterwards, and the doctor told us it was a small stroke: "a little warning – obviously stress-related".

She seemed to recover, but then two days after I saw her at the Tom Williams event she died suddenly after a huge stroke on 4 September 1992. She was sixty-seven years old. Her life was filled with stress and her health was never the best, but her going was so unexpected that even yet, at certain times, it is hard for me to come to terms with her non-presence.

My mother had thirteen children, of whom I am the eldest. Three boys died at birth. The rest survived, five boys and five girls. When I was born, she was twenty-three, and a child came every year after that. I don't know how she coped. We were poor, and she carried our family. When the ten of us moved out, the grandchildren started to move in and the cycle started again.

My ma loved dancing and she had a terrific sweet tooth. She read a lot, as did many of her generation, and she sang around the house most of the time. All of these habits I have inherited, although my singing is not as good. I may have inherited other habits or traits; I hope so. One thing my mother gave me without being conscious of it is a deep appreciation of the unselfish, unconditional and undying nature of mother love. I told her that a few times over the years. Half joking, and serious as well. But when she died, I wasn't with her.

She was rushed suddenly to the City Hospital. Our family gathered at her bedside, including our brother Sean who was released from prison, handcuffed to a prison officer. If I had gone, it might have posed a danger for those who were staying. My ma would have understood. But I am sorry I didn't get to tell Annie Adams just how much I love her.

# Chapter Twelve

## *British Pre-conditions*

In October 1992, the British government's representative told us that the Mayhew talks with the other parties were going nowhere. We were given a two-page document: an assessment of existing problems. More importantly, the British representative also gave us a preview of a speech that Patrick Mayhew was to make in Coleraine in December in which he would say that the British had "no pre-selected constitutional outcome" in any talks. At the same time a message accompanying the draft speech reiterated the exclusion of Sinn Féin from talks and restated the pre-condition that only in the context of an end to violence would we be able to participate. The message also spoke of no "imposed solution"; no "preconceived master plan"; that any "new structures for the government of Northern Ireland must be acceptable to both major traditions"; that the British government also accepted the need for a "new North/South arrangement adequately to cater for and express both traditions"; and that negotiations would centre on the three main relationships "within Northern Ireland, within Ireland, and between the two governments".

Initially a Sinn Féin response was issued which rubbished Mayhew's speech. Our press officer, Richard McAuley, for once, was too early. But subsequently I made a considered response. This was the way of this process of private teasing out and public semaphore that we were now engaged in with the British government

Richard McAuley had been the prisoners' press officer in Long Kesh when I was there and he had taken great delight in editing – that is, censoring – my limited publicity work. He was the originator of the idea of forming Relatives' Action Committees in support of the H-Block men and the Armagh women. Back on the outside again, he did sterling work in the Sinn Féin press centre. He and Chrissie McAuley, also a former prisoner, were now husband and wife, with a family of young children.

They were both extremely hard-working and dedicated activists. Later I asked Richard to come and work directly with me, and he went on to become the best press officer in the business, the envy of other parties. And governments also.

In my response to Mayhew, I criticised the exclusion of Sinn Féin from the talks process, repeating my earlier assertion that we had a democratic mandate which had to be respected. I made the point that any "precondition on Sinn Féin participation serves only to delay our inevitable involvement. That Sinn Féin will be involved in talks is absolutely certain." Most political observers and media commentators rubbished this.

Censored, demonised and under physical attack, nevertheless we seemed to be making progress. Even though the violence remained at a high level, at least the commencement of meetings with Dublin was a positive development which could lead to the breaking of the cycle. But then . . . disaster. The Fianna Fáil/Progressive Democrat coalition government in the South fell over a row between Albert Reynolds and the leader of the Progressive Democrats. It was a tense time and the outcome of the elections was disastrous for Reynolds and Fianna Fáil. They lost many seats.

On this occasion, the winner was the Labour Party led by Dick Spring. A new Labour/Fianna Fáil coalition came to power in early January 1993, with Spring securing six of the fifteen Cabinet seats for his party. He took the post of Tánaiste (Deputy Prime Minister), as well as Minister for Foreign Affairs, with responsibility for the North and Anglo-Irish relations. Reynolds briefed Spring on the work to produce a joint declaration and the meetings with Sinn Féin. They agreed that Albert would continue the private discussions with Sinn Féin, work on the joint declaration, and the related issues of "structures, processes and measures". Dick Spring would, at the same time, pursue a separate path, placing an emphasis on talking to unionists.

We continued to push for direct face-to-face meetings with the British government. The British representative kept telling us to be patient. In February 1993, the "rep" became more upbeat about the possibility of delegation meetings. The government was serious, he said. "The IRA needs to provide the space to turn the possibility of meetings into a reality. A suspension is all that is required of them." According to the Derry link, the British "believed that two or three weeks was a sufficient period to convince republicans . . . Reciprocation would be immediate; troops withdrawn to barracks, checkpoints removed . . ."

We received all of this cautiously. We passed the information back to the IRA without comment. By the end of that month, the Derry link reported that the British representative had said that the British government had agreed to talks with Sinn Féin. They needed a "no violence" understanding over two or three weeks of private talks and no public declaration of this.

The talks, involving two or three delegates, could be held in Sweden, Norway, Denmark, Scotland or the Isle of Man. Martin asked who would represent the British side and they identified Quentin Thomas, the deputy secretary to Sir John Chilcot, the British permanent secretary to the NIO – the man most involved with Brooke and Mayhew in the back channel with Sinn Féin.

John Major authorised the sending of a nine-paragraph document to us, outlining the basis on which his government would enter into talks and emphasising that "there should be no deception of either side". The document stated that the British government "has no blueprint. It wants an accommodation, not an imposed settlement, arrived at through an inclusive process in which the parties are free agents." Martin McGuinness stressed the need for no pre-conditions to such a meeting and reported back to our core group.

By now we had formalised the remit of the core group which was handling these contacts for us. It was now a sub-committee of the Ard Chomhairle with a broad remit to make recommendations to the Ard Chomhairle in relation to all areas of work. This included the work with John Hume, with the Irish government and with the Brits, our contacts with unionism and our outreach in the USA.

The sub-committee, chaired by me, which was initially made up of Martin McGuinness, Aidan McAteer, Mitchel McLaughlin and Pat Doherty, had been joined since by Ted Howell, Siobhán O'Hanlon, Gerry Kelly and several more. Others were to join our ranks later. As the work increased we formed a negotiations committee, which was more nationally representative and in which some had formal responsibilities: for example, for keeping records, keeping the party informed, handling publicity and so on, as well as the actual negotiations themselves. The contact with the IRA was through Martin McGuinness and myself. The issue of what the IRA should do was rarely discussed by our group. Although I have no recollection that we ever decided on that, it was the way the group evolved. It was taken for granted that the IRA would take and keep its own counsel. Our task was to get the optimum position out of our work and pass it back into the party structures to whatever level was appropriate for clearance. The army tie-in was left to me or Martin.

The elements of our strategy were clear. To persuade the British to change their policy of supporting the union, including repealing the Government of Ireland Act by which Britain claimed sovereignty in Ireland; to persuade the Irish government to defend and promote Irish interests; to persuade unionists that their future lay in a new all-Ireland context; to initiate a debate leading to dialogue with unionists and Protestants; to win international support; to mobilise support for the Irish position, particularly in the USA; and to establish a democratic structure by which all of this could be agreed, implemented and overseen.

The next few months saw a continuation of discussions behind the scenes. These included more meetings between Martin McGuinness, Aidan McAteer and Martin Mansergh. John Hume and I kept in close touch and I met regularly with the Sagart. I also met privately with Michael Lillis, a former Irish diplomat who had played a key role in the negotiations leading to the Anglo-Irish Agreement. The engagement, a result of a personal initiative by a mutual acquaintance, was useful in giving me an insight into the mind of Irish officialdom.

Around this time, the IRA met with Gordon Wilson, father of Marie Wilson – one of those killed at Enniskillen. In the immediate aftermath of her death, Gordon Wilson had moved everyone by his poignant account of his last minutes with his daughter as she lay buried in the bomb rubble, and by his forgiveness. I met him myself some time later for a private one-to-one chat on the margins of the Forum for Peace and Reconciliation, and I found him to be a thoughtful and thoroughly decent Christian.

On 20 March two small IRA bombs exploded in Warrington in Lancashire killing two young boys, Jonathan Ball, aged three, and Timothy Parry, aged twelve. There was widespread outrage. The death of anyone is tragic, but the deaths of children cause an emotional shock which strikes hard. For my part, I was devastated.

The following day Martin McGuinness and Gerry Kelly met the British government representative, Colin Ferguson. Denis Bradley and his colleagues were also present. Gerry Kelly had spent over fifteen years in prison for bombing London, had escaped from prison and was eventually recaptured in Amsterdam from which he was extradited. He was now a key member of our core group. Martin told me later that Colin Ferguson had been keen to persuade him and Gerry that the British side was serious, that Mayhew accepted there could be no progress without Sinn Féin and that

*Bobby Sands*        *Francis Hughes*        *Ray McCreesh*

*Patsy O'Hara*       *Joe McDonnell*         *Martin Hurson*

*Kevin Lynch*        *Kieran Doherty*        *Thomas McElwee*

*Mickey Devine*

THE TEN REPUBLICANS WHO DIED ON HUNGER STRIKE IN 1981 (AP/RN)

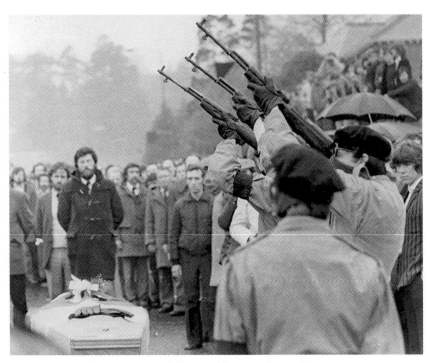

*Firing party and Gerry Adams at funeral* (AP/RN)

*Rioters target an RUC vehicle* (AP/RN)

*Fr Alec Reid* (Andersonstown News)

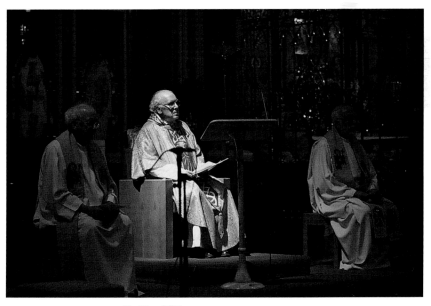

*Fr Des Wilson* (Andersonstown News)

*Sean Savage*

*Mairéad Farrell*

*Dan McCann*

THE GIBRALTAR THREE (AP/RN)

*Milltown funeral attack* (Pacemaker)

*RUC presence at a funeral* (AP/RN)

*Dáithí Ó Conaill* (AP/RN)

*Ruairí Ó Brádaigh* (AP/RN)

*Pat Finucane* (AP/RN)

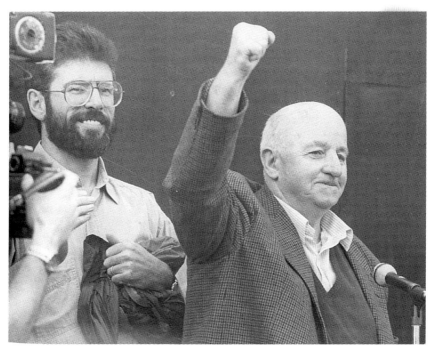

*Gerry Adams and Joe Cahill* (AP/RN)

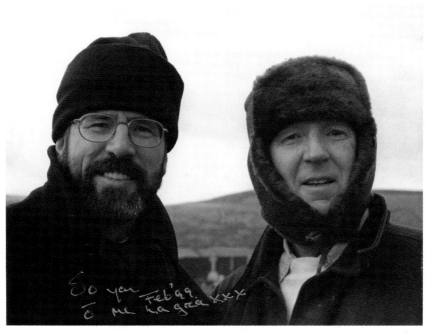

*Gerry Adams and Terence "Cleaky" Clarke* (AP/RN)

*Gerry Adams speaking outside Connolly House after the IRA cessation was announced*
(Brendan Murphy)

*Gerry Adams hemmed in on Ormeau Road*
(Brendan Murphy)

*Gerry Adams and Martin McGuinness at gates of Stormont* (Pacemaker)

the "final solution is union" between the North and South. His exact words were that the British accept that "Ireland should be one". Colin Ferguson argued for a two week break in operations from the IRA. He said that the delegation meetings would provide an opportunity that must be grasped quickly. Confidentiality he said was "of the utmost importance. Only Major, Mayhew, Hurd [the British Foreign Secretary] and the Secretary to the Cabinet know anything about this."

We were sceptical. The British had just spent twenty-five years trying to defeat the IRA – not trying to find a deal. And there was always the possibility that Colin Ferguson was speaking out of turn and that his views did not reflect those of his bosses.

Colette and I planned to spend the Easter weekend that year in Buncrana with my cousin Mary and her husband Tommy. I was to speak at the Easter commemoration in Drumboe in County Donegal, where four IRA volunteers had been executed in 1923 during the Civil War. En route, I met with John Hume at his home. I was spotted at the Hume household by a friend of a local journalist who passed the news of my visit to the Belfast correspondent of a Dublin Sunday newspaper. That journalist began to make enquiries of both our respective press offices.

Our office tracked me down. Mary did not have a phone, and I spent what seemed an eternity on Easter Saturday evening in the phone box outside a public house on the main street in Buncrana trying to work out a line with both our own people and with John Hume. I was enthusiastically encouraged in my endeavours by the pub's Easter holiday customers. They came out periodically from the bar in sizeable delegations to cheer me on. One man who was up from Belfast for the weekend later introduced himself to me. We were old school friends, and I was delighted to meet up with him again.

Eventually, I abandoned my high profile Main Street telephonic vigil, and John and I agreed to meet at Mary's later that night. We did so briefly. John was a bit unsettled. Part of his problem was that he had not briefed many, perhaps not any, of his own people about our dialogue. I did not have the same difficulty. A core of senior Sinn Féin people were fully informed of our deliberations, and once I got wind of the press enquiries I also tried to make sure that as many of them as possible had notice of the upcoming news story.

The revelation that John and I were still talking caused the usual political outcry. When that abated, and with the Easter break over, our core group reviewed the situation. From our perspective, while the dialogue with the Irish government was better since Albert Reynolds became Taoiseach, the discussions on the joint declaration had made little real progress. The feeling was that a public debate around a peace initiative could be productive. The popularity of a peace initiative could help inject a momentum that might make progress easier.

Of course, it could all go badly wrong. The Irish government might be spooked and pull out of the joint declaration project. The Brits might close down the back channel. Although this was not the most important dimension of our work we did not want to do anything silly to close down any avenues for potential progress. The Hume axis, the work with Dublin and our limited success in the USA were more important. But at the same time, few knew or could be told the true extent of the discussions, including some key players. It was all very delicate and tentative, and we did not want to make a mess of any of it. However, we felt a public dimension could be useful. I put some of these arguments to John Hume. After a thorough discussion, we agreed to release a joint statement on 23 April.

In it, we accepted that the most pressing issue facing the people of Ireland and Britain was the question of lasting peace and how it can best be achieved. We agreed that we needed a process of national reconciliation. We also ruled out an internal Six County-based settlement and asserted that the Irish people as a whole have a right to national self-determination. We saw the task "of reaching agreement on a peaceful and democratic accord for all on this island, as our primary challenge".

We concluded by revisiting Fr Reid's basis for the Sinn Féin/SDLP talks five years earlier, setting as our objective the development of an overall strategy to establish justice and peace in Ireland. We did not reveal the depth of our discussions or that we were negotiating with the Irish government for a joint declaration to be issued between the two governments. But the public mood, at least on the nationalist side, was good as the two leaders of nationalist opinion in the North appeared to be holding out the prospect of progress.

While all this was going on, the IRA leadership was considering whether it would provide the space for us to explore the British government's position. In principle, the IRA was against a ceasefire as part of a British government pre-condition for talks with Sinn Féin. Sinn Féin was against pre-conditions off any sort. If we didn't defend our mandate and the rights of our electorate, no one else would. At the same time, there was a duty to be positive and constructive if there were genuine goodwill efforts to get dialogue going.

If the British were looking for space for talks in order to avoid upsets, there were lots of opportunities for this if the will was there. In the ebb and flow of armed resistance, there were natural breaks in IRA activity. There were all sorts of reasons for this. Enemy activity or logistical or supply difficulties all had effects on how guerrilla war was conducted. Occasionally, the IRA command structure would order a halt to operations if it had any of these reasons for doing so. On the negative side, this happened rarely. On the positive side, when it did happen, depending on the reason and on obvious security grounds, no explanation was offered to volunteers or expected by them as long as the lay-off was not too long.

Unless the problem was huge, the IRA's Army Council would seldom be involved in these matters. They were essentially matters for the Chief of Staff and the army's command structure. But the Army Council had been told that the British government was thinking along new lines. No matter how sceptical republicans might be about that, London had already taken a step forward by authorising the meeting between its representative, Colin Ferguson, and Martin and Gerry. There was a need to explore what was being hinted at by the Brits and a duty on any responsible and thoughtful leadership to make it as easy as possible for all involved. To its credit, that's what the IRA leadership decided to do: to take a risk and make it as easy as possible for all concerned.

On 10 May, a message was passed by Martin via the Derry link to the British government informing Major and Mayhew that Sinn Féin "had sought and received a commitment which will permit you to proceed so that we can both explore the potential for developing a real peace process". In other words, the IRA had agreed to a two-week undeclared suspension of military operations. The message spoke of the need to agree agendas and formats for meetings and for the British to nominate someone to liaise with Martin McGuinness. We also urged that the meetings proceed speedily, stating that Sinn Féin had prepared our response to the British paper and this would be presented at the first meeting of a proposed joint secretariat.

This decision by the army leadership was the biggest breakthrough so far. I felt cagey. I knew it was the right thing to do, and there was a sense of satisfaction that we had persuaded people to take this step. It had been accomplished by dint of a lot of very hard work and some innovative thinking by those involved. But I didn't feel elated, except perhaps in the way a chess player may feel when he plans a move whose outcome depends on how the opposition reacts. What happened now was totally dependent on the British government proceeding as they had promised. This was new ground. I have never developed any sense of reliance on the British government. Until now, this was a long game, played slow. Now, the Sinn Féin leadership had delivered. More importantly the IRA leadership had stuck its neck out. It had moved first. Granted it was a defensible position, but it was one that the rank and file were not aware of, nor could they be, at least not until the exploratory phase was finished. In the meantime, a speedy response and secrecy by the Brits were essential. The secrecy lasted one day.

The following day, we had to contact the British expressing concern about a report out of Washington that a reporter working for an English paper had been briefed by British sources on the talks. Two days later, the British confirmed that one of their people was responsible but that it was under control. They said, if asked their press people would deny it. Almost two weeks later, the Derry link reported back that the British representative, Ferguson, had spoken to them on 24 May on his return from holidays. He gave a long account of support from officials for the IRA offer and of the debate around it.

Apparently the issue was discussed at a specially convened meeting involving Hurd, Major himself, the most senior of their officials and another senior minister Kenneth Clarke. There was indecision and objections, particularly we were told from Ken Clarke. Mayhew was wobbling between "pushing for acceptance and wanting a safer, longer period of cessation". John Major, we were told, had instructed his secretary to draw up a programme which he would be able to announce in parliament. It was obvious that the British had backed away from their proposal, and their representative was deeply apologetic about this.

Martin and I decided that we weren't going to accept this as a proper response to what we had achieved. The very least we would do was wait for a formal attitude to the 10 May proposition.

Meantime, there was a vile, vicious kick-back from some of the professional Southern "opinionators" – particularly in the Independent Newspaper group – against the initiatives by John Hume and me. John was subjected to a particularly personal, totally unfair campaign of vilification that was sustained for a considerable time by sections of the Dublin media. This campaign was out of sync, in my experience, with popular nationalist opinion. But it did have its effect on the politicians, particularly in the Irish government. By May 1993, there was little progress in our discussions with Dublin on a joint declaration.

Given that this was a Fianna Fáil led administration, we knew they were producing a more advanced version than any declaration which would have been provided by the other parties. At the same time, we were also conscious that the position being pressed on us was a dilution of the usual Fianna Fáil rhetoric. This was not on. We pushed hard for the Irish government to engage with the British on the Hume/Adams position. We were putting it up to the Reynolds administration.

So was the IRA. Its leadership wrote to the Irish government, expressing their seriousness about the project and giving its assessment of the various drafts that we had now worked our way through with Dublin. The army said, "We recognise that what is required is a package that creates (what is) a political dynamic for irreversible change, and whose objective is the exercise of the right to national self-determination. We see this as the basis for democracy and the beginning of the process of national reconciliation and a lasting peace." The army rejected the Irish government redrafts of the document which John and I had signed off on, saying that it didn't believe that these would produce the necessary dynamic. It stated its support for the Hume/Adams draft of June 1992 and proposed that the Irish government endorse this.

It is difficult to see whether any other approach was feasible. Unless the government was prepared to press the British to move beyond the Anglo-Irish Agreement position, there was little point. Whether the British could be moved or not was one thing, but an effort had to be made to get them to move. It was crucial for the Irish government to have as advanced a position as possible. Its position was even more important than the British one. A British government cannot be expected to define and promote Irish national interests. That is the function and the duty of an Irish government. The problem was that, since partition, successive Irish governments, for a multiplicity of reasons, had no cohesive strategy to bring about the imperative of its own constitution. In many ways, the government was now being challenged to start that process.

The reality is that when it came down to the nitty gritty of what was required to build an unarmed strategy for the goals of independence and unity, the Dublin establishment was on a learning curve, having to consider all kinds of options for the first time. Up to this point, there had been no strategy. There were other matters that needed agreement as well. There was the issue of republican prisoners. And the proposed peace convention. Censorship was a problem. Albert Reynolds responded to these matters in a paper entitled "Steps Envisaged", which he gave to the Sagart in May. This said that censorship would be ended in the wake of a

123

joint declaration. There would also be consultation on a peace convention, and every effort would be made to deal with the issue of prisoners.

Eventually, after further drafting and redrafting around the putative joint declaration, a slightly amended version of the June 1992 document emerged. Reynolds undertook, despite his own reservations, to try to get John Major on board. The British Cabinet Secretary flew into Baldonnel Military Airport outside Dublin to pick up the draft document. On 10 June, we sent an oral message to the British expressing concern at the protracted delay by them in formally responding to the IRA and reminded them of the progress that was being made in the discussions between John Hume, myself and the Irish government.

On 14 June, the British faxed us a copy of the document they had been given by Albert Reynolds a few days earlier. They asked us to authenticate it. As well as sending confirmation of this through the back channel, I also told John Hume to tell the British that the document they had received had republican support. At John's request, I told him that he could tell the Brits that I thought the document had the potential to get the IRA on board. I told John that Sinn Féin was authenticating the document ourselves through our own line of communication. Later, when John Major publicly denied knowing the detail of Hume/Adams, we knew he was lying. Apart from everything else, we had their faxed copy of the document as proof.

# Chapter Thirteen

# *President Robinson Comes to Belfast*

In 1993, the different strands of our work began to converge. John Hume and I had concluded a big chunk of the task we set for ourselves seven years earlier. The Irish government was starting to focus on its bit of the jigsaw. We urged it to deliver on its responsibilities to people in the North by developing strategies for equality across a range of issues, alongside outreach to the unionists. The Irish American axis was starting to shape up.

Unionism was the one big part of the jigsaw not even on the table. Not surprising; if the British were not prepared to dialogue with us, political unionism didn't even need to consider such an option. But if the search for peace and national reconciliation were to succeed, they had to be part of it. That was probably the biggest challenge of all, and it was a central theme in all the Hume/Adams statements.

The Sinn Féin outreach to unionism had been limited to a small section which was prepared to meet with us. In the 1970s there had been some dialogue between republicans and representatives from some of the unionist paramilitary groups. The reader will not be surprised to learn that much of this took place through the efforts of Fr Reid and Fr Des Wilson. It also involved Nobel Peace Prize winner Seán MacBride – the former IRA leader of the 1920s and 1930s who became an Irish government minister, international jurist and eventually UN Commissioner for Namibia.

Regrettably, none of these discussions achieved much. Our inability to develop a real dialogue with political and civic unionism and the Protestant Churches was a constant source of frustration. The realpolitik, of course, was that the unionists refused to talk to us. We were the enemy. Many unionists saw the IRA war against the British as a war against them. Republican efforts, whether military or political, were seen by many unionists as a direct assault on them. Some of the violent actions carried out by republicans reinforced this view.

For Sinn Féin, the imperative of talking to unionists grew as our peace strategy evolved. How could we unravel centuries of conflict if we didn't talk to each other? All sides had done terrible things. None could be ignored. Centuries of hostility and powerful emotions were clashing with each other at an individual and at a community level. There were bitter memories of hurt and pain. How could we bridge this chasm of distrust?

Our public outreach to ordinary unionists over the heads of their political leaders and appeals to Church leaders of all denominations were creating ripples. In March 1992, I received a letter seeking a meeting from two former Presbyterian Moderators, the Revd Jack Weir and the Revd Godfrey Brown. Weir had been one of a group of Protestant Church leaders who met the IRA in December 1974 at Feakle in County Clare. That meeting led to a prolonged truce, which came to an end around the summer of 1975.

Both Jack Weir and Godfrey Brown were impressive people. Tom Hartley and I met the two clergymen for the first time over tea and homemade scones on a bright spring morning in the parlour of Councillor Marie Moore's home on the Glen Road in West Belfast. By such niceties are barriers broken down.

The former Moderators released details of our meeting on 23 April 1992. They were viciously criticised for breaking the public political consensus of not talking to Sinn Féin. However, out of this dialogue grew other avenues of engagement with Presbyterian clergy, in particular the Church and Government Committee of the Presbyterian Church. Over the following years, Tom Hartley, Jim Gibney and Mitchel McLaughlin, among others, worked hard at meeting representatives of the other Protestant Churches, including the Methodists and the Church of Ireland. And there were the meetings in Clonard Monastery. We also made limited contacts with unionist business people, mainly through our local councillors who were involved in economic committees at local government level.

From our fragmented discussions with this range of groups and individuals, we had a picture of a community under siege, much different from the belligerent and dogmatic image presented by its leaders. Like most nationalists, we had what could be described as a paternalistic view of unionists. We considered them to be misled and mistaken, their dependency on the union arising from colonial connections. In our eyes, they were part of what we were, almost prodigal nationalists. But the small "u" unionists we were meeting professed Britishness. On closer examination and discussion, this seemed in many cases to be more an alienation from things Irish than a real sense of things British. In some ways, it depended on what being Irish meant.

We needed to reach out to unionists and to explain what sort of Ireland we envisioned – one that is inclusive, built on equality and justice and human rights. We needed to look at ways in which unionists could find a place in a new Ireland. We needed to listen to what they meant by their sense of "Britishness". And they needed to tell us.

We also felt uptight at the bullish denials by unionist leaders that there was anything wrong with their little statelet. They even denied that there was discrimination. We wanted them to face up to the role they played in sustaining the conditions for conflict and their responsibilities for finding a resolution to the conflict. The issues are interlinked. If we are in denial about our responsibility for a problem, we will feel no compulsion to find its solution. We could only address these issues through dialogue, but there was no dialogue with political unionism. Most of the time they didn't even reply to our letters.

At least there was some progress on the nationalist side. How would the British government respond publicly to the Hume/Adams proposal for a joint declaration? Downing Street was proving less than enthusiastic about the potential that had emerged out of the secret dialogue. Would Major be more thoughtful about an initiative and a draft paper which had the endorsement of the Irish government?

Major's response was heavily influenced by his own situation in Westminster, where he held only a slender majority. There was also growing opposition within his party to developments within the European Union. This came to a head in a vote on the Maastricht Treaty, which took place in July 1993. It looked like Major would lose the vote and be forced to resign. He needed the nine votes in the British parliament held by the Ulster Unionist Party. It was being suggested to us by Ferguson that this is why Major had failed so far to respond to the IRA initiative.

There were other issues, of course. British strategy, developed over the previous twenty years, was a series of integrated counter-insurgency policies with maintenance of the union the objective. Within this, the favoured British option was for the emergence of a coalition of the unionists and the SDLP in the Six Counties to outmanoeuvre republicanism and nationalism politically, while the securocrats defeated the IRA militarily. For so long as this eluded them, the British controlled everything. This meant their system – the permanent government – was in charge. The officials ran most of the politicians posted here by Downing Street. Security interests were the priority and the security and intelligence agencies dominated.

Peter Brooke's remarks and Patrick Mayhew's Coleraine speech had indicated a possible move away from this. But was it real movement or a more sensitive approach by more thoughtful British Consul Generals? With strategic planning from the Irish side based upon a consensual and inclusive way forward, and consistent and sustained work, it might be possible to explore and build upon the most progressive aspects of "Brookespeak". If the remarks by Brooke and Mayhew could be developed, there were possibilities. The prize from a British point of view was a big one. The IRA campaign was having a real effect, particularly now in recent months in Britain itself. Ten years after Thatcher had boasted that the hunger strikes were the IRA's last card, the army was resurgent.

Maybe Colin Ferguson represented the emergence of more advanced thinking within the British system. Maybe someone was starting to consider that British interests could be best served by peace in Ireland. If this was so, and if it amounted to more than a different tactical approach, this would require a shift away from a policy of political containment and the primacy of militarism. Was London up to this? Was John Major? Was Albert Reynolds? It would require bravery and vision. And an ability to see beyond the difficulties and priorities of the moment.

It didn't take long for John Major to indicate, at least privately to Albert Reynolds, his rejection of Hume/Adams. Within days of receiving it, he told the Taoiseach that there were aspects of the paper that the British could not accept.

Meantime, in the midst of these discussions with John Hume, the secret negotiations with the Irish government, secret negotiations with the British government, and secret discussions internally about these secret negotiations – two events occurred to remind me of the genuine warm-hearted goodness of most people and the downright stupidity and irresponsibility of some others in authority.

The first was the visit by the President of Ireland Mary Robinson to West Belfast. The second was about an advertisement for a book of short stories I had written.

In any other country, a visit by the President would be a source of great enjoyment and delight. But this was West Belfast – a part of Ireland under

British jurisdiction. A visit here was beyond the pale. Even more alarming in the minds of the tabloid media, Mary Robinson was scheduled to shake my hand! Instead of dealing with the plusses or indeed the minuses, if that was their view, of an Irish presidential visit to West Belfast, the media trivialised the engagement. Of course, the subtext of all of this was that some of us were not worthy enough to have our hands shaken. We were beyond the norms of good manners and civilised behaviour.

Mary Robinson had been elected Irish President three years earlier. She was a well-known and respected human rights lawyer and former member of the Irish Labour Party. She had resigned from that party in 1985 over its support for the Anglo-Irish Agreement, which she felt was unfair to unionists. However, as the Labour candidate she had succeeded in winning the Irish Presidency in December 1990. Her elected platform promised she would be a voice for those who were deprived and marginalised, and as President she had already made several visits to the North. So far, these had ensured that she met non-controversial "safe" groups. Early in 1993 on a visit to a peace conference in Derry, she had even refused to meet the relatives of the fourteen men killed by the British army on Bloody Sunday 1972. This caused outrage among nationalists.

Some time after this a longstanding activist on justice and equality issues approached one of our leadership team with the suggestion that a presidential visit to West Belfast, including meeting with me, was possible if it could be organised on a community platform. Such an initiative would, our friend thought, be useful in breaching the wall of exclusion which had been built around Sinn Féin by the establishment. It would also be important for the people of West Belfast.

We put the idea to a range of West Belfast community groups, and they issued an invitation for the President to visit. They invited her to see for herself the work of that community in its battle against endemic unemployment, discrimination, poor housing and repression, and to celebrate the many positive aspects of their work. Called "A Celebration of Culture and Creativity", it was to be held in the College of Further Education on the Whiterock Road, beside Ballymurphy, my home area. As a member of the management committee of Féile an Phobail, the West Belfast festival, I was on the list of people to be invited.

The British policy was to marginalise and demonise republicans and the community within which we took our support. West Belfast was in many ways the pulse of our struggle. One British Secretary of State had already referred to the people there as the "terrorist community".

129

At first, the Brits said the President couldn't come because she had not gone through the proper channels. When that failed to deter her, they refused to provide diplomatic security protection. One poor Irish government official who travelled to Belfast to discuss the matters with his British counterpart was left waiting for two hours in his car.

The response of the Irish establishment wasn't much better. The leader of the Labour Party Dick Spring made several efforts to persuade Mary Robinson to pull out of the visit.

Though due to come on Friday, 18 June, by Wednesday the community groups had still not received confirmation of her visit. Eventually, as the deadline for the last post arrived, they decided to go ahead and mail the invitations to the hundreds of other people who were to come to the event. As far as we were concerned, the event was going ahead. A short time later, Aras an Uachtaráin, the President's residence in Dublin, phoned to confirm her visit.

That wasn't the end of it. The next day two Irish government representatives landed in West Belfast and tried to reorganise the entire structure of the event. Their purpose was obvious: to persuade the event organisers to stop me coming. When that failed, they tried to ensure that I was placed so far from the President that we wouldn't see each other, never mind actually meet and shake hands.

All of this was going on in the background. The public knew none of it. The unionists, the British government and some Southern politicians and newspapers whipped up a storm of protest. Most of it centred around the handshake. The British Prime Minister John Major spoke to the Irish Taoiseach Albert Reynolds. The British Ambassador in Dublin sent a "stiff" diplomatic note. The Democratic Unionist Party described the visit as a propaganda boost for the IRA.

The real agenda of the British was to maintain what had been a solid, cohesive opposition to anyone having anything to do with republicans even though, at this very moment, they were secretly talking to us.

The Belfast Institute of Further and Higher Education college on the Whiterock Road was formerly Saint Thomas's Secondary School. Many of its pupils were imprisoned, some were killed, particularly in the 1970s. Most of my brothers had been pupils there. Among a fine teaching staff at one time were numbered the Nobel Laureate and poet Seamus Heaney and the writer Michael McLaverty.

The day the President came was a great day. She was greeted by a welcoming party of enthusiastic pupils from the local Irish language schools. The McPeake family and friends entertained us all with some of the best Irish music to be heard anywhere. Sean Maguire, another legendary figure in Irish traditional music, followed. It was terrific. The renowned St Agnes's Choral Society rounded off the entertainment with bits of *Madame Butterfly* and other operatic delights.

"Up the Aria!" a local wag exclaimed to me.

The meeting with the President was little more than a few friendly words, a handshake and a *"céad míle fáilte"* – a welcome from me. More important than anything I could have said was the plea from Emma Groves, who was standing beside me. Emma had been blinded by a British army rubber bullet in November 1971. She had been shot in her living room by a British paratrooper, who fired through her open window as he stood eight yards from her. A mother of eleven children then, at the time of writing she is eighty-two, a grandmother of forty and a great-grandmother of thirteen. All this time Emma has been a wonderful campaigner for an end to plastic and rubber bullets. She eloquently appealed to the President to support this campaign.

Mary Robinson's visit was an important initiative. I have always felt that she did not get proper recognition for the stand she took. It sent a timely signal of the need to treat people with respect. It was also hugely popular throughout Ireland.

But it wasn't popular with everyone. The *Sunday Independent* called on Mary Robinson to resign, and the following Monday's edition of *The Irish Times* carried eight critical articles on our handshake. But perhaps most telling of all was the opinion poll that revealed that 77 per cent of people in the Twenty-six Counties backed President Robinson.

A few weeks after the furore around Mary Robinson's visit, I found myself again the centre of attention as another part of the marginalisation and censorship process kicked in. I had written a book of short stories – *The Street and Other Stories*. My publisher, Steve MacDonogh of Brandon, decided to go for a short twenty-second radio advertisement on RTÉ. The advert was as follows: "This is Gerry Adams speaking. My new book is called *The Street and Other Stories* and it's on sale in good bookshops in the thirty-two counties. Most of the stories are about ordinary people and everyday events, and there's a fair bit of *craic* in them also. That's *The Street and Other Stories* and this is Gerry Adams. I think you might enjoy it. *Slán*."

RTÉ refused to carry the ad and Steve took the case to the Dublin High Court. The former Labour Party minister – Conor Cruise O'Brien, who had been the architect of Section 31 in its current form when introduced in 1972 – testified in defence of banning the advertisement. He claimed my short stories were thinly disguised propaganda for the IRA. O'Brien argued that while the advert was not political, the opening words would offend and corrupt the Irish public.

"I have in mind," he said, "the opening words: 'This is Gerry Adams speaking.'"

His claim that the book was propagandistic was rubbished by a large number of book reviews in Irish and British periodicals and newspapers, which specifically said the book wasn't propaganda. I felt a little divorced from all this. I have long considered Conor Cruise to be a dangerous crank, but there was a method to his madness. Republicans are not supposed to be able to write books, and if some of us occasionally do, then no one is supposed to get wind of it. How could we be treated as pariahs if our little efforts at literature were advertised on mainstream radio? And, on a personal level, the message was obvious. If you want to be a writer, change your politics.

Steve MacDonogh has been publishing my books since 1982. I like the challenge that writing presents and I feel extremely privileged to have my work published. Some of my books, *The Street* especially, are a kind of therapy, a sideline and, in the middle of all the other madness, an outlet. I enjoyed the public reading of my modest penmanship in the court in Dublin. I was only sorry that I wasn't there. As it was, the High Court judge in his ruling on 16 July decided that my public persona was such that I could not be divorced in the public mind from Sinn Féin. He therefore determined that it was for RTÉ to decide whether the advertisement breached Section 31. I was not surprised that the advert was never broadcast.

The then minister responsible for Section 31, Michael D. Higgins – a decent man and a good poet, who was later to end Section 31 – and I shared the same publisher. In an ironic twist, three days after the High Court judgement, on 19 July, Steve MacDonogh hosted an event at the Galway Arts Festival where Michael D. read from his latest collection.

Meanwhile, back in the real world there was no clue as to what was happening to the Hume/Adams proposal. Over the summer we continued to push the British government for a formal meeting in the context of the IRA's initiative. In September, we received a message back which fundamentally changed everything. Now we were being told that "the government side has not asserted a belief that a two weeks suspension" was enough for talks. The secret talks were in trouble, and the British were indulging in bad faith.

On 10 September, we wrote back expressing our disappointment. A few days later, John Hume went to Downing Street to meet John Major, urging him to respond positively to the draft of the joint declaration. He also wanted to determine where the discussions between the two governments were. We were getting little real information on their deliberations. Despite John's efforts, nothing new emerged from the Downing Street meeting.

After a lot of discussion within the Sinn Féin core group, we decided that it was necessary to win public support for the Hume/Adams initiative in order to increase political pressure on the British and Irish governments. Consequently, I put a proposal to John Hume for a further Hume/Adams statement that would seek to inject a new dynamic into the process without breaching any confidences. I gave a draft statement to John for his opinion. He made a few changes and, when we had agreed a text, we released it to the media on Saturday evening, 25 September.

In the statement we said that our efforts to create a peace process had "made considerable progress" and that we had agreed to forward a report on all of this to the Dublin government. We acknowledged that the broad principles involved would be a matter for wider consideration by the two governments, and we expressed confidence that a peace process could be put together.

The general reaction reflected the heartfelt desire of the vast majority of Irish people for progress towards real peace. There were inevitably negative, even some hysterical, reactions, mostly from the usual suspects. Ulster Unionist MP Ken Maginnis said that if the Hume/Adams talks were about joint authority, it would bring the North closer to war than ever. DUP MP Peter Robinson spoke of civil war, while John Taylor threatened that the talks would lead to a loyalist backlash. Some claimed that I was playing John Hume as a pawn in order to get Sinn Féin a place at the conference table. All nonsense, of course: John Hume was too wise to be anyone's pawn. They knew and I knew that Sinn Féin would have to have a place at the conference table if a real agreement was ever to be reached.

The Dublin-based *Evening Press* described our joint statement as not just a significant advance, but also an important window of opportunity for both Dublin and London. The London *Observer* described it as one of the most hopeful developments in recent history. The two governments, perhaps mindful of the real story, were more muted in their responses, although Patrick Mayhew stressed the importance of the consent of unionists to any constitutional change while reiterating British policy of not talking to Sinn Féin. The media focus then shifted to the report which John and I had said we would give to the Irish government.

John Hume went off on a pre-arranged visit to the USA with an arrangement to see Albert Reynolds and Dick Spring when he returned. While John was in the States, we had agreed that I should inform the IRA of developments and attempt to get a positive response. The IRA subsequently issued a public comment welcoming our efforts. In a statement on 3 October it said: "This is the first statement issued by Óglaigh na hÉireann [the IRA] on this initiative. The leadership of Óglaigh na hÉireann welcomes this initiative. We are informed of the broad principles which will be for consideration by the London and Dublin governments. It is unfortunate that the British government reaction to this initiative, so far, has been negative and has fuelled unionist reaction. Nonetheless, if the political will exists or can be created, it could provide the basis for peace. We, our volunteers and our supporters, have a vested interest in seeking a just and lasting peace in Ireland. Our objectives, which include the right of the Irish people to national self-determination, are well known. Our commitment remains steadfast."

All of this, it has to be remembered, was played out publicly in a situation in which broadcast restrictions prevented the media in the South from carrying any interviews with Sinn Féin spokespersons. In the North, our voices could not be broadcast. The consequence of this was that people were getting little or no information regarding the efforts by republicans to achieve peace.

Despite this, I made it clear that I was prepared to go to the IRA with a package if one could be produced. To be successful, any package had to allow the IRA to consider the future of its armed campaign. But I repeated time and time again that, whatever happened, I would not mislead the IRA, nor would I mislead others about the IRA. For its part, the IRA could speak for itself. In early October, in a lengthy interview in *An Phoblacht*, a spokesperson for General Headquarters staff said, "If the political will exists or can be created, then there is some hope that the situation can be moved forward."

While John was away, Dublin government sources briefed that it had no report from John. Media reports alluded to this. But, of course, John had kept the government fully briefed on his work. The Sagart also had been in continuous contact and Sinn Féin had met Dublin directly. Instead of an effort to get agreement by the two governments on a joint declaration, we were getting media disinformation from Dublin.

I spoke to John by phone in the USA and filled him in on what was happening in his absence. When he returned, he and I met before he went off to see the Taoiseach and Tánaiste on 7 October. In our view and in the short term, the onus was on the two governments – especially the Irish government. Dublin wasn't a spectator in all of this; it was a player and it had a responsibility to move the initiative forward. The imperative for that was apparent even in the public opinion polls, which, since our September joint statement, reported that 72 per cent of people supported the Hume/Adams initiative. When John met Albert Reynolds and Dick Spring it was a cool encounter. Dublin was unhappy that our joint statement, and the public support it received had injected urgency into the process. The popular imperative was for the pace to be speeded up.

The Hume/Adams initiative was therefore at the centre of discussions between Albert Reynolds and John Major when they met at an inter-governmental conference on 13 October in London. The British had reached a point where they didn't really want to progress with the joint declaration proposition. Major held a number of meetings with other ministers and officials in the days after this to discuss Hume/Adams and what should be done with it. On 19 October he wrote a letter to Albert Reynolds: "After giving it very careful consideration, with all the intelligence at our disposal, we have very reluctantly concluded that it will not run at the present time."

We weren't told this, of course, at the time, but on the same day the British Home Secretary Michael Howard signed a banning order against me under the provisions of the Prevention of Terrorism Act. I was banned from travelling to Britain. It was a particularly appropriate day, in that exactly five years earlier the British government had introduced its broadcast ban against Sinn Féin. Now the British government had decided that, in addition to censorship, people in Britain shouldn't have the opportunity to meet Sinn Féin leaders. If any were so minded, they would have to come to Ireland. It was a British version of the internal banning orders used against political dissidents by the apartheid South African government and the old Soviet Union government. We truly were as British as Finchley.

## Chapter Fourteen

# *The Downing Street Declaration*

The Sinn Féin organisation was starting to have some impact on issues of inequality. The exclusion of republicans and nationalists and the denial of basic rights and entitlements took many forms. In Belfast, one of these involved the banning of republican and nationalist demonstrations from the city centre. These streets were the sole property of the Orange Order and the unionists. Several years earlier, Belfast Sinn Féin had initiated a campaign to reclaim the city centre and Belfast as "Our City Also".

August 1993 saw the campaign achieve its goal: a major republican march to the City Hall. It was an emotional experience for everyone who took part. Joy mingled with determination as thousands converged from four different parts of the city. As each contingent approached the City Hall, they burst into spontaneous applause. The atmosphere was electric as wave after wave of cheers and clapping rippled back through the huge crowd. I saw many a grown man and woman crying. Others hugged each other in sheer joy. The older generations of Belfast republicans never thought they would see the day. It was a great occasion. Belfast city centre belonged to everyone. In our public comments, we made it clear that we desired a shared city, a peaceful city.

Three weeks earlier, loyalists had thrown a bomb at a local Sinn Féin advice centre while North Belfast Councillor Bobby Lavery and several others were working there. The bomb failed to explode. Nine months earlier, Bobby's brother, Martin, was killed by loyalist assassins in front of his five-year-old daughter as he sat with her wrapping up Christmas presents in the living room of their home. Now, the UDA struck at the Laverys' home just hours after the march ended.

Nationalist Belfast was celebrating the last night of city-wide festivals. As part of their contribution, Cleaky and a few other former political prisoners had organised a reunion, complete with their version of the illicit *poitín* that kept prisoners periodically sane. I succumbed to his invitation to attend, though my intention was to do no more than drop in. I was barely in the door when we got the news that a death squad had sprayed the Lavery home on the Antrim Road with up to thirty shots, as Sean Lavery, aged twenty-one, sat watching the television. Accounts of the attack were confused, but we knew it was serious. As Cleaky's event was abandoned, news came that Bobby's son had been hit. He died on the way to hospital. The anger within republican Belfast was palpable. We had asserted and won our right to freedom of assembly in our own city, but at a terrible price.

The Maastricht vote earlier in the summer had shown how vulnerable Major was within the British parliament and how dependent he was on unionist votes. Some unionist leaders felt liberated enough to engage in the traditional unionist sport of making provocative and offensive anti-Catholic comments. Following the killing of a Catholic man, Sean Hughes, a father of three at his hairdressing salon on the Falls Road, former unionist minister John Taylor MP, himself a victim of a gun attack in the early 1970s, remarked, "In a perverse way, this is something which may be helpful because they [Catholics] are now beginning to appreciate more clearly the fear that has existed within the Protestant community for the past twenty years."

There was widespread nationalist outrage at Taylor's comments, seen as an encouragement to loyalists to carry out further attacks. The killing also raised again the spectre of collusion between the loyalist death squads and the RUC. It became clear that, after the murder of Sean Hughes, the RUC placed roadblocks on every road leading from the scene of the killing, except the road the gang had taken back into a nearby loyalist area.

As the peace initiative appeared to falter, on the streets the outworking of British forces' involvement in the various unionist death squads was taking its toll. Since August, ten people had been shot dead by them, nine in Belfast. Many others were wounded. There were daily attacks. In one incident, a black taxi was targeted in North Belfast. Claiming responsibility, the UDA said: "It was an attempted mass murder but the weapon jammed." On the same day that John Major's private message rejecting Hume/Adams was delivered to Albert Reynolds, the UDA Inner Council told the London *Guardian* newspaper: "We are out to terrorise the terrorists. To get to the stage where old grannies up the Falls will call on the IRA to stop, because it is ordinary Catholics that are getting hit."

Several days later, shortly after lunch on the Saturday, Richard and I were working on a statement on the state of the peace initiative. I turned on the radio to listen to the news and heard the first reports of an explosion on the Shankill Road in West Belfast. Over the next few hours the horror of what had happened unfolded. The IRA had placed a bomb in a fish shop below rooms used by the UDA leadership for meetings. There was no one there at the time of the attack. It was a busy time on the Shankill Road. It was thronged with shoppers. Two IRA volunteers – dressed in white coats, to give the impression that they were deliverymen – entered the shop. The bomb exploded prematurely. One of the two, Thomas Begley, aged twenty-two, was killed instantly. The old building collapsed, trapping shoppers.

Out of the rubble and devastation were taken the bodies of eight local people, among them Michelle Baird, aged seven, and Leanne Murray, aged thirteen. A ninth person, Wilma McKee, was to die the next day. Fifty-seven others were injured. The emergency services and local people used bare hands, axes and crowbars in a desperate attempt to rescue the injured. I was shattered by the news reports, and my first thoughts were for the families of those who had been killed and injured.

I was also conscious of how damaging this was going to be to our efforts to breathe life into a peace initiative that appeared close to collapse. The Shankill attack reinforced my view that we had to use all our energies and efforts to save the peace initiative. We had to redouble our efforts. Clearly, the attack made this more difficult. Those who were opposed to what Sinn Féin, John Hume and I were trying to do seized upon the Shankill bombing. The IRA operation on the Shankill was wrong; there can be no doubt. The IRA intention was to kill the gang leaders supervising the deadly killing campaign against Belfast nationalists and republicans and any available Catholics. But the IRA operational plan had little regard for the civilians in the vicinity, or indeed even for the IRA volunteers involved in the operation.

The opportunity of wiping out the UDA leadership blinded the IRA to the consequences of their actions if anything went wrong. In reality, everything went wrong. Ten people died in the bomb blast that day, including four women and two children.

Four days later, IRA volunteer Thomas Begley was buried. In the intervening days, loyalists had killed four Catholics. Another man was shot and seriously wounded outside Thomas Begley's home by a British soldier. Fear stalked the streets. Begley's funeral was huge, with thousands of nationalists and republicans stepping out in solidarity with his family. At one point, I carried the coffin. Photographers and camera crews rushed to snap the moment, and it appeared on television news programmes and newspaper front pages everywhere. I was the target of some vicious comment. Much has been made about my attendance at Thomas Begley's funeral. I can understand why the families of the victims of the IRA bomb would protest at my presence. I accept no such protestations from others who exploited my attendance for their own narrow political ends.

While Thomas Begley, like everyone else, has to take responsibility for his actions, a twenty-two-year-old born into and reared in a situation of conflict can hardly be held to blame for difficulties created and sustained by older and more powerful people. Unlike them, Thomas Begley paid with his life.

Before the end of the month, another nine people were killed by the UDA and UVF. Seven were killed – six Catholics and one Protestant man – when a UDA gang entered the Rising Sun bar in the small County Derry village of Greysteel, midway between Derry city and Limavady. Two men, masked and carrying an AK47 assault rifle and a Browning 9mm automatic pistol – both part of the South African weapons shipment – walked into the crowded bar around 10 p.m. It was Halloween evening. Local people were out for a quiet night when one gunman shouted "Trick or treat!" and then both opened fire. The pistol jammed after one shot, but the gunman using the rifle emptied his magazine and then reloaded before opening fire again. Forty-five shots raked the room. When it was over, seven people were dead and nineteen injured. It was the worst October in almost twenty years of conflict. Twenty-eight people had died. The sense of shock and bewilderment and grief was everywhere.

Martin McGuinness appealed for calm. "Emotions are running very high in the present climate and the Protestant community may now fear a possible retaliatory attack. I readily understand these feelings and I am stating with all of the authority of my position with Sinn Féin that such actions are totally contrary to republican philosophy."

Martin also sharply criticised the British government over political events in the days immediately prior to the Greysteel attack. On 27 October, Tánaiste Dick Spring made a speech to the Irish parliament in which he set out what he described as his six principles for progress. He gave unionists the right to withhold their consent to any agreement, thus reinforcing the unionist veto over political or constitutional change. This position differed fundamentally from the usual formula, which spoke of a majority having the right to withhold consent. This shift caused a storm of protest from nationalists and republicans. In addition, Spring made no mention of the role and responsibilities of the two governments, and especially of the British government. He threw the onus entirely on to nationalists and unionists living in the North, effectively letting both governments off the hook.

The British government jumped on Spring's "principles". The Taoiseach had just been told by London that the joint declaration idea was dead. Now the Tánaiste provided an emphasis on issues that the British felt more comfortable with. Spring also appeared to commit the Irish government to changing the Irish constitution. I felt that this was a step beyond which any Irish government, but especially a Fianna Fáil led government, could go. And within hours of his speech, Spring was forced to clarify his remarks about the rights of unionists, consent and the responsibilities of government. But the damage was done. The British were determined to kill off Hume/Adams, a joint declaration and any hopes for a peace process.

Mayhew began to plan and organise a new round of inter-party talks, and Major arranged meetings with the North's political leaders. British opposition to the Hume/Adams position had also been voiced when, during questions in the British House of Commons, John Hume had called on the British government to respond quickly. He didn't know that the British had already told Dublin no! Mayhew denied knowing anything about Hume/Adams. And then in a move clearly designed to win unionist approval, Major allowed the Procedures Committee in the House of Commons to discuss the proposal for setting up a "Select Committee on Northern Ireland". This had been a unionist demand for years.

All of this came to a head when Reynolds and Major met on the margins of a European Community meeting in Brussels on 29 October 1993. The statement which emerged from their forty-five-minute meeting was a determined slap in the teeth to all whose hopes were pinned on Hume/Adams. The two governments publicly ruled out adopting or endorsing the report of the dialogue between Hume and myself as the basis of any initiative that might be taken by the governments. They said that negotiations on a political settlement could only take place between democratic governments and parties committed exclusively to constitutional methods. Consequently there could be no talks or negotiations between their governments and those who used, threatened or supported violence for political ends. There could be no secret agreements or understandings between governments and organisations supporting violence as a price for its cessations.

The offer of talks and the request for an undeclared IRA stoppage of operations was buried. It was also evidence, if evidence were needed, that the British government was the senior partner in the relationship between the two governments.

All of this was spun to the media as "no talks with Sinn Féin". It ignored the reality that each government had been talking to republicans privately for years, in the Irish government's case, only a few days earlier. The communiqué concluded with a paragraph supporting a resumption of the inter-party talks. The spin from the governments to the media after the Brussels summit was that the governments had decided that they wanted nothing to do with anything that had "Gerry Adams's fingerprints" on it! The following Monday, Major restated his position in the House of Commons. As unionist MPs looked on, he commended the Irish government for its acknowledgement of the right of the unionists to give or withhold consent and he praised Dick Spring's six principles. When pressed by John Hume and asked why he had rejected the Hume/Adams initiative, Major said, "I realised the conclusion, as we set out in the statement over the weekend, that that is not the right way to proceed."

The secret talks came back to haunt Major and Mayhew and to point up the hypocrisy of their stance. During the summer, there had been reports in the media speculating about behind-the-scenes talks. We had complained to the British government about these because they were clearly coming from that side. The story eventually began to break. Belfast journalist Eamonn Mallie, who had been pursuing the NIO for several weeks only to be rebuffed and repeatedly told that there had been no talks and no meetings, was given a British government document by the DUP MP Revd William McCrea revealing that talks had taken place between the British and republicans and that it had been cleared by the British Secretary of State Patrick Mayhew.

Mallie ran the story of talks. The NIO responded in a hard-hitting and arrogant response which rubbished the story, claiming that it belonged more properly in the fantasy of spy thrillers.

Several days later, John Major told a meeting in London that he would never talk to organisations which did not renounce violence. Denials by him and Mayhew continued for the rest of the week, sometimes on a daily basis. In the meantime, the *Sunday Observer* was planning to run Mallie's story and to publish the government document. As the newspaper hit the streets late Saturday evening, the British issued a statement admitting that there had been contact with Sinn Féin. Mayhew claimed that the contact had arisen because of a message sent from the IRA via Martin McGuinness in February that the conflict was over. There was no such message. Martin was clear about this. So was I. All written messages, and this was allegedly a written message, were put together by the two of us and one or two close members of the core group. We also kept a record of all these messages. Furthermore, to guard against such an eventuality, if the message was an oral one, we gave Martin a speaking note. This was a practical measure to avoid mistakes. It was also our way of watching his back. It was a risky business dealing with the British government. One of our obligations was to protect our man.

I also was very perplexed following the 1974 truce between the IRA and the British government, and the confused period which followed this, when we could find no record of any of the discussions or commitments which underpinned this. My concern about this wasn't because I didn't trust the people involved. On the contrary, I knew they were doing their best. But I felt that we needed to learn from these experiences. If negotiations were a form of struggle, and it was increasingly the case that they were, then there needed to be an institutionalised memory available to leaderships from which lessons could be drawn. I also felt that these matters were part of the history of our struggle.

For all these reasons, once the early discussions with the Sagart led into talks with John Hume and the Irish government, and when the back channel reopened, we established a practice of recording almost everything. We were glad we did. To me it seemed as if the British were trying to undermine Martin McGuinness and to discredit him in the eyes of other republicans. We were not going to let them away with that.

The next morning, Sunday, the media descended on Stormont Castle outside Belfast for a press conference during which Mayhew was to give the British version of events. No one was impressed by his performance as he stumbled through his explanation for contact with us. We listened intently to the news reports, and when Mayhew announced that he planned to place a record of the exchanges in the Commons Library, we decided to produce our own record.

In an initial response to Mayhew that afternoon, I rubbished the British account of a message in February from the IRA. I revealed that during the discussions outlines of policy positions were exchanged and that the British government had rejected the proposal put forward by John Hume and myself. I accused Major and Mayhew of telling lies: "They have lied to their

142

own parliament, to Jim Molyneaux (the UUP leader) and to the Irish and British people about the existence and nature of their contact with Sinn Féin. Now that they have been forced to admit talking to Sinn Féin they are continuing to lie about what is involved . . . These lies and the patent dishonesty of the British position make a difficult situation worse."

That evening we came together in a Sinn Féin office in Turf Lodge in West Belfast to collate the bits and pieces of documents and messages that had passed between us and the Brits. The race was on! We were trying to put our record of the exchanges into the public arena before they produced their own account. In one room, Aidan McAteer, me, Siobhán O'Hanlon, Pat Doherty, Gerry Kelly, Ted Howell and Síle Darragh were sifting through pieces of paper. In another room, Martin McGuinness and Richard McAuley slaved over a hot computer. When were messages passed? When were meetings held? What was said?

It was cold, dark and wet outside. Inside, portable gas fires held back the draughts. At some point during the evening, someone had the bright idea of ordering pizzas, which were quickly consumed, along with huge amounts of tea and coffee. The work went on into the wee hours until we were satisfied that we had put together an accurate account of one of the most closely guarded secrets of twenty-five years of war – that talks between the British government and Irish republicans had been going on for over three years, including Margaret Thatcher's term as Prime Minister; that these discussions had held out the prospect of face-to-face negotiations between the two sides and an IRA ceasefire to facilitate these.

The following morning, Martin McGuinness and I held a press conference in Conway Mill in West Belfast. We released our record of the exchanges, including photocopies of most of the documents that we had received and notes of minutes of meetings between the Derry link and the British representative. There was one document which we dated and titled but did not publish because of its sensitivity and the ongoing efforts to build a peace process. This was the Hume/Adams document.

I told the assembled press corps that up to now we had declined to be drawn on press queries about talks with the British government because we wanted to protect the back channel. This had always been dependent on confidentiality, and we had hoped to maintain that secrecy because the line could help in the search for a viable peace process. I confirmed that there had been contact between the British government and Sinn Féin and I gave a short history of its existence. I pointed out that, in the course of our dialogue, outlines of British government and Sinn Féin policies were exchanged and discussed. This process was not an alternative to the discussions which I was conducting with John Hume. Indeed, on a number of occasions Martin McGuinness instructed his contact that the Hume/Adams discussions were dealing with the substantive issues and that they were a serious effort to reach agreement on the principles, the dynamic and the process required to bring peace to Ireland. When John Hume and I reached agreement, the British were informed of this. The IRA's positive attitude to this development was also conveyed to them. There can be no doubt that Mr Major and his colleagues knew that the Irish peace initiative had the potential to move all of us towards a lasting peace.

I drew particular attention to the request from the British for us to seek a suspension of operations by the IRA for two weeks and the army's positive response. I surmised that the British government's decision to renege on its position was due – in part, at least – to political difficulties in the House of Commons. I accused the British government of trying to sow confusion and division, and of actively trying to thwart the Irish peace initiative by denying knowledge of its content.

That afternoon Mayhew placed his documents in the Commons Library. To no one's great surprise, the two sets showed remarkable differences. Journalists spent the next few days poring over the two versions, trying to determine which was true and which false. The general assessment favoured Sinn Féin's account as the true version. Then, on 1 December, Mayhew admitted that a number of errors had emerged in the British account; he claimed twenty-two in all. This further reinforced the already widespread view that the Sinn Féin account was true. Sinn Féin subsequently produced our own assessment of the two versions and all of this was placed in the National Library in Dublin.

Two years later, the former British Secretary of State Peter Brooke confirmed that he had given clearance for the reactivation of the back channel in 1990.

While Sinn Féin generally felt vindicated by the turn of events, the job of making peace was now more difficult. The possibility of negotiations between Sinn Féin and the British government had been lost, at least for a while. There was even greater distrust between us. This was particularly true because of the allegation that the IRA had sent a surrender message through Martin to the British in February: it further soured the relationship between us and the Brits. Future relationship building between us became more problematic than it might otherwise have been.

Subsequently, Denis Bradley – one of the trio of Derry people who made up the back channel – revealed that he and the British representative had been responsible for the February message. This was a breach of the trust which the British government and we had placed in them. It transpired that the Derry trio were so incensed by the British government's rejection of the IRA's positive response to its ceasefire request that they informed John Hume of the existence of the back channel, and of what had transpired in the three preceding years. This was another potentially dangerous and foolhardy decision, breaking all the rules which go-betweens must adhere to. It happened because Denis Bradley was genuinely upset at the arrogance of the British. He also thought he knew better than the Sinn Féin leadership how we should deal with the Brits. In other words, he had started to take decisions for us. This could well have resulted in a serious breach in my relationship with John and irreparable damage to the search for peace. It didn't, because of John Hume's acceptance that Sinn Féin had a right to do what we had done. His focus was on trying to find a way forward.

The Derry group's actions convinced us that this was not the way to build the kind of understanding that a peace process required. The Sagart was still the only go-between we had encountered who fully understood the role of channels of communication. The Derry trio were well intended. These mistakes to one side, they had given good service and we were grateful to them. But the back channel had had its day.

We were collectively at a point where we needed to see beyond the lies, deceptions and breaches of trust. The Irish peace initiative had reached a defining point. The process was in trouble.

There was increasing public support in Ireland for the Hume/Adams initiative and criticism of the two governments. I gave vent to some of that when I remarked that I was of the opinion that John Major was "not interested in peace but with holding on to power". I repeated my belief that the onus was on Albert Reynolds to lead the Irish efforts to achieve peace. I said that republicans would give a fair hearing to any proposals he might have, but in the absence of any other initiative "the process advanced by Mr Hume and myself contains the substantive issues and the dynamic required to advance all parties to the conflict towards a meaningful peace process".

John Hume also used every opportunity to argue in support of our project. The pressure on both of us was intense, but it was John's instinctive, emotional and tearful response to relatives at the funeral of one of the victims of the Greysteel attack, which in many ways captured the public mood. The Dublin-based papers had intensified their attacks on our efforts. John was particularly targeted, as if they saw him as a traitor to their conservative view of republicans. The *Sunday Independent* in one edition ran seven separate articles attacking him – some in the most vitriolic and offensive language. The result was that John collapsed and was rushed to hospital.

But on the streets a different mood was evident. As the government's stance against Hume/Adams grew in intensity, so too did public support for it among nationalists. Perhaps people were fed up after twenty-five years of listening to the same speeches and promises from the governments – knowing they would go nowhere. Perhaps it was because a lot of people thought what John and I were saying made sense. Perhaps we had just succeeded in catching a mood and a desire for change.

Whatever the truth, broad nationalist popular endorsement of Hume/Adams grew by leaps and bounds. This presented a particular problem for Albert Reynolds who, in early November, faced his party delegates at the Fianna Fáil Ard Fheis. An *Irish Press* report of the debate on the North at the conference recorded that "The debate, one of the two most spirited of the weekend, gave overwhelming support to John Hume's initiative with the Sinn Féin President Gerry Adams. Delegate after delegate questioned why there hadn't been a more fulsome [sic] and wholehearted support for Mr Hume in recent weeks." A delegate from Buncrana, in County Donegal, captured the mood of the conference, as well as being wildly applauded when he remarked, "All this nonsense about talking to terrorists – the British Commonwealth Heads of government contains more 'reformed terrorists' to the square inch than a Sinn Féin Ard Fheis."

The groundswell of support at the Fianna Fáil Ard Fheis in favour of our efforts was replicated in local government council chambers and at public meetings across the island. Reynolds's office was flooded with letters and phone calls from voters angered at the stand of his government and in support of Hume/Adams.

The result was a more public upbeat attitude by the Irish government to Hume/Adams. We were back in fashion. A few days after his Ard Fheis, Reynolds now swung so far in the other direction that he told a couple of Dublin journalists that "I will walk away from John Major and put forward proposals myself. I am not prepared to let this opportunity pass." The British were annoyed by this. They believed that they had shifted Dublin away from the idea of a joint declaration and on to the safer ground of inter-party talks. They thought they had broken the nationalist consensus, which they saw as a threat to their own interests.

Then followed a series of private meetings between officials from the two governments. At this time the unionists – whose votes in the British parliament were so important to John Major – demanded that the British should abandon the process entirely.

John and I met again on 20 November and, in an attempt to maintain the public focus and pressure on John Major, we issued a further joint statement in which we said that we hoped that "the British government will respond positively and quickly to the clear opportunity for peace which this initiative provides . . . We are personally greatly encouraged by the popular and widespread support which has greeted the initiative and by the personal messages of support and encouragement that we have received."

The IRA, in only its second intervention in the public debate, again welcomed the Hume/Adams initiative and reiterated both its support and desire for a peace process.

The response of the two governments came on Wednesday, 15 December, when at a joint press conference John Major and Albert Reynolds produced the Downing Street Declaration.

The two leaders committed themselves to fostering agreement and reconciliation leading to "a new political framework founded on consent". On behalf of the British government, John Major reaffirmed "that they will uphold the democratic wish of a greater number of the people of Northern Ireland on the issue of whether they prefer to support the union or a sovereign united Ireland".

He said that Britain had no selfish or economic interest in the Six Counties and that their "primary interest" was to see peace established by agreement among all the people on the island and to work with the Dublin government to achieve an agreement "which will embrace the totality of relationships".

The two governments committed themselves to seeking to create new institutions and structures to enable the people of Ireland to work together "in all areas of common interest". The two governments reiterated that the achievement of peace "must involve a permanent end to the use of, or support for, paramilitary violence" and confirmed that "in these circumstances, democratically mandated parties which establish a commitment to exclusively peaceful methods and which have shown that they abide by the democratic process are free to participate fully". The

Irish government proposed the establishment "in consultation with other parties, of a Forum for Peace and Reconciliation to make recommendations on ways in which agreement and trust between both traditions in Ireland can be promoted and established".

The media spotlight shifted almost immediately to republicans. With no time to analyse or assess the Declaration, the media were demanding of Sinn Féin: was it enough for us? More importantly, was it enough for the IRA? Whatever view the IRA might take of it, I was determined that Sinn Féin weren't going to be bounced into anything. Mitchel McLaughlin, our Six County chairperson, made it clear that we would "be studying in depth this morning's joint declaration . . . we will be comparing this with the Hume/Adams initiatives."

Within hours of the Declaration being launched, Taoiseach Albert Reynolds and Prime Minister John Major returned to their respective legislatures to seek endorsement of the document. Almost immediately, public statements by the two leaders and the members of their Cabinets indicated that real differences existed between both governments – not only on the actual meaning of significant and substantial parts of the Declaration, but on its stated objectives. Clarifying the Declaration in the House of Commons for Ulster Unionist Party leader James Molyneaux, the British Prime Minister said: "What is not in the declaration is: any suggestion that the British government should join the ranks of the persuaders of the value or legitimacy of a united Ireland . . . In sum, the Declaration provides that it is and must be for the people of Northern Ireland to determine their own future."

The Taoiseach addressed the Dáil with an entirely different emphasis. He asserted that "for the first time ever, the right to self-determination of the people of Ireland is acknowledged subject only to the question of consent". He said, "There is no unionist veto, only the requirement for the consent of a majority", and went on to say that "the door is open on one hand to a united Ireland if it can be achieved by unity and consent".

The following day, at a meeting of Sinn Féin's Ard Chomhairle, I pointed out that the difficulties involved in trying to build a peace process on a foundation of confusion and contradictions must be abundantly obvious to everyone. There was an obvious need for clarification. Major rejected my request, declaring that the Declaration was non-negotiable. He said: "There is a gauntlet down on the table. It is there for Sinn Féin to pick up. The onus is on them."

Within days, Major also published an article in a Belfast newspaper, aimed at clarifying unionist concerns. He claimed that the Declaration reaffirmed the constitutional guarantee to unionists that the North would remain part of the United Kingdom. That same day, Albert Reynolds said that there was a constitutional onus on John Major "to pursue unity".

Clearly the peace process required an initiative to break the deadlock. Did the Downing Street Declaration do this? Sinn Féin's peace strategy had taken years to evolve. Our dialogue with Irish religious, business, community and political representatives was protracted. The Hume/Adams position had taken years to arrive at. The Downing Street Declaration itself was the result of all of this, as well as some frenzied activity after John Hume and I had focused them on this issue.

We sought to find what part the Downing Street Declaration could play in this phase of the peace process. Was the Declaration evidence of a real political will to build a genuine peace process or was it just two governments trying to placate the public mood without really getting to grips with the causes of conflict? Was this as far as the British would go? How did it match the Hume/Adams initiative? Was it a staging post?

There was nationalist rhetoric in the document, but was this the British conceding the rhetoric of certain irresistible concepts, and then, by qualification, rendering them meaningless? One commentator had already called the Declaration a masterful piece of ambiguity. But this was a life and death situation that affected everyone on the island of Ireland.

We also had to examine the commentary that ran alongside the Declaration. John Major had put his unionist spin on it. In addition, as part of the attempt to put pressure on republicans, both London and Dublin hinted in leaks to the media that if republicans refused to accept the Declaration, there would be a crackdown. The London media quoted British government sources talking about internment without trial being reintroduced North and South, alongside the sealing off of the 300-mile border.

The British also rejected any notion of an amnesty for political prisoners. British Foreign Secretary Douglas Hurd threatened republicans that, unless we stopped prevaricating, we could expect no quarter. The British also told us that exploratory talks with Sinn Féin would begin only after a period of decontamination. Obviously, the issuing of ultimatums and the use of gratuitously offensive language while we were looking at the Declaration was not helpful. In the midst of all of this manoeuvring, core issues were being obscured in a frenzy of speculation and rumour. The two governments needed to recognise and acknowledge the right of republican voters to have their views represented in the broadcast media and in direct dialogue. I made it clear publicly that there could be no negotiated agreement that did not address the symptoms of conflict, as well as the causes. The equality issue was central, as was the release of political prisoners.

We decided to establish a Peace Commission. Its objectives were straightforward: to assess the Downing Street Declaration in terms of our overall peace strategy; to consult the widest possible spectrum of public and private opinion on how to establish a lasting peace in Ireland; to create a dialogue around the issue of peace and to make its findings public. Mairéad Keane, a member of our Ard Chomhairle, was given responsibility to convene the commission.

Internally, within Sinn Féin and our activist base, we also had to seriously engage in a wide-ranging process of briefings and discussion. This was made a little easier when the Irish government moved in January to scrap the censorship laws – Section 31 – in the Twenty-six Counties. For the first time since 1972, people in the South could see and hear a republican representative on radio and television.

In an effort to break the impasse, I wrote to John Major. But he was not for moving. Meanwhile, the loyalists were whipping up tension. The UDA leaked what they described as their doomsday scenario – full of talk of ethnic cleansing and repartition, conjuring up images of the horror happening in the Balkans. At the same time, Ian Paisley launched his "Save Ulster Campaign", declaring that the Downing Street Declaration "rolled out the red carpet for the IRA".

We received unexpected support of a sort from my old sparring partner Cardinal Cahal Daly. He said, "Channels exist whereby clarification can be given, without the principle of negotiation being conceded." But the British chose instead to relaunch their flawed, failed inter-party talks strategy. No one on the nationalist side thought this strategy capable of going anywhere.

It wasn't only clarification the British were saying no to. Behind the scenes, they were battling Irish America over efforts to secure a visa for me to travel to a conference in early February. Another new area of struggle was about to take centre stage.

# Chapter Fifteen

## *Americans for a New Irish Agenda*

The British Tory attitude to international – and especially US – efforts to find a resolution to the conflict were best summed up by the late Lord Hailsham. *Irish Times* journalist Conor O'Clery recalled: "I once asked the former British Lord Chancellor, Lord Hailsham, back in the 1970s, if the intervention by Irish Americans such as Senator Edward Kennedy on Irish issues made any impression on the British government. His face reddened and he slapped an open palm on his polished desk. 'Those bawstards', he cried. 'Those Roman Catholic bawstards! How dare they interfere!'"

But dare they did, as historically they had so often done; perhaps that's why Hailsham was so outraged. For over 200 years the Irish diaspora in the USA – Irish America – played an important supportive role in the Irish nationalist and republican cause during key periods of the Anglo-Irish conflict. Many Irish – some Presbyterians at the end of the eighteenth century, but mainly Catholics in the nineteenth and twentieth centuries – had fled to the United States to escape poverty and hunger, discrimination and oppression. Like many other nationalities fleeing to the "new world", they brought their language, music, dance, literature and their politics. Those who fled the Great Hunger in the 1840s helped to found, then fund, arm and train the Fenian Movement. A few short years later, they were giving money to ex-Fenian Michael Davitt's Land League, which successfully demanded fundamental changes to the ownership and distribution of land.

Their children helped Ireland achieve a measure of independence in the period from the Rising of 1916 to the Civil War six years later. Irish Americans always lobbied to win US government support for the Irish position as against that of Britain. After the partition of Ireland, Irish America split – as did republican Ireland – along Civil War lines. The Civil War itself saw yet more Irish republican exiles fleeing to the USA. In some cases, these were disillusioned, embittered and disappointed activists. Others continued solidarity work. Irish America itself was fighting its own struggle for recognition and rights in America.

Irish American politics on the national question reflected the situation back home. While support for an end to British rule was strong, it was not well organised. The main political connection from Ireland to the USA was from the Irish government, particularly Fianna Fáil. This was the case when the current phase of conflict erupted in 1969. By that time, the lot of Irish America had improved. The election in 1960 of John F. Kennedy ushered in a new era. Still, the failure of the Irish government to defend Irish national interests in the USA gave the British a largely free hand in promoting its propaganda. A consequence of this was that successive US governments followed the British agenda, banning senior republicans from travelling into the United States.

After the civil rights struggle of the late 1960s and the start of the war in the North, senior US politicians like Ted Kennedy, Daniel Moynihan, Tip O'Neill and Hugh Carey tended to support the approach favoured by the Irish government and John Hume. In the absence of a clear strategy to advance Irish nationalist goals, their engagement was often presented by the Irish and British governments and perceived by republicans as simply anti-republican.

Other Irish American figures – like Paul O'Dwyer, a leading New York lawyer – and Congress members – including Peter King, Richard Neal, Ben Gilman, Tom Manton – lobbied, campaigned and challenged British propaganda. Organisations like Irish Northern Aid and Clann na Gael highlighted justice issues and raised funds for political prisoners and their families. And there were those who followed the timeworn path of sending weapons to Ireland. A myriad of campaigning groups also mushroomed during this period, some focusing on single issues – like the Birmingham Six or the strip-searching of women republican prisoners – while others tackled issues like discrimination.

The Sinn Féin leadership knew the Irish cause needed to be internationalised. This lesson was apparent in the developing peace process in South Africa. Our leadership had long appreciated the importance of international opinion, but when we came to explore the potential for engagement with the international community, we didn't understand how to lobby this opinion in a strategic way.

Sinn Féin was a small party, under-resourced, under-developed and with no significant financial backing. True, we did have an international section – then called the Foreign Affairs Bureau – but this was essentially a one-man or one-woman show: good people doing their best to get information out of Ireland and to build contacts. How could we build an international dimension, especially when the British had the resources of their Foreign Office and embassies to promote their analysis and national interests? The countries of the European Union saw the conflict in Ireland as an internal matter for the British government. The United States, under President Reagan and then President Bush, had seen its role as one of working with its oldest European ally. This was nothing new and is well documented in Sean Cronin's fine book on the matter, *Washington's Irish Policy*.

The Irish government had no independent strategy to promote Irish national interests. But the USA was the one region in which there was a natural hinterland for the Irish cause.

Despite obvious hurdles, it was our view that the Irish American community presented us with our best chance of internationalising the issue of peace in Ireland. It had the most developed of our support groups and, within the Irish American community, there was a deep interest in Ireland and a genuine desire to see peace achieved. Unlike the Irish anywhere else, Irish America had considerable influence – not just in politics, but in the business world as well.

The US government's visa ban on senior Sinn Féin members entering the USA required that the bulk of the party's discussions, reviews and analysis of its involvement with organisations in the USA took place in Ireland. Successive leaderships of Irish Northern Aid were involved in these discussions, and, less publicly, prominent Sinn Féin members continued to visit the USA to brief supporters and encourage their work. But this was no effective substitute for the consultation and debate that was required. It often gave rise to mistakes in the political handling and management of the effort to build a wider support base. Inevitable tensions and misunderstandings arose from all of this both in the USA and between some activists in the USA and the Sinn Féin leadership. There was also some political disagreement. Old loyalties and friendships with longstanding members of Sinn Féin who had left the party after the 1986 Ard Fheis debate on abstentionism had an effect.

In April 1992 a well-known Irish American, John Dearie, organised a forum on Irish issues in Manhattan's Sheraton Hotel for Democratic presidential hopefuls Jerry Brown and Bill Clinton. Asked by one of the panellists if he would appoint a peace envoy for the North, Clinton said he

153

would. Martin Galvin of Noraid asked the presidential candidate if he would authorise a visa for me and other Sinn Féiners to visit the USA. Clinton replied, "I would support a visa for Gerry Adams." Clinton went further and endorsed the MacBride Principles. His response received loud applause.

Out of this Chris Hyland, Clinton's deputy national political director with responsibility for engaging with ethnic groups, approached *Irish Voice* owner Niall O'Dowd about creating a committee to win support for Clinton within the Irish American community. The first chairperson of "Irish Americans for Clinton" was former US Congressman and Connecticut lawyer Bruce Morrison. As a member of Congress, Morrison had steered legislation through that secured thousands of new visas for Irish people. He was consequently well known and respected within the Irish American community.

When Clinton returned to New York in October, he met O'Dowd, Boston Mayor Raymond Flynn and Paul O'Dwyer. All of them were impressed by him and by his commitments. Several days later, one of Clinton's aides, Nancy Soderberg – who had formerly worked for Ted Kennedy – drafted a letter to Bruce Morrison that was effectively Clinton's manifesto position on Ireland. In it, he went further than any previous presidential candidate. He committed himself to a more active role in working "with the leaders in those nations to achieve a just and lasting settlement of the conflict."

He acknowledged that: "A permanent and peaceful solution to the crisis in Northern Ireland can only be achieved if the underlying cause of the strife and instability is dealt with vigorously, fairly and within a time-frame that guarantees genuine, substantial and steady progress . . . I believe the appointment of a special US envoy to Northern Ireland could be a catalyst in the effort to secure a lasting peace." For many Irish Americans, and those of us watching in Ireland, his comments on collusion broke new ground: "We also believe that the British government should establish more effective safeguards against the wanton use of lethal force and against further collusion between the security forces and Protestant paramilitary groups."

The letter was viewed as a major breakthrough, although those who had formed "Irish Americans for Clinton" knew campaign promises don't always translate into policy. After Clinton was elected, "Irish Americans for Clinton" became "Americans for a New Irish Agenda". Within weeks they travelled to Little Rock, Clinton's home and campaign headquarters, to talk to his aides about putting promises into action. It was the first time that any grassroots Irish American lobby ever engaged with an incoming administration. After Clinton's installation as President, "Americans for a New Irish Agenda" continued to press the White House for implementation of the election promises. They also argued that a new US Ambassador to Ireland should be someone with clout and an understanding of the situation.

The British went on the attack. The day after Clinton was sworn in as President, the British government told journalists in London that its priority would be to have the envoy idea scrapped.

The first evidence that the "Americans for a New Irish Agenda" were having some success came over the St Patrick's Day period with the appointment as Irish Ambassador of Jean Kennedy Smith, Ted Kennedy's sister. A widow, she had founded the Very Special Arts programme for the mentally disabled and had overseen its growth across the USA and into fifty-five countries. However, hopes of an early appointment of a peace envoy were dashed when Taoiseach Albert Reynolds on his St Patrick's Day visit to the White House told Clinton that he was against the idea.

One of the new wave of activists who emerged in the 1980s was Ciaran Staunton. A Mayo man, he was a resident in Boston, an immigration reform activist and a Noraid member. His work with the immigration reform movement had put him in contact with a wide range of Irish and Irish American political opinion. One of these was Niall O'Dowd, originally from Thurles in County Tipperary but raised in Drogheda, owner of the *Irish Voice* and *Irish America* magazine. (They were later to become brothers-in-law when Ciaran married O'Dowd's sister Orlaith).

Not long after Clinton took up residence in the White House, Niall O'Dowd travelled to Dublin where he met with Ted Howell. Ciaran Staunton arranged for the Dublin meeting at which O'Dowd asked for an IRA halt to operations to facilitate him bringing a delegation of senior Irish American figures, all of whom were members of "Americans for a New Irish Agenda". Niall travelled to Belfast for his first meeting with me in twenty years. We discussed at length the problems and the possibilities open to us in the USA. We also gave him some sense of what we were trying to do, without telling him about the secret discussions then taking place separately between us and the Irish and British governments.

Niall felt that there were now opportunities of bringing a new dimension of Irish America into the frame. It was now time to get delivery on Clinton's election commitments. Niall thought a section of corporate

America in particular could be persuaded to play a role. "Americans for a New Irish Agenda" would come to Ireland to meet with a wide range of opinion. On its return to the USA, the group would report to the White House. In order to enhance the visit, but in particular to send a message to the delegation and the White House, Niall was advocating that the IRA have an operation-free period.

There was initial resistance in the army leadership to another request for an undeclared short halt to operations. Following the British bad faith response to the earlier IRA offer, there was a distinct concern that its willingness to contemplate these departures would be misread by its enemies. When the IRA eventually agreed to facilitate the visit, it was on the clear understanding that this was to be no more than a gap in operations timed to coincide with the visit. Its purpose was to empower the delegation.

Bill Flynn was chairman of the board of Mutual of America Life Insurance Company. He is also, among a host of other commitments, Chairman of the National Committee on American Foreign Policy. He had helped organise and fund a peace conference in Derry in 1992 called "Beyond Hate". He met and was impressed by Martin McGuinness at that time. Later he travelled to Belfast where he and I had tea in the dilapidated Sinn Féin offices at Sevastopol Street on the Falls Road. Bill came to the Irish cause through the Peace People, but quickly realised that there were huge issues of injustice underpinning the conflict. He came to visit many times, accompanied by his friend Bill Barry, who told me later that they had security concerns at that time about Bill wandering around Belfast. They established contact with the loyalists and began important, largely unrecognised work reaching out and supporting political developments in that constituency. I brought Bill to Clonard Monastery to meet the Sagart. His interest and involvement grew and continues to this day. Tom Moran, who now runs Mutual of America, has also played a key role.

When O'Dowd asked Bill Flynn to take part in the delegation, he readily agreed. Chuck Feeney was another businessman. He owned Duty Free Shoppers Ltd, the biggest duty-free shopping company in the world. Chuck, a billionaire, is one of the most remarkable men I have ever met. A private man who always shunned the spotlight, he was totally committed to our efforts to build a peace process. He cared little for the personal aspects of wealth. Some time after we first met he gave over three and a half billion dollars away to worthy causes. We got to know each other when Chuck contacted Niall O'Dowd to find out what was happening in Ireland.

156

Niall arranged for us to meet. In Chuck, I found all the things that are good about America. He was humanitarian, down-to-earth, concerned about the world and deeply interested in Ireland. Again, when O'Dowd asked him to get involved in the delegation, he immediately agreed.

Bruce Morrison was the main spokesperson for the group. Joe Jameson and another labour official, Bill Lenihan, made up the labour section. Niall O'Dowd was the facilitator for the group. The Irish Americans met a range of groups and individuals, including the two governments, but eventually they made it to Connolly House for their first ever meeting with us. Within Sinn Féin circles, the group for ever became labelled the "Connolly House group". They also met with a range of community groups in Conway Mill and heard the personal accounts of discrimination – in jobs, lack of investment, poor housing, bad health and deprivation – faced by nationalists each day.

On their return to the US, Niall O'Dowd arranged for a meeting between Ciaran Staunton and Bill Flynn to plan their next move. The three went to Famous Original Ray's Pizza at 688 Third Avenue in Manhattan. They decided that Bill Flynn would ask the National Committee on Foreign Policy – a non-profit-making organisation of which he was chair – to hold a peace conference on the North of Ireland. They would invite all party leaders from the Six Counties, including me.

Several weeks after the meeting, it emerged that the pizza parlour was being used by the Mafia as a centre for a major drugs operation. The organisation running the drugs was run by Aniello Ambrosio, who owned the pizza parlour. He arranged drugs shipments and stored drugs in his basement. And for some time his parlour had been under surveillance by the Federal authorities. In fact, the pizza parlour where the three conspirators had gone to have their quiet meeting was at that time probably the most heavily bugged place in the country!

Meanwhile Tony Lake and Nancy Soderberg met the Congressional Ad Hoc Committee on Irish Affairs in the Capitol, including Ben Gilman, Peter King, Tom Manton, Richard Neal and others. This was a first, and Lake told the group that the White House intended to give the issue more attention. Not long after this President Clinton, asked by *Irish Times* reporter Conor O'Clery about a visa for me, said that he would keep the issue under review, especially in the light of events flowing from the 15 December Joint Declaration by Prime Minister Reynolds and Prime Minister Major.

In Dublin, Jean Kennedy Smith asked the Taoiseach what he thought of the US giving me a visa. Reynolds said he had no objections. The new

Ambassador also asked John Hume, who also said he had no objections. She herself expressed her support to her brother, Ted Kennedy, and to the White House.

On 14 January 1994, I applied for a visa to attend the conference organised for 1 February. Jean Kennedy Smith sent a cable to the State Department endorsing the visa application. Some members of her staff sent a dissenting cable to express their opposition. The visa battle had begun. The British government began an intense private and public campaign to keep me out. The British Embassy and its ambassador worked round the clock arguing that a visa for me would be a diplomatic catastrophe. They sought and received the support of the House Speaker Tom Foley. The Secretary of State Warren Christopher opposed granting a visa, as did the Attorney General Janet Reno and the head of the FBI Louis Freeh. On the other side, Ted Kennedy and three Democratic Senate colleagues, Chris Dodd, John Kerry and Daniel Moynihan, wrote to President Clinton backing the visa. Others in Irish America rallied to the issue. In addition, full-page advertisements appeared in the *New York Times* calling for US support for efforts to find peace. The advertisement was signed by the Chairs or CEOs of eighty-five leading American corporations and over 100 other prominent Irish Americans.

On 28 January, I visited the US Consulate in the centre of Belfast and met the Consul General Val Martinez. He had been instructed by the White House to ask me two specific questions about my attitude to violence and the political process. I arrived around 9 a.m. and spent over an hour talking to Martinez. As I walked from Queen Street where the Consul office is sited, I was stopped by the RUC. The officer who stopped me ordered me to assume the search position. I told him to give my head peace. We had a little stand-off at the street corner, watched by a growing crowd of interested citizens, before someone more sensible or senior instructed my officious officer by radio to do something more productive.

Later, we issued a statement to the media about the engagement with the Consulate. I was mindful that the State Department questions had already been published that morning in *The Irish Times*. I faxed the statement to Niall O'Dowd, who passed it on to Trina Vargo, who then passed it on to Nancy Soderberg in the White House. Later the following evening, a news report emerged out of San Diego in California claiming that the "Southern California IRA" had placed hoax bombs at British stores in that city. No one in Ireland would have taken the story seriously even if they had been aware of it, but with a decision imminent from the

White House, Nancy Soderberg rang Niall O'Dowd to contact me to condemn this threat. It was 2 o'clock in the morning when Niall got through to me in Belfast. I listened to what had happened and to the White House request and, basically, I told him to tell the White House people to get real. I couldn't be issuing statements every time these silly stories appeared. I was moved to ask, "Does this mean I have to apologise every time an Irishman gets into a fight with an Englishman in a pub?"

Niall persisted. He agreed with me that this was nonsense. But as the President was going to make a call on the visa shortly, he argued that we should leave no excuses for others to trip us up. Eventually, I agreed to issue a statement condemning the bomb threats, which Niall worked out with me.

The next morning, President Clinton spoke to Warren Christopher and to Janet Reno, both of whom were still against giving me a visa. At 10.30 a.m. he told his staff he was going to authorise the visa. It was to be a restricted visa for two days only and I had to remain within New York. The next morning, Monday, I picked it up at the US Embassy in Dublin before just managing to get the midday Aer Lingus flight to New York.

I was surprised at the furore my visit created. It was an education. The British government's hysterical handling of the issue had ensured that the trip was a huge international media story. I didn't quite realise how big until I landed in New York. There were television crews there from all over the world. I did more interviews than I could count in the next two days. People have said to me that I was calm. I was too tired to get excited. One of the most important interviews was with Larry King. He opened by pointing out that it was against the law in Britain to put my voice on television. His remarks immediately highlighted the use of censorship laws by the British government. For his show to be broadcast in Europe, which covered Britain, an actor's voice had to be used – in this case, an American actor. Most US journalists and broadcasters were not even conscious of the broadcast restrictions and many could not understand the logic, nor did they approve of this denial of a basic civil right.

On Tuesday, 1 February, John Hume, John Alderdice of the Alliance Party and I attended the National Committee on American Foreign Policy conference at the Waldorf Astoria. DUP leader Ian Paisley and UUP leader James Molyneaux had declined to participate because of my presence. In my speech, I gave an overview of the situation back home. I finished by saying, "It is our intention to see the gun removed permanently from Irish politics."

After more interviews, I went to an event sponsored by "Americans for a New Irish Agenda" at the Sheraton Hotel, which was attended by a capacity audience of cheering, shouting, excited Irish Americans, and some more recently arrived Irish. The meeting was chaired by Bruce Morrison, and Paul O'Dwyer shared the platform with me. It was a powerful, emotional event. The best part was the question and answer session. The *craic* was mighty.

"Where did you get that tie?"

"Dunnes Stores." Which was the truth.

"Do you like New York?"

"If you can make it here, you can make it anywhere."

"Can you sing that?"

The event was a celebration, a vindication of the refusal of the New York Irish to give up on the Irish cause. It was great.

When Brian McCabe – the New York cop who was looking after me – deposited me back on the Aer Lingus jet bound for Dublin, I was barely in my seat before I fell fast asleep. When I awoke, the plane was making the approach to Shannon. It had been a mad whirlwind few days. An unprecedented number of people had heard the Sinn Féin message. The door into the USA had been opened. Irish American opinion was invigorated and informed. That potentially powerful community had a real sense of what was possible, and there were new players – particularly within corporate America – who were prepared to play a new role.

In the meantime, the British media and political establishment went wild in their condemnations of the New York visit. UUP MP Ken Maginnis said, "In the future, deaths in Northern Ireland will be Clinton deaths." The *Daily Star* commented that it would love to see me in a coffin with a gap where my face used to be. *The Sunday Times* referred to "gullible Americans". Hurd and the British Ambassador in Washington attacked the US media. Ambassador Renwick told CNN I reminded him of Hitler's propaganda chief: "When I listen to Gerry Adams I think, as we all do, it's reminiscent of Dr Goebbels."

I suppose, if I took it too seriously, this type of personalised hatred could have an effect. To tell the truth, the first time many, many moons ago that I heard myself described in these terms, I thought they were talking about someone else. The reality is that I have always felt very much a part of a community in struggle. Undoubtedly, not everyone in this community agrees with me, but most of the expressions of odium and contempt come from outside as part of the wider propaganda campaign. I

160

regret the loss of anonymity, but compared to what others have lost, I can't really complain. The fact is republicans have challenged the status quo. We are seen as a threat. Others see me, and the likes of me, as a front man for terrorism and respond accordingly. All of this goes with the job that I am trying to do, but Irish people especially know that standing up to colonialism brings its own punishment and reward. I am rewarded with the support and protection of our community in struggle.

After the US trip, some Conservative politicians demanded that the censorship ban be tightened. Others in Britain, including the London *Independent* and the *Guardian* called for its removal. The *Daily Telegraph* described relations between Britain and the USA as "The worst rift since Suez."

Douglas Hurd rushed to the US to meet with Vice President Al Gore. On his return to London, he attacked me as a "failed politician".

Major spoke of my "smokescreen of evasions and falsehoods".

Back home, as this tide of hysteria broke over me, I asked Colette what she thought.

"You must be doing something right," she said.

# Chapter Sixteen

# *Party Conferences*

When I arrived back from New York, the peace process was still in crisis. The British government was adamantly refusing to provide clarification on key aspects of the Downing Street Declaration for Sinn Féin. Instead it met with the SDLP, the UUP, the DUP and the Alliance Party. There was no package to take to the IRA leadership. The British forces intensified their operations. The conflict continued.

Major's government stumbled on, dangerously close to collapse as a result of political scandals and a wafer-thin majority in parliament. The UUP MP John Taylor reminded the British Prime Minister that the nine unionist votes might be withdrawn if Major moved against unionist interests. The British were again pushing their inter-party talks idea. And, in a one-week period from 27 January to 3 February, the first casualties of 1994 occurred with the deaths, in three separate attacks, of three Catholic men.

A sad and tragic reminder of the longevity of the conflict and of its human cost emerged with the death of Arthur McDonnell from West Belfast. He died from wounds he had received nineteen years earlier when shot by British soldiers. In July 1975, he was sixteen years old. McDonnell and another sixteen-year-old youth, Charlie Irvine, were in a car which back-fired as it passed a British army foot patrol at the corner of Clonard Street and the Falls Road. The soldiers opened fire, killing Charlie Irvine instantly. Arthur McDonnell was hit several times and went through the windscreen when the car came to a halt. Nineteen years later, blood clots which had formed in wounds in his calf travelled to his lungs and killed him.

The same week Arthur McDonnell died, the UDA planted one of their South African-imported fragmentation hand grenades at Connolly House. The grenade was tied to bushes and a trip wire placed across the path leading to the front door. A few days later, the UDA returned and fired an RPG rocket into the building. The RUC arrested Joe Austin, now a Sinn Féin councillor, when he arrived at the scene. And the UDA weren't finished. A week later, they returned and shot three men carrying out repairs to the building.

In February, Amnesty International once more voiced its concern that "Members of the Security Forces used their official status to target suspected members of opposition groups for murder."

But the same week brought a glimmer of hope. In reply to a letter I had sent him, Albert Reynolds outlined his views of the Downing Street Declaration and provided clarification of the Declaration from the Irish government's perspective. But John Major continued to refuse to follow the lead provided by the Taoiseach. He demanded that we make our minds up – or else! I made it clear, privately and publicly, that the British government approach was unacceptable and irresponsible, especially when the contradictory interpretations of both governments on key aspects of the Declaration were so apparent.

But for some on the British side, the idea of a peace process was anathema, especially to the "securocrats" – those faceless men and women who run Britain's various military and intelligence agencies. Their idea of peace was the defeat of republicanism. For some, like Tory MP Terry Dicks, the answer was even simpler. "The only place for Gerry Adams," he said, "is six feet under with a bullet through his forehead."

Then another little glimmer: some of Patrick Mayhew's speeches appeared to be aimed at publicly clarifying some aspects of the Downing Street Declaration and British policy.

Towards the end of February, Sinn Féin held our annual Ard Fheis at the Killinarden Community Centre in the Dublin suburb of Tallaght. There was still considerable pressure on public buildings, hotels and others to refuse us the use of their facilities. Public buildings were denied us by councils with local representatives acting under instructions from their party leaderships. Commercial premises were visited by the Special Branch, and if the visit itself didn't succeed, owners were often told that a Sinn Féin event could create problems when it came to licence renewals or Garda monitoring of other regulations.

Despite similar pressure, the Killinarden Community Centre opened its doors to us. The working-class people of Killinarden opened their homes to Sinn Féin delegates from all across Ireland. They made us very welcome indeed.

There was a larger than usual number of journalists and TV cameras present, and, for the first time, because of the lifting of Section 31, RTÉ and other Irish broadcasters could now broadcast coverage of the speeches, Ard Fheis debates and developments.

This was a crucial juncture in the internal politics of Irish republicanism. Many of the delegates attending the Ard Fheis had watched the political events of the past six months. They saw the process moving forward at a breathtaking pace. At the centre of this whirlpool of developments was the prize of peace, but at its core also was the work and determination of Irish republicanism. The reality was that for twenty-five years the political landscape had been frozen over – no real movement, no real progress. Now people saw the ice thawing and, in the last six months, had witnessed the beginnings of a public debate on the causes of conflict where none had existed before.

It was also the first opportunity I had to speak to such a widespread representative gathering of activists since the Hume/Adams initiative had become public, since the secret negotiations with the British had been revealed and since the Downing Street Declaration. It was important that both activists and the public realised the pivotal role we had played in all of this. We could also take some satisfaction from the international focus on our peace strategy, particularly in the United States and Britain.

We had identified British government policy as the major cause of conflict in Ireland. The British government had the power and the responsibility to move things on. Irish republicans by ourselves simply did not possess the political strength to bring about our objectives. That reality had to influence our political and strategic thinking. Consequently, our strategy was both politically defensive and offensive. We had defended our own political and organisational integrity and cohesion, even at a time marked by murderous attacks on us and our families. We had also endeavoured at all times, and failed sometimes, to prevent confusion in our membership and base, especially in the developing situation.

I told the Ard Fheis that we needed to measure progress in the context of how our strategy affected our opponents and possible allies. British strategy had, since the early 1970s, been based on marrying a section of "pragmatic" unionists and the SDLP in an arrangement to govern the Six-County state. The Hume/Adams initiative and our engagement with Dublin, had, in my view, reversed that. The Irish peace initiative, primarily built by us, with John Hume and the Irish government, was confronting the British government for the first time with a consensus – shaky and at

164

times superficial perhaps – but it was putting London on the defensive. The conflict and the peace efforts had also acquired a measure of consistent international attention not seen before.

In my Ard Fheis address I spoke directly and at length to unionists. Our demand for British withdrawal was not aimed at unionists. It was a demand for the right of everyone on this island to control and shape our own destiny. The civil and religious liberties of Northern Protestants must be guaranteed and protected. I also spelt out our vision of the future of Ireland.

I told the Ard Fheis that for the Downing Street Declaration to address the issue of Irish national self-determination was a significant departure for the British government. I said: "A nation cannot have half a right or a quarter right to self-determination. There can be no justification for trying to instruct the people whose right to self-determination you have just conceded, how they are to use it . . . having addressed the issue the British should now move to permit the Irish people to take up that challenge and they should see to persuade the unionists that their future lies in that context."

It was clear to me that the Downing Street Declaration marked a stage in the slow and painful process of England's disengagement from her first and last colony, Ireland. It might be a small step, as was the Anglo-Irish Agreement of 1985 which – leaving aside justifiable republican criticisms – gave Dublin, for the first time, a foot inside the door in the Six Counties. That door now needed to be opened wide.

The issue of an IRA cessation focused the minds and the scripts of those journalists covering the Ard Fheis. But for Sinn Féin, the concept of a peace process and its objectives had a much wider agenda. I outlined a range of equality issues and demands for citizens' rights right across all aspects of political, social, economic and cultural life. These were for basic entitlements like the right to live free from sectarian harassment or an end to discrimination in employment.

The unionist response to all of this was published in two papers. Both argued for the status quo.

In the meantime, unionist death squads targeted Catholics, and the RUC and British army intensified their harassment of nationalists and republicans. The IRA continued to wage war against British targets. In March there was an unprecedented series of IRA mortar attacks on London's Heathrow Airport. The first occurred on 9 March. Coded warnings were telephoned to news organisations and then four mortars were fired. The following evening, and again after coded warnings, another four mortars were fired at Terminal 4. By this stage, Heathrow was in turmoil and had been turned into an armed camp. Despite this, a third attack took place when a further four mortars were fired in the early hours of Sunday, 13 March. That evening, more coded warnings were given, but no mortars were fired. The impact was the same: the airport was brought to a standstill. The next morning Scimitar light tanks were deployed, along with units of the SAS.

Martin McGuinness and I held a number of meetings with the IRA leadership during this period to update it on current developments within the process and to put to them our views on the potential of all of these.

Some commentators, in reporting this period, suggest that the IRA had already privately agreed to call a cessation, that it was just a matter of time as the game was played out. This is not the case. The IRA's position was to continue the war. The Army Council had no other position. There is no doubt that the army leadership was open to the idea of supporting a genuine peace process, but it also remained committed to pursuing the armed struggle, and units generally operated at will within ordained guidelines. There was a debate, of course, within IRA ranks, but this was informal and was not leadership led. How could volunteers be motivated to risk life and limb by a leadership encouraging them to think about cessation? In IRA eyes, there were no grounds to consider such an option. Neither were there any grounds for supposing that this situation might change in the short term. But with so much speculation, and given the number of unprecedented IRA moves, there was a lot of discussion within IRA ranks. And there was, wisely, no attempt to stifle this.

Essentially, IRA discussions centred on whether the process had the potential to advance republican and democratic goals or whether it could have the opposite effect. The majority of IRA volunteers were sceptical about any notion of a ceasefire. Some had come to a position where they were prepared to see armed struggle not as an unshakeable principle but rather as a tactic to be used when no alternative existed. But there were others who just did not see any other way to get the British establishment to change its attitude. And there were others still who thought, even if there was reason for a cessation, it would only give the advantage to opponents and enemies.

All of these options were set against the risks involved, especially the impact they might have on the internal cohesion of the army. There was also a concern about the impact on Sinn Féin, on activists and the republican and nationalist support base.

166

Consequently, in our conversations with the army, it was clear that there were IRA leaders who felt the Downing Street Declaration was no advance but rather a trap. Some felt that there were no circumstances at this time which would justify the army having a cessation. There was a fairly widespread view that a lot more needed to be done on all of these matters. What was certain was that there was no possibility of an IRA ceasefire on the back of the Downing Street Declaration.

Within Sinn Féin there was a lobby arguing for a complete rejection of the Downing Street Declaration, with or without clarification. But the greatest support was for two options, which were not mutually exclusive. One was that we should continue in the short term to edge forward in the politically cautious manner we had adopted since 15 December. The other, slightly less cautious approach required building on the conditions created by Sinn Féin's peace strategy, the Irish peace process and the Downing Street Declaration. I favoured this approach and began a letter-writing campaign to Major and other British political leaders.

We needed to take initiatives, risky though this was, to inject momentum into the process. Writing to John Major and the other British political leaders may not have been much of an initiative, but it signified that we had not given up. If making peace needed tenacity, Sinn Féin had endless supplies of that.

The IRA had put on its thinking cap also. On 30 March there was an announcement by the IRA of a three-day ceasefire – from 5 to 8 April, coinciding in part with the Easter period. Christmas ceasefires were now generally seen as seasonal gestures of goodwill. This, however, was more than a gesture. For the first time in twenty years, the IRA had decided on a unilateral suspension of hostilities for the express purpose of creating space for political developments to take place. The six-day advance notification of the IRA initiative provided the British government with an opportunity to give clarification to republicans. Martin McGuinness, in a press conference in Belfast the day after the IRA announcement, described the IRA move as the first brick in the process. He asked who was going to lay the second brick. That was the question for the British government.

Martin and I knew that we had the real possibility of achieving significant progress if we could move John Major. In my letter to the British Prime Minister, I had asked him to authorise direct talks with Sinn Féin only in the context of clarification – not negotiation. Major was, as ever, having difficulties in the British parliament. He risked alienating his right wing with an initiative on the North.

Seven days later, on 6 April, with the three-day ceasefire in place, I wrote to Major again. He hadn't replied to my first letter. I asked him to reflect on his government's refusal to provide Sinn Féin with clarification while being prepared, as he had been, to speak to every other party. I told him we were not interested in bilateral negotiations with the British government. Negotiations were properly the business of talks involving the two governments and representatives of all the Irish people – including Sinn Féin.

The following day, I received a letter from Roderic Lyne, John Major's private secretary. All this did was to tell me to read the Declaration. He repeated the pre-condition in his letter that there had to be a permanent end of violence before the London government would speak to Sinn Féin. Publicly, Major described the three-day IRA cessation as a cynical ploy and a public relations gesture.

The loyalists continued to target Catholics, throwing bombs into homes, attacking taxi depots, and in one particularly brutal case, torturing for several hours and then shooting dead a thirty-one-year-old Protestant woman, Margaret Wright, mistaking her for a Catholic. A week later Theresa Clinton – the wife of Sinn Féin activist Jim Clinton and mother-of-two – was sitting in the front room of her Balfour Avenue home in South Belfast when her killers fired at her through the living room window. They must have seen her. She was hit by fourteen bullets. The attack on the Clinton family was the fifth attack in as many days by loyalists. A few nights earlier, eleven children had narrowly escaped death or injury when, in two attacks, grenades were hurled into their homes.

Martin McGuinness and I attended Theresa's funeral on a bleak, cold spring day. As we left the beleaguered streets of the nationalist lower Ormeau and made our sad way down the deserted main road, the tension was intense. My heart went out to those brave people who served our cause in vulnerable communities.

Theresa's death brought to twenty the number of Sinn Féin activists and family members killed by loyalists in the previous five years. Scores more had been injured. Theresa Clinton was the fourteenth person to be killed since the start of 1994. Nine of these had been killed by loyalists. There was also a campaign of attacks on the homes of SDLP members. Although there were no fatalities and guns were used only on a limited basis, the effect was terrifying for SDLP families. For many, the hand of the securocrats could be seen in the actions of the loyalists. Neither wanted the peace efforts to succeed.

But we persevered. Martin McGuinness and Aidan McAteer held a series of meetings with Martin Mansergh. Of course, the Sagart was constantly on the road between Belfast and Dublin. In late April, I forwarded to the British government – through Taoiseach Albert Reynolds – a document detailing the clarification of the Downing Street Declaration which Sinn Féin required from London. It contained twenty questions.

It was important that the British government respond positively to this initiative. There was an increasing sense of public desperation, a real fear that an opportunity to achieve peace might be lost. The previous year the British had talked to Sinn Féin. Now Major was refusing to do so at this crucial point – what was the logic in this?

During that week the South African peace process took another giant step forward. In the first ever all-race elections 22.7 million voters went to the polls. There, too, they faced difficulties and uncertainties – not least the gun and bomb attacks against ANC activists and the black majority. There were also powerful elements within the South African system trying to prevent progress.

As we waited for John Major's response to my letter, the unionist death squads kept up their unrelenting campaign against Catholics. At the beginning of May, a UVF death squad walked around the side of an isolated home in East Tyrone under cover of darkness and opened fire through a living room window, killing seventy-six-year-old Roseanne Mallon. The family and local people immediately accused the RUC of collusion in her death. While the predictable denials were made, subsequent events and new facts surrounding the murder supported the family's view.

Several months after her killing, high-powered surveillance cameras were discovered dug into the earth just 400 yards from Roseanne Mallon's home. Also discovered was a transmitter, which sent pictures back to a monitoring station run by British military intelligence and the RUC Special Branch.

Shortly after local people had removed the cameras, a large number of troops and RUC personnel saturated the area. It was widely believed that this was to recover and remove other equipment. The RUC Chief Inspector in charge of the murder inquiry told the media that no one in British intelligence or Special Branch had informed him that they had cameras monitoring the house. But events added to the reality of collusion. Three weeks prior to her death, members of the RUC Special Branch had detained a relative of Roseanne Mallon's at a checkpoint. Twenty minutes later Billy Wright – the leader of a loyalist death squad in Portadown reported to have been personally responsible for over a score of Catholic dead – arrived and spoke to the RUC Special Branch officers. Wright then told Mrs Mallon's relative that he was going to be killed. The day before the killing, two young boys disturbed a number of armed men in an old house near the scene of the murder. The boys' parents informed the RUC soon after the incident. The RUC claimed that the men were a hunting party.

A few hours after the killing of Roseanne Mallon, two men were arrested near Portadown. They were released after several days.

It also emerged that six British soldiers, almost certainly the SAS, were watching the house at the time of the attack, but were ordered "not to react". Material recorded by the cameras was also kept secret. Up to fourteen hours of tape for the day before the murder were missing. Military logbooks were also "unavailable". At the time of writing, there has been no inquest held into Roseanne Mallon's murder.

Within days of her killing, loyalists killed another four Catholics, including two teenage boys. Many more were lucky to escape injury or death in these and other attacks, including one in which loyalists – using AK47 rifles – opened fire on a Sinn Féin march going into Belfast city centre.

I was on that march up towards the front when the shooting started. We were in Divis Street adjacent to the Shankill area and close to the city centre. There was a *crack-crack-crack* of automatic rifle fire. The bulk of the people in the demonstration scattered for cover, but a group of young people almost instantly headed towards the area where they judged the shooting had come from. Sinn Féin stewards moved quickly to disperse them. It was a sign of the times. A peaceful, almost carnival march was suddenly transformed into a frightened, angry group of people. Mothers grabbed for their children. People everywhere ran for cover. The younger elements were trying to get to where the gunman or gunmen were positioned. Even though they had probably withdrawn immediately after opening fire, it was highly dangerous. I turned to head off some of the youngsters. Cleaky blocked me. As soon as the shooting started, he stuck to me like glue. In fact, he tried to force me to leave the scene – which would have been a sensible move. As it turned out, we quickly got the young people back. No one was hurt and the march quickly regrouped and made its otherwise uneventful way to a rally at the City Hall.

Cleaky wasn't long out of prison. He had put together a team of drivers and minders, mostly former prisoners, to look after Sinn Féin representatives. They were extremely brave people who put their lives on the line every day for us. That day was one of their first tests.

Early in July, the IRA killed a UDA leader. Several weeks later, they killed two other senior members of the UDA in South Belfast who, it was claimed, had been involved in the attack on the bookmakers shop on the Ormeau Road in 1992 in which five Catholics were killed.

Finally, the British government replied to my letter. Their response reached me in Turin, where I was fulfilling speaking engagements. Its twenty-one pages were certainly at odds with London's previous assertions that no clarification was necessary or indeed possible. Their response, therefore, marked a small but important step in the slowly evolving peace process.

By the time I returned to Ireland, the British had published their response. And Sinn Féin was in the throes of a European election campaign. Consequently, the internal discussion on the British government's clarification letter was going to take a little time. In addition, we were still negotiating with the Irish government on related matters. The Ard Chomhairle of Sinn Féin decided to hold a special delegate conference in July to examine the Downing Street Declaration in detail and agree our formal attitude to it and its relationship to the peace process.

Inevitably, the conference attracted huge media interest. Speculation and predictions were rife: we were going to reject the declaration, we were going to accept the declaration, the IRA was going to announce a ceasefire. These and other stories filled the newspaper columns. But for anyone who was following the story closely it was obvious that the package was still not in place for Martin and me to take to the IRA.

Clarification from the two governments, and especially the British, now that it had eventually been provided, tended to support the case that the Downing Street Declaration was in many ways an ad hoc and not so well drafted response to Hume/Adams. The flaws in the drafting were not the fault of the drafters. They were evidence of the different types of pressure on the two governments. So while the declaration was a significant development, that was all it was.

In the weeks leading up to the conference, we were privately pressing the Irish government to bring forward its position on a range of issues including prisoners and demilitarisation. Publicly, headlines were dominated by stories of death and destruction as the unionist death squads killed Catholics across the North. One incident in particular stood out. I had been in Dublin for a meeting of our Ard Chomhairle to discuss developments in the peace process, including our plans for the July conference in Letterkenny in County Donegal. Dublin was ablaze with colour as Ireland was that day playing Italy in a World Cup soccer match in the United States. There was a hardly a soul to be seen. They were all in watching the drama unfolding on their television screens. But a different drama was taking place in the North. Shortly after the match, and as Dubliners were out on the streets celebrating a famous victory, I got a call from our press officer Richard McAuley. A loyalist death squad had walked into a pub in Loughinisland in County Down and slaughtered six men.

Before the conference, Sinn Féin published the report of our Peace Commission. Some submissions focused on the need for the British government to withdraw its support for the unionist veto. Some reflected the fears of the nationalist community regarding British intentions in Ireland and its links with the death squads. Many nationalists, particularly at the hearings in Belfast and Derry, had expressed the view that they had no rights in the Six County state and that nationalists' rights and the unionist veto could not co-exist. They did not trust the British government. There were some significant submissions from Northern Protestants which outlined their concerns and hopes.

One theme dominated all others: the belief that a viable peace process was possible. Somehow, we had to make that belief a reality.

The conference met on 24 July in the disco of a hotel outside Letterkenny, guests of the owner, who was prepared to take a stand on our right to free assembly. A number of us were cramped together on the small stage while delegates were seated on the dance floor below flourescent disco lights. It was an interesting ambiance for a party conference. People were generally in good form. One of the highlights was the attendance of Pat Treanor, a councillor from County Monaghan. Pat had been arrested several days before while showing some visitors around fortifications on a cross-border road, which had been closed by the British military.

Pat was taken by RUC vehicle to a barracks in County Tyrone. On route the vehicle was attacked by an IRA unit operating from the back of a lorry. Pat lost a finger in the attack. No one else was hurt. When he rose to speak at the Letterkenny conference, he was warmly greeted by delegates. He then went on to regale us all, and an obviously puzzled international media contingent, with an account of his exploits.

That to one side, the conference was uneventful. We had tried to dampen media expectations, and the Irish government was alerted to the fact that there would be no major announcements.

If the Declaration was a step in the peace process, we were now looking to the next steps. These had to deal in a fundamental way with the core constitutional issues, as well as the secondary issues. For most of the media, our considered position spelt rejection –that's how many chose to report it. Some went so far as to proclaim that the peace process was dead and it was all the fault of republicans. As was so often the case, the truth was very different.

# Chapter Seventeen

# *A Space for Hope*

Sinn Féin emerged from the Letterkenny conference united and confidant. It was difficult at times for all our activists to keep pace with the developing situation, and this could be unsettling. The Letterkenny conference brought everyone up to date. A few years before, Sinn Féin strategy was limited. Now that we were driving a process, our activists had a real sense of being agents of change, and of the party being at the centre of developments. So while there were uncertainties and doubts, morale was good.

Progress was also being made behind the scenes in the meetings and discussions with the Irish government. We were in the final stages of putting together a position with the Connolly House group. And the peace process was now on the agenda in the White House, where President Clinton's National Security Advisor Tony Lake and his deputy Nancy Soderberg were keeping a close watch on developments.

Martin and I gave the IRA another assessment of the situation in early August. It was coming to the point of deciding if this was the right time to start putting the jigsaw together. Timing was critical. If we pulled everything together and the army said no, the process was over before it really started. I was able to tell the army people of the progress that we had made. In my opinion, there was an identity of view between Sinn Féin, the SDLP and the Irish government on a range of issues. Commitments given were about a programme, a process for change.

How deeply committed Dublin and the SDLP were to this would emerge in due course. There was considerable tension still within sections of the SDLP leadership. Contrary to some stated views, the disscussions within the SDLP were not in Sinn Féin's interest. A united SDLP supporting its leader was more suitable to us and our enterprise. Because we had vested so much in the Hume/Adams axis, any distraction was counter-productive. At different times in the process, the Sinn Féin core group applied itself to considering how to reduce the SDLP's internal difficulties.

While Sinn Féin was supportive of what I was trying to do, sizeable sections of the SDLP did not give John the same back-up. In fact, at different times we had a sense of efforts to knobble him. Notions of a pan-nationalist alliance were fanciful and the stuff of unionist press statements, although that, of course, was what was required. But the tensions within the SDLP leadership and the deeply ingrained anti-republican hostility of some of its leaders made this impossible. It is a credit to John Hume that he persevered despite all this and that we were able to find agreement on a range of important issues.

These included, for example, an acceptance that partition had failed, that the present structures were inadequate and had to be changed, that there could be no internal settlement within the Six Counties, that the Irish people as a whole have a right to national self-determination and must be able to exercise this right freely and without external impediment, and that this was a matter for agreement between the people of Ireland alone. We also agreed that the unionists could have no veto over discussions or the outcome of those discussions, and that a negotiated settlement required fundamental constitutional and political change.

There were differences of opinion on how a number of these principles could be interpreted, but there was also sufficient commonality of view to allow us to move forward. There was also a need to address a number of areas of immediate and practical concern to nationalists living in the North. These included parity of esteem, equality of opportunity, and equality of treatment for Irish culture and identity.

Martin was able to report that, after a long process of negotiation with the Irish government, Dublin had provided written assurances that if there was a cessation there would be an immediate response on practical matters. Sinn Féin would be treated like any other political party – not subjected to harassment and marginalisation. The immediate effect of this would include a meeting between Taoiseach Albert Reynolds, myself and John Hume. There would be a meeting soon after between myself and Albert Reynolds and regular consultation between us after that. There would also be consultations between Irish government officals and Sinn Féin as regularly as required.

There would be immediate bilateral discussions between Irish government representatives and Sinn Féin representatives on the proposed Forum for Peace and Reconciliation, which was how the Sagart's original idea for a convention had turned out. We would participate in the Forum on the basis of our electoral mandate. The Irish government was also committed to seeking to influence the British government and to encourage the US administration to take a more positive approach to the issue of visas for republicans.

The Connolly House group had also passed back to us a document which set out a serious programme of work and commitment from them and Irish America. Entitled "Policy Statement by Irish American leaders", it said that in the event of a ceasefire they would commit themselves to "the creation of a campaign in the United States dedicated to achieving" a number of specified goals. Among these were:

- An immediate end to all visa restrictions imposed by the US government on Irish republicans.
- The provision of unrestricted access for the Sinn Féin party leader; including access to the same level of the administration and members of the House and Senate as is available to all other major political party leaders.
- The creation of a staffed, representative office in Washington DC to educate and inform American media and influence public opinion on the peace process.
- They would act as guarantors insofar as they could, and do their best to get the US government to act as guarantors, so that any agreements entered into by the governments were adhered to.
- A campaign to stimulate private and corporate investment in the North of Ireland.
- An effort to get the White House to provide new forms of aid from the US.

The Connolly House group was committed to exerting maximum American pressure on the British government, and to use every means possible to prevent loyalist murder gangs from operating. They also committed themselves to seeking to end the harassment and surveillance of members of the Irish community in the USA.

The IRA meeting to which we reported all these matters had a new, different quality. It was obvious that matters were coming to a head, although there was still work to be done. The army people agreed to meet again within days to receive an update from us of our last-minute deliberations. It was coming close to make-your-mind-up time. Everyone knew this. What was not so clear was how the Army Council would formally deal with a proposition for a cessation. Some were prepared to support the idea if it was a launching pad to drive the struggle forward. But these were hardheaded people. They could see the political landscape changing as a result of Hume/Adams and other initiatives. Some of these initiatives had been authorised and devised by them. But short-term tactical initiatives, even risky ones, were nothing compared to a decision to call a halt to operations.

Some of the leadership were against a cessation. They had been frank about that. And they were good people. Long-time, sincere, serious and committed activists. People you could rely on. People you could trust with your life, provided you were straight with them. They would be disciplined and committed enough to accept whatever decision was made, but they would do their best in a totally honest and democratic way to ensure that that decision was one they favoured. It was going to be a close call.

Arrangements for meetings with the IRA were always problematic. Martin and I both knew that our movements were constantly monitored, phones and homes and offices were bugged. We had to be very careful. This made for some torturous travel arrangements.

One meeting Martin McGuinness and I had with the IRA sometime later illustrates the lengths to which secrecy was maintained. We had already been in three different cars and then we had to climb into an old van. The floor of it was dirty and covered in old straw, dried clay and what looked suspiciously like sheep shite. Martin wrinkled his nose and grinned at me. He was jet-lagged, having just returned from the USA. His dark lounge suit looked out of place. So, I am sure, did mine. We sprawled on the floor of the van. The driver flung a few empty bags towards us.

"Here, sit on these. Sorry youse are in your good clothes."

He pulled the van door closed behind him. The windows were blacked out. As the door slammed shut, we were plunged into darkness.

"Last night the White House," Martin chuckled as the van lurched forward, "today this."

Meanwhile back in Belfast, our core group met again to review the situation. These meetings also had a security element to them. Our concern that the British should not know what we were discussing meant that we held the most important meetings outside of our offices or other places which would be obvious targets for electronic surveillance.

So it was that our group crowded into supporters' bedrooms or spare

177

rooms to plot the next steps. I was of the firm view that we needed to choreograph a series of statements – actually more public initiatives than statements – from John Hume, Albert Reynolds and the Connolly House group, which would actually signal the coming together of the different pieces of the package. Privately I thought that such a public manifestation of support for an alternative approach might persuade republicans that there really was the possibility of another way forward. It certainly would provide a new context into which the IRA could enter.

We needed a visa for Joe Cahill. A veteran activist and senior Sinn Féin figure, he had spent over fifty years of his life in struggle against the British. Party colleague and Monaghan Councillor Pat Treanor was to travel to the USA to make preparations for Joe's tour. Pat was an important representative in his own right, but he would also be a travelling companion in the USA for Joe, who was not in good health.

The IRA wanted to see whether the Irish government was prepared to take on the British on this issue and if it could win such a political battle with the British within the US administration. It would also be an important indicator of how seriously the Clinton administration intended to take the issue of peace in Ireland. If the visas were denied, the IRA would weigh that heavily in any decision about the potential for the peace process.

The Sagart's support was enlisted. He had modified his role in recent months to doing follow-up with all of us. He kept me on my toes, pushed the Irish government, and kept in constant touch with John Hume. The Sagart had a great affection for the Holy Spirit. At different times over the years when the situation appeared dire, he would remark to me. "It's up to the Holy Spirit now."

A year or so before in a telephone conversation he was trying to find out from me how things were going. The two of us were very conscious of phone lines being tapped. We were being cagey – especially me – and the Sagart could not ascertain whether the particular business I was involved in was going well or badly.

Eventually he asked, "Do we need the Holy Ghost on the field?"

We are both big hurling and Gaelic football fans.

"I have him playing in goals," I answered. He knew we were under pressure.

That became an accepted code between us. I don't know what the code-breakers of GCHQ in Britain made of it. If the Holy Spirit was on the team at all, we were in trouble. His position on the field indicated the state of play. So, if he was in backs, we were on the defensive. Forwards, we were on the attack. In goals, we were in real trouble. If he was on the bench, things were progressing well. Once I told the Sagart the Holy Spirit had transferred to the other team. Another time he, or she, as the Sagart reminded me, was injured. In one memorable conversation the Holy Spirit was sent off for fouling. That was against Dublin. The Sagart thought the ref was too harsh. These conversations invariably occurred at points of great tension after crisis meetings.

By now, the Sagart was a firm friend of Jean Kennedy Smith. He undertook to lobby her, and the Taoiseach as well, to get Joe Cahill an American visa. In his telephone conversations with me during that episode the Sagart had the Holy Spirit playing in every conceivable position. President Clinton is said to have looked at Joe's "CV" – as a young man in the 1940s he had been sentenced to hang. His sentence had been commuted, but a comrade, Tom Williams, was hanged. In 1974 Joe was caught smuggling several tonnes of weapons into Ireland from Libya. He had also been deported from the States. Since his release from prison some time after this, he had been a senior figure in Sinn Féin and a key proponent of the peace process. The US Ambassador to Ireland, Jean Kennedy Smith, supported the request for a visa, but the pressure from the British was intense and the Taoiseach and Ambassador fought a determined battle.

The Connolly House group returned to Ireland on 25 August. They met the Taoiseach on their arrival. The following day, Friday, they were at Connolly House again where they met with a senior Sinn Féin delegation including myself, Martin McGuinness and Mairéad Keane. The outside of the building still bore the scars of the loyalist rocket attack months earlier. Inside, we discussed the policy statement they had signed up to and sought assurances from them that this would be followed through on. The establishment of the Washington office and its funding was particularly important. I also told them that it was my view that the IRA was moving toward taking a decision on a cessation. But I pointed out that no decision had been made and there was no certainty about the outcome of that decision. I asked them to respect the confidentiality of the meeting. Outside speaking to the media, Bruce Morrison told them that he was encouraged and that the group felt that the process was moving in a constructive direction.

I saw the meeting as an important contribution to our efforts to convince other republicans that a strong international element did exist and could be brought to play in support of the Irish side in any negotiations with the British. This would be significantly reinforced by the visa for Joe Cahill. Pat Treanor now needed one as well. On the day that the Connolly House group arrived in Ireland, Pat had left for the States. He had been stopped by Immigration and sent back. This wasn't good.

Albert Reynolds was pushing Clinton hard. Jean Kennedy Smith in particular was pulling out all the stops. So was London. The visa issue was now the subject of a pitched battle between Ireland and Britain or at least between the diplomatic services and governments of both countries. I felt my visit to New York was wee buns compared to Joe's travel plans. I was a bit like John the Baptist.

The following Sunday, John Hume and I met and issued another joint statement. We recapped the work done thus far. We restated our view that agreement on a peaceful and democratic future was no threat to anyone. We also put the onus on the British government to respond positively.

Later that evening Taoiseach Albert Reynolds issued a statement in which he also expressed a belief that a historic opportunity was opening up. He too said that the British government had a heavy responsibility. He wanted to see an all-round demilitarisation of the situation and the full participation of all parties on equal terms in talks leading to a comprehensive political settlement.

The pieces of the jigsaw were together. It had taken a frenzy of work since last we met the army leadership. Martin and I met the Army Council again. The meeting was inconclusive. People needed more time to cogitate over all the issues. And while Joe's visa would not have broken the deadlock, it certainly was a test of whether we could deliver. I relayed all this back to the Taoiseach. Then, late on Monday night, 29 August, the President gave his authorisation for the two visas. The Taoiseach rang the Sagart who was staying in the same house as Joe in expectation of this. The next morning Joe and Pat picked up their visas from the US Embassy in Dublin. By lunchtime they were on an Aer Lingus flight to New York. Subsequently Joe's five-day visa was extended to allow him to travel across the USA.

To those in the know, it may have seemed obvious that there was going to be an initiative by the IRA in the form of a cessation. While we were able to report at a special meeting of our party's Ard Chomhairle on the gathering together of the various pieces of the jigsaw, everyone understood that the army would make its own decisions.

I had always argued that a changed political climate could create the potential to eradicate the underlying causes of conflict. It would take time, but those who took the initiative would have the advantage – at least for the opening rounds. I did not underestimate the difficulties involved.

On the way to see the Army Council again, I was preoccupied with all these issues and probably a little withdrawn. Whatever way this meeting went, a Rubicon had been crossed. It was now over to the IRA leadership. Would the army give our package space? The direction of politics could be changed irrevocably if it did, but there were no guarantees. There were powerful forces against change – not only within the British establishment and within unionism. The Irish establishment had its interests as well. History told us that the Irish government could not be relied upon.

The army meeting was tense. I had some sense of the way people might vote by the way they had spoken at other meetings and by their attitude to the reports we had been giving them, but there had been no individual lobbying and it was impossible to predict the outcome. Martin McGuinness spoke eloquently, as did others both for and against a cessation. About the overall struggle. About the army and the strains and stresses on it. About the British government's attitude thus far in response to IRA initiatives. What would happen to the struggle if the British spurned a cessation by the army? How would volunteers react? Or that wonderfully resilient and loyal support base which had sacrificed so much over the decades? About the families of volunteers who had been killed. I thought about the prisoners and their families. And what if the army split?

One of Martin's great qualities is his sense of conviction and confidence. He can bring a strength to a debate which is very compelling. Even if you might not agree with him, you know he is going to deliver on any commitment he makes, or die trying. He spelt out how the last few years had been the education of a lifetime for many people. The Hume/Adams initiative had given people hope. More and more nationalists were seeing republicans making a real effort to build peace. Republicanism was stronger. There was a sense of Irish nationalism reasserting itself. And there was a strong and growing Sinn Féin party with a sense of itself and of what it should be doing.

The struggle wasn't ending, we told them. They knew that, of course. In its public statements, the British government had spelt out its commitment to dialogue with Sinn Féin and to addressing other matters, including cutting back on the British military presence. These were all on the public record. If the Brits reneged, as they might, then *they* would be seen as spurning the possibility for peace.

The difference between this cessation and any other one, we argued, was that in the past these were bilateral arrangements which were negotiated out, usually in secret between republicans and the British. Now any arrangements would be multilateral. At other times, the IRA had been the main – in some places the only – manifestation of republican struggle. The armed struggle was *the* struggle. Now the struggle was bigger than the army.

There was also the question of the unionists. We were being told that elements within unionism wanted peace. Republicanism in its essence is a generous philosophy. Well, let's see, we said, if between us all we can reach out to the unionists to build that peace. John Hume had remained true to the process, despite all the problems, and now Dublin was giving firm commitments. A powerful element within Irish America was prepared to play its part. All of this had come to be because we and people like us created the space and the conditions for all these possibilities.

In many ways, I said, the easy decision was for the IRA to continue to fight. Then, when eventually it was all over, those republicans who survived would meet at each other's funerals or at commemorations, like we had been doing over the decades, and we could reminisce about how we had kept the faith. We could swap yarns and loose talk and take certain succour from being old irreconcilables. That was the low-risk option.

The high-risk option was the one we were arguing for. It meant uncharted waters. It would involve compromises. It could mean risking – and losing – everything. And unlike others, who had lost in the past, we would be seen as responsible for the loss. We would be the ones to blame. We who had taken the wrong path. But we could also be the generation who would win freedom. We could set in place a process which could create new conditions for a genuine and just peace, and from there build a pathway and a strategy into a new all-Ireland republic.

A formal proposal was put to the meeting. In essence, the army was going to give the process a chance. It would cease its military operations, go to the sidelines and monitor progress. Each Army Council member spoke in turn and declared their vote. The proposal was then formally put to the meeting. The cessation was on. The vote would remain secret. Those who voted against pledged their support to the new position. Unity was essential. I have always considered that the peace process and the republican cause, and the IRA, owes a special debt to those Army Council members. It could be argued that those who proposed or supported the proposition for a cessation deserve credit, and that may be fair enough. But to be passionately against a position and then to go and argue and debate and defend and promote that position with your peers is worthy of credit and commendation also.

The Army Council had to bring forward its proposal to the Army Executive. All commands had to be instructed. It was to be a busy, unsettling time for the people involved. There was also a statement to be written. Some sources have suggested that the army were considering a different kind of a statement from the one which was released. This is not the case. According to these sources, Albert Reynolds sent a strong message that nothing less than a full cessation would suffice. But no such message was ever given to the Army Council. It was not needed. In fact it would have been counter-productive.

Such was the significance of the IRA initiative that the IRA's publicity director could not draft anything which would undersell or allow opponents of the peace process to pick holes in what was being announced. On Wednesday at noon the IRA declared its intentions:

"Recognising the potential of the current situation and in order to enhance the democratic peace process and underline our definitive commitment to its success, the leadership of Óglaigh na hÉireann have decided that as of midnight, Wednesday, 31 August, there will be a complete cessation of military operations. All our units have been instructed accordingly . . .

"Our struggle has seen many gains and advances made by nationalists and for the democratic position. We believe that an opportunity to create a just and lasting settlement has been created. We are therefore entering into a new situation in a spirit of determination and confidence: determined that the injustices which created the conflict will be removed and confident in the strength and justice of our struggle to achieve this."

## Chapter Eighteen

# *America Again*

The IRA cessation was the opening of a new phase of struggle. It was, as the Irish Nobel Poet Laureate Seamus Heaney was to write within days of its announcement, "a space in which hope can grow". Our task was to deepen that space, and to widen it so that hope would flourish. We had to fulfil the potential that the IRA initiative had created: a mighty task given the range of political and military forces opposed to our efforts and the shaky consensus on the nationalist/republican side.

We had to hit the ground running. Dialogue with our activists, with our support base, and with wider public opinion was now imperative. In the immediate hours after the statement became public, and as it was being flashed around the world, Martin McGuinness and I, along with other senior Sinn Féin leaders, arrived at Connolly House for an impromptu rally. There were hundreds of people there. As we pushed our way through the cheering crowd, I was struck by the awesome responsibility of it all. The hopes and aspirations of all the people who were clapping us on the back and the dreams of the many others who would be watching this unfold were now pinned to our ability to deliver. Someone thrust a bottle of champagne and a bunch of flowers into my hands as I climbed on to the small platform that had been erected outside Connolly House.

I praised the IRA leadership for its bold and decisive initiative. They had created a crucial moment, a decisive moment in the history of Ireland.

The crowd was enthusiastic. Many of them were friends and activists I had known for years. Some had lost loved ones in the struggle. Among them was Paddy Mulvenna. The anniversary of the killing of his son, Patrick, an IRA volunteer and my brother-in-law, was that day. For the Mulvenna family and others like them, this was going to be a difficult time. "The freedom struggle is not over," I said. "We must develop an irreversible momentum for change, which will move the British government away from the failed policies of the past."

I also took the opportunity to speak to unionists. Their leaders had been quick to condemn the IRA's move. Ian Paisley claimed that unionists now faced the worst crisis in Ulster's history. Jim Molyneaux said it was a destabilising move. In his view, it was not an occasion for celebration, quite the opposite.

I appealed directly to the unionist section of our people to join with the rest of us in creating a new democracy.

In the middle of all of this, I took time to single out and to thank one individual, a private citizen, who has played and who will continue to play a crucial role in this process. I was, of course, referring to the Sagart. Mindful of his desire for privacy, I declined to name him. As the speeches finished, a cavalcade of black taxis and cars – all crammed full of people waving flags and cheering – sped off to travel throughout nationalist Belfast.

Our spontaneous public event had one unexpected side effect. Sky Television, which decided to carry it live, had to use actors' voices for Martin McGuinness and myself because of the British government's broadcast restrictions. But Pat Doherty and Bairbre de Brún were broadcast using their own voices. Perhaps they ran out of actors!

There was another private and, for those involved, undoubtedly a personal demonstration of the effects of the IRA announcement. All that week, scores of people visited the Republican Plot in Milltown Cemetery. Friends and presumably relatives of the patriot dead buried there made their pilgrimage to mark what was a deeply emotional development. My wife Colette met Mairéad Farrell's mother, who was uplifted by the army's move. "I'm only sorry my Mairéad isn't here for this," she said.

The new South African government, led by a recently elected President Mandela, lauded the decision. Archbishop Desmond Tutu described it as absolutely unbelievable news. He told reporters that his excitement was similar to the day that Nelson Mandela had been released from prison. In the United States, President Clinton expressed his delight at developments.

But while the rest of the world welcomed and applauded the IRA move, the usual begrudgers issued dire warnings of doom and gloom, and the British government went into prevarication overdrive. The voices of the past were shouting loudly. According to Conor Cruise O'Brien, it was all a clever IRA plot to create a civil war; it would end with the collapse of democracy in Ireland and the IRA in control. One of his articles in the

London *News of the World* was headlined "IRA Will March into Dublin". His answer to this devious republican master plan was simple – internment.

The British government played for time. Having spent months arguing over clarification of the Downing Street Declaration, the British now engaged in a new word game around the IRA statement. The statement they said did not include the word "permanent"!

I set out the Sinn Féin stall at a packed press conference in Dublin two days after the IRA announcement. Sky News was again going to take it "live", albeit with an actor's voice. So the first thing I did was to call on John Major to end the nonsense of the British broadcasting restrictions and lift the banning orders against Sinn Féin leaders travelling to Britain. I went on to urge the creation of inclusive all–party negotiations as the first crucial step in any conflict resolution strategy. I also called for visible and speedy progress on the many issues which had contributed to the conflict.

We were aware of the dangers to the peace process posed by a British government still locked into a war mindset. Part of the Sinn Féin strategy, in our discussions with the Irish government, had been to agree a number of confidence-building measures – what I referred to at that time as "the strategy of alternative initiatives" – which did not require British involvement or approval.

The first of these – a meeting with the Taoiseach and John Hume – was set for Wednesday, 6 September. But already only a day or so after the cessation, there was trouble. Dublin contacted me to ask if that meeting could be rescheduled. Seamus Mallon apparently was demanding that there be an Irish government/SDLP meeting before our get-together. I said it wasn't on. We had just done the impossible and now I was being asked to rearrange one of the commitments that had persuaded the IRA. Eventually, when it was obvious that we were not going to budge, the meeting at Government Buildings between John, the Taoiseach and myself went ahead as had been agreed.

A small group of us, including Rita O'Hare, Sinn Féin's Director of Publicity, and Jim Gibney accompanied me. It was a "*lá stáiriuil, cruinniú stáiriuil*" – an historic day, an historic meeting. I wore a Bobby Sands T-shirt under my shirt and tie. The meeting itself was relaxed. Albert Reynolds was very down-to-earth. I liked him. There was tea and buns all round. John seemed a little under pressure. None of us mentioned the attempt to rearrange our get-together.

The main item for discussion at our meeting was the proposed Forum for Peace and Reconciliation, scheduled for late October. Afterwards the three of us spoke to the media and we were photographed shaking hands. The significance and symbolism of this was enormous. I was conscious about how unionists might perceive the public coming together of nationalist Ireland. Already one young Catholic man, John O'Hanlon, had been killed on the first day of the cessation by loyalists. I spoke of extending in generosity the hand of friendship to my Protestant brothers and sisters.

I also extended a word of thanks and appreciation to the government officals. While there were obvious differences of disagreement between Sinn Féin and Irish government officials, throughout this process the officials engaged with us and continue to engage with us, in a constructive and positive way. As the story developed, Seán Ó hUiginn and Martin Mansergh were joined by others, like Tim Dalton, Paddy Teahon, Tim O'Connor, Ray Basset and Dermot Gallagher. There were at least a dozen other very committed civil servants who were less senior but no less important.

There was an air of quiet celebration afterwards in the foyer of Government Buildings as we said our goodbyes. Away from the media, Cleaky was busy getting photographed with everyone, including the Taoiseach. I had arranged to see the Sagart and we picked him up en route through Dublin city centre. We chose a pub at random in Dorset Street to have a quiet yarn; it was Joxer Daly's. I had never been there before, but it is a fine pub with old-fashioned snugs. It was also fitted out with memorabilia of the 1916 Rising. Cleaky and our security team took this as a good omen as we crowded into a quiet corner surrounded by photographs of the leaders and the events of the insurrection.

I was moved to buy a drink. Some of our company thought that was just as much history as one day could contain. I didn't mind. The Sagart was a teetotaler. The rest of them were on duty. So it was soft drinks all around. Except for me. My work was done for the day, so mine was a pint.

Beneath the benign gaze of Pearse and Connolly and the other 1916 leaders, we raised our glasses to one another.

"*Sláinte!*"

It was a good day's work.

\* \* \* \* \*

In the meantime, local communities along the border began to take their own initiatives. The border separating the North from the South stretches for over 300 miles and cuts across several hundred major and unapproved roads, some of them little more than country lanes and cow tracks. Over the preceding years, the British army had used a variety of devices – large concrete blocks, miles of razor wire, the cratering of roads with explosives – to prevent traffic moving back and forth. The impact on local communities was enormous. Economically, towns were cut off from their natural hinterlands. Farmers sometimes had to make detours of scores of miles to get from one piece of their land to another. Families also found retaining social contact more difficult, often necessitating going through British army checkpoints where harassment and delays were frequent.

This caused a range of community and action groups to regularly play a cat-and-mouse game with the British forces. Suddenly, they would appear and fill in a crater or, using large trucks and lifting equipment, remove concrete bollards. Occasionally, they built a new road around a particularly well-constructed block. It would stay open for a while, and the Brits would move in, swamp the area and block the road again.

On Sunday, 4 September, in an impressive demonstration of people power, community associations in Derry, Donegal, Fermanagh, Cavan, Monaghan and Tyrone converged on closed cross-border roads and began reopening them. At the same time, Sinn Féin produced our first ever detailed breakdown of the extent of the British military garrison in the Six Counties. It was a colour map with an area-by-area itemisation of the British presence. Queen's University lecturer Mike Tomlinson estimated that 1994 troop levels were now such that there was one British army/RUC member for every 3.7 Catholic males between the ages of sixteen and forty-four. Estimating the full costs to the British government of its garrison in Ireland was a difficult task. However, it was conservatively estimated that over the previous twenty-five years the cost was probably somewhere around £20 billion. The RUC had 161 installations throughout the Six Counties. The British army had 135 fixed military installations and structures. Between them they had 32,000 people under arms. We were the most militarised area in western Europe.

Ten days after my meeting with Albert Reynolds and John Hume, British Prime Minister John Major announced the lifting of the broadcasting restrictions and the opening of ten of the 250 closed border roads. It was a small but welcome first indication by the British government that it might be prepared to move beyond prevarication. But, predictably, in dealing with the British government you always have to watch for the negative message. That came during a visit by Major to

South Africa on 22 September when he ruled out the release of political prisoners. He went further. He told his hosts, most of who were ex-political prisoners themselves, "In the UK people are not in jail as political prisoners." When South African President Nelson Mandela was a political prisoner, he was described by Major's predecessor Margaret Thatcher as a "terrorist". That was the reason she gave for not talking to him.

Major's officials in the British Embassy in Washington were lobbying the White House and State Department *not* to give me a visa for a return visit to the United States. When this failed and a visa waiver was issued, the British then briefed the media that they had achieved a "diplomatic breakthrough" by succeeding in preventing me from meeting President Clinton. I was surprised to hear this, as I'm sure the President was, as we had no arrangements to meet!

Richard McAuley and I left for Boston on Saturday, 24 September. By this point, Mairéad Keane was our representative in Washington. She was busy planning to open an office there, working out the details of this trip and discussing with Larry and Sean Downes, Ciaran Staunton, Fay Devlin, Shannon Eaton, Sean Mackin and many others, the establishment of a "Friends of Sinn Féin" group in the USA.

This first major trip was for three weeks – beginning in Boston, and then travelling throughout the USA and to Vancouver and Toronto in Canada. Each day was a blur of meetings, media, dinners and receptions. Our objectives were straightforward: to put the Irish republican position on the political agenda in the USA; to influence opinion makers in support of the peace process; to build relationships with political leaders and business leaders; to hold discussions with existing Irish American organisations and to clear the way for Americans to fundraise for Sinn Féin.

It was an exhilarating and exhausting three weeks. Everything was new and everyone wanted to help. Senator Kennedy was a gracious host in Boston, taking time out of his senatorial election battle to meet us at Logan Airport and later to host a public event. Congressman Richard Neal brought us to Springfield in Connecticut, where the first words spoken to me were by a Kerryman speaking in Irish. Here were the last people to leave the Blasket Islands off the coast of Kerry. Others were from West Mayo. In Philadelphia, the people were from Tyrone. In Cleveland, they were from Mayo. And on and on it went. I asked an old Clare man in Detroit how come people from the same area in Ireland settled in the same place in the USA.

"Did you ever see a flock of birds flying? One comes down, then another, then another till the whole flock lands."

We also met Italian Americans. In New York, Comptroller Alan Hevesi arranged a meeting with the Jewish business community. We met Native Americans and African Americans.

The visit to Cleveland was a personal highlight for me. There I had the honour and privilege to meet Mrs Rosa Parks, whose stand against racial prejudice and her refusal to sit at the back of the bus is credited by many as sparking the American Civil Rights Movement. We also held a large meeting with the local Irish American community, which was almost entirely judges and police officers. I joked to them that here in the United States I was enjoying a new, completely different relationship with judges and police from that which I had back home.

It had been eight months since my previous visit into New York. Again, the reception was overwhelming. Six of us travelled across the USA, and those travelling with me for the first time in the Big Apple were amazed by the number of New York cops who met us at the airport and took us in a convoy of lights and sirens into the city. I told the press conference that when we stopped Richard got out of the car with his hands up! The last time I had that sort of escort I was on my way to jail.

In New York we met the Connolly House group and discussed the help they had promised to provide. There were also public meetings with capacity crowds of cheering and jubilant Irish Americans, and our team did the rounds of the media stations and editorial boards. My friend, Big Brian, arranged for the Harbour cops to take us in one of their patrol boats to Ellis Island in offshore Manhattan and close to the Statue of Liberty. Ellis Island is the place that was used to process all of the emigrants to the USA. About one million Irish passed through there.

Amid the exhibits of clothes, photographs, family heirlooms from Italy and Germany and Poland and Latvia is a little delft plate of the four provinces of Ireland. In another section there is a shillelagh. One could imagine that anyone going away for good would take their most treasured possessions – a photograph of parents or family, a grandparent's walking stick, a favourite item of clothing, a little personal memento. It is little wonder that the first person processed through Ellis Island was an Irish woman, Annie Moore.

A few days later on 1 October in Philadelphia, I wrote to the White House requesting a meeting with government representatives. We had already been given to understand that a meeting would take place, but no arrangements had been finalised and US policy still banned meetings with Sinn Féin.

The week before I travelled to Washington, a unionist delegation had visited the White House where Vice President Al Gore had met them. Our efforts to secure equality of treatment by the Clinton administration were to be eventually played out in the unlikely setting of Hickory Hill.

Hickory Hill: the very name resonates with American history. The home of the late assassinated US Attorney General Robert Kennedy. The place where he and his older brother, US President John F. Kennedy, spent a lot of time during the harrowing days of the Cuban missile crisis. We had been invited to spend our first night in Washington in Hickory Hill by Robert Kennedy's daughter Courtney Kennedy when we arrived in Boston on 24 September and were formally welcomed by Senator Edward Kennedy and his wife, Vicky. I was told then that there would be no meeting at the White House, no meeting with the Vice President, and that we would have to make do with a meeting in the State Department.

To be denied by the White House the same access afforded to the unionists risked inflicting a serious blow on a fragile peace process. I made this clear to the National Security Advisor Tony Lake and Nancy Soderberg, Staff Director of the National Security Council, through Niall O'Dowd, who was the conduit for messages between us. I told them also that I was prepared to picket the White House when our group arrived in Washington.

It took most of our visit and a series of phone calls between myself, O'Dowd and Soderberg as we toured from city to city before we got an acceptable outcome on this issue. I put a compromise proposition to the White House from Philadelphia, that I should speak to the Vice President over the phone and that this would be publicly announced as the end of the ban on White House contact with Sinn Féin. It took time to get someone to close on this, and our telephone calls punctuated our journey towards Washington, from airport to airport, and eventually on the last leg of our journey, by car. At one point, we stopped in a lay-by on the side of the Potomac river – which some in our exhausted group kept referring to as the Pontiac – and continued to negotiate the following day's arrangements. As luck would have it, our mobile phones were as tired as we were: one after another the three we had with us died, their batteries drained. The White House thought we were hardballing. They were right, but the poor health of the mobiles added tension to the dialogue. Plus, Jack, our driver, couldn't find Hickory Hill. So it was much later when we finally arrived in the dark outside the white stone Georgian house that is Hickory Hill, home to Ethel Kennedy and her clan.

Courtney and her husband Paul Hill were there to greet us. Paul was one of the Guildford Four. He had served almost twenty years in jails in England on trumped-up charges. Using the house phone, we concluded an agreement that would result in a five-minute phone call with the Vice President the next morning and a White House announcement that the ban on contact between Sinn Féin and the US government was lifted.

I slept that night in Robert Kennedy's room and awoke early to discuss with our little group how we would approach the pending phone call with the Vice President.

At 8.35 a.m., Sunday, 3 October, the White House rang. Courtney wanted me to take the call in her father's study, so I was sitting at Robert Kennedy's desk when Al Gore came on the line. The significance of the call and of the location was not lost on any of us.

After the initial "How are you?" we discussed developments, and I explained to the Vice President the significance of the IRA cessation, Sinn Féin's objectives and our view of the administration's role in the peace process. At the end of our allotted time, as he thanked me for our efforts, I took the opportunity to invite him to Ireland.

A few minutes later, a fax letter came through from the White House, from Tony Lake, officially telling me that the ban on direct US-Sinn Féin contacts was lifted and inviting me to begin a process of engagement with the White House. This was to include Nancy Soderberg's participation in the State Department meeting that was to take place the next day.

A short time later, we drove into Washington. Courtney invited us to stop along the way and visit her father's grave and the grave of President John F. Kennedy. I thought of Milltown Cemetery in Belfast where so many of my own family, friends and comrades are buried. But Arlington was unlike any other cemetery. It stretched for miles and miles. Thousands of white crosses for the young Americans who lost their lives in Vietnam faded towards the horizon. Courtney knelt and prayed at her father's grave. She had brought flowers from the house and gave me some to lay at his memorial. We stood about her in silent reflection. Like so many families in Ireland, the Kennedys had been touched by violence and suffered much.

At the State Department it was a friendly, relaxed and businesslike meeting. We put to the US government directly our need for their support to build confidence in the peace process and to keep it moving. I pressed the need for inclusive negotiations. We also visited Capitol Hill where we met a range of Irish American Congressional members from the Ad Hoc Committee on Ireland and the Friends of Ireland. Republican Congressman Peter King and his staff had been enormously helpful. With no Sinn Féin office yet in Washington, he and his people worked long hours with Mairéad Keane to ensure a successful visit.

Before we left Washington, it was arranged that I would do an interview on *The Larry King Show* with Ken Maginnis of the Ulster Unionist Party. The British government had been loath to send a minister to visit the US at the same time as I was there, but they wanted a contrary voice and arranged for Michael Mates, a former Conservative party minister at the NIO, and Ken Maginnis to travel there. Both men, who would not speak to me back home, never mind go into television studios to debate the issues, crossed the Atlantic to do exactly that in America. I did an interview for a BBC programme out of New York with Mates and subsequently *The Larry King Show* in Washington with Maginnis. When I offered to shake hands with Maginnis, he refused. Many Americans later told me that for them that was the point Maginnis lost the debate.

What neither Ken nor Larry King nor the millions watching knew was that just prior to entering the studio the zip on my trousers had broken. It happened when I was clowning about in the reception room where our group was waiting for our segment of the programme to begin. I was trying to get focused and was looking for a quick brainstorm, but of course everyone ignored me, as was their wont. I jumped up on to the table, emulating Robin Williams in *Dead Poets Society*.

"Captain, my captain," I cried.

They continued to ignore me, as was also their wont.

I dropped my trousers. That got their attention. Unfortunately, when I pulled them up again, my zip busted. There was a frantic few minutes as we tried to repair the damage or find a pin – to no avail. Time ran out and I had to go into the studio. During the programme that wasn't too much of a problem as we were sitting at a desk. However, when the discussion ended, my plight was obvious. I stood exposed. I picked up a newspaper that Ken had brought with him, folded it and held it strategically before me. When Richard and I arrived downstairs in the huge CNN lobby, there were six or more television crews interviewing Ken about the programme. Keeping the newspaper carefully placed, I walked across this huge wide-open lobby, stepped up behind Ken, put my hand on his shoulder and asked him how he was doing. He rushed off as if stung by a bee. Richard, I and Ken's newspaper followed in his wake.

Then it was off to the West Coast. We were met coming off the plane by the usual contingent of police officers. There was a familiar face among all the uniforms: Jack Webb, a regular visitor to Belfast and a long-time activist for the Irish cause. He was a retired police officer. In fact, local rumour had it that the Clint Eastwood character "Dirty Harry" was based upon Jack's police exploits. He certainly looked the part and carried the firepower to prove it. I was delighted to see him, and as we walked towards the terminal he filled me in on the upcoming events. My attention was caught by a passing group of bigwigs.

"Who are they?" I asked Jack.

"Assholes!" he hissed in true Dirty Harry style.

And that's the way the rest of the visit went.

There is an active Irish republican activist community in San Francisco, and they pulled out all the stops. I spoke at Berkeley University in Oakland, where the packed audience had been primed by our hosts, including Angela Davis and Rene Castro, to sing "Happy Birthday" to me. It was 6 October. I was forty-six.

The next day, with California State Senator Tom Hayden, we travelled to Los Angeles. That evening Fionnuala Flanagan, the well-known Irish actress, and her husband Garrett O'Connor hosted a party at their home in Beverly Hills. Among those who attended were Gabriel Byrne, Sean Penn, Martin Sheen, Angelica Houston, Barbara Hershey, Colm Meaney and others. Midway through the proceedings, Fionnuala produced a birthday cake. I shared it with another of the guests, Pedro Meyer, whose birthday it was also. Pedro is a renowned photographer; his wife Trisha Ziff has had a long interest in Ireland. The evening ended with Irish, American, Mexican and Irish American voices raised in song and recitation. The *craic* was mighty.

Outside, a reporter for *The Sunday Times* was skulking around, trying to identify those attending the party. He needn't have bothered: they were all quite pleased to be there. So were we. Especially Aidan McAteer, friend of the stars.

And then for most of my colleagues, it was back home. Gerard McGuigan and I travelled on to Vancouver before Toronto. The Canadian events were as well attended, celebratory and enthusiastic as the American ones. In Vancouver, just in case we were homesick, a small crowd of unionist supporters barracked us on our arrival. More moving was the welcome by a group of native people who recognised us on the plane, and as we made the approach run into Vancouver airport, they sang a native

194

song of welcome. It wasn't only a fitting beginning to the Canadian events, it was also an evocative and poignant end to the US trip. I also had the bonus of reconnecting with my Aunt Rita and my cousins in Toronto. It was the first time that I got to meet with them on their home turf.

The day before I left Canada for Dublin, the various loyalist paramilitary organisations – united under the title of the Combined Loyalist Military Command – called its ceasefire. It was a direct result of the IRA's cessation, but it was a mighty step in any case, marking the possibility of new thinking within unionist paramilitarism. I welcomed it.

# Chapter Nineteen

# *Seizing the Moment*

John Major was under enormous pressure by those in Britain and Ireland and internationally who wanted progress. In the aftermath of my three-week trip to the USA and Canada, the order barring me from travelling to Britain looked more ludicrous than ever. It was 21 October before Major announced he was lifting the banning orders on Martin McGuinness and myself. In the face of a mounting campaign by local people along the border, he also announced the opening of all cross-border roads.

Exactly one week later, the political representatives of 82 per cent of the Irish people – that is, everyone except the unionists – came together at Dublin Castle for the inaugural meeting of the Forum for Peace and Reconciliation. It was chaired by Catherine McGuinness, a wonderful and exemplary Irish woman. Dublin Castle had been the administrative centre of British rule in Ireland for centuries. It had witnessed many dark deeds. Now, from within its opulent splendour, we were building a process which I believed would lead eventually to the end of British rule in Ireland. One of my memories of this time was when one of the attendants ushered me into a side room to use the toilet. To my surprise, a wall plaque proclaimed that this was the room in which the badly wounded 1916 leader James Connolly was held before his execution.

Two days later, nationalist children on the lower Ormeau Road were batoned by the RUC as they protested against a planned Orange march through this nationalist area. The RUC's political bosses raced to defend this action. Patrick Mayhew assured unionists that he had no plans to change either the name or the structure of the Royal Ulster Constabulary. Instead, Mayhew chose to press the issue of IRA weapons and to erect it as an obstacle to substantive negotiations.

The peace process suffered its first serious blow with the unexpected resignation on 17 November of Albert Reynolds. The collapse of his

Coalition government centred around a controversy involving a Catholic priest, Fr Brendan Smyth, who subsequently served a prison sentence for sexually abusing children. There were allegations that someone in Dublin had tried to prevent Smyth's extradition to face these charges in the North. Reynolds's Fianna Fáil party and Dick Spring's Labour Party came to loggerheads on the issue, and the Labour ministers in the government resigned. Reynolds resigned as leader of Fianna Fáil and was replaced by Bertie Ahern. In the weeks that followed, intense negotiations took place between the major parties in the Irish parliament. I was concerned that the loss of Reynolds at a time when John Major was still not engaged in the process could seriously, or even fatally damage what had been put together. Our assessment and calculation prior to the cessation had been that the Reynolds government was the strongest government in more than twenty-five years. That stability and leadership had been crucial to persuading the IRA that the peace process, and the nationalist consensus that had created it, was a viable alternative to the armed struggle. Now this important element in our strategy was gone.

In my dealings with Albert Reynolds, I found him practical and straightforward. He had a positive attitude to life and, at times, a happy-go-lucky approach. We got on well. He and Martin McGuinness in particular struck up a good rapport. It was to Albert's credit that he instructed his own system to engage with us, that he took risks that his predecessors had shied away from. He deserves great credit for this. I am more critical of his handling of the Hume/Adams propositions and how the British were able to collapse this down to the Downing Street Declaration. He defended this to us on the grounds that he was dealing with the practical politics of the time. He has a point, of course, and everything is relative. For many in the Irish establishment, the Downing Street Declaration was an advanced document. To republicans, it was a stopgap of sorts, an advance perhaps, but significantly short of what was required. Still, there is no doubt that Albert did his best, which was significantly more than any other Taoiseach before. I got to know his wife Kathleen and his family. They were good *craic*, without any pretensions, a warm and friendly family who made me feel at home. They were deeply upset by Albert's fall from power. One of his daughters was especially outraged by what she saw as Dick Spring's role in this. Albert was more philosophical, on the surface at least.

Negotiations to form a new government took almost four weeks. There was also a coalition, but this time it was led by John Bruton, the leader of

Fine Gael. Bruton was seen by many republicans and most nationalists living in the North as pro-unionist. It was unlikely that he would see himself as the leader of Irish nationalism in negotiations with the British government. Faced by a British government and unionist parties seeking to either reduce the potential of the process or collapse it entirely, Bruton's attitude was likely to prove disastrous.

Even as this crisis was playing itself out, we were trying to maintain pressure on the British government. The day Albert resigned, I was in London for my first visit there since the exclusion orders were first imposed in 1993. I had a series of meetings with British MPs from the three main parties – the Conservatives, Labour and the Liberal Democrats – and the inevitable media interviews. I also did my first ever book reading to a packed room at Waterstones Bookshop in Charing Cross Road in central London. The crowd outside was so large that we needed the help of some pleasant London "Bobbies" to make it back to our car.

There was still no sign of Major's government setting a date for the promised talks with Sinn Féin. Indeed, we were informed that we would not be invited to an economic conference in Belfast on 13 December at which John Major would be speaking. In interviews and articles, I made it clear that we would not accept any pre-conditions being placed upon our electorate or upon us.

John Hume and I added our joint voices to a call for the British government to move more speedily. On 30 November we warned against stalling. The British by this stage were suggesting 15 December as the date for a meeting between us, but the row over our exclusion from the economic conference and the public and private uproar and criticism from nationalist Ireland and Irish America forced them into a rethink. Roderic Lyne, Major's Private Secretary, replied on 1 December to my letter to Major informing us that Quentin Thomas, Deputy Secretary at the NIO – one of the senior people involved in the messing around of the secret talks between us – would lead their delegation. They suggested 7 December as a date for our first meeting. Although I would not be participating in these talks myself, it was felt that we should seek a two-day postponement to allow me to return from the USA where I was scheduled to meet President Clinton's National Security Advisor Tony Lake at the White House.

The British moved to resolve the row over the economic conference in a typically offensive fashion. They said that six Sinn Féin councillors on six local council economic committees could attend for two and a half hours. We rejected this. Several hundred people subsequently picketed the conference.

I arrived in Washington on Monday, 8 December, and held a series of meetings with senior political figures, including Senators Ted Kennedy and Chris Dodd and Congress members Peter King and Ben Gilman. I asked for a meeting with the State Department and spoke also to Martha Pope, Secretary of the US Senate. In January, she would be taking up her new post working closely with Senator George Mitchell – who had been appointed President Clinton's Secretary of State on Economic Initiatives in Ireland. During my meeting with Martha, Senator Mitchell – in Maine getting married – rang and we spoke for a few minutes.

The next day Mairéad Keane, Richard McAuley, Ciaran Staunton and I went to the White House. It was another first in a year bursting with these. I gave Tony Lake and Nancy Soderberg our assessment of the peace process and expressed our concern at the British government's reluctance to take up the challenge and engage meaningfully. I stressed the importance of the role of the US in helping to resolve differences that might emerge. We needed someone outside the frame, friendly with all sides, and with the ability to exercise influence and persuasion.

As evidence of the administration's increasing interest in the process, the Commerce Secretary Ron Brown dropped by to discuss the investment conference in Belfast. Ron was an African American who entered politics through the Civil Rights Movement. In the time ahead, he was to play an important supportive role in seeking to improve US economic ties with the North and the border counties. As our meeting concluded, he asked me what the US government could do to help, and in an obvious reference to Mrs Rosa Parks, I told him not to ask me or Irish republicans to sit at the back of the bus. He laughed and from that moment we had an important ally in the US government.

Ron Brown was to visit Ireland many times. It was clear both from the speeches he made and from initiatives of which he was part that he identified with the battle against discrimination. Working closely with him were Virginia Manuel and Chuck Meissner. Both spent a lot of time in Ireland on economic initiatives and ensuring that trade missions from the US visited economically deprived areas in Belfast and along both sides of the border. Tragically, Ron Brown and Chuck Meissner were later killed in an aeroplane crash in the Balkans.

Before we left the US, I held a meeting with colleagues who had formally incorporated "Friends of Sinn Féin Inc." as a not-for-profit corporation in the state of New York. Our goal was to raise funds, which would help us run an office in Washington, organise public tours of the US for Sinn Féin spokespersons, and provide the financial back-up necessary for Sinn Féin in Ireland to build our party. We had already complied with US Department of Justice requirements for registration under the Foreign Agents Act. The right to fundraise was going to be another battle. Already the British Embassy was lobbying hard against the administration giving its approval, even though Sinn Féin could fundraise in Britain.

I returned to Belfast in time for our first publicised meeting with the British government. It took place at Parliament Buildings, Stormont. Our delegation was led by Martin McGuinness and included Sean McManus from Sligo, Lucilita Bhreatnach, Siobhán O'Hanlon and Gerry Kelly, who was secretary to our delegation. Quentin Thomas led the British delegation.

Martin began by remarking on the absence of women within the six-man British delegation and then asked after "Fred" – Colin Ferguson – the British representative in the secret talks. He read prepared opening remarks and handed over a submission by us which set out, from our perspective, the causes of conflict: Britain's claim to sovereignty over a part of Ireland. Martin welcomed the resumption of discussions between us, but criticised the British government's continued failure to properly recognise our democratic credentials.

As far as we were concerned, these were merely preliminary discussions – exploratory talks – which should conclude quickly in order that we could move on to inclusive peace talks led by the two governments and addressing the three broad areas of political and constitutional change, democratic rights and demilitarisation and associated issues. But it was quickly clear to Martin and the others that the British government was not prepared to move to substantive negotiations. Instead they were making the surrender of IRA arms a prerequisite for that.

The Sinn Féin delegation raised the related issues of prisoners, Irish language rights, harassment, border roads and more. A few days later, on 15 December, John Bruton was elected as the new Irish Taoiseach. The next day he and I met at a session of the Forum for Peace and Reconciliation in Dublin. There was real concern within wider nationalist opinion about Bruton's approach to the peace process, to the British government and the unionists, but it was a situation we simply had to cope with as best we could. He was obviously aware of his reputation. Both of us went out of our way to have a good meeting. No matter about our differences, I always found Mr Bruton to be courteous.

The British had provided two written submissions to our team. The first outlined its basis for entry into dialogue. The second was a broad, non-definitive response to a number of questions we had put in our submissions. The British delegation had been quite frank in putting the position that Sinn Féin was not to be accorded equal treatment, despite the acceptance of their delegation leader, Quentin Thomas, that our party threatened no one and that Sinn Féin was a main political party with an electoral mandate. London had responded to our verbal submissions on such matters as equality, prisoners and cultural discrimination. But the overwhelming focus of the British delegation was on IRA weapons.

As 1995 began, it was obvious that the British government was engaged in a strategy that involved – at best – stalling the process through the deliberate erection of barriers and – at worst – attempting to create and sustain a crisis around the issue of IRA arms. They did this in a way which would portray Sinn Féin as being the unreasonable and inflexible party. For me the logic of a peace process was that – through talks – we would arrive at a settlement which removed the causes of conflict and for ever took the guns from the political equation in Ireland. In our submissions to the British government, we made this clear.

Not good enough, or so the Brits said. At the 16 January meeting, the British government paper stated that "As a matter of principle and of political reality substantial progress on the issue of decommissioning would be necessary before Sinn Féin could and would be included in such a dialogue."

To add insult to injury, as the sixth meeting between the delegations was to begin on Thursday, 9 February, Cleaky's security personnel, who travelled to and from Stormont meetings with our delegation, found an electronic listening device in offices allocated to us in Parliament Buildings. It was mutually agreed with the head of the British delegation to postpone the meeting. Clearly, this was a serious breach of trust. But more importantly, we were still being treated differently from the other parties, our electoral and democratic mandate was not being respected, and no British political representatives had been introduced into the discussions. We spent the next two months trying to reverse that situation. I wrote to John Major and Patrick Mayhew, and Martin wrote to and met British officials privately, along with Siobhán O'Hanlon, to try to break the deadlock.

At the end of February, the British and Irish governments produced a discussion paper titled the "Framework Document". This had been under discussion for over two years, and it was supposed to set out their joint view of future developments. In their words, it outlined "a shared understanding between them on the parameters of a possible outcome to the talks process".

We saw it as an opportunity for the British to move into a proper engagement with Sinn Féin. However, it immediately ran into a storm of controversy and protest because it envisaged new political structures in an all-Ireland context. This was too much for the unionists, who rejected it outright. The UUP threatened to pull down the Major government. Major moved quickly. He tried to reassure them: "Northern Ireland is a central part of the United Kingdom . . . for my part, I cherish the United Kingdom and Northern Ireland's part in it."

# Chapter Twenty

# *Major Mistakes*

Having pulled back from the Framework Document, John Major's tactical and negative approach to the process became ever more apparent in his government's public efforts to blame republicans for the difficulties.

British briefings to the media claimed that we were refusing to discuss decommissioning. Martin McGuinness publicly and privately told the British that we wished to engage in serious, substantive and constructive discussions with British ministers on all relevant issues – including the decommissioning of weapons.

Speaking on a visit to Washington for the St Patrick's Day celebrations, I expressed our willingness to discuss every issue, including decommissioning. But the British government was going out of its way to make things difficult. The British Embassy in Washington lobbied to prevent me getting a visa – no surprise there. They lobbied to prevent me getting an invitation to the Speaker's Lunch – to which the Taoiseach and other Irish political leaders are traditionally welcomed. They lobbied to prevent the White House inviting me to the President's St Patrick's Day event. They lobbied against Sinn Féin getting the right to fundraise. They lobbied Congressional and Senate members not to meet me. Patrick Mayhew travelled to Washington in early March for meetings with Vice President Al Gore and Secretary of State Warren Christopher. He told them that there would have to be decommissioning of weapons by the IRA before Sinn Féin would be allowed into substantial talks.

At a breakfast meeting with journalists on 7 March, Mayhew spelt out three pre-conditions which Sinn Féin would have to satisfy before we could enter into all-party talks. With impeccable audacity, these pre-conditions were presented as the Washington "principles". These demanded that the IRA disarm progressively; that it spell out what this would entail; and that it actually decommission some arms to start the process. Mayhew told the journalists that only by agreeing to these could republicans remove what he described as "their self-imposed disqualification".

The British Secretary of State left Washington apparently satisfied that he had achieved his goals. But he had failed to take proper account of the many political and business leaders now solidly behind the peace process, who believed that the British approach was wrong and who wanted their government to take a different tack. Congressman Ben Gilman and three other co-chairs of the Ad Hoc Committee on Irish Affairs, Peter King, Tom Manton and Richard Neal – Republicans and Democrats – sent a letter to President Clinton supporting my visa. Senator Chris Dodd spoke to the President during a round of golf on the same day Mayhew was talking to the journalists and came away convinced the President was open on the issue of fundraising. Ted Kennedy phoned President Clinton and other Irish Americans rowed in behind. Sinn Féin's commitment to seriously discuss every issue was good enough for the White House. The President agreed to Americans having the right to fundraise for Sinn Féin, and I was invited to the White House St Patrick's Day event. The British were furious. Clinton sent a letter to John Major explaining why he had done what he had. But for five days the British Prime Minister refused to take a telephone call from the President of the United States.

When I arrived in Washington on 14 March my first job was to open a Friends of Sinn Féin office. The battle line was drawn: one Mayo woman versus hundreds of British diplomats. The Brits were in trouble. Then it was off to the Speaker's St Patrick's Day lunch, to which I was accompanied by Congressman Peter King.

As well as Peter, Republican Congressman Thomas DeLay of Texas and Susan Brophy, Deputy Assistant to President Clinton on legislative affairs, were at our table. I had expected to meet the President once the media were ushered out. But there appeared to be some problems. Someone said that the Irish Embassy and the Irish Department of Foreign Affairs had vetoed a meeting. Then we were told that the veto had come from one of Newt Gingrich's staff. This was getting to be a surreal situation. The harpist in the corner, strumming away, guests eating their corned beef and cabbage and President Clinton and me sitting a few yards apart without a word passing between us. So I asked Peter King to tell someone in authority that I was going home.

Peter and Susan and the US Ambassador to Ireland, Jean Kennedy Smith, went off and cornered Gingrich's aide. They then came and told me that John Hume would be introducing me to the President. Whether there was any real problem or not, I don't know. A few minutes later Peter told me that they wanted me to meet the President now.

I couldn't resist staying put.

"They want you now," Peter repeated anxiously.

I looked him straight in the eye. "He'll have to hold on," I said jokingly, "till I finish my dinner."

John did the introductions. Many of the seventy-six assembled guests started to applaud when they saw what was happening. Clinton told me the British government was beating up on him, and I remarked, "Now you know, Mr President, what we have to put up with!"

Bill Clinton was enthusiastic about the peace process. I was impressed by his commitment. In time, as I got to know him, I was impressed also by his grasp of the detail, the personalities, the politics and the strategies involved. In subsequent meetings, it was clear that he understood and had a real insight into the scheming and game playing. I became convinced that his engagement was genuine and committed.

That evening Mairéad, Richard and I attended the annual American Ireland Funds dinner in Washington, and Taoiseach John Bruton was guest speaker. We were amazed, and Irish Americans around us were outraged, when Bruton made remarks that put him firmly on the British side in the arms debate. He called for the IRA to move on weapons and, in interviews with the media in the coming days, suggested that the White House was putting us under pressure to secure movement by the IRA on this issue – which wasn't true.

The next evening I visited the White House, accompanied by Mairéad Keane. We were standing in line, along with Richard who had come over to drop us off and make arrangements to pick us up again. We were spotted by a very pleasant sergeant in the Secret Service who came over, introduced himself and took us out of the line to get us into the White House more quickly! Richard was delighted when the sergeant handed him a business card with his number and told him to ring if he needed to contact me. The incongruity of it – a Secret Service agent who gives out a business card! And to Richard McAuley, the most subversive public relations person in town. Some secret!

Before formalities commenced, I had a chance to speak to both the President and First Lady Hillary Clinton. The "Celebration of Ireland" was a fine St Patrick's Day affair. An entire floor of the White House had been opened up for the event. A senior official told me that such affairs were normally restricted to about a hundred guests, but with the Irish that wouldn't work: it took about three hundred invitations to get proper representation.

The White House was designed by Irish-born architect James Hoban, who won a gold medal for his effort. And the first President to live in it was an Adams! – President John Adams. In the library, we saw an old weapon which had been found hidden in the chimney – undecommissioned. We were also told of how the British burned the building in 1812 and how some fine paintings were saved from the blaze.

The schedule, as was the norm at any Clinton event, ran overtime. At 10 p.m. when we were supposed to be finishing, the President was just beginning to speak. Back at our hotel Richard, Ciaran Staunton, Shannon Eaton and Kieran Clifford, a young Irish American woman who helped run our Washington office, were watching *The Quiet Man* on television – it was St Patrick's Day after all. Ciaran, a Mayo man, was getting quite sentimental. Especially over the sheep.

Richard was worried that we were standing outside the White House waiting for our lift, so he decided to ring Mairéad's mobile. She had forgotten to switch it off, and as President Clinton spoke it started to ring. Everyone shifted uneasily. We knew instinctively it was Richard. He is famous in our circles for his attachment to telephones. The phone kept ringing. The audience was visibly discommoded. Richard was being persistent. The phone stopped briefly. The President kept talking. The phone started again. The President concluded his remarks. The phone continued. Eventually it too gave up. Some time later when she hoped no one was looking, Mairéad slipped her hand into her bag and turned the phone off.

After the speeches and entertainment, Eileen Ivers and Joe Derrane led other musicians into a *seisiún*. It was a lively evening. And, as with so many Irish events, it ended with singers from the floor giving their rendition of a favourite song. John Hume, who has a good voice, began to sing "The Town I Love So Well" about his native city of Derry. I joined him, and together we cleared the building.

During my time in the States, I remained in regular contact with Siobhán and Martin. Apart from lobbying against us in the USA and their refusal to introduce a minister into the talks, the British were objecting to us raising the issue of demilitarisation in the discussions. They resented us equating British violence and British weapons and British armed organisations with all of the other armed groups in the conflict. Then, when it appeared that we might have agreement on an agenda for a meeting involving Michael Ancram, a British minister at the NIO, this collapsed. Patrick Mayhew rejected my commitment to seriously discussing all issues on the basis that this did not provide the clear and reliable assurance which the British government needed.

Meantime, Ancram had no difficulty meeting with loyalist representatives – none of whom had any electoral mandate and all of whom had said that no weapons would be handed up until a political settlement was reached.

Martin and Siobhán continued to battle away in letters and in smaller private meetings with Quentin Thomas and Jonathan Stevens. In an effort to clear a way through this impasse, Martin suggested that there should be no formal agenda but that the meeting would be preceded by an exchange of letters. Both sides would set out their own view and address each other's concerns. On 12 April, Patrick Mayhew announced that the British government would soon be holding bilateral meetings with all parties – except Sinn Féin. Martin wrote to Quentin Thomas accusing the British of establishing a two-track approach to talks, with Sinn Féin in a second track, at a different level and pace from the other parties. A week later he wrote again, pointing out our concern at the continuing discrimination against our party and electorate.

Then on 24 April 1995, almost eight months after the IRA's cessation began, the British announced that following intensive exchanges with Sinn Féin, the government believed a sufficient basis now existed for the entry of ministers into the exploratory dialogue with us. I welcomed this move, although it was obvious that the British government was still treating our party differently. This was reinforced two days later when Mayhew sent out invitations to all the other parties, except Sinn Féin, for bilateral meetings. We were still being kept within a process of "decontamination". The Irish government moved to blunt the British approach by also issuing invites to all the parties for bilaterals – including us.

Most people knew the process was in trouble. Former Taoiseach Albert Reynolds summed it up when in an interview with the London *Observer* on 23 April he remarked: "There was supposed to be a generosity from both governments. The Irish government has shown it, but the British have not. The British may have miscalculated that they can sit back and do nothing. But if they [the IRA] went back to the armed conflict people won't blame them because they have shown good faith."

A meeting with Michael Ancram was unlikely to speed up the process.

We had to keep pressure on the British government. All of our experience to date was that they still had no real political commitment to the peace process. British strategy was still focused on defeating republicans. The stalling and prevarication were about reducing expectations, diminishing hope and encouraging schisms among our ranks.

That was always a danger. There was quite a lot of justifiable grumbling within the wider republican community. Certainly, the behaviour of the RUC and British army did not give cause for hope. The raiding of homes was still commonplace. A remilitarisation programme – especially in the South Armagh area and in Fermanagh and Tyrone and in Belfast – was taking place. Worse, many nationalist and republicans were now having more unwanted attention from and unwelcome contact with the British army and RUC than they had had before. These forces were taking advantage of the IRA cessation to travel in and patrol and harass residents in areas where until now they would rarely have stayed for long because of the fear of attack by the IRA.

We needed to regain momentum. We also needed to get through to the British political leadership that their approach was wrong and, if it was based on a genuine fear or a concern about republican intentions, to try and tackle that through direct dialogue with them. Talking to Michael Ancram wasn't going to achieve that. I therefore wrote to Major in early May asking him to clear a meeting with Mayhew.

We were all conscious that President Clinton's economic conference in Washington was now looming. Unlike the British one in Belfast, this conference was all-inclusive. How could Mayhew and I be in Washington, in the same hotel at the same conference and not meet – even accidentally in the corridor? Was he going to hide behind the potted palm trees? Were British minders going to be clearing hotel corridors and lifts to try and prevent us bumping into one another? What message would it send to people about the peace process if we were sitting in the same conference hall and Mayhew was surrounded by handlers trying to stop me walking over to shake hands? So, I put it to Major, as Martin McGuinness had in February, that there should be a formal meeting between Mayhew and myself.

On 8 May, I was off to the United States for a three-week speaking tour that would conclude at the economic conference. Twelve cities – no breaks – from the East Coast to the West. This was a US traumatised by the Oklahoma bombing of a federal building the month before. The British government and sections of its media sought to exploit this tragic event to attack republicans and embarrass me. I had already written to President Clinton extending my sympathies and condolences to the families of the dead and injured.

Richard and I landed in Boston. We did an event there and then flew up to Portland, Maine, in a small two-engined plane. We hit a lot of turbulence and for some time it was a white-knuckle ride. Shannon Eaton, one of our key workers in that region, had organised a number of really good events. Our guests included the legendary Irish musician, Tommy Makem.

And then it was down to New York on 10 May where we held our first annual Friends of Sinn Féin dinner at the Essex House Hotel, with Fionnuala Flanagan. It was $1000 a plate and 400 people packed into the event.

"Far from it we were reared," I told our guests.

The same day in Belfast, Martin McGuinness, Siobhán O'Hanlon, Lucilita Bhreatnach, Sean McManus and Gerry Kelly met a British government delegation led by Michael Ancram. Our submission and message to Ancram stressed the importance of equality for our party and electorate and the urgent need to work out the logistics for all-party talks. Ancram, however, was still locked into Mayhew's Washington pre-conditions.

By now the British knew that there was no way of Mayhew avoiding me in the Sheraton Hotel, the location of the economic conference. This was confirmed when Ancram started to talk about the possibility of a meeting between Mayhew and myself in Washington, but only in the context of exploratory talks – not as part of his bilaterals with the other parties. Ancram refused to be definitive, but it appeared to us that the pressure on the British had to be considerable.

By the time I had travelled back and forwards across the USA and reached Washington, Mayhew had asked for a meeting. Speaking at the Washington Press Club on 23 May, I welcomed this, pointing to the fact that for the first time ever all the main players, the Dublin and London governments, the unionists, the smaller loyalist parties and nationalists and republicans were all under the one roof.

The conference billed as the "White House Conference on Trade and Investment in Ireland" was hosted by President Bill Clinton and organised by Senator George Mitchell, along with Commerce Secretary Ron Brown and his colleague Chuck Meissner. Vice President Al Gore and a range of US political leaders and business people attended. It was scheduled to take place over three days, during which time participants would explore business possibilities in the North's Six Counties and the six border counties in the South of Ireland.

My meeting with Patrick Mayhew was scheduled for Wednesday evening, 24 May. Richard handled the arrangements. This wasn't easy, as he was now being followed around the hotel by a media team who assumed that where Richard was, I would eventually be – and so would the meeting. Richard had several discussions with some of Mayhew's PR people about the venue and press access. At one point, the British wanted to move the meeting out of the hotel entirely. Richard refused.

At around 7 o'clock in the evening Richard and Mick Conlon – another of our group – went to Suite 6006, followed by the media. The lobby and corridor outside the room where the meeting was to occur were packed by journalists, camera crews and photojournalists.

Richard and Mick were met in an outer room by British Ambassador Sir Robin Renwick and his embassy colleague, Peter Westmacott. They discussed the arrangements for the meeting, which was to include myself, Richard and Mairéad Keane, and which would take place in an inner room. There was to be no coffee, tea or anything stronger. Just a quick handshake – in private, no cameras – and a fifteen-minute meeting.

Richard left to report back to me, and Mick remained, using the time to discuss with the British Ambassador the merits of fly-fishing and whether the best location for this was the West of Ireland or Alaska. Renwick preferred Alaska, and Mick remarked, "Maybe sometime we could share a fly there." Mick also told the assembled British officials after Richard left that he felt like a hostage being left behind as evidence of good faith.

Mairéad, Richard and I left our room and, followed by journalists, camera lights bright in our faces, we fought our way through the media throng into Suite 6006. Here we were shown into the backroom, where Patrick Mayhew and James Cran waited to greet us.

The handshakes were brief but cordial. Mayhew, using a written speaking note, told us why the British government would not allow Sinn Féin into all-party negotiations. He was visibly shaking and nervous as he spoke and he stuck rigidly to the text of his note, which the British issued afterwards, almost word for word, as a public statement.

I leaned forward, almost touching Mayhew, telling him that it was very important that he understood that we were serious about making the peace process work. We accepted that there were differences in our positions, but

210

we had to see beyond these. The peace process, I told him, was a personal priority for me and *the* political priority for Sinn Féin. The great achievement had been the silencing of the guns, and we needed to build on that. There couldn't be a two-speed process, inequality was wrong, the open-door policy of President Clinton and the Irish government were the way to move forward. We needed to secure an agreement. That meant taking risks. We were taking risks with our lives. The British government needed to seize the moment.

Mayhew insisted we couldn't move into substantive talks unless there was movement on decommissioning. I remember wondering how could I break through this British mantra. I had to try and ensure that after our meeting Mayhew was left with some food for thought. I said, "We're both political creatures and there is a temptation to lock horns. We have to avoid this. You did the right thing by agreeing to do this meeting. Let's keep doing the right thing."

The meeting was longer than the allotted fifteen minutes. It lasted about thirty-five minutes, and at the end of it we met the media separately. Almost a hundred journalists trapped in the hotel corridor desperately tried to make sure they heard every word or captured every move on their cameras.

Richard was left to brief the media. The rest of us went off to network with business people, US, Irish and British politicians, and others at the conference. We also had our first face-to-face meeting with loyalist political representatives, including David Ervine and Billy Hutchinson of the Progressive Unionist Party, which represents the UVF, and Gary McMichael and Davy Adams from the Ulster Democratic Party, which represented the UDA. The three Dunfey brothers from Boston – Bob, Jerry and Jack – facilitated the meeting. Mitchel McLaughlin, Caoimhghín Ó Caoláin and Shannon Eaton represented us. The Dunfey family, originally from County Kerry, are well known through the Boston-based Global Citizens Circle for their support and work for democracy and human rights in South Africa. Over the years, they have also been supportive of the Irish peace process.

There was a lesson in the Washington experience, especially for the British government. The US had arranged this event, had pushed and sold it to the parties and to public opinion. The result was, no one could resist attending. Could the same be true of inclusive talks? But London wasn't interested. The dynamic in the process was coming from the Clinton administration when it should have come from Downing Street.

The meeting with Mayhew and the networking on the margins of the economic conference, including the meeting with the loyalists, all pointed to the importance of the US involvement. The British government's decontamination period was not only highly insulting; it also caused real resentment among republicans. So whatever the substance of the meeting with Patrick Mayhew, the fact that it took place was important in getting the British government to face up to the unworthiness of their position. More importantly it also soothed some, though not all, republican sensitivities.

# Chapter Twenty-One

# *My Hero, Nelson Mandela*

Nine months had passed since the IRA cessation. I returned from the USA encouraged but apprehensive. Our core group decided to strike while the iron was hot and see if my meeting with Patrick Mayhew had had any effect other than giving the media a front-page story. I wrote to him on 2 June, asking for a further meeting. Days later, a letter from Mayhew's private secretary informed me that there would be no substantive political talks for Sinn Féin without progress on the issue of decommissioning.

Martin and I then did a run of meetings with the Irish government and other political parties in the South. Bruton's Washington speech was evidence that he was shaky on the process. We made it clear to him that we could not deliver the British government's demands on weapons.

The reality was that the demand for a surrender of IRA weapons was never mentioned by the British government before 31 August 1994. In fact, the British had been engaged in secret intensive contact and dialogue with us from 1990 until November the previous year, never at any time raising the issue of decommissioning. Had a surrender of IRA weapons been imposed as a pre-condition to peace negotiations prior to the cessation, there would have been no IRA cessation announced at all.

We were totally committed to the permanent and effective removal of all guns from Irish politics. The British government had said that the holding of illegal arms and the use of violence and threats had no place in a peaceful, democratic society. We agreed, but the North was not yet a peaceful and democratic society. It was born out of violence and sustained by violence, mostly directed against the nationalist people. Against this backdrop of conflict, which had frequently seen loyalist pogroms against Catholics in the past, supported by state forces, the pre-condition of surrender of the IRA was unrealistic.

The fact was, there were many armed groups – British, unionist, as well as republican. There were 19,000 members of the British army; 13,000 members of the RUC; approximately 140,000 legally held weapons – the vast majority in the hands of unionists. There were large stockpiles of sophisticated weapons in the possession of loyalists, much of which had been brought into the North with the collusion of British intelligence; and then there were weapons held by the various republican organisations – the IRA being the largest – and a number of smaller organisations. The depth of insecurity for nationalists living in the North could not be underestimated. Removing weapons from Irish politics had to be a goal of the process, not a pre-condition.

This realpolitik had to be understood and accepted if we were to make progress. The important thing was to build on the potential and advance to where all guns were not only silent but obsolete. The British were treating the arms issue as a one-item agenda in their discussions with Sinn Féin. Irish Foreign Minister Dick Spring, speaking in Washington earlier in March, warned that, "If we take the attitude that nothing will happen unless there is a surrender or decommissioning of arms then I think that is a formula for disaster."

The practical aspects of decommissioning were, of course, an entirely separate matter. The modalities of decommissioning were practical matters which could be resolved quickly in my view in the right conditions. The most important thing was to create those conditions. The problem was that John Major still had a war mentality when what was required was a peace mentality.

Dick Spring had come to exercise a steadying influence on John Bruton. He suggested that one way out of the impasse over weapons might be for the two governments to establish an international commission for peace and disarmament in Ireland. He also expressed concern that this would only get over the weapons issue if the British really wanted to.

As this was going on Rita O'Hare, Chrissie McAuley, then our national director of education, Richard, our Gearóid and I were 4000 miles away in South Africa. We were invited by the ANC – with whom Irish republicans have long enjoyed fraternal relations – to visit their country. We arrived on 14 June 1995 and stayed for a packed week of meetings and travel across a beautiful country still trying to come to terms with the enormous changes of the past year. In truth, we saw less of the country than I would have liked – Capetown by moonlight; Pretoria, a pretty tree-lined city; Durban Beach on a stormy, late-night, two-minute stop. Johannesburg was the only place where the sun shone. It was winter in South Africa – weather-wise, that is. Every other way, it was spring. There was a sense of a new beginning, of a new South Africa.

On our first day, we were met at the airport by ANC Deputy Secretary General Cheryl Carolus, ANC Secretary for International Affairs Yusof Saloojee and Robert McBride, a former ANC prisoner who had been condemned to death by the apartheid regime. We were taken to have lunch with the ANC's National Executive at their party headquarters in Jo'burg. To our great surprise and honour Walter Sisulu, the grand old man of African resistance, made a special point of coming to the lunch. Afterwards I presented him with a wooden Celtic cross carved by the republican prisoners in Long Kesh. It was one of several gifts made by the prisoners that we had brought with us – some of which were damaged when the British opened our baggage in Heathrow airport. An ANC former prisoner helped repair them.

Walter Sisulu spoke of his own time in prison and of his memories of the hunger strike in Ireland in 1981. He was in prison then and told us of the great solidarity that existed between ANC prisoners and the republican prisoners. ANC members had watched events unfold in our prison struggle. It was a moving, emotional speech in which he recalled hearing of the death of Bobby Sands and of the silent tribute ANC prisoners across South Africa paid a fellow freedom fighter. Most of our delegation was in tears by the time he finished. Later, another ANC activist, who had spent fifteen years on Robben Island, was to tell us that from that point on ANC prisoners never spoke of "a hunger strike"; they always referred to "a Bobby Sands".

I was impressed by the ANC leadership. In many ways, President Mandela was a first among equals. We met Cyril Ramaphosa, Secretary General of the ANC and the party's main negotiator with the apartheid regime. We also met Thabo Mbeki, Deputy President, and Jacob Zuma, National Party Chairperson. Women were represented in every delegation: at national, regional and local level. In other meetings we learned of how the ANC were planning the course from conflict to democracy.

Of all of the political leaderships I had met up to then and since, never have I met a group as cohesive, articulate and far-seeing as those in the ANC leadership.

We also encountered a range of political opinion. In a strange way, the engagement with the Afrikaner representatives was a revelation to us. We first met with General Constand Viljoen, a retired chief of the South

215

African defence forces and leader of the Freedom Front Party. The general had come into party politics on the eve of South Africa's historic election of Nelson Mandela.

A small man, white-haired and about sixty, he had told the white right wing that he believed the ANC was still an organisation pursuing a revolutionary strategy. His followers, mainly white farmers, had wanted him to lead them into a "third Boer war" to defend and save the Afrikaner *volk* from being sold out by the traitors in the National Party led by de Klerk. Then – four days before the election, following twenty meetings with the ANC – he opted for a negotiated settlement.

I again met Roelf Mayer, who as the apartheid regime's chief negotiator played a pivotal and positive role in the transitional process. Another meeting took place with a more shadowy figure from the apartheid era, Dr Niel Barnard. At one point, he had been the South African government's chief "spook", its head of the National Intelligence Service – South Africa's equivalent of the CIA. In 1987, while Mandela was still in prison, Barnard was one of a committee of senior officials set up by the South African government to conduct private discussions with the imprisoned ANC leader. Barnard told me that the first issue for them was the armed struggle. They put it to Mandela that the ANC would have to renounce violence and give up armed struggle before the government would talk to it. They had a discussion over many months in which they argued that ANC violence was criminal and in which Mandela spoke about the violence of the state. It was an argument that continued right up to the elections when Mandela became President.

Barnard also told me that his government went into negotiations with the ANC believing that the ANC would fragment and that they could string out the negotiation process for years, perhaps decades. They misunderstood the dynamics for change within a peace process and the ANC's careful management of their part of it. They underestimated the ability of the ANC. When I put it to him, he conceded that maybe they believed their own propaganda. They didn't commence negotiations to bring an end to apartheid, though that was the outcome. The South African experience had all sorts of lessons for us.

The day after we arrived in South Africa we went to the South African Parliament Building in Capetown where I addressed the Parliamentary Select Committee on Foreign Affairs and met senior ANC and other figures. I was amazed to find the old apartheid paintings, statues, murals and hangings still in place. No matter where we went, no matter how salubrious or palatial our surroundings, I was conscious that only a short time ago black people had been excluded.

Sitting drinking tea and coffee before a huge window with a magnificent view of Table Mountain, our conversation was suddenly interrupted by the arrival of an ANC women's delegation. The ANC had arranged for us to meet a delegation of their women activists, but this was much more than that. One woman swept in ahead of the group. A striking black woman, in the most colourful dress and headdress that I had yet seen, she looked around her with the most authoritive glance and asked, "Who's Chrissie McAuley?" Looking at Chrissie and Rita, ignoring me, she said, "Which one?" Chrissie looked at me, surprised that anyone should be asking for her. The woman scooped her up and hugged her hard. She then introduced herself as Adelaide Tambo, wife of former ANC President Oliver Tambo who had died in 1993.

Mrs Tambo heard of Chrissie from her friend and ANC exile Sadie Forman in London. She sent word that we were coming. Chrissie and Rita and Adelaide got on famously – women in a common struggle. They had a most enjoyable meeting. We men quite wisely took a back seat.

The purpose of our trip was for us to learn the lessons of South Africa's approach to conflict resolution and to brief people on our process. It was an emotional experience. My first protest against apartheid had been in 1970 against the South African Springboks rugby team. There was almost a sense of completing that circle because our hosts arranged for us to attend the semi-final of the Rugby World Cup between South Africa and France. Now, here in South Africa, I was going to support the Springboks.

The atmosphere within the stadium in Durban was electric – in every sense of the word. There was a thunderstorm replete with thunder, lightning and sheets of rain, the like of which I had never seen before. It looked as if we, and the tens of thousands of almost entirely white spectators, would be disappointed and the match cancelled. But the rain stopped and the match began. The stadium was a riot of colour – the rainbow colours of the new South African flag – green, black, white, gold, red and blue. It was everywhere. There were a few old South African flags, but these paled into insignificance against the cheering chants of tens of thousands of South Africans exuberantly waving their new flag and urging their team on to success. When South Africa won, the emotional outburst was overwhelming. South Africa went on to win the World Cup.

Later that night, we made dinner for our ANC hosts and then spoke into the wee hours of the morning about the similarities of oppression, resistance, interrogation and jail. All of our delegation had been imprisoned, both Rita and I had been shot, and Chrissie had been hurt in a bomb explosion. Rita had been grievously wounded in 1972, and she and an ANC comrade had this surreal conversation in which he showed her one injury he had received and she showed him a better one, he showed off another injury and she topped that. She was always a show-off.

Sunday saw us travelling back to Jo'burg and a tour of some of the townships – Soweto, Alexandra and Phola Park. Everywhere we went, the ghost of apartheid stalked us. Everywhere, except in the townships and squatter camps. Here the obscenity of apartheid howled at us and the fortitude and patience of the black majority humbled us. The conditions in the squatter camps were pitiable. The sights we witnessed there have stayed with me and have reinforced my conviction that the first world has to do more for the Third World.

In Soweto, we were taken to the grave of Joe Slovo. Slovo had been General Secretary of the South African Communist Party and a member of the ANC's NEC. When the ANC decided to adopt armed struggle as a means of struggle in 1961, Joe Slovo was recruited by Mandela along with Walter Sisulu to form the high command of Umkhon to we Sizwe (The Spear of the Nation) or MK. His first wife, Ruth First, was killed in 1982 by a parcel bomb sent to her office in Maputo, Mozambique. He rose to become Chief of Staff of MK.

He died six months before our visit. As we made our way through the huge Soweto cemetery to his graveside, we were accompanied by hundreds of local ANC activists, mainly women. At the graveside, I made a few remarks about Joe Slovo's life and example. The crowd sang "*Nkosi Sikelele*", the South African national anthem. It was a touching moment.

Then it was on to a short tour of the vast township that is Soweto – over one million people – and Alexandra township. And then Phola Park. As we arrived there we were surrounded by hundreds of people waving spears and shields in the air. They sang a song of greeting, and then we slowly made our way along a dual carriageway towards the squatter camp, our hosts dancing and chanting as they went. This tradition of *toyi-toyi* was impressive, in stark contrast to Phola Park, which was a terrible sight. Makeshift homes of corrugated tin, held together with bits of rope or wire. A row of latrines and a water tap. All of it covered in a blanket of dust. And the children – hundreds of children everywhere – clothed in worn and torn jerseys and shorts. Most wore no footwear.

Later that day, back in our hotel, Chrissie and I were sitting talking to our South African police guard and driver. The police squad was made up of both white and black members. We were amazed to learn from two of them – one black, one white – that during the apartheid years the white officer had been responsible for the interrogation of his black colleague. At one point during this torture – for that was what it was – the white officer had held his black colleague by the ankles out of a window high above the car park of the police barracks. He taunted him with racist language. Scores of ANC activists died this way when they were dropped from such interrogation rooms. Fortunately, on this occasion the black activist wasn't dropped because his white colleague told him that he wanted to torture him some more. As a result of the changes brought about by the negotiations and the election, the black ANC activist ended up in charge of the same police squad as the man who had tortured him. The most amazing part of this story was that they and their families now socialised together outside of their jobs.

The meeting with President Mandela on Monday, 19 June, was the highlight of all our meetings. The president was self-effacing in his humour, totally relaxed, but focused. Robert McBride brought us up a little earlier than expected to the office Mandela used when he worked out of the ANC's headquarters at Shell House in Jo'burg. As usual, much had been made about whether there would be a handshake, would we be photographed together, would we be photographed shaking hands and so on? The British government had been involved in a heavy lobby against our visit, especially against our meeting Mandela. Everyone else saw this trip as good for the peace process, as consolidating the peace process, but not the British government or the unionists: for them, it was still about victories and defeats, and they reacted to us on this basis.

As we entered his outer office, Mandela was leaving to go to a quick meeting down the hall. His face lit up into that bright, warm smile that hundreds of millions around the world have come to know, respect and love. As he shook my hand, he grinned mischievously and said: "Ah, comrade Gerry, I'll not wash my hand for a week." He also shook hands warmly with our Gearóid, bantering with him about having a subversive father.

Later we spent almost two hours with Madiba – as he is called by his friends and comrades. During our meeting, he recalled how he was castigated when he visited Ireland in 1992 because he publicly called for talks between the British government and Irish republicans. Good humouredly, he recollected how, while he was being publicly condemned

219

for his audacity, the British were secretly talking to us. His commitment to a peace process and a peace settlement in Ireland was obvious. The meeting itself was good humoured, funny, serious and uplifting for us.

Richard had prepared a draft joint statement to be issued by Madiba and myself. I put it to the President and, following slight changes, the statement was released. At the press conference afterwards, Mandela fielded questions with ease. The South African President said that he was sure Sinn Féin and the British government would find a way to resolve difficulties in our process. Then he added, with an impish smile, that while the ANC suspended its armed struggle unilaterally, it never surrendered its weapons. I have met Mandela many times since. Even today we still seek advice from the ANC. Madiba remains one of my heroes and in my view the greatest political leader of our time.

All too soon the five of us, exhausted but elated, returned home. Our peace process was still in trouble. The British were not for lifting the pre-condition. In South Africa I had warned of the danger and risk of slipping back into conflict. Martin McGuinness repeated that view. Some journalists and, predictably, the unionists chose to interpret these remarks as a threat. It was simply the truth. We wanted to avert a crisis, but we could not do it on our own. Martin made it clear that, as far as Sinn Féin was concerned, exploratory talks were now over. It was time to move on to the next and most dynamic stage of the peace process.

Easier said than done. We were now into the marching season of the loyal orders – the Orange Order, the Apprentice Boys and the Royal Black Institution. The marches, which celebrate the victory of King William of Orange in 1689, are fundamentally sectarian and triumphalist. They are about one section of our people expressing their superiority over their neighbours. The loyal orders brought together all trends and strands of unionist opinion.

Most nationalists tolerate these parades, despite their offensive nature. We accept that the Orangemen have the right to march, but not in areas where they are unwelcome. There were and still are a small number of parades, less than a dozen of over three thousand, where the loyal orders are determined to march through nationalist neighbourhoods. And so once again as Orange marches were shepherded through these areas, nationalist residents were batoned and beaten off the streets. Many were arrested.

Mayhew added to the deepening crisis on 28 June when he told the media that his talks with the other parties would go ahead without Sinn Féin. And then he released British paratrooper Lee Clegg from prison!

Clegg had been one of ten paras who, on 30 September 1990, had opened fire on a car containing teenage car thieves in West Belfast. Thirty-six shots had been fired, nineteen hit the vehicle. According to the lone survivor, there were two distinct bursts of gunfire, the second after the car was stationary. When the shooting was over, two teenagers were dead.

The soldiers claimed the car had struck one of their number, injuring him in the leg. But an RUC man, who initially backed this account, then made a new statement saying no soldier was at risk or injured. The soldiers had deliberately injured their colleague's leg after the incident to cover-up what they had done and to lend credibility to their concocted story. In June 1993, Clegg was convicted of murdering Karen Reilly and attempting to murder Martin Peake. Another soldier was jailed for seven years for the attempted murder of Peake, but was freed on appeal after his conviction was reduced to malicious wounding. Four other paras were cleared of charges relating to the incident. The officer in charge of the squad of soldiers – a lieutenant – was promoted to captain before his case went to trial.

Clegg appealed his conviction to the Appeal Court in Belfast and to the British House of Lords, but lost. There was a vigorous public campaign in England to secure his release. It was supported by most of the British right-wing broadsheets and tabloids and by the Conservative Party. On 3 July, Clegg was released from prison after serving just over two years of a life sentence for murder. There was uproar in nationalist areas. Firstly, at another example of the British system protecting its own, but also because after almost one year of the IRA cessation, the British had refused to make any move on the issue of republican political prisoners – some of whom had already spent over twenty years in prison.

Hundreds of vehicles were destroyed in some of the most vicious rioting witnessed in years. Republican activists on the streets trying to calm the situation were told to fuck off by many of the young people.

Later, to add insult to injury, Clegg was promoted from private to lance corporal. In prison, he had remained on full army pay. Then it emerged that the paras had built a large model of the car in their canteen at Hollywood Barracks, just outside Belfast, along with a papier-maché head covered in blood. A large notice stuck to the wall above the model car read: "Vauxhall Astra. Built by robots. Driven by joyriders. Stopped by A Company."

The crisis was worsening. Speaking on 7 July at a meeting of the Forum for Peace and Reconciliation in Dublin, a few days after Clegg's release, I reminded the assembled political leaders that many in the room used to claim that an end to the IRA's campaign would see prisoners released and the start of real talks. This had not happened.

A few days later, thousands of Orangemen gathered at Drumcree, a Church of Ireland church on the outskirts of Portadown in North Armagh, demanding that they be allowed to walk down the Garvaghy Road, a nationalist area. The Unionist MP for the area, David Trimble, insisted that the Orangemen had the right to march to Drumcree Church by one route and return to the town by the Garvaghy Road. That there were now six nationalist housing estates along this return leg of the march meant nothing. This was a "traditional" route and the Orangemen demanded to march it.

A deal was done which allowed 500 Orangemen to march down the Garvaghy Road provided they took a different route for the 12 July march. There was to be no triumphalism, but as Paisley and Trimble entered Portadown, to the cheers of supporters, they strutted in a triumphalist little tango along the last few yards. A delighted and beaming David Trimble told the media that the unionists had won the day, that there would be no negotiations and no compromise and that they would be back again.

The next day, the RUC placed the lower Ormeau Road under curfew. The media were barred. Residents were denied milk or breakfast supplies. This situation continued for some hours until, despite the protestations of the local people, an Orange parade made its way down the road. Baton-wielding RUC officers attacked the local nationalists.

To many nationalists, the peace process seemed to be dying on its feet. Loyalist arms factories were uncovered in County Down and in England. In Scotland other loyalists were charged with attempting to obtain weapons for the UVF.

In an effort to lift the growing sense of despondency, I met with John Bruton, John Hume and Dick Spring on 14 July at the final meeting of the Forum for Peace and Reconciliation before its summer recess. In a joint statement, we said the impasse had to be overcome and that meant starting talks quickly. The Fianna Fáil leader Bertie Ahern warned Major that peace must not be allowed to founder.

On 18 July, Martin McGuinness and I met Patrick Mayhew and Michael Ancram privately in Derry at our request. We arranged a quiet, away-from-the-media get-together in the home of a senior churchman. He and his wife greeted us with genuine hospitality. The meeting was relaxed and I warmed a little to Mayhew. I thought he was out of his depth, unsuited to the demands of this process and unable to adjust to it, or to the reality that it was driven by upstarts like us. He was very much of the establishment: pampered and probably unused to being challenged. When he could not defeat our arguments, he seemed surprised and perplexed. I did get the sense that he knew we were genuine, as well as serious, about out position.

News of our meeting, including its venue, was leaked to the media. I suspected it came from Mayhew's security detail, who saw Martin and me, or from the NIO, which must have known we were meeting. Despite this, we met again on 27 July. After hours of discussion, the British position appeared to be set in stone. We suggested that the two governments should organise a conference to be held in September to initiate all-party negotiations as the best way of overcoming the present impasse. But the British remained stubbornly inflexible.

The Sinn Féin core group was talking itself hoarse and burning up brain cells trying to break the impasse. Mairéad lobbied our US friends and the White House to see if they could help. I wrote to President Mandela asking him to speak to John Major. Our party sought to mobilise public opinion in Ireland.

There was, of course, always the possibility that the British government and others might be genuinely miscalculating the IRA's position on decommissioning or Sinn Féin's ability to manoeuvre on this issue. We weren't trying to be clever. The reality was that an objective of a conflict-resolution process could not be made a pre-condition for that process.

The issue of an international commission on arms was now gaining currency, and, in an article in *An Phoblacht*, I warned that it was a non-starter if this commission idea was merely a device to process the British government's pre-condition. In a letter on 6 August, John Bruton told me that the commission would hold discussions with all the parties, and make recommendations to the governments on the modalities of decommissioning in the right circumstances. This commission would work side by side with a new phase of political talks, to be conducted by the governments on a "triangular" basis with the parties. From the moment these talks began, he said, all the parties would be treated with absolute parity of esteem.

Bruton argued that these triangular talks would represent an initial phase of the all-party talks themselves. We were fast approaching the first anniversary of the IRA cessation and Mr Major's government was strangling the peace process. The London *Independent* called on Major to lead from the front. Its editorial said, "Nearly a year after the ceasefires, with a general election at most eighteen months away, this is the moment for the British government to set a more ambitious political pace."

The first anniversary of the IRA cessation was at the end of the month. One year after the exuberance and enthusiasm of 31 August 1994, we did not even have peace talks and no one knew when or if these would begin.

The Irish government and Washington were pressing London for agreement on inclusive talks and the international arms body. A summit was set for September for Bruton and Major. Before it took place, David Trimble was elected leader of the Ulster Unionist Party. His triumphalist dance with Ian Paisley at Portadown had appealed to the intransigent majority within the UUP.

I flew off to the USA on 11 September for a series of meetings in Washington. We needed the USA putting the maximum pressure on Major so that, if an international body was to be established, it was set up for the right reasons. I met National Security Advisor Tony Lake and Nancy Soderberg. Vice President Al Gore dropped by. I also met George Mitchell, and a variety of senators and congressional representatives. The Americans now publicly set a date for President Clinton's first ever visit to Ireland, and the first visit by a US president to the North. It was to take place between 28 November and 2 December 1995.

The White House was mindful of the President arriving in the midst of a crisis or worse, and therefore had a real interest in pushing for a resolution of the impasse. The twin-track approach – an international body and substantive bilateral and trilateral talks between the parties and the government – was now acknowledged as the best, probably the only way out of the growing mess. The White House was keen to push ahead with this, as was I. But we had to get it right, and that meant we were now engaged in a negotiation over the details.

I had arranged a second visit to the White House, but the British got wind of it and briefed some journalists that I was being summoned back there to have the riot act read to me. I cancelled the meeting and arranged to meet privately with Tony Lake and Nancy Soderberg. It was a good meeting.

As usual, our US trips weren't all about briefing political leaders and negotiation. I visited Georgetown University and gave a lecture to a packed hall of keenly interested students. There was also some time for a bit of *craic* with those we were talking to in the White House. Tony Lake was an avowed baseball fan. He commended baseball to me as a metaphor for the need for rules in the peace process. I succeeded, thanks in the main to the efforts of Brian McCabe, to get a video of the all-Ireland hurling final. Off it went to the West Wing, with a note from me: "These are the rules we play by." Later he told me he enjoyed the video: "It's a wonderful game," he said. And he was right. Hurling is the best game in the world.

September was a month awash with speculation of a breakthrough. There were news reports that there was to be a substantial communiqué, and rumours of a British commitment and a date for all-party talks. All of this was because of the upcoming visit by President Clinton.

London and Dublin were indeed working on a draft communiqué. A draft of this in early September acknowledged that the two governments had agreed to create the conditions for all-party talks in round table format, aimed at reaching an agreed political settlement based on consent. These could commence before the end of 1995. The British were apparently hinting that 15 December might be a good date. Meetings would take place with all parties to lay the groundwork for these talks. The draft also said that the governments had agreed to establish an International Decommissioning Commission. This commission would have the initial and limited remit of reporting to the two governments by mid-November 1995, on whether it had established that a clear commitment existed on the part of the relevant paramilitary organisations to the full and verifiable decommissioning of all illegally held arms in the appropriate context and manner. The two governments aimed to meet before the end of November 1995 to agree the appropriate way forward.

Along with some colleagues, I was now immersed in private meetings with Irish government officials trying to make sense of this proposal and to ensure that the British would not seek to manipulate it and turn it back on us. We were now working with Paddy Teahon and Tim Dalton along with Seán Ó hUiginn. John Bruton had a special adviser, Sean Donlon, who dipped in and out of our discussions without any real effect. We told them that the draft was not acceptable. It wasn't specific enough in terms of an agreed date for all-party talks; the remit of the international body was too vague; there was nothing guaranteeing that the British would use this to get off the "Washington 3" hook (outlined as pre-conditions for Sinn Féin by Patrick Mayhew) or that Sinn Féin would be treated on the same basis as all of the other parties. I told the governments and the White House that any international body – and George Mitchell was by this stage in the frame as its chair – had to be a political body: that is, political parties would make submissions. I also argued strongly that the initiative, if it was to have any hope of working, needed a guarantor.

As a consequence of all of this, the proposed summit between Bruton and Major was cancelled, but work on a text for a joint communiqué continued. The IRA gave its own verdict of Britain machinations in a statement on 27 September. It described the decommissioning issue as a deliberate distraction and stalling tactic by a British government acting in bad faith. It declared that there was no possibility of the IRA meeting these demands.

A new draft on 25 September elaborated on the role of an international body. It would now have three members and would ascertain and advise on whether and by what means the question of arms could be settled to the satisfaction of both governments and all parties. Accordingly, the body would report by a date unspecified whether it had established that a clear commitment existed on the part of the relevant paramilitary organisations to a satisfactory process for the full and verifiable decommissioning of all illegally held arms.

Bruton then had a series of meetings with John Major to discuss the details of the twin-track approach. Nancy Soderberg arrived on our side of the Atlantic in early October for meetings with the two governments and ourselves. I met her on 4 October. The British were now shifting the December date, moving it back. But discussions on what the twin track would involve, how it would work and who it would involve continued. So too did our efforts and the efforts of others to push the British in the right direction.

Diplomatic activity between Dublin, Washington, London and us was now intense as President Clinton's visit drew nearer. On the streets, Sinn Féin was holding demonstrations calling for the peace process to be saved. John Hume and I met to discuss how the impasse could be ended. On 6 October we put together our own proposed draft of a joint communiqué for the two governments. It set 30 November as a date for the commencement of substantive talks, removing any pre-conditions, and was broad enough in its description to include the issue of all arms. We asked for a meeting with John Bruton to give this proposition to him. Bruton refused to meet us. This caused consternation and raised the real fear that he was preparing to do a deal with the British without reference to his two partners in the nationalist consensus.

Martin McGuinness then passed our proposals to the British government at a meeting with Michael Ancram on 20 October. In an effort to move the process on, and to demonstrate our willingness to be flexible, Martin told Ancram that we had commissioned a paper which would deal with a range of issues – including decommissioning and a response to the British government paper on modalities – as part of a submission to an international body – should one ever be set up. Martin told Ancram that we would be willing to give serious consideration to the recommendations of an international body on its merits. We wanted such a body to deal with the issue properly. That meant removing it as a pre-condition. We needed to be assured that the twin track was serious and genuine and that the governments would ensure that substantive talks would begin not later than Hume and I proposed, or the 15 December date being suggested by the British. To our alarm, Ancram now put a different timetable. The British were now arguing that three months was needed for the twin track to reach all-party talks. This would put talks well into the New Year!

Without prejudice to the discussions, Martin and Ancram also discussed who would be on the international body, how long would it sit, would its hearings be private or public, where would it sit, and what would its terms of reference be? The British indicated that they were still only looking at submissions from loyalists and republicans. Martin firmly told them that other parties had to be able to make submissions. The British still also wanted to keep the remit to a narrow definition focused on "illegal" weapons. We argued for a wider, more open definition.

Most importantly, we wanted to know if the demand for actual decommissioning was now off the screen. Would the British accept recommendations from an international body which disagreed with the British position? The British conceded that while "Washington 3" was still their position, an international body might produce a new position. At a subsequent meeting with Irish government officials, it emerged that London was now going to produce a concepts paper. In their discussions with the Irish government, there appeared to be no urgency on the British side.

Towards the end of October, the British sent us and the unionists a copy of their concepts paper – now called the building blocks paper – which set out their view of the twin track. It was an amended, slightly longer draft of the last draft joint communiqué discussed by the two governments. Nowhere in the paper did the British government commit itself to a firm date for the commencement of substantive all-party talks. It continued to limit the scope of discussions to what was described as unauthorised arms.

Moreover, the British made it clear that they would not set a date for all-party talks unless the unionists were on board. This provided the unionists – and, in particular, David Trimble – with a veto over talks.

The diplomatic discussions continued through November. John Hume and I tried to give the process a much-needed kick in the pants by publicly releasing our proposals to the two governments. John Major again added to the sense of political crisis by rejecting a call – made by the Taoiseach in a speech in London on 11 November – for a date for all-party talks. The toing and froing over the detail and a text for the joint communiqué led to some of the bitterest words from Irish government sources about the British. The media were told of "blatant lies", of "cynical manipulation" and "disinformation", as well as the British trying to "dump the blame for failure on John Bruton". They were right. They were also far too slow figuring this out.

In a last-ditch effort to resolve matters and as President Clinton's plane, Air Force One, was in the air on its way to London, the Taoiseach and the Prime Minister met at Downing Street for discussions, which lasted until midnight on 28 November. I tried in vain throughout the day to talk to the Taoiseach. I began ringing his office at 9.45 that morning. I was worried that Dublin would move too far towards the British position. A joint communiqué was eventually produced by the two governments, shortly after 10 o'clock that night. We received our first copy of it from the media. We were deliberately kept out of the loop.

The joint communiqué was, at best, a fudge. Dublin had blinked first. Major, by deliberately taking the negotiations to the wire and with President Clinton on his way, had succeeded in facing down the Fine Gael Taoiseach.

Dublin had signed up to a joint communiqué that failed to meet even the minimum standards it had itself set. There was no firm date for substantive negotiations. The discussions period set for the twin track was twelve weeks, not the six that the Irish government had argued for. Dublin had also argued that the international body should take the entire weapons issue within its purview, but the communiqué reflected the British definition that the discussion of weapons would be limited to those held by the IRA and loyalists. The third pre-condition – which demanded the actual decommissioning of weapons – wasn't mentioned, but John Major reiterated it at the press conference of Tuesday night, 28 November.

The British had reinforced the unionist effort to thwart progress into substantive talks. In addition, unionists had been stridently demanding an election to an assembly or convention in the North. The Irish

228

government's view was that, if any elected body was to be flagged up, then any joint text must adequately reflect the consistent view of nationalists on this issue. The communiqué did not do this. Unionists could take succour from a paragraph that said that the participants to the talks, along with the governments, would properly take account of democratic mandates and principles, including whether and how an elected body could play a part. There was no recognition of Northern nationalist opposition to this position.

The issue of arms decommissioning featured in nine out of the twelve paragraphs. The role of the international body – to be chaired by Senator Mitchell – was advisory, with neither government bound by its conclusions. The two governments proposed to meet again in mid-February to review progress and to consider the recommendations of Mitchell's body – due to report in mid-January.

We did not think the joint communiqué and its proposals would break the impasse. But the peace process was at a defining point: it was a time to take more risks. The test would be whether this development removed the weapons pre-condition and how quickly it would lead to all-party talks.

Before engaging in the twin-track process and meeting the two governments and the international body, we had first to meet President Bill Clinton as he made his triumphant visit to Ireland.

# Chapter Twenty-Two

# *President Clinton on the Falls Road*

President Clinton arrived into Belfast early on 30 November 1995. It had been a long evening and night before as we negotiated the format of our meeting. It was almost a rerun of Clinton's Irish counterpart Mary Robinson's visit to West Belfast two years earlier.

The British were, predictable as ever, trying to block all of this. They did not want a photograph of the President and me shaking hands. I wanted a meeting on the Falls Road. Some of the White House people wanted it at the Mackies engineering plant on the Springfield Road between nationalist and unionist West Belfast. Given Mackies sectarian history, whatever changes had come about in recent years, it would not go down well within nationalist opinion if our meeting took place at a factory renowned for discrimination.

The eventual outcome of the late night calls was an agreement that the President would make a stop on the Shankill to visit a unionist working-class district, then travel to Mackies where he would speak at a public event. After that, on his way across the city, he would stop en route at the junction of the Falls Road and Springfield Road and meet me. There would be a public handshake outside McErlean's bakery shop.

President Clinton arrived in Belfast International airport about ten miles to the north-west of the city. He travelled into Belfast in his bullet- and bomb-proof Cadillac limousine. He first went to Violet Clarke's fruit shop on the Shankill. He next travelled to Mackies, which provided one of the most poignant points in the trip when two young children – nine-year-old Catherine Hamill, a Catholic, and eleven-year-old David Sterrit, a Protestant, read letters they had written to welcome the President. Standing on a wooden box so she could reach the microphones and be seen, Catherine said, "My name is Catherine Hamill. I live in Belfast. I love where I live. My first daddy died in the Troubles. It was the saddest day of my life. I still think of him. Now it is nice and peaceful. I like having peace and quiet for a change instead of having people shooting and killing. My Christmas wish is that peace and love will last in Ireland for ever."

Catherine's father, Patrick, was shot nine years earlier in his home a few hundred yards from where Catherine was now standing speaking to President Clinton. He died the next day in hospital. Catherine was six months old at the time. Sometime after Clinton visited, it emerged that her father had been targeted for murder by the British intelligence agent Brian Nelson.

While the President was visiting Mackies, I went to the Culturlann, an Irish language centre on the Falls Road with Richard and Big Eamon to meet Blair Hall, a political counsellor at the US Embassy in London. Blair was dressed up for the day with trench coat, hidden walkie-talkie, an earpiece and a microphone attached to the inside of his coat sleeve. We were about a half a mile from the spot where the meeting with the President was to take place. We had coffee and Danish pastries while I listened to live radio coverage on my Walkman. I gave one of the earpieces to Blair. He now really looked odd sitting with two earpieces.

We were the only four in the place, and occasionally Blair would use his walkie-talkie to check how the President's schedule was going. We left the Culturlann and walked down the Falls Road. We were accompanied by Allison Hartley, one of the pupils from Meanscoil Feirste, the Belfast Irish language secondary school, her mother Liz and one of the teachers, Cahal. We had arranged for them to be in McErlean's to make a presentation to the President about the lack of British government funding for Irish language education. At that time Irish had no legal status, and the burgeoning nursery and primary schools sector was entirely dependent on voluntary donations raised by parents and supporters. The North's Department of Education was notoriously biased in its attitude to requests for money for the Irish medium sector.

As we approached the junction of the Falls Road and the Springfield Road, we could see that the road was blocked by hundreds of people. A US official, dressed in the compulsory trench coat, emerged from the throng and told us that the President was running slightly late. So we went for a walk in the grounds of St Dominic's High School for girls. It gave me a chance to gather my thoughts. The peace process was in trouble. The two governments had produced a twin track which leaned too close to the British position – with no evidence that the British would use it to get the process off their hook on the weapons issue. The President's visit had the potential to kick-start the process and save it from collapse. His presence – what he said and how he used his influence – was crucial.

A US official arrived and asked if we would take a car round to the back of the bakery. There were some concerns about the interaction and the hostility between the RUC and the hundreds now gathered to greet the President. I knew it would be OK and refused the car. We walked through the crowd over to McErlean's. Richard and I went in and spoke to some of the customers sitting at tables having tea. Among them were Marguerite Gallagher and Pat McGivern, who run the Green Cross bookshop, and Chrissie McAuley. They were there to make sure that everything ran smoothly when the President entered the bakery. I also arranged with the women behind the counter to have some local bread in a bag ready to present to the President.

Outside, Richard, Big Eamon and I waited with the White House people and Blair Hall for the President to arrive. As the limousine swung round to stop in front of the bakery, a black van pulled between the lorry carrying the camera crews and photographers, and me and the President – probably the vehicle carrying the critical care nurses whose job it is to stabilise the President in the event that he is shot or hurt or takes ill. Working on the old Irish maxim "Murphy's law – if it can go wrong, it will" – Richard was prepared. He pulled from his pocket a small camera he had borrowed the previous night from a photojournalist. He took several photographs of the President and me shaking hands and talking. The media were furious at having been prevented from getting the shot they all desperately wanted. There was even talk that the White House had arranged for the van to deliberately pull in front of the press. Richard had also arranged to have the engagement video-recorded. When it was over he gave the camera to the press photographer from whom he had borrowed it and his photo was flashed around the world.

"Hi ya, Gerry," the President said with a smile.

"*Céad míle fáilte*," I said. A hundred thousand welcomes.

He told me that he had been reading one of my books – *The Street and Other Stories* – as he flew into Belfast that morning.

"Now I know where you get your inspiration from," he said.

The President went into McErlean's. I stood outside talking to Tony Lake. Inside, President Clinton was given a bag of soda farls, bannocks and wheaten bread. Liz Hartley and Allison and Cahal got the chance to make their presentation to him. The people inside were delighted. Outside, the crowd was enthusiastic. Clinton drove his security people crazy when he decided to do an impromptu walkabout. He went to the chemist's next door and then walked about fifty yards down to a barrier that had been erected across the road where hundreds of hands were outstretched for the shaking.

There was no security problem. The biggest danger to Bill Clinton was when it appeared that he might go into the Seán Mac Diarmada Gaelic Athletic Club. The Macs are one of Belfast's premier hurling and football sides, as well known for their hospitality as their exploits on the field of play. If the US President had ventured into the clubrooms, it is likely he might be there yet. But the press of people as well as the security barrier prevented that possibility.

It was a big day for the Falls Road – the scene of so much resistance, so much sorrow and anger. The people here had suffered. Pilloried, demonised, disenfranchised and targeted by British Crown forces and their surrogates in loyalism, they were now host to the most powerful man in the world.

Below where the President received a warm welcome from local people, Nora McCabe had been killed by an RUC plastic bullet; below that was the battle-scarred Sinn Féin office, the scene of the killing of Paddy Loughran, Pat McBride and Michael O'Dwyer. The crowd around Bill Clinton were not star-struck groupies. Many of them would have concerns about US foreign policy. But they were genuinely pleased to see the US President. They recognised the role he was playing. They understood the significance of his visit and they felt he was on their side. He had come to visit them in their own place.

As President Clinton left to travel across to East Belfast and on to Derry, I met Niall O'Dowd and Bruce Morrison, who were part of the presidential entourage. We walked up to the Springvale Training Centre, where a lunch had been arranged for US Commerce Secretary Ron Brown. It was like meeting an old friend. We hugged, shook hands and went in to listen to the speeches. Afterwards, along with Bill Flynn, Niall, Bruce and I walked over into the Kashmir Road where, in the living room of a small terraced house, I told our Irish American friends that, while Sinn Féin would engage in the twin-track process, every political instinct and our experience talking to and dealing with the British convinced us it was unlikely to work. Everyone was elated by the President's visit, but there was still much work to be done.

That evening the President turned on the Christmas tree lights in Belfast. There were people as far as the eye could see outside the City Hall, and they gave him and the First Lady a tumultuous welcome. The 49-foot white pine tree had been felled in Al Gore's home state of Tennessee in November. Later that evening, there was a reception in the Whitla Hall at Queen's University. As the President rose to speak, someone, thinking ahead to the presidential re-election campaign, shouted out "Four more years." The hall erupted in applause and laughter. The President, smiling, said, "The plane for America leaves tomorrow. I want you on it." His speech fitted the moment. He looked to the future. And he pledged America's support: "The question of whether you will go forward is all up to you, but if you do we will be proud to walk with you."

I stood with several Sinn Féin representatives as the President and Hillary Clinton made their way along the rope line, greeting and talking to the scores of guests present. Later, we met for twenty minutes of small talk and a photo opportunity for the media.

The next day the Clinton entourage headed to Dublin for another tremendous welcome. It was clear that Ireland had carved a huge place for itself in the hearts of President Clinton and Hillary. The following year the video footage of his reception in Ireland became a central part of his campaign for re-election.

Now it was back to the grindstone, and seeing what we could do to make sense of the twin track. The two governments had sent letters of invitation to all the parties for meetings. I had met George Mitchell privately for an hour on 2 December, along with Fr Reid, and given him a brief background of the situation. The Sagart had spent longer with him. The Senator formally wrote to me on 7 December to arrange a publicised meeting. That same evening the IRA declared that there was no question of the IRA meeting the ludicrous demand for a surrender of weapons either through the front or back door.

Sinn Féin was doing its best to defuse the crisis over arms. We met the international body at 8 a.m. on Monday, 18 December, in Dublin Castle. We arrived much earlier at the front of the building and had a little distance to go to get to the commission's office towards the back. It was a sharp misty morning as we made our way through the cobbled courtyards of the Castle. We appeared to be the only ones about the place. Martin McGuinness recited poetry for our edification. Lucilita Bhreatnach remarked that the last time republicans were in Dublin Castle at such an early hour was during the Easter Rising.

Senator George Mitchell had been joined by the former Finnish Prime Minister Harri Holkeri and Canadian General John de Chastelain,

Canada's Chief of Defence Staff. Mitchell's chief aide, Martha Pope, was also in attendance. Rita O'Hare, Martin, Lucilita and I were there for Sinn Féin. We presented them with a comprehensive and detailed submission, entitled "Building a Permanent Peace in Ireland". We also gave them a collection of videos as information. We reminded them that the British government said in September 1993 that there would be no attempt to impose prior restrictions on the agenda of any talks. Our meeting lasted over two hours. It was a good engagement. I formally requested that they should ask the British government for copies of various reports on collusion, shoot-to-kill and other matters which had been suppressed.

Our submissions took the view that there would be no unilateral surrender of arms by any of the armed groups. However, given an acceptable political scenario, the practicalities of disarmament could be worked out without any great difficulties. We also pointed to one of the methods raised by the British themselves; that was the destruction of arms by those in possession of them. It was Sinn Féin's hope that the international body would clear away the British government's obstacles to inclusive talks. I was impressed by the speed and urgency with which the Senator and his colleagues approached their task. These very busy people had come from all parts of the world and in a hectic round of talks over four days met more people and received more submissions than the British government had in the previous sixteen months.

A few days later, I wrote to George Mitchell with additional information he had requested. The international body was being given conflicting positions by us and the British on whether the decommissioning of IRA weapons had been raised prior to the IRA cessation. I provided him with a quote from the Fianna Fáil leader, Bertie Ahern. On 20 June 1995, Ahern, speaking in London, said that decommissioning had not been raised as a pre-condition for Sinn Féin's admission to full talks before the IRA ceasefire.

We met with the Irish government in the twin-track process the same day that we met the international body. We met the British government the following day, 19 December. I put to Mayhew as forcefully as I could that there should be no pre-conditions, no vetoes, no precluded or predetermined outcomes to negotiations. A framework should be established and ground rules worked out by agreement between the party leaders and the governments. We proposed that he and Dick Spring host multi-party discussions immediately after the New Year.

December was also the month which saw John Major's parliamentary majority reduced to five as a result of deaths and defections. The Ulster Unionists' nine votes put them in an even stronger position than before. John Taylor, their deputy leader, put it bluntly, firing a warning shot over Major's bow. He announced that there was no reason to bring about a premature election so long as the governments acted in the best interest of the UK in general and of Northern Ireland in particular.

As we entered 1996, all eyes were on George Mitchell and his colleagues as we awaited the outcome of their deliberations. The British gave no hope for progress. George Mitchell returned to London on 11 January for meetings. Mitchell later recalled telling Major that the international body was not going to recommend prior decommissioning. He was going to propose parallel decommissioning during the political negotiations. Major told Mitchell that if they did, he would reject the report.

Meanwhile, David Trimble demanded elections for an assembly or convention. The Irish government, the SDLP, Fianna Fáil and ourselves all rubbished the idea. Michael Ancram in a dinner conversation with George Mitchell and his colleagues said that the British wanted some reference to an election in the international body's report because the unionists were insisting on an election and an assembly before any negotiations. Ancram also suggested that the issue of parallel decommissioning should be placed in a separate section of the report. On 23 January, the international body produced its long-awaited report. It rejected prior decommissioning and offered an alternative proposal containing three elements which came to be known as the Mitchell Principles. Firstly, to participate in negotiations, parties would have to promise to adhere to six fundamental principles of democracy and non-violence. Secondly, the parties should consider parallel decommissioning, and thirdly, the report set out a detailed process to achieve decommissioning.

In a short paragraph, George Mitchell, Harri Holkeri and General John de Chastelain said: "Several oral and written submissions raised the idea of an elected body. If it were broadly acceptable, with an appropriate mandate, and within the three strand structure, an elective process could contribute to the building of confidence."

The unionists were elated. The rest of us were worried. And with some justification. The following day, John Major spoke in the British House of Commons. He took the one paragraph on elections out of the sixty-two paragraphs in the report and told his colleagues: "[W]e believe that, in the light of the Mitchell Report, there are two ways in which all-party

236

negotiations can now be taken forward. Both are fully consistent with the six principles set out in the report. The first is for the paramilitaries to make a start to decommissioning before all-party negotiations. They can if they will. If not, the second is to secure a democratic mandate for all-party negotiations through elections specially for that purpose."

The Mitchell Report had been effectively dumped. The commitment to all-party talks contained in November's joint communiqué had been brushed aside. There was widespread nationalist anger. A week before this, at a trilateral meeting between Sinn Féin, the Irish government and the British government, Patrick Mayhew had told me that the two governments would consult with all the parties before responding to Mitchell's report. It would, he said, be greeted only with a holding statement. Some consultation – some holding statement!

John Hume accused Major of playing politics with people's lives, of buying the votes of the House of Commons in order to keep his government in power. He was right. The Unionist votes were more important to the Tory government than anything else. Hume went on to accuse Major of seventeen months of time-wasting. Dick Spring described British tactics as divide and conquer. It was obvious that the Tories were not prepared to alienate the UUP votes in the British parliament and the twenty or more right-wingers in the party who were quite capable of bringing it down. London would string out the process in the hope that republicans would splinter and lose credibility and support. It wanted unilateral control of the pace of events in a way that suited its needs and objectives. It was also obvious that the British Labour Party was not prepared to take a different approach this side of a British general election.

At the end of January, I flew to Washington to provide the White House and senior political, business and labour leaders with our assessment of the situation. Major had binned the Mitchell Report. He had abandoned the twin-track approach, and the February date for all-party talks and imposed a new pre-condition – the unionist demand for an election to an assembly.

I met President Clinton and Tony Lake and engaged with a wide range of US political opinion. I repeated the urgent need for substantive talks. I left my meeting at the White House with the clear impression that President Clinton had not signed on for Major's election idea.

On 7 February, in an effort to break the logjam, Dick Spring suggested to Mayhew at a meeting in Dublin that the two governments should convene talks similar to those held at Dayton in the USA – which had been held to resolve the Bosnian conflict. This would involve a two-day multilateral proximity meeting. Spring failed to get agreement from Mayhew. Michael Ancram later described the proposal as premature.

Two days later at around 6 p.m., Richard received calls from several journalists asking him about reports from Dublin that there was an IRA statement saying the cessation was over. By the time he and I met shortly after, most of the media had heard that the cessation was over. He was inundated with calls for a Sinn Féin line. While he worked on this, I alerted some of those we had been working with. I rang John Hume. I rang John Bruton's office and I phoned Tony Lake at the White House. I knew that Dick Spring was in Washington, and I rang the Irish Embassy in Washington to get a message through to him. Then the media queries about an IRA statement became reports of a bomb alert in London.

The IRA statement announcing, with great reluctance, the end of its cessation, with effect from 6 p.m. on 9 February 1996, was issued at 5.30 p.m. Asserting that its objective had been to enhance the democratic peace process, it accused the British government of duplicity. Shortly after 7 p.m. a huge IRA bomb exploded at South Quay station beside Canary Wharf on the Isle of Dogs in London. Two people died and there was massive damage running into tens of millions of pounds.

In the immediate aftermath of the attack, I had little time to reflect on what had happened. I was stunned. The collapse of the process need not have happened. The IRA had to take responsibility for the bomb, but the British government's refusal to grasp the historic opportunity which had been handed to it guaranteed such an outcome. My big regret was that people died, and that Sinn Féin strategy was once again relegated to the passenger seat.

The Sinn Féin peace strategy remained the right strategy. We couldn't afford to become fatalistic or despondent. We needed a peace process and a negotiated peace settlement. At a personal level, as television footage showed the extent of the damage the bomb had caused, I felt overwhelmed. This one explosion cost the British Exchequer more than all the other bombs of the previous twenty-five years. There was bound to be fallout over that. I was also bound to get some of the blame.

The reaction of the two governments was also predictable. Within days, the establishments in Dublin and London were back to the old agenda of trying to isolate Sinn Féin. The Irish government announced that there would be no more ministerial meetings with us. The British also refused ministerial contact. I wrote to Major and Bruton asking for urgent meetings. I still had the hope that there were some within the governments who had been persuaded by the peace process that the only way to end this conflict was through dialogue.

The Irish government agreed to meetings between Sinn Féin and officials. Subsequently, the British government also agreed to meetings with officials. We told both that rebuilding the peace process required dialogue – as soon as possible and with no pre-conditions. On 18 February another bomb, smaller this time, exploded on a bus in Wellington Street near Covent Garden in London. One person, IRA volunteer Edward O'Brien, aged twenty-one, died. The bomb had exploded prematurely as it was being transported. The day before, two square miles in the heart of London, including Trafalgar Square, Pall Mall, Piccadilly Circus and Oxford Street were all closed off after a bomb warning from the IRA. A small bomb was defused, but not before it had caused chaos.

Ten days later John Major and John Bruton held a summit in London. In a joint communiqué afterwards, they finally announced a date, 10 June, for the commencement of all-party talks. An election was to be held, details to be worked out in the course of multilateral consultations. The two governments would meet the parties at Castle Buildings at Stormont. All the parties, that is, but Sinn Féin. We were again excluded.

The irony wasn't lost on most people. For eighteen months, we had tried to get the British to remove pre-conditions and to set a firm date for negotiations. All to no avail. Now, two weeks after the IRA cessation ended, a date was set. The same day Major and Bruton met, John Hume and I met also. We then travelled to meet representatives of the IRA leadership.

# Chapter Twenty-Three

# *Towards All-Party Talks*

During the meeting with a seven-strong IRA delegation, we heard the news that the governments had set a date for all-party talks. The meeting lasted several hours. John Hume and I had prepared our arguments, as had the IRA. All of the IRA volunteers spoke, although their contribution was led mostly by two people. John was on form. He was articulate, focused and persuasive. Both of us acknowledged the difficulties and bad faith created by the British, but we also put a strong case for the restoration of the IRA cessation.

The IRA representatives detailed at length how the leadership had been won over initially by the agreements and commitments made in the run-up to the cessation. It had been a leadership decision within the authority of the Army Council, but nonetheless IRA volunteers had to be brought on board. This meant the army leadership placing its credibility and leadership on the line.

The IRA had finally agreed to the complete cessation of military operations because it believed that a determined approach would be made by the breadth of Irish national political opinion. John Bruton had fractured this. In the IRA's view, he paid more attention to the British agenda, supported its position on arms, refused to meet John Hume and me and publicly supported the unionist demand for elections to a forum.

The British had reneged on their public commitments. The refusal to demilitarise, the continuing ill-treatment of prisoners especially in Britain, the release of Lee Clegg, and the decision around the Garvaghy Road were all cited. As one of the IRA delegation said: "We sued for peace, the British wanted war. If that's what they want, we will give them another twenty-five years of war!" But the meeting had its positive moments, as well. The most important of these was when we were told that the IRA leadership was prepared to restore the cessation if a viable alternative could be produced.

John and I pushed for the meeting to be made public, for the army and John and myself to make separate statements giving our views of our discussions and of our hopes arising from it. The next day an IRA statement said that it had listened attentively to the case presented by us. The IRA restated its commitment to republican objectives and placed the responsibility for the breakdown of the process firmly on the shoulders of the British government. It added that it was prepared to face up to its responsibilities.

John Hume separately told journalists that he hoped the initial consultative talks involving all the parties and the two governments, scheduled to begin on 4 March, would help create a situation in which a new cessation might emerge. I made it clear that Sinn Féin was prepared to participate in these discussions positively and in the hope that they might move the situation forward. John Hume's hopes were quickly dashed when the British minister, Michael Ancram, declared, "There would be no meetings [with Sinn Féin] before a ceasefire." Consequently, no invitation was issued to us to participate.

Not having an invitation was no reason not to turn up. On Monday morning, I led a Sinn Féin delegation to Castle Buildings in the Stormont estate. Patrick Mayhew and Irish Minister for Foreign Affairs Dick Spring, who were available in the conference room to hear the views of the parties, refused to talk to us. The two unionist parties, the UUP and the DUP, refused to attend because of the presence of the Irish government representatives. The unionists, now faced with the prospect of talks beginning on 10 June, were trying to exclude or sideline the Irish government.

The hard-line approach of the British government toward republicans was especially evident at this time in its treatment of republican prisoners. Harry Duggan, from County Clare, who was in his twenty-first year of imprisonment in England, was refused compassionate parole to attend his mother's funeral. Harry hadn't seen Bridget in twenty years.

But most concern centred on the condition of Paddy Kelly. While held in prison in England, he had been diagnosed with skin cancer. Prison authorities had refused, even while the IRA cessation was in place, to provide him with proper medical treatment. He was subsequently moved to Maghaberry prison in the North, but we were campaigning to have him repatriated to Portlaoise prison outside Dublin, closer to his partner and family. We also believed that the Irish government would be more amenable to ensuring that he received the medical treatment he needed, although our information suggested that he was now terminally ill. The British refused to move him.

On 11 March, a Sinn Féin delegation privately met with senior officials in the Irish government to identify the gaps in our respective positions and to see what could be done to bridge those gaps. John Hume and I met with a senior Irish government official some days before this. The delegation meeting focused on the failure of Taoiseach John Bruton to defend and assert Irish national interests. The officials claimed that in their discussions with the British government on the proposed Forum, the Brits had worked hard to ensure that it would have no administrative or legislative power. The problem was that most nationalists and republicans believed the unionists were getting their own way, aided and abetted by John Major, assisted by John Bruton.

These issues underpinned a series of meetings between Sinn Féin and the Irish officials throughout March. We were also meeting with Fianna Fáil's Martin Mansergh on the same agenda.

Meanwhile, three and a half thousand miles away, Richard and I arrived once again in the USA for a series of public and private meetings. There was no invitation to the St Patrick's Day event in the White House. The British made much of this. But I now had the opportunity to do something many of my friends always wanted to do – to attend the St Patrick's Day parade in New York.

But first there was a round of meetings, mainly with Irish America. These engagements gave me an opportunity to gauge at first hand the response of Irish America to the end of the IRA cessation. I wasn't disappointed. Irish America, like Irish political opinion at home, understood that, while the IRA had to take responsibility for its own actions, blame for the collapse of the peace process was laid firmly at the door of the British government. I also met with most of the Connolly House group. They had deep concerns at the ending of the IRA cessation and its likely impact on our project in the United States.

While the IRA cessation was over, I believed it could be restored. I told them confidentially that we were already in discussions with Dublin in an effort to rescue the situation. The White House and Irish America continued to be main players in all of this, in my opinion, and we needed their help in removing the roadblocks to progress. Specifically, while there was now a date for all-party talks, it was wrapped with barbed wire in an effort to keep Sinn Féin out. The process needed a dynamic built into it, and that required a time-frame, as well as an inclusive agenda. This was where the White House could play a crucial role and the Connolly House group could educate and help mobilise opinion.

A few days later in Washington DC, Mairéad Keane, Richard and I met with Tony Lake, Nancy Soderberg and Maryann Peters, a senior aide. I made it clear from the outset of our meeting that I wanted to be able to go to the IRA with a package that would address all of the uncertainties. I pointed out that the British had now, apart from the restoration of the cessation, imposed three new pre-conditions on Sinn Féin: decommissioning, the Mitchell Principles and participation in an elective process that we were very much opposed to. Bill Clinton's National Security Advisor told us that he talked to the British about all of this on a recent visit to the Middle East, and that the President spoke to John Major. He urged us to participate in the elections and argued that the Mitchell Report was about dismantling the issue of arms as a pre-condition. I emphasised my need for clarity from the British. I warned of the dangers of establishing a Forum which reasserted unionism's demand for majoritarian politics. Such a development was intended to keep Dublin out of the situation; to internalise the problem and allow the British to off-load any failure on to the people in the North. Asked by Nancy Soderberg about the Mitchell Principles, I pointed out that I had already publicly said that we would approach this issue positively.

The next morning it was the early train to New York to take part in what is probably the most famous St Patrick's Day parade in the world. New York Governor George Pataki generously hosted a St Patrick's Day breakfast at the Rockefeller Centre from where I travelled to St Patrick's Cathedral for Mass. I was told it was a typically cold, sharp March day in New York. But the warmth of the tens of thousands of people crowded along the pavement made up for the nip in the weather.

At St Patrick's Cathedral Cardinal O'Connor greeted our party and everywhere there were cheers of encouragement. It was a great day. For some, it had even more profound consequences. I was later told by some of the New York cops – who I have come to know well on my many visits – that one of their number, Ed Lewis, broke ranks from the marching phalanx of New York police officers to speak to his girlfriend, Eileen Breslin. He dropped to his knee, pulled out an engagement ring and proposed. A shocked Ms Breslin broke down into tears and said yes. Richard suggested that we should send Ed to speak to John Major.

At the end of the march, we headed off for Scranton in Pennsylvania where the Friendly Sons of St Patrick packed into a hall in their hundreds for a wonderful event. The next morning, we drove back to New York to catch the flight home. We also tried to see the matinee performance of *Riverdance* at Radio City Music Hall. As luck would have it, our driver got lost coming back in from Pennsylvania and we arrived late. We were ushered in to the top balcony for a brief twenty minutes to see the closing sequences from the show. The dancers and music were brilliant. We left Radio City regretting that we had not seen the whole production. At least I was able to buy the CD on the plane home – a small consolation.

Back in Ireland, the two governments had published a consultation paper entitled "Ground Rules for Substantive All-Party Negotiations". The paper said that the agenda for the 10 June negotiations would begin with an opening plenary session, in which the participants would address the report of the international body on arms decommissioning. All participants would make clear their total and absolute commitment to the principles of democracy and non-violence set out in the Mitchell Report.

The unionist parties reacted angrily. Both Trimble and Paisley warned Major that they were not prepared to accept the format for the negotiations. Paisley claimed that it was "Nothing less than an attempt to muzzle the elected representatives of the Ulster people and find a way of delivering our province into the hands of the Dublin dictatorship." Paisley said that the Irish government had now been given the right to challenge the North's constitutional position within the United Kingdom.

Less than a week later, on 21 March, John Major published his proposals for an elective process to the Forum. He also decreed that the negotiating team for each party would be drawn from those elected to the Forum, but the Forum itself would have no power to intervene in the negotiations. The paper reaffirmed the British government's position that no invitation would be issued to Sinn Féin to select a negotiating team or to participate in the negotiations.

We had decisions to make around participation in the May election, in the Forum, the negotiations and the Mitchell Principles. Our annual Ard Fheis was upon us. Delegates from all over Ireland crammed into the Ambassador Cinema, at the top of O'Connell Street, to debate these issues. Many of the delegates made clear their preference to boycott both the elections and the Forum. They were not prepared to allow others to impose conditions or restrictions on our endeavours. After an intense debate, an emergency motion was endorsed. This mandated the Ard Chomhairle to take the necessary steps to ensure the voice of our electorate was not isolated. Two other emergency motions were passed, endorsing the party's peace strategy and committing us to continue with our efforts to reach out to the unionist and Protestant section of our people. Tom Hartley spoke about our efforts to meet with unionists. He reported that there were now four sections within the broad family of unionism who were willing to engage with us; the Churches, the business community, the community organisations and the loyalists.

The question uppermost in most people's minds was could we restore the peace process? It was my view that we could. Part of this meant having a strategic sense of what was actually going on. The British government was indeed involved in a real negotiation, but it was not with us. Their negotiation was with Dublin, the SDLP, the unionists and the USA government. That is, bigger players with – from our perspective – weaker positions than ours who the Brits believed would accept less. London's aim was to lessen our influence by doing a deal without us and to concede the minimum possible to achieve this.

However, the combined weight of the political parties in Ireland, even if exerted in a cohesive way, was probably insufficient to determine that the outcome of negotiations would be an Irish national democracy. A first step had to be getting the Irish government back to the private agreements that had created the August 1994 opportunity. We were sceptical about our ability to do this, but were morally obliged to try. Even if we were successful, the IRA might not buy into it. The experience of the last eighteen months had soured the situation badly. Achieving a restoration of the cessation was not going to be easy.

Toward the end of March, Mitchel McLaughlin and Gerry Kelly privately met the former Conservative minister Michael Mates. Interestingly, he acknowledged that unionists didn't want all-party negotiations because they believed it meant having to give things up.

Six days later, I wrote to Michael Ancram at the NIO in response to the British paper. Essentially, I told him that Sinn Féin was opposed to elections in advance of and as a pre-condition to negotiations; opposed to a unionist Forum; opposed to the exclusion of any party from the election; and opposed to the exclusion of any party with a mandate from the negotiations.

In our discussions with Irish government officials, we discovered that Dick Spring had suggested to Patrick Mayhew that George Mitchell be brought in to chair the negotiations. The British Secretary of State had dismissed this because the unionists would not accept a role for Mitchell.

However, Spring had since written to the British, again proposing George Mitchell for this job.

Out of the blue, SDLP Chief Whip Eddie McGrady announced that his party intended to stand in the elections and to participate in the Forum. This was a complete U-turn. When the UUP leader David Trimble had first proposed elections and a Forum, McGrady had slammed it, describing it as a unionist demand and an expression of unionist policy to prevent a real settlement taking place. However, following McGrady's announcement that the SDLP would take part in the elections and Forum, I convened an urgent meeting of our party leadership. On 24 April, we reluctantly announced that Sinn Féin had decided to enter the election contest. With the SDLP contesting, we had little choice – unless we were prepared to give them a free run. It was still our view that the election and the Forum had no useful role to play, but we felt that it was important to give leadership, to secure an endorsement of our peace strategy and to return a strong republican voice to prevent any attempt to return to the bad old days of unionist domination and majority rule. I made it clear that we would not be participating in the Forum.

The same day I wrote to the Revd Martin Smyth, the unionist MP for South Belfast and Grand Master of the Orange Order. I was worried that the summer marching would see a repeat of the violence of previous years. I felt that a dialogue between us could be helpful. I acknowledged in my letter to him that the Orange Order had the right to march. But Orangeism had to accept that citizens also had the right to withhold their consent to marches.

With only six weeks to go before the 10 June date for negotiations to begin, a senior party delegation met with senior Irish government officials. We told them that we were there to try, even at this late stage and despite the obvious difficulties, to produce a package which we could take to the IRA. They were unlikely, I said, to accept anything less than what was put together in 1994. Consequently, we needed to work out with the Irish government a common view on political change, demilitarisation and democratic rights. There could be no impediments to progress, and a time-frame was necessary if it wasn't to drag on indefinitely.

I put to them the widely shared view that the Clinton administration could only intervene when given a choice between an Irish position and a British one. The problem was that John Bruton often took up positions identical to the British and occasionally – from our point of view – even more British than the British! We had to use the good will internationally to help move the British and to ensure that they kept commitments made.

Of course, we needed to make every effort to get the unionists or a section of unionism on board, but they couldn't have a veto.

Making this happen over the next six weeks would not be easy. Convincing people, especially a sceptical IRA, would be difficult. I suggested that there needed to be a public dimension to this. For their part, the officials sought to assure us that the government was working with the British government to ensure that the negotiations were reasonable and not a charade. They also told us that there was no higher priority than creating the conditions in which Sinn Féin could participate in the negotiations and that, while the Irish government believed the arms issue would be addressed at the outset of discussions, it would not be a blocking mechanism or a pre-condition. This was not yet agreed upon with the British government.

They were pushing for George Mitchell to chair the talks. There was resistance from the unionists and the British side. However, the British had a problem. Senator Mitchell had produced the report of the International Body on Decommissioning which they were now using as part of the negotiations process. How could they explain to President Clinton that they didn't want someone of Senator Mitchell's obvious stature? One official suggested that we come back with an a,b,c,d of what we wanted the Irish government to do. And I thought that idea had merit. I also suggested that they should do the same thing.

Some of our discussion focused on the proposed method of agreement in the negotiations – sufficient consensus. What did this mean? Who would define it? One Irish government official argued that the one lever we and they had in this process was that nothing was agreed until everything was agreed. I asked if they had a time-frame in mind, and they responded by saying if Mitchell was in the chair there would be a limit to the amount of time he could devote to this.

The day of these discussions was the day the IRA placed its biggest ever explosive device in England under London's Hammersmith Bridge. The bomb failed to detonate.

Our round of intense discussions continued on 27 April with a meeting with the US Ambassador in Dublin Jean Kennedy Smith and, via secure phone link from the Embassy, with Tony Lake at the White House. I briefed them on our efforts to get a restoration of the cessations, and they were very positive about this.

Around this time, Taoiseach John Bruton made a speech which sought to address the concerns of nationalists living in the North. He ruled out any internal Six County settlement or the re-establishment of a unionist-dominated administration in the North. He also said that he wanted to ensure that an exclusive focus on this issue of decommissioning did not prevent parallel progress on other issues. He argued that the negotiations would be real, covering all the issues, including equality, and he raised the need for an indicative time-frame to help ensure momentum and dynamic.

This gave a spur to our private discussions with Irish government officials. The Irish government people were trying to pin the British down on how they would handle the arms issue and the question of the Mitchell Principles in the negotiations, as well as the role of George Mitchell himself. By the beginning of May, the British were amenable to George Mitchell, General de Chastelain and another as chairpersons. There was also now talk among the officials about an indicative time-frame, and they told us that the onus for confidence-building measures would not just be laid at the door of republicans. It would also involve the two governments. Our team welcomed this, but the reality was that it was all still a negotiation in progress. While the Irish government officials were placing as optimistic a spin as possible, none of it was tied down.

We believed that there would be no decommissioning of IRA weapons outside of a settlement, and that there would be no parallel or prior decommissioning. Our discussions on the weapons issue dealt with the establishment of a new commission to handle it and the remit and legislation covering it. Much time was also spent on the mechanics of the negotiations process: for example, how meetings would take place, who would meet with whom, who would chair what session, what was the function of the business committee and who would chair it, how would referendum work if there was an agreement, and much more.

Martin and I tried to persuade the Irish government officials to set out all of this in a paper. We wanted the British position tied down. Initially, we were told no. There was a worry that a paper might become public, or another party in the Irish parliament might ask about documents, forcing the Taoiseach to reveal the extent of our deliberations.

I suggested to them that even a non-paper setting down the Irish government strategy in respect of core issues and its approach to talks, including decommissioning, would be helpful. I had been amused sometime before to discover that non-papers were sometimes described as "angel" papers. That quaint and whimsical title brought a different and wry note to the boring detail and tedium of the endless paper chain that made up most of the negotiations.

On 10 May, on a secure line from the US Consulate Office in Belfast, I spoke to Tony Lake in Washington. I reflected on my most recent conversations with the Irish government and the suggestions on the table for dealing with the arms issue, including the notion of a commission. I advised him that we were trying to formulate a position which made the Mitchell Principles and Sinn Féin's attitude to them more positive. And I sounded a note of warning over an article to be published in *The Irish Times* by John Major in the following days, which was being flagged up in advance. To be useful, it needed to deal with all of the issues.

"We still have a lot of convincing to do," I told Lake. "I am encouraged by the meetings with the Irish government. Sometimes meetings can be unhinged, but these meetings have been very useful and constructive."

The pace of events and meetings, always pretty frenetic, moved up a gear. Sunday, 12 May, saw the newspapers full of speculation about an imminent IRA cessation. No evidence was offered by those who ran the stories, and I knew that this was not even on the radar screen at this point. But someone, in one or the other government, and possibly both, was trying to increase public pressure. Once again, it was said that much of the pressure was coming from the United States. Again, not true.

A second draft of the non-paper was produced. It drew on public agreements, documents, speeches, assessments of the commitment and positions of the British government, covering matters such as the agenda, how the various strands of the negotiations would work, how roadblocks in the negotiations could be avoided and the timetable for talks. There were assurances to nationalists in the North that the political process would be meaningful and that we would never again be marginalised. However, there was no sense or vision of a United Ireland.

I made it clear to the officials that I did not see the IRA agreeing to reinstate a cessation short of a recommitment by the Irish government to the position agreed by it in the 1994 discussions prior to the IRA cessation. We gave them a copy of this. Some of the Irish government officials baulked at the 1994 position, and one admitted bluntly that the objective of an "Agreed and independent Ireland", centred on the 1994 position, would not get past the government.

I gently but quite firmly told them that this was a real concern for Irish republicans. We were not interested in finding a better way of governing "Northern Ireland" in a British jurisdiction. There had to be an all-Ireland context.

Martin McGuinness, not one for mincing his words, warned the officials about the media spins coming from the governments. He said, "People are saying no to a ceasefire now and are definitely saying don't decommission anything. An accumulation of demands by whoever, the Taoiseach, John Major, the President of the United States or the Pope in Rome, won't have any effect on the IRA leadership. The only thing that will affect them is the work we are doing now and if we can put together a package."

We agreed to meet the following week.

In the meantime, Paddy Kelly, the terminally ill republican prisoner, was flown by helicopter on the Tuesday to Portlaoise prison. While this was good news for his partner Angela Rice and their child Sarah, the truth was that Paddy was coming home to die.

In an effort to try and create a more positive atmosphere, to tackle another of the pre-conditions laid down by the governments head-on, as well as signal our serious intent, I issued a statement which spelt out Sinn Féin's willingness to endorse the Mitchell Principles.

This was a major step for us, but we felt that it was a necessary initiative to reach out to unionists and others. It also meant that a potentially difficult initial discussion on the agenda for the negotiations was defused before we reached it.

Six days before the election, there was another meeting with Irish officials. We were flabbergasted when they told us that, as far as the Taoiseach was concerned, no deal had been done between the previous government and Sinn Féin in 1994. Their instructions were to make this clear to us. Whatever had been said then was of no consequence and would have no bearing on this government. Martin placed on the record our firm belief that a deal had been done with the previous government.

The officials also informed our delegation that their last meeting with the British government was difficult. They still didn't have a clear scenario with the British on the weapons issue. It was also clear that, with the elections only days away, there was no real prospect of getting the British to focus on the issues, although the officials from both governments were meeting the following week.

The status of the non-paper was changed to a speaking note, presumably a device for allowing the government deniability in the event it became public. But, in effect, it remained an outline of the Irish government's negotiating position on many key issues. We agreed to come back with a view – and amendments – of it for the next meeting.

The election was now dominating our work. For my part, my role as party leader was to be everywhere, to rally the organisation and to convince the electorate that a vote for Sinn Féin was a vote for peace, for real change and for inclusive peace talks. I travelled the length and breadth of the Six Counties. On the eve of the election, I went into the Ulster Television studios in Belfast for an unusual party political broadcast – to the USA. The thirty-minute broadcast was watched in over thirty states and in Canada. It was a unique, successful experiment in speaking to Irish America without actually travelling there.

And then it was 30 May: time to count the votes.

To the consternation of our opponents, people chose Sinn Féin in greater numbers than ever before.

We won 116,377 votes – that is, 15.5 per cent of the poll or 42 per cent of the nationalist vote. It was the highest vote we had ever achieved in this period of our history. The pundits had to go back to the 1955 Westminster election to find a better Sinn Féin result. In West Belfast, we picked up four of the five seats and confirmed our status as the largest party in the city of Belfast with over 21 per cent of the vote.

Across the North, we won fifteen seats, three times what we took in the Assembly elections fourteen years earlier. With our increased mandate, we picked up an additional two seats in the "top-up list", making a grand total of seventeen seats. The SDLP won twenty-one, the DUP twenty-four and the UUP thirty. The Alliance Party vote dropped badly and it emerged with only seven seats.

The "top-up list", providing two seats each to the ten parties with the greater share of the vote, meant that for the first time the UVF-aligned Progressive Unionist Party had two representatives and the UDA-aligned Ulster Democratic Party also got two. The three other parties to benefit from this unique electoral system were the Women's Coalition, the Labour Party and the UK Unionist Party. The leader of this latter party, Bob McCartney, was elected in North Down, giving them a grand total of three seats.

So the stage was set for the negotiations on 10 June. The people had spoken, the winners had been chosen. All it needed was for the parties to sit down in their new configurations and do the hard bit – reach an agreement.

John Major said, "Once the elections are over, the route to negotiations is clear, direct and automatic." But that was before the elections. The count was not long finished when Patrick Mayhew made it clear that no IRA cessation meant no invitation to the talks for Sinn Féin. For the

251

governments, our voters were second class – our mandate less legitimate than anyone else's. The pre-conditions on our entry to negotiations remained in place. For both governments, that meant a new IRA ceasefire. For the British, it also meant decommissioning. Our behind-the-scenes discussions had failed to breach these positions.

In the immediate aftermath of the election, our discussions intensified with the Irish government around possible positions for it and the British government. We only had days before the start of talks to construct a package which we could take to the army leadership and persuade it to reinstate its cessation. Despite some pretty brazen media stories – planted by either or both governments to exert pressure on Sinn Féin – the reality was that we were under no pressure from within our section of the community.

At the beginning of June, there were intensive talks between the two governments led by Patrick Mayhew and Dick Spring in London. John Bruton and John Major also took part in the discussions, which were reported to be in difficulties over the role to be allotted to Senator George Mitchell. The general shape of what was being agreed seemed clear enough. The talks would open on 10 June with a plenary session. Decommissioning would be considered by a sub-committee, and while it proceeded, agreement would be sought between the parties and the governments on the agenda and the procedures for the talks, including how decommissioning could be dealt with. This process – with many breaks – would last until September. Then the decommissioning obstacle would be erected again.

This led to a "senior IRA source" telling the *Irish News* and BBC that a ceasefire before 10 June was "extremely remote". The IRA source went on: "We remain ready and willing to continue with our position of enhancing the atmosphere for proper and meaningful negotiations. It would appear there is absolutely no likelihood of any substantive IRA move this side of 10 June."

Dublin officials told us that it would be for George Mitchell to call time on the decommissioning issue when all parties had shown good intent. But when we asked if the British were committed to this approach, we were told "No". There were many other issues which the officials had no answers to. At the end of a long, tiring discussion, I told the officials that I thought it unlikely that we could discuss all of this with the IRA and for that organisation to consult its volunteers and for us to get a positive response before Monday, 10 June.

The next day the process was thrown into turmoil. Political and public opinion was outraged when Garda Jerry McCabe was shot dead and a colleague seriously wounded in an armed raid in Adare in County Limerick. They had been escorting an An Post truck which was distributing around IR£100,000 in pension and social security money to post offices in West Limerick. The IRA moved quickly to deny that any of its volunteers or units were involved. But the allegations increased in ferocity. Some time later, after carrying out its own internal inquiry, an embarrassed IRA acknowledged that some of its members had indeed carried out the attack without authorisation of the Army Council. The operation had been cleared at a lower level.

Sinn Féin was the inevitable target of a political and media storm, especially in the South. I and other party colleagues faced a barrage of criticism. We repudiated the killing in the strongest possible terms, but the damage done to our efforts to restore the peace process was considerable.

The two governments, meanwhile, had sent out invitations to the other parties to participate in the negotiations. So I wrote to both Mayhew and Dick Spring complaining about this.

The day of 10 June dawned. All-party negotiations – minus Sinn Féin – were about to begin. It could have been a historic day if common sense had prevailed.

# Chapter Twenty-Four

# *"Putting It Up to a Bully"*

Sinn Féin was excluded from the talks, but we decided to go anyway. Early on 10 June our successful Forum candidates and a sizeable contingent of other elected representatives gathered at Conway Mill in West Belfast to drive in a motor convoy across the city to Stormont. Cleaky, our chief scout, preceded us by several minutes. As we left Conway Mill, our long line of cars was led by carloads of camera crews. Some were hanging out of sunroofs. One enterprising cameraman was riding pillion, wrong way round, on a motorbike.

Our convoy drove down the Falls Road, on to the west link and across the M3 bridge into the loyalist heartland of East Belfast. The mood was buoyant. We knew we would be turned away, but there's nothing quite like putting it up to a bully, and for the Sinn Féin delegation that morning, that's exactly what it felt like. We also knew our exclusion would be *the* story, and especially the international story of the day.

To make matters worse for the governments, they decided to pull the plug on John Major and John Bruton's opening speeches, which were to have been televised live. They were worried that Paisley was going to upstage them by heckling during the live transmission. They also decided to exclude the press from the plenary session, leaving the media with nothing to report except the arrival of Sinn Féin representatives.

Cleaky arrived at Stormont's main gate a few minutes before we did. He radioed back to inform us that the gates were being closed in anticipation of our arrival. The government's gameplan was to keep us at some distance from the main action at Castle Buildings. We got out of our cars and Martin McGuinness and I led the Sinn Féin delegation across to the locked barriers, adorned with a British coat of arms. I demanded entry. In response, a security man arrived with a chain and padlock to make doubly sure we couldn't get through the gate.

This was a bit daft. The two side gates, through which pedestrians could walk, were still open. The Stormont estate – which includes Parliament Buildings, Stormont Castle, Castle Buildings and other civil service buildings – is open to the public. As we stood waiting to talk to a British official, joggers and people walking their dogs passed by us and into the estate.

All of this fitted into the mood of our group. We knew we weren't going to be permitted into the talks and presumed that we would be locked out of the venue itself. But we were not even being permitted to drive into what is a public area. Someone, somewhere in the bowels of the Brits' great political machine had thought to keep us away from the sizeable international, as well as local, gathering of media. It was not a well-thought-out position. It underestimated Richard's ability to use a telephone – always a mistake.

Richard is famous for his attachment to his phone. He used it to alert some of his press contacts who were standing around outside the talks venue. Meanwhile, Cleaky conducted a negotiation of sorts with one of the officials at the gates while our delegation massed in front of them. As has happened many times in this process, it was a bit like *Monty Python's Flying Circus*. Cleaky would leave our group, walk through the side gate to the other side of the barred gates and talk to the official. He would then walk back out again and consult with us. After much of this, it transpired that we would be allowed to walk to the talks building.

"No," we said. "We want to drive up the main avenue."

By now, the media had arrived in hordes. The street theatre at the gate was acted out in the full view of television cameras. An NIO official had also arrived. He was obviously more PR sensitive and conscious of the impact of images of the Sinn Féin grouping being held at the barred gate. Martin McGuinness held out his hand to the unfortunate official, an adviser to Patrick Mayhew, who seemed relieved not to have to deal with Cleaky. His relief was short-lived.

"I come in peace bearing the hand of friendship and representing over 116,000 voters," Martin told him. The official, with no mandate, tried to persuade us that only six of the Sinn Féin representatives elected to the Forum would be allowed through, and pointed to the side gate.

Martin replied, "We are not second-class citizens, and will go through the front gate."

"Right on!" Cleaky agreed.

So it went on for another thirty minutes. Then suddenly the RUC opened the gates and our convoy recommenced its interrupted journey up the Prince of Wales Avenue to the negotiations building. By this time, the photographers had their front page photos.

We were blocked again when we arrived at the talks venue at Castle Buildings. The gates were not to be unlocked this time. As our group and the large crowd of media people pressed against the wire fence, I bantered with Gerry Kelly – who has a deserved reputation as a jail-breaker – that it was the first time he had ever tried to break into a British compound.

A second, rather sheepish NIO official was dispatched to talk to us from his side of the wire. As he told us we couldn't get into the talks, his every word was recorded, while I defended Sinn Féin's mandate and our right to be part of a peace process.

It would have been impossible for this to happen in South Africa, commented one Reuters correspondent. "Could you picture peace delegates there being kept out. The ANC took part without a ceasefire being in place. The British could have started all this last year. What a bloody farce."

The two governments then offered to give us their position formally. The first ever Sinn Féin delegation to enter Castle Buildings – Martin, Siobhán and Richard – walked through the gates into the talks building. There they were told by an Irish government and a British government official that we were barred.

Meanwhile outside, the rest of us distributed copies of a text of a speech I would have given had we been allowed entry. Our spokespersons were busy for an hour or so moving from one camera crew to the next explaining our position to a range of media outlets.

The talks themselves weren't any great shakes, anyway. The unionists persisted with their reluctance to accept George Mitchell as the chairperson. The ever-patient and unfortunate senator spent two days closeted in a side room while "Groundhog Day" was played out in the main talks room.

David Trimble's deputy leader John Taylor's view was that giving George Mitchell the job of chairing these talks was "the equivalent of an American Serb presiding over talks on the future of Croatia . . . It is a non-runner." Ian Paisley, as usual, went further. He said Mitchell would be "some sort of Pope sitting over all the talks".

They were determined to prevent the appointment of someone perceived as being in any way outside their influence. Their concern was not that Mitchell was too close to Irish America or the Vatican. They were against a US involvement, particularly since the change of policy initiated by Clinton. In fact, Mitchell had no record of involvement in Irish affairs and no history of involvement in Irish America.

His background was in liberal Democratic politics and the law. He was a former Senate majority leader and brought a huge amount of experience as a facilitator to Ireland. He needed all of it, and lots of patience as well. When he eventually took his seat as chair of the talks in the early hours of 21 June, Paisley's DUP and the smaller UKUP protested.

It is said that the two parties had planned to occupy Mitchell's seat but were frustrated in their efforts by a British official who was given the onerous task of sitting in it until Mitchell was appointed. In any case, they walked out in high dudgeon. Later they walked back in again.

The two governments and the nine participating parties then agreed to the Mitchell Principles of non-violence and democracy. The talks were adjourned until the following Monday.

On Friday, the Forum met for the first time in Belfast. We boycotted the meeting as we had promised during the elections. The SDLP and Sinn Féin had already agreed in the Hume/Adams talks that an internal settlement was not a solution. It would have been illogical to participate in what was clearly an internal or Six County forum. The SDLP attended, but to their chagrin they sheepishly withdrew the following month, vindicating our position.

In the meantime our behind-the-scenes discussions with the Irish government officials continued. We tried to find a nationalist consensus position around which a co-ordinated strategic approach by the Irish side could be developed. Reaching a nationalist consensus with a government which barely acknowledged nationalism was no easy task. There were difficulties also for Dublin in the way London was conducting the negotiations. But in fairness to the Irish civil servants, they persisted. So did we. The day after negotiations opened in Belfast, they broadly accepted changes we proposed to the positions we were both working on. There remained areas of disagreement, and we continued to discuss these.

Then the IRA bombed Manchester city centre, causing a huge explosion outside the £200 million Arndale Centre. Initial damage to it and to surrounding businesses was estimated at around £300 million. Although warnings of almost two hours were given, the blast injured scores of civilians. These events sent shock waves through the Irish government system. The talk was of Dublin cutting off all contact with us. Bruton, we were told, thought it was over, that there was no hope of an

IRA cessation, and that the IRA never had any intention of calling one. He was already under pressure from former PD leader Des O'Malley over the killing of Garda McCabe to cut contact and go on without Sinn Féin. Unionists were demanding internment. Others were seeking a return to the old policies of condemnation and the marginalisation of republicans.

The prevailing mood among nationalists was for no doors to be closed. Inevitably, the media and public political pressure was on Sinn Féin to get the IRA to call another cessation. Despite being fully briefed on our engagement with the IRA leadership, John Bruton raised the temperature by demanding to know whether I had yet gone to the IRA to ask for a ceasefire. If not, why not? And did Sinn Féin support the armed struggle of the IRA?

I stated publicly that the Taoiseach and his department were fully aware of our efforts to restore the peace process and to achieve an end to all armed actions. More importantly in view of Bruton's challenge, I also revealed that the government knew that I had been in regular contact with the IRA leadership in an effort to restore the peace process.

Sinn Féin was not the IRA. We were not involved in armed struggle, nor did we advocate it. On the contrary, we were absolutely committed to democratic, peaceful methods of resolving political problems. I acknowledged the difficulties – especially for the Irish government – caused by the killing of Garda Jerry McCabe and the Manchester bomb. I made it equally clear that we were not walking away from our efforts, and I restated my confidence in our ability to achieve what previous generations had failed to win: a permanent peace.

Meanwhile, unionists continued to attack the ground rules and procedures for running the talks. Their objective was to reduce the power and authority of George Mitchell. Against this background, there was an IRA mortar attack on a British army base at Osnabrück in Germany.

John Hume and I decided to undertake a private initiative. He agreed to carry a letter from me to John Major. This letter, written on 26 June, was an attempt to persuade Major that, despite the difficulties, I believed we could still devise a way out of the impasse. I acknowledged that recent IRA attacks created grave difficulties for him. I sought to persuade him that the best way of his government convincing republicans of its sincerity was through direct dialogue; with political will, we could find an agreed means of doing this.

On 2 July, John gave Major my letter. The British Prime Minister replied to John six days later. He rejected both ministerial dialogue and meetings with officials. He did so in a qualified way, but the message was clear. He restated the British government's pre-condition of an unequivocal restoration of the IRA ceasefire and for decommissioning to take place during the negotiations.

I wrote to John Hume on the back of Major's response. I told John that, even if Major wanted to move in a positive way to restore the process, the situation arising from the Orange Order's protests now dominating the situation gave him little room to manoeuvre. I also said that John and I should get together as soon as possible to figure out the next step.

This was played out against the background of increasing tension around the Orange marching season. As ever, the main focus of confrontation was the lower Ormeau Road in South Belfast and the Garvaghy Road in Portadown. The latter had been the scene of Paisley and Trimble's now infamous jig the previous year.

This year, RUC Chief Constable Hugh Annesley announced that he was banning the 7 July Orange march down the Garvaghy Road. The Orangemen could return from Drumcree Church by the same route they had taken to get there. The reaction of unionists was ferocious. Another siege of Garvaghy Road began, with unionist leaders calling on supporters to join the thousands now camped at Drumcree Church. The situation was becoming increasingly fraught. District Orange Master Harold Gracey described Drumcree as Ulster's Alamo. Speaking outside the Church of Ireland at Drumcree he declared, "We will not be giving in to Dick Spring, John Bruton, Gerry Adams, Martin McGuinness, or any other spokesperson for Jesuit priests." Trimble described the decision to reroute the Orangemen as an affront to religious and civil liberties. He also warned that if the Orange march did not go ahead then the loyalist ceasefire might not hold.

That night, a Catholic taxi driver from Lurgan, Michael McGoldrick, was shot dead a few miles from Drumcree. It was widely believed that the killing had been planned by Billy Wright – believed to have been involved in the killing of over a score of Catholics and who later broke from the UVF and formed the Loyalist Volunteer Force. Wright, whose nickname in the media was "King Rat", held several meetings with the Orange Order in Portadown. He also held at least one meeting with David Trimble. Across the North, unionist paramilitaries began blocking roads, closing rail lines, sealing off towns and villages, attacking Catholic houses, businesses, schools and churches. The North's two main airports were blockaded and Larne, the main port, was closed. More than thirty families were forced from their homes in North Belfast, Lisburn and Ballymena. Two Catholic schools were substantially damaged in firebomb attacks.

And then on 11 July, Annesley changed his mind and agreed to the Orange march. Two thousand RUC officers and one thousand British soldiers attacked several hundred men, women and children on the Garvaghy Road and forced a march of a thousand Orangemen through the area. There was pandemonium. Plastic bullets were fired. The anger within nationalist areas raged across the North. That night, the RUC attacked young people in Derry leaving pubs and clubs. Within several hours, 900 plastic bullets were fired.

The following night, thousands more plastic bullets were fired in Derry as running battles were fought in the streets. One young man was killed when a British armoured vehicle drove over him. This was in marked contrast to the attitude to unionists and loyalist rioters in the preceding week of unionist violence and intimidation.

On the same night that the RUC turned on Garvaghy Road residents, convoys of battleship-grey RUC Land-Rovers sealed off streets on the lower Ormeau Road. The area was effectively put under a state of martial law. Anyone wishing to enter the streets had to prove they lived there, and RUC officers checked people's identities against their intelligence files. It was obvious that the RUC was planning to force an Orange march through their area the following day.

I was asked, as were other nationalist politicians, to come to the area and monitor events. I telephoned the RUC at Donegall Pass barracks to inform them of my plans to travel into the area. I asked to speak to a senior officer, but the constable who answered the phone couldn't find one. He suggested I go to the roadblock on the lower Ormeau Road and speak to the senior officer there.

Richard, Big Eamon and Paul Hamilton accompanied me. We stopped briefly at Cromac Street, a short distance from the lower Ormeau, where several hundred nationalist residents from the Market area were holding a protest against the curfew. I asked them to disperse peacefully, which they did.

At the roadblock, we left our car and I spoke to an RUC sergeant who advised me that the media, public representatives and residents were permitted access. As I was about to proceed through the block, an RUC inspector arrived. He stopped me and told me I could go no further. I was immediately blocked in by a few burly, heavily armed RUC men. I asked the inspector for his name. He refused to give it. I explained why I was there and pointed out that other elected representatives were allowed in. He told me again that I was not to move, he was preventing me from moving under common law. I asked what statute. He refused to say, and then he refused to speak to me.

By this time, I was squeezed between several armoured vehicles and surrounded by a scrum of RUC men. They stood inches from me, staring into my face. Indeed, at one point a sergeant had to order them to move back. Then it started to rain. Another inspector arrived. He refused to speak to me also. I asked again to be allowed to proceed. No, I was told. The stand-off continued. So did the rain. Then, to our surprise, a voice pealed out theatrically from above us.

"What is this we have here, Mr Adams? An evening out with the constables? How very jolly."

Our tightly pressed group, RUC officers and Shinners alike, craned around and looked up in amazement.

"Aha," the voice proclaimed, "I see I have your attention. This is a sorry state of affairs. Unhand that constable, Mr Adams. You know you should not be consorting with the enemy like that. Back off, sir. Down, boy."

The voice belonged to a passing and very unsober middle-aged man. He was addressing us from the top of an armoured vehicle. As he continued his commentary, our group, captives and peelers, united in laughter. Behind the good-natured drunk, the Belfast skyline was illuminated by the Orange bonfires, and the ratatatat of Lambeg drums made its mark in the night air.

Richard phoned some contacts in the media as well as the office of LORAG (Lower Ormeau Residents Action Group) to tell them what was happening and where we were being held. Subsequently, another line of RUC was established a short distance up the road to stop residents coming down to us. It wasn't long before TV cameras, journalists and photographers turned up to record this surreal scene: the armed ranks of the RUC surrounding me, and our small group, the rain, the drunk sitting on top of an armoured vehicle singing rebel songs, the sound of the Lambegs and the occasional bangs and flashes of fireworks from the nearby loyalist Donegall Pass area. It certainly ranks as one of the most bizarre press conferences I ever attended.

Four hours later, at around 1 o'clock in the morning, I was released. We made our way up the road to the office of LORAG. We stayed the night. Early the next morning, hemmed in by hundreds of RUC, we watched as an Orange parade walked through a Catholic area which resented and

261

objected to its presence. I was nose to nose with a line of RUC officers. Other observers were allowed through to the pavement, but a senior RUC officer ordered his men to keep me behind the line. He brought forward one guy with a plastic bullet gun to keep me in my place. I spent a long time pretending I was as hard as nails as I stared into the muzzle of the deadly weapon while its owner encouraged me to give him a chance to use it.

The parade passed without incident. My overwhelming feeling was of great sadness as I watched the bowler-hatted, besuited and besashed brethren make their way past us.

Later, when the area was clear of the military and RUC presence, we bade farewell to our brave and beleagured friends in the lower Ormeau. Getting back to West Belfast was a problem, but eventually – by dodging Orange parades and driving a roundabout route through an otherwise deserted city centre – we made our way back to the Falls.

A week later, I was in Dublin with a Sinn Féin delegation meeting with Irish government officials. Our objective was to focus the government on the dangers of more street violence in August during planned marches in Derry and along the lower Ormeau Road, as well as on the peace process itself. We saw the crisis around the Orange marches as an opportunity to find an overall resolution to the small number of contentious parades.

No matter how difficult things became, farce was rarely far away. Lots of the contact between us and others was discreet. Once during a particularly fraught period, Martin McGuinness and Rita O'Hare were slipping into Iveagh House, the Department of Foreign Affairs headquarters at St Stephen's Green in Dublin. A Dublin city tour bus was passing at the same time. As our two intrepid negotiators entered the building the tour guide's voice boomed: "And there we have the Sinn Féin leader Martin McGuinness going into Iveagh House." Martin and Rita spun round in surprise to be caught in the flashes of numerous tourist cameras.

As for the negotiations, I told the officials that nationalists generally had no confidence in the talks. One senior Irish government official said that the government was pushing the British to talk to Sinn Féin at official level and to publicise this. I surprised the officials by telling them that if bilateral meetings between the Brits and Sinn Féin was the difference between moving the British government and getting the right conditions for all-party negotiations then there need be no bilaterals.

The officials acknowledged what we already knew: the Stormont negotiations had made no real progress. It was widely accepted that if the talks recessed during August only to come back to more arguments over procedural matters, public confidence would evaporate. The imminent possibility of a Westminster general election was now hanging over all our efforts, having a detrimental effect on the British government's approach.

The priority was to sort out the marches. The difficulties this involved were brought into sharp relief by Patrick Mayhew, who made some public comments in which he refused to rule out forcing another march down the Garvaghy Road.

Despite this, I wrote to Revd Martin Smyth, Grand Master of the Orange Order, to Alistair Simpson of the Apprentice Boys of Derry, and to Jim Molyneaux, former leader of the UUP but still in charge of the other loyal order, the Loyal Black Preceptory. I acknowledged the right of the loyal orders to march, but I urged them to engage in dialogue with residents of Catholic areas they wanted to walk through as a way of finding an accommodation. I told the three leaders of Orangeism that I would be happy to meet with them to discuss these matters. The only one to reply was Martin Smyth. He said no.

As we reached the end of July, the two governments and the parties in Castle Buildings formally agreed a compromise document on the rules of procedure governing the talks but failed to reach agreement on the agenda for talks recommencing in September. The unionists were insisting that decommissioning be top of the agenda. The death of George Mitchell's brother, Robbie, meant the senator had to travel to the US for the funeral.

It had been a bad July – one of the worst I could remember. When it was over, David Trimble and Ian Paisley and the Unionist parties – who had brazenly flouted the Mitchell Principles – were welcomed back into the talks as if nothing had happened.

For nationalists, their worst fears had been realised by the capitulation of the British government to the campaign of mass intimidation, murder, violence and threats of violence orchestrated by unionist political and paramilitary leaders. I appealed, especially to nationalist young people, not to get drawn into confrontation with the British army and RUC or sectarian conflict with the unionists. I also welcomed John Bruton's public criticism of the British government's collapse in the face of unionist intransigence. The Taoiseach's remarks were entirely valid, but the British government probably didn't take them too seriously. It knew it could depend on the Irish government to stick with the exclusion of Sinn Féin from the talks.

August, which threatened a repeat of the street violence of July, passed relatively peacefully. That was in the nature of this place. Sometimes when mayhem threatened, it was all sweetness and light. Other times, when calm was expected, were overthrown by madness. Most of the Orange marches were peaceful as a result of either locally based deals or imposed rerouting of marches by the RUC. One of the features of August was Féile an Phobail, which had been established as a consequence of the demonisation of republican West Belfast following the killings in Gibraltar and the funerals afterwards. This community response, in the form of a people's festival of music, song, poetry, drama and sport, had become an annual expression of solidarity and creativity, one of the most important aspects of community life I have been involved in.

There was still violence, of course. A young Catholic man was stabbed to death in North Belfast. It also emerged that the British intelligence agent Brian Nelson had been released from prison six months earlier. The antipathy of the British system towards republican prisoners was again evident in the treatment of Ella O'Dwyer. She was in the twelfth year of a discretionary life sentence. Her father was critically ill, but despite repeated and urgent requests, she was refused compassionate parole. On the other hand, Torrens Knight, who was serving twelve life sentences for his part in the sectarian murders of twelve people in Greysteel and Castlerock, was quite properly released twice to visit his sick grandmother. When she died, he was released to attend her funeral.

A few days later John Major wrote again to John Hume, who had been in regular contact with him. In his letter, Major outlined what he said was Sinn Féin's position as presented by John Hume. It was not our position. Maybe Major misunderstood John, or maybe he didn't *want* to understand him. I urged John to write to Major and correct this. I also felt it was necessary for me to present Major with a point-by-point position.

But August also saw the core group within Sinn Féin complete a formula of words – including commitments, for the two governments – which we felt could significantly advance the efforts to restore the peace process. We were not going to make it easy for either London or Dublin to dodge their responsibilities.

# Chapter Twenty-Five

# *Talks at Last*

The words presented by us were in the form of a draft statement by the two governments. On 5 September, I told Irish government officials I thought we could secure a renewed IRA cessation if the two governments signed on to these very detailed draft words. Among other matters, they committed the governments to an "agreed time-frame for the conduct of the negotiations" and went on to tackle the issues of decommissioning and confidence-building measures.

The draft statement was based on inclusivity, an end to pre-conditions and equality for all parties. The negotiations would address all issues, including the international body's proposals on decommissioning.

The most senior Irish government official we were talking to thought it was "90 per cent doable", but that the British would baulk at some things. The White House was briefed on our endeavours. We encouraged Dublin to seek active support from the administration there while we commenced a series of intensive meetings with Irish government people to tease out the areas of difficulty.

As this initiative was being processed, the Castle Buildings talks recommenced on 9 September, immediately running into another crisis. The DUP brought forward a motion calling for the expulsion of the two parties representing the unionist paramilitaries – the PUP and the UDP – on the basis that they had breached the Mitchell Principles. The Combined Loyalist Military Command, the umbrella group for the unionist paramilitaries, had issued a death threat against Billy Wright as a result of an internal loyalist feud. Wright was opposed to the peace process and to the continued ceasefire by the unionist paramilitaries.

Given that Revd Willie McCrea of the DUP had shared a platform four days earlier with Billy Wright, it smacked of the worst hypocrisy. One of the smaller unionist parties, the Alliance Party, made similar charges against the DUP, the UUP, the PUP and UDP over the events of the summer. It was getting messy. But Senator Mitchell structured the debate, set time limits on it – to frustrate any efforts to spin this crisis out – and then passed it back to the two governments for deliberations. Not surprisingly, the governments refused to expel anyone.

Of greater concern for me were remarks by John Bruton in Washington, in which he gave an upbeat assessment of the possibility of an IRA cessation. I can only assume he made these remarks in the context of our confidential efforts. The result was enormous speculation – much of it mischievous and damaging – making my job much more difficult.

The following weeks were filled with private meetings, telephone calls and faxes as we tried to make a go of this latest initiative and, in particular, to get John Major to engage in good faith. Interestingly, it was one senior Irish government official who best summed up the British government's approach when he said, "There is no way that this British government is ever going to move other than crab-like."

As ever, events on the ground complicated our endeavours. Towards the end of September, British police stormed a house in London, killing an unarmed IRA volunteer, Diarmuid O'Neill. Others were arrested in separate raids, and in North London explosives and weapons were found. In North Antrim, the UVF and DUP were involved in orchestrating the blockade of Masses in Catholic Churches in Bushmills, Dervoch and Ballymena, and the intimidation of thousands of Catholics mostly in North and East Antrim.

Following talks with David Trimble, the two governments produced a joint paper on decommissioning. I was told by Irish government officials that David Trimble wanted to do business, but needed cover on the decommissioning issue. They had shown him draft legislation prepared for an International Commission on Decommissioning. Trimble needed more. He wanted a verification committee. The Irish government had made it clear to Trimble that this would be a voluntary process. More discussions were planned and the officials were hopeful.

When the two governments eventually produced this paper, the unionists rejected it. John Major responded to our initiative in a letter to John Hume on 27 September, rejecting any notion of a time-frame for the negotiations and questioning Sinn Féin's commitment to the peace process. Despite this rebuff, we continued to talk to Irish government officials in an effort to secure an agreed text. Pat Doherty stood in for me at this point because I was in the process of promoting a book, *Before the*

*Dawn*, and understandably my publisher, Steve MacDonogh, wanted it to get the best send-off possible. His schedule included launches in Belfast, Dublin and London, as well as a host of radio, television and media interviews. At one signing in Waterstones in Dublin I arrived just before 1.30 in the afternoon to find several hundred people queueing. The signing was due to last 1–2 hours, but people kept turning up so that I finished eventually at 9 that night.

In early October, Richard and I travelled to Frankfurt to the International Book Fair. It was an amazing place with thousands of publishing houses filling huge halls with all sorts of books. As we were unpacking bags in our hotel room in Frankfurt, we got a telephone call telling us that our friend and colleague, Councillor Pat "Beag" McGeown, had died. Pat had spent nine years in prison. I first met him in the cages of Long Kesh, and then after a failed escape attempt he was moved to the H-Blocks. Pat was on hunger strike for forty-seven days in 1981. When he lapsed into coma and started having severe convulsions, his wife, Pauline, asked the doctors to intervene. The damage done to Pat's heart then was grave. Now, fifteen years later, it had finally given out. Two days later, Richard and I flew back to Ireland for more book signings. A week later, we travelled to Paris and Amsterdam. It was a hectic time sprinkled with numerous phone calls with Pat Doherty and other comrades involved in the secret negotiations.

During one meeting, Pat was advised by a senior Irish government official that the possibility of the British moving was not high due to Major's weak position in Westminster. The Brits were intent on keeping Sinn Féin out of the talks and were trying to move on without us. This peace-making business was not for the faint-hearted.

That same day I sent a letter to John Hume to pass on to Downing Street. I consciously described Major's response – but in particular his draft words – as inadequate, rather than a negative response. I then set out in a memo only the most essential amendments, in the hope that we could overcome the differences between us. Ten days later, the IRA – having so far restricted its actions to attacks in Britain itself – now struck for the first time since the ending of its cessation at a British military target in Ireland. It was all the more devastating because it was the British army's military headquarters at Thiepval Barracks at Lisburn. Lisburn HQ was the nerve centre of the British military presence in Ireland. In addition to several army regiments, the base also housed special military intelligence units, which directed agents and informers – mainly working within loyalist death squads.

Twenty British soldiers and a number of civilians working at the base were injured. One British soldier, Warrant Officer James Bradwell, died. John Major in his response to these events departed from his prepared script at his party conference in Bournemouth in England to launch a personal attack on me. Major said that Warrant Officer Bradwell had been murdered in cold blood: "I sent him there, Mr Adams, so spare me any crocodile tears. Don't tell me that this has nothing to do with you. I don't believe you, Mr Adams, I don't believe you!"

Behind the rhetoric, indirect negotiations over a possible formulation of words and commitments continued at a painful pace. Drafts were being exchanged, and the tedious chore of parsing and amending them took a lot of our time. The devil was in the detail; our experience with the British showed that their interpretation of word formulae in agreements tended towards the minimal rather than the generous side. There was a consensus view on the Sinn Féin side that the British would drive a coach and four through any gap provided in any text. They loved ambiguous texts which left them wriggle room. We wanted direct, non-complicated, tied-down commitments.

There was no commitment or agreement between the two governments on a time-frame. The British seemed to oppose the Irish language in a completely irrational way. They removed the issue of Irish from the draft we gave them. Their wording on policing was also so non-committal as to make it pointless. Subsequent drafts from Downing Street served only to make matters worse, not better. The pre-conditions became harder and more difficult to deal with – especially the setting of an unspecified period of time before Sinn Féin could enter negotiations, even if the IRA were on cessation. The Dublin officials gave their view that it was all still open and up for consideration, but they warned that the talk now was of a British general election in February. We persevered.

However, by now there was increasing public speculation around what some in the media called Hume/Adams Mark II. On 21 November, Major met David Trimble, Ken Maginnis and Patrick Mayhew in his rooms at Westminster. Afterwards, Trimble was confident that there would be no forward movement from Major. He told a British Sunday newspaper that he believed Major was going to sign off on his exchanges with John Hume and that he would be doing so by sending him a restatement of policy. That weekend John Hume received a letter from Major, which set out the British government's position as defined by them in early November. One week after his meeting with Trimble and Maginnis, Major publicly responded to the behind-the-scenes efforts in a reply to a planted parliamentary question. He set out his position on the basis that it was a response to John Hume and others about the possibility of a new IRA ceasefire. In other words, it was London's response to our work. Dublin was furious. Major called for the unequivocal restoration of the ceasefire and set down an unspecified period of time in order that he could make a credible judgment that it was lasting. He also published the text of the letter he had sent the previous week to John Hume.

A few hours later, Rita O'Hare and I met with the group of senior Irish government officials who had represented the government throughout this period. They arrived late. We were told that Major had phoned the Taoiseach around noon that day to tell him he was publicising his draft of the position of the two governments. Bruton strongly objected and said that the governments should work together. Major refused. He rebuffed the Taoiseach after what was described as tough talking. Bruton put to Major an alternative scheme in which the talks in Castle Buildings would break for Christmas, if possible an IRA cessation would be achieved and announced, Sinn Féin would then sign up to the Mitchell Principles and we would then go straight into the talks when they recommenced. Major said he had gone as far as he could.

I bluntly told the officials that Major had consciously broken confidence on a largely private effort to get the peace process back on track and create real talks with real potential. He had chosen to tell the unionists. He had then publicly rejected all we had been working to achieve. What Major had now put out in the public domain was a process that effectively ruled out the swift entry of Sinn Féin into all-party talks after a new cessation. The British position amounted to a new obstacle course without a time limit. There would be unlimited scope for more stalling and prevarication on the part of the unionists and the British government – even worse than the shenanigans which followed the first ceasefire.

We had to pick ourselves up and go back at it. But that, as ever, wasn't being made easy by events on the streets. Five hundred reactionaries tried to prevent Catholics going to Mass at Harryville in County Antrim. They hijacked and burned vehicles and dragged people from their cars, then assaulted them. The blockade of Harryville chapel continued for over a year. There were other sectarian attacks against Catholic property in Belfast. The RUC also stepped up its actions against nationalists. In a concentrated series of raids throughout West Belfast, over a dozen homes were raided by squads of RUC officers who used sledgehammers and crowbars to rip up floors and drive holes through walls and ceilings. Furniture, chairs, TV units were all destroyed as some of the houses were made uninhabitable. IRA operations against the British forces also continued with mortar and gun attacks.

Then a bizarre crisis emerged in the talks at Stormont. Towards the end of November, members of the UKUP and the DUP started asking Senator Mitchell had he or any of his staff been in touch with Sinn Féin? At one point during a debate in the Forum, Ian Paisley said, "I want to go further and put on record in this House that I believe certain people in Mr Mitchell's office are talking with the IRA."

We figured that members of the British intelligence establishment were winding the unionists up about something – but what? We discovered what it was all about when the London-based *Daily Mail* and the Dublin-based *Sunday World* produced headline stories alleging that George Mitchell's chief aide Martha Pope was having an affair with Gerry Kelly!

British dirty tricks were at work again. The story was clearly intended to damage the process and undermine George Mitchell's integrity as chair of the talks. The two newspapers carried reports by anonymous "security sources" claiming detailed knowledge of weekend meetings between Kelly and Pope. They even claimed that Gerry – who has a deserved reputation as a poet – wrote romantic poetry for Martha Pope! The truth was that Martha Pope had never met Gerry Kelly. She quickly moved to take legal action against the newspapers involved. And although both papers printed retractions and apologies a week later – although not with the same prominence used in running the story – a lot of damage had been done. For many unionists, their confidence in Senator Mitchell and his staff – never high – now reached a new low. Senator Mitchell tried to ascertain from Patrick Mayhew if there was indeed any intelligence report, only to be told that the British government did not comment on matters of intelligence. Mayhew wouldn't even confirm to Mitchell if such a report existed.

The same week Bruton and Major met in Downing Street for a summit. According to Irish government officials, Bruton had argued strongly for a date from the British government for Sinn Féin's entry into negotiations in the event of a cessation. Major wouldn't budge.

I was told that President Clinton was equally unhappy with Major's stance. According to one official, Major was acting unilaterally, based on ensuring his own survival.

In order to circumvent this, we suggested that the Irish consular services lobby all the parties in Britain on the admission of Sinn Féin to all-party talks after the upcoming British general election. This was, we thought, one way of opening up a dialogue with Tony Blair and the Labour leadership.

Increased IRA activity, and the fact that there had been no substantive progress in achieving an IRA cessation, led John Bruton to take an increasingly belligerent stance toward Sinn Féin privately and publicly. The British especially were pushing the line that Sinn Féin was not serious and that the IRA had never any intention of renewing its cessation. Bruton, who on occasion had expressed the same opinion, was susceptible to this argument and the pressure from London that normally accompanied it.

In a telephone call, one Irish government official told Rita on 6 January that there was now a strict "no contact edict" in place between Sinn Féin and the government. A few days later when Rita turned up at his door, she was told that he had been instructed not to see her. Bruton, it appeared, had formally decided to close down contact, and we were told that officially in a letter on 10 January. The letter said that the Irish government was unable to agree to a further meeting between Sinn Féin and officials unless we could give assurances on an imminent IRA ceasefire. In light of Major's rigid position, this was clearly beyond our ability. The government also poured cold water on the notion of opening discussions with opposition parties in Britain.

I met John Hume and provided him with amendments to the 10 October position we had given to Major. With colleagues, I had reworked that position so that if the British government was interested in real negotiations, this document could yet become the vehicle to do so.

I stressed to John that this was a without-prejudice attempt to break the stalemate London had created. In other words, the 10 October position was unaffected by this exploration. These suggested amendments had no status. Only when we were assured that the British government was willing to move into a credible talks process would I have any hope of persuading people to look positively at them.

I made it clear to John that the British government would also need to outline, clearly and in detail, the substance of the programmatic approach they intended to take. John and I also discussed other ways of keeping this effort alive and of trying to engage with Major. We decided to send a list of questions to the British. To be workable, this initiative would also require a negotiation with the British over the answers to the questions. In this way we could still deal with word formulas and substance, but using a

271

different method than we had been trying for six months now. I suggested to John that he seek to obtain from the British, without prejudice, the "possible answers" to our "possible questions".

The five questions we eventually settled on covered the British government's attitude to inclusive and comprehensive negotiations; the implications of this position for Sinn Féin's entry into talks; what assurances could London give on pre-conditions; what assurances could it give that unionists wouldn't be allowed to thwart progress; and how would the British government deal with the issue of confidence-building measures in the event of a ceasefire?

The next weeks saw John and I work on draft responses to the questions. We drew heavily on the 10 October position to Major. Towards the end of January these were faxed to the British. Around the same time, I wrote directly to Major pointing out the hypocrisy of the British position in refusing to exclude the unionist paramilitary representatives from the talks in light of obvious breaches in their conditional ceasefire during the violence of the summer. I wasn't arguing that they be excluded, but that Sinn Féin – with our substantial mandate – should be included.

The ironic part of all of this, and I suppose a measure of our strong personal relationship, was that publicly John Hume's and my political parties were competing in the forthcoming general and local government elections. The battle opened early in January with an article in a Sunday newspaper in which John linked any possible electoral pact with Sinn Féin in the Westminster election to the need for us to end our abstentionist policy toward the Westminster parliament and the announcement of an IRA ceasefire. The SDLP seemed to think that their attendance at Westminster was a plus in any election battle with us, and they would push it heavily in their canvasses on the doorsteps and their soundbites to the media.

The only problem for them was they were almost an abstentionist party themselves. That certainly was the de facto outcome of the dismal record of attendance for their four sitting MPs. Out of 659 members, the four SDLP members ranked bottom in terms of attendance. Some had an attendance record of only 4 per cent – hardly a great advertisement for the benefits of attending the British parliament! We won this debate by publicising their attendance record.

We also proposed that an electoral pact between our two parties could maximise the nationalist vote and allow Sinn Féin and the SDLP together to take up to 8 out of the 18 seats allotted to the North in the British parliament. We had argued for this for many years. The problem was that since its creation in 1970, the SDLP was never prepared to countenance any other nationalist party sharing its position. It would split the nationalist vote and see unionists elected rather than tolerate any political alternative to its political hegemony.

There was an equally fierce battle going on within unionism, primarily between the UUP and DUP, and with the smaller parties, like the Alliance party and McCartney's UKUP, or the loyalist parties, all vying for slices of the unionist cake.

On 11 February, Amnesty International issued only its second ever "urgent action appeal" in respect to the Irish situation. It was made in respect of Róisín McAliskey, the twenty-five-year-old daughter of former MP and political activist Bernadette Devlin McAliskey. Róisín had been arrested in November 1996 and was being held in appalling conditions in Holloway prison in London. The German government was seeking her extradition in connection with the bombing of the British army base at Osnabrück. Amnesty called on its entire membership to lobby in support of Róisín.

According to the International Secretariat of Amnesty, Róisín, who was entering the sixth month of her pregnancy, was strip-searched twice a day, morning and evening, as well as before and after visits, even though she had "closed" visits – meaning that there was no possible physical contact between her and her visitor. She was also refused access to the pregnancy unit in the jail. Her case had become something of a *cause célèbre*, and there were weekly, sometimes daily, protests in Ireland, Britain and the United States demanding her release.

On 14 February, the British government sent six questions to John Hume to be passed to me. Downing Street had not yet answered our questions, but someone within the British system had clearly decided to apply the old maxim that attack is the best form of defence. So, while we got no answers, even this presented an opportunity to tease out the British position.

I replied six days later, three days after John Holmes, Major's private secretary, had told me in a letter – released to the media – that before Sinn Féin could enter negotiations, the IRA must declare an unequivocal restoration of the ceasefire. I used my response to set out again the areas which we and the British government needed to focus on and resolve: the removal of pre-conditions; the need for a time-frame for the talks; the timing of Sinn Féin's entry into the talks; and confidence-building measures.

Meanwhile, like our process, the talks at Castle Buildings were just limping along. With two elections pending, there was little prospect of getting the participants to focus. So on 5 March the talks were put into cold storage until 3 June. There was widespread pessimism, and few thought that the deeply flawed process could survive for long.

Sinn Féin and the SDLP were by now locked into a bitter electoral contest. We eventually ended up standing in seventeen out of the eighteen constituencies. It was a crucial election and, while I was hopeful of retaking West Belfast, nothing could be taken for granted. After long and very serious consideration, we stood Martin McGuinness in Mid-Ulster against the DUP's Willie McCrea, and Pat Doherty carried the flag for Sinn Féin in West Tyrone. Although the SDLP had ruled out an electoral pact between us, we continued to press the matter. A strong nationalist vote would be good for the peace process. And a strong Sinn Féin vote would empower us in our negotiations with the two governments.

The Irish establishment, which had a long association with the SDLP and was aghast at the growth of Sinn Féin in the North and the example that was setting for the electorate in the South, quickly came out in support of the SDLP and against Sinn Féin. John Bruton had accused republicans of having a nightmare version of unity. He compared republicans to the traditional version of unionism and said we did not recognise "the possibility of multiple allegiances. Republicans had a territorial concept of unity," he alleged. A short time later, the Fianna Fáil leader Bertie Ahern wrote an article for the pro-SDLP Belfast *Irish News* which was headlined – "Tell Sinn Féin No Ceasefire No Vote".

Electoral contest or not, John Hume and I continued our efforts to engage the British government. The Irish government was still in its no-contact mode with Sinn Féin. In an effort to draw the British out on our questions, John Hume formally wrote to Patrick Mayhew in early March. He sent Mayhew our five questions. Mayhew replied a week later and John passed the correspondence back to me. I set to work right away drafting a response and approaching Mayhew's letter in a positive way. I did so in the clear belief that our collective efforts were about providing clear and unequivocal assurances that a genuine process of negotiations was on offer. So I answered Mayhew's letter, and sent it back to John twenty-four hours later.

As John and I waited for Mayhew or Major's response, Sinn Féin was busy trying to reach out to the British Labour Party. It was widely expected that it would win the British general election and form the next government. But having been on the opposition benches since 1979, its leadership was making sure it said, or did, nothing that would provide the Tories with anything that might be used against them.

One of several efforts we made involved a friend of one of our senior people who knew one of Tony Blair's people. At our request, he asked about Blair meeting us. While ruling out a meeting at this time, the reply was a positive one. According to our friend, Blair said that people who thought he would not take an interest or would not add fresh impetus were wrong. "I will take the issue very seriously indeed and I have a far clearer understanding of it than people might think. But it would be electoral suicide to have such a meeting at the moment and could not be justified in principle."

Blair said he had new ideas. Our contact wrote back to us: "He has commitment. But nothing, as far as he's concerned, can be done in advance of the election. He understands how eager you are to meet him, claiming that I am the fifth such approach." So, here was some sign of other possibilities. A signal of a different approach by a new British government.

US Senator Ted Kennedy entered into the fray in a major speech in New York on 14 March. Niall O'Dowd's *Irish America* magazine runs a gala event each year – America's Top 100 Irish Americans – which usually attracts significant media attention. Ted Kennedy was proclaimed "Irish American of the Year" and used his speech to urge the British to remove any pre-conditions to Sinn Féin's entry into talks in the event of an IRA cessation. He also rounded on those in "high places who do not to admit or accept their responsibility for failing to respond to the (first) IRA ceasefire". The British moved quickly to rebuff Kennedy's call and restate their pre-conditions.

At the end of March, I had a meeting with the Fianna Fáil leader Bertie Ahern and several of his shadow cabinet. A general election was also pending in the South of Ireland. There was a strong expectation that Fianna Fáil would form the next government in Dublin. I was therefore keen to get some sense of Ahern's likely approach. He had already met Tony Blair, and Martin Mansergh was keeping in touch with Mo Mowlam – Blair's spokesperson on the North and the person most likely to emerge as Secretary of State in the aftermath of a Labour victory. Ahern appeared ready to pick up the peace process as a priority and suggested that Martin Mansergh should meet us soon to talk about rebuilding the Irish nationalist consensus position.

Rita moved quickly to follow up that suggestion and met Mansergh within days. He told her that a Fianna Fáil government would renew contact with Sinn Féin, although whether Bertie Ahern as Taoiseach could meet me publicly in the absence of an IRA ceasefire would be dependent on the situation.

The situation was not good. Loyalist attacks on Catholics were running at a high rate. Among these, one man, John Slane from West Belfast, was shot dead during March at his home by the UDA. His killers carried out their attack and fled in full view of a British military base on top of a nearby nurse's residential block of flats. This prompted renewed claims of collusion between the loyalists and the British army. In North Belfast, a 100-pound car bomb was left outside the Sinn Féin office in Lepper Street.

After mounting speculation, John Major finally announced the date for a general election – 1 May. It was to be the longest run-in to a British general election in memory. Major needed the time to galvanise his party and its support if he was to have any chance. Everybody went into election overdrive.

Except, that is, for a bunch of republican prisoners held in H-Block 7 in Long Kesh. They were busy taking part in "Operation Tollan". Tollan is the Irish word for a tunnel, and that was exactly what they were constructing by digging their way through fourteen inches of concrete flooring, down eight feet, and then excavating twelve metres of rocks, clay and soil in atrociously wet and dangerous conditions. The tunnel was only discovered when a major subsidence, caused by flooding, led to a hole appearing in the yard above. In the inevitable furore that followed, the prison administration unleashed its riot squads, and over sixty prisoners were beaten in follow-up searches.

IRA attacks continued. Among these were bombs on the London to Glasgow rail line, an RUC officer seriously injured in a sniping attack in South Armagh and the discovery of a 1,000-pound landmine near the British army base at Ballykinlar in County Down.

Unionist hackles were raised by Labour's Mo Mowlam when she told a BBC interviewer that Sinn Féin could be in the talks on 3 June if the IRA called a ceasefire. This was the first real public indication that a British Labour government might be prepared to approach all of this differently from John Major. The DUP and UUP predictably threatened to pull out of the talks if Mowlam's scenario came about.

I was on the campaign trail. It was at times like this that being the only all-Ireland party put all of us to the test. We had to fight three major elections on the island within a six-week period. No easy task. We had an ace up our sleeves for the Northern elections. We had discovered under an old rule in the British parliament that members who didn't take the oath of allegiance to the monarchy could still have offices and use of the facilities at Westminster but without pay. This rule was created to deal with English republicans or atheists, but it suited us as well.

When Richard did publicity on this, it caused a stir. Some republican opponents warned that this was the slippery slope to Sinn Féin taking the oath of allegiance and sitting in the chamber. It wasn't. Apart from constantly seeking to improve our ability to more effectively represent our constituencies, we had a major project of reaching out to political and public opinion in Britain to persuade it of the merits of leaving Ireland. Facilities at Westminster could be used as a beachhead to promote this.

The Sinn Féin organisation was at full stretch and vigorously electioneering. There was a buoyancy, a confidence about the campaign. The response we were getting was remarkable and, if truth be told, a little frightening. Expectations of success – of a breakthrough election – were everywhere. The party had caught a fever, and I was worried that if we failed to match these expectations we would face a serious morale and political problem later. At the same time, the atmosphere and the response we were getting was good – so, we had to go for it.

Our Ard Fheis that year was a short one-day event in Monaghan, but there was a real sense of energy buzzing around the room. The constant refrain of the delegates outside the conference hall, and even quietly to each other inside, was to get the Ard Fheis over so they could get back to canvassing and the elections. And that's what they did – breaking again only briefly to lodge nomination papers for the elections to local councils on 21 May.

On 1 May, the voters made their way to hundreds of polling stations across the North – and made history. When the vote was counted, the Sinn Féin share had jumped from 10 per cent in the 1992 Westminster election to 16.1 per cent. It was the largest vote we had taken out in the North in four decades. We won two seats. I had the great honour to be re-elected for West Belfast. Martin McGuinness comfortably took Mid-Ulster. And Pat Doherty came close in West Tyrone. He fell this time, but his day would come.

Every constituency saw an increase in the Sinn Féin vote, pushing us into position as the third largest party in the North. The SDLP vote generally held also. They took 24.1 per cent, and together our two parties pulled out 40.2 per cent of the total vote. It was the highest nationalist vote ever recorded in the history of the state.

On the unionist side, David Trimble's UUP won 32.7 per cent of the vote and ten seats, seeing off the DUP challenge. Paisley's party won 13.6 per cent of the vote and two seats.

In Britain, the Conservatives were trounced. John Major resigned as leader of his party and Tony Blair came to power with an unprecedented 179-seat majority.

The Westminster election results created a new sense of hope. But could the governments and parties meet the challenge?

*Gerry Adams, Albert Reynolds and John Hume* (Photocall)

*Gerry Adams surrounded by cameramen* (Brendan Murphy)

*Aidan McAteer, Courtney Kennedy, Gerry Adams, Mairéad Keane and Richard McAuley, at Hickory Hill on receipt of fax from Tony Lake announcing end of ban on contacts with Sinn Féin.* (AP/RN)

*Gerry Adams with Rosa Parkes* (AP/RN)

*Moments before Gerry Adams and President Clinton met on the Falls Road:
Eamon McCaughley, Tony Lake, Nancy Soderberg and Gerry Adams*
(Richard McAuley)

*President Bill Clinton and Gerry Adams shake hands on the Falls Road*
(Richard McAuley)

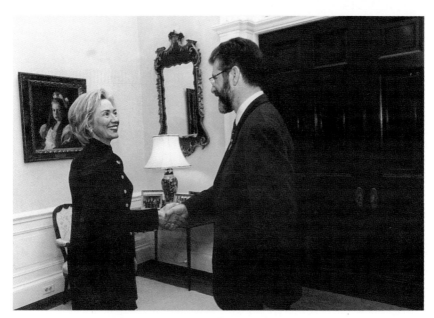

*Hillary Clinton and Gerry Adams* (AP/RN)

*Martin McGuinness and Gerry Adams with President Bill Clinton* (AP/RN)

*Police intervention during republican protest march* (AP/RN)

*Terry Enright's funeral* (AP/RN)

*David Trimble addresses the media at Hillsborough Castle at the end of the Easter talks while Gerry Adams looks on from the steps.* (Photocall)

*General John de Chastelain, Mo Mowlam, David Andrews, Martin Mansergh and Liz O'Donnell look on as Bertie Ahern and Tony Blair speak to the media at Hillsborough Castle.* (Photocall)

*George Mitchell* (Pacemaker)

*Gerry Adams and schoolchildren approach a British army post in Crossmaglen*
(Brendan Murphy)

*Sinn Féin at No 10 Downing Street: Martin Ferris, Michele Gildernew, Martin McGuinness, Gerry Adams, Lucilita Breathnach, Siobhán O'Hanlon and Richard McAuley* (Photocall)

*Martin McGuinness, Nelson Mandela and Gerry Adams* (AP/RN)

# Chapter Twenty-Six

# *Barred from the Mother of Parliaments*

I wrote to the new British Prime Minister on 2 May, congratulating him on his success, wishing him well for the future and assuring him of Sinn Féin's commitment to rebuilding a credible peace process. I asked him to authorise meetings as soon as possible. I wrote in a similar vein to Mo Mowlam.

Many republicans and nationalists didn't really expect a lot of difference under a Labour government. Labour had been in power in 1969 and had failed to defend human rights, promote equality for all citizens and to effectively challenge the one-party rule of unionism. The criminalisation of political prisoners was devised and introduced under a Labour government and overseen by Merlyn Rees. And, of course, there was the little Labour Führer from the North of England, Roy Mason, who unleashed the SAS and the torturers within the RUC.

It was Labour's Don Concannon who visited the hunger strikers on 1 May 1981, four days before Bobby Sands died, carrying a message from Labour leader Michael Foot telling the prisoners that Labour supported Thatcher's intransigence and that the men should abandon the hunger strike. He met Francie Hughes in his H-Block cell, and Francie asked him did he support the prisoners' five demands. When Concannon said "No", Francie told him to "Close the door after you."

Traditionally, Labour had been for a united Ireland. Much of its early support was in the Irish immigrant community and among their descendants who fled to England in the nineteenth century to escape starvation and poverty. In 1981 it became a "unity by consent" party. But there was a strong lobby within what was now called "new" Labour who wanted to change even that. They wanted to help build a new Union. They were not united Irelanders; they were British unionists.

Despite this and despite Labour's disgraceful record on Ireland, I was pleased to see Blair elected. Whatever way it affected Ireland, the change was good for the British people. After almost twenty years of Tory rule, the Brits deserved a break. The dismal decline and obvious corruption of British politics in the last years of that government was in direct contrast to the image of the Blair family as they made their almost presidential way up Downing Street through cheering crowds. That was bound to be good for Britain's morale. The people who had voted in huge numbers for an end to the nastiness and sleaze of the Conservatives had something to cheer them up.

Signals from Downing Street after the election were not good. There was an immediate flurry of meetings between the UUP, DUP, Alliance, SDLP and the new British Secretary of State. Trimble also met Blair. Sinn Féin was excluded. New guidelines drawn up within the civil service continued to strictly circumscribe contact between Sinn Féin and British government ministers and officials, despite our substantial new electoral mandate.

Dublin's position was no better. Taoiseach John Bruton was still refusing to authorise meetings between his officials and us. However, we knew that these officials were more upbeat following Blair's overwhelming victory. Our feedback on the conversations between the two governments was that both Mowlam and Blair were positive, although cautious.

And then, unexpectedly, Siobhán O'Hanlon got a call on her mobile phone. Public transport in West Belfast is mostly provided by London-style black taxi cabs, known locally as black hacks or black taxis. Siobhán was travelling to the Sinn Féin office when the call came through on 9 May. It was Quentin Thomas, one of the two most senior civil servants at the NIO. He asked if Siobhán could take down a note for me, which in the crushed confines of a packed black taxi wasn't possible. She arranged to ring him back from the office.

His message, for a British civil servant, was straightforward. He acknowledged my two letters to Blair and Mowlam and said: "They are being studied and they are being taken seriously. It is helpful that they have not been published. The new government are finding its feet. They are focusing on the Queen's speech (when a government traditionally sets out its plans for the year ahead) and other things. We will be replying before too long. We hope something positive can be done. I have noted Gerry Adams's remarks about confidence-building measures. Obviously this is a two-way street, and it is essential that events on the ground, any terrorist act in GB or Northern Ireland, hoaxes or otherwise, make it difficult. We will be responding, but these events make it difficult."

Eventually Siobhán managed to reach me in Dublin and together we agreed a speaking note for her to pass back to Thomas. It said: "Siobhán has passed on to me your comments. I want to assure you of our desire to make progress. We wanted to make an early and direct approach, but we appreciate the need for sensitivity, so let me assure you that there is no intention on our part to make any of this public. Our desire is to help create the conditions in which real progress can be made. The sooner this is done the better. We share your concern about events on the ground, which are beyond our control. There are grave difficulties on our side also, not least among these is the treatment of the remand prisoner Róisín McAliskey, the delay in transferring sentenced republican prisoners in Britain back to Ireland and their conditions, the events surrounding the killing of a young Catholic, Robert Hamill, in Portadown, the action of the RUC and British army and the ongoing loyalist attacks on our party and community."

The Robert Hamill killing had generated enormous anger among nationalists and republicans. A twenty-five-year-old Catholic with two young children, he had been one of two men attacked by a loyalist mob in Portadown town centre on 27 April. They were beaten unconscious by the mob while in plain sight of an RUC patrol parked near by. The RUC failed to intervene. Eleven days later, Robert Hamill died. His partner later gave birth to their third child. The Hamill family organised a justice campaign around the case, demanding an independent inquiry. Their campaign continues today.

A few days after Robert Hamill's death, a sixty-two-year-old Catholic father of six, Sean Brown, was kidnapped by the Loyalist Volunteer Force as he locked up the GAA club in Bellaghy in County Derry. He was later found shot dead. This, and two election campaigns – one in the South and the local government elections in the North – was the background against which we were working to get the process back on track.

John Bruton was doggedly sticking to his "no contact" with Sinn Féin position. Publicly, he defended his advice to the electorate in the North not to vote Sinn Féin. In one interview, he proudly proclaimed that he would never be neutral as between Sinn Féin and the SDLP. That was fair enough. Indeed all the main parties in the South supported the SDLP and campaigned for it during elections. But at least Fianna Fáil kept contact with us. They also knew the mind of the Southern nationalist and republican electorate. Bertie Ahern met publicly with us on 14 May.

As is often the case in our dealings with London, it was two steps forward, one step backward. So, while there were now some encouraging signals coming from the Blair government, the Speaker of the House of Commons Betty Boothroyd succumbed to unionist and conservative pressure and announced that she was overturning over 100 years of British parliamentary tradition and refusing Martin McGuinness and me the use of facilities at Westminster. If we wanted the facilities after this, we had to take the oath of allegiance to the British Queen. Boothroyd's ruling was due to come into effect at midnight on Tuesday, 20 May. If we went to Westminster before this, we would get to use the facilities and to use the publicity around this as a platform for our cause. Martin and I discussed this and decided we should travel to London and highlight the hypocrisy and stupidity of a system that was prepared to turn its own traditions on their head because they were afraid of two duly elected Irish republican MPs.

But before we could go to visit the "Mother of all parliaments", Tony Blair came to Belfast on his first official visit as Prime Minister. The speech he delivered in South Belfast repeated much of the failed rhetoric of the past. I could understand his "I believe in the United Kingdom" remark. He was, after all, the Prime Minister of a government pledged to uphold the union. However, his assertion that "I value the Union" was at odds with successive claims of neutrality by British governments and was offensive to republicans and nationalists who wondered what there was about this corrupt little state to value.

The double standards of previous British governments were also evident in his speech. It was insensitive of him to commend unionist paramilitaries for their "restraint" on the very day that the people of Bellaghy were burying Sean Brown. Blair raised the old unionist war cry for changes to the Irish constitution while indicating no comparable willingness to change the British constitution. Apparently it was all right for the British to occupy and lay claim to a part of Ireland by force, but the Irish had to yield our claim to nationhood.

Many nationalists and republicans were understandably disappointed by Mr Blair's remarks. In truth, we should not have been. The British government will always defend British national interests. Our job is get them to change policy, especially on the question of the union. The responsibility of any Irish government should be to defend and promote Irish national interests – including the central issue of unity.

However, while the rest of us were parsing the speech for evidence that it differed in some way from those delivered by Major, there was one difference that jumped out and which focused the media: Sinn Féin was invited to meet government officials. Within an hour, I received a fax from

Mo Mowlam confirming the invitation to talks. Siobhán faxed our acceptance.

I subsequently wrote to the new Secretary of State. I acknowledged that she had a difficult job and I told her I hoped her tenure would usher in a new beginning for both our peoples.

Perhaps realising that Fianna Fáil were electorally outflanking him because of their more positive stand on the peace process, or more probably because of the upcoming meeting in the North between us and the British government, Bruton now agreed to a meeting between his officials and Sinn Féin.

The briefing to the media from Irish government sources around this meeting was unhelpful and untrue: they claimed this was a meeting to discuss an imminent ceasefire. I told the officials when we met on 17 May that this was unacceptable and counter-productive. There was no imminent ceasefire, but there was an opportunity and we should get down to the business of dealing with the issues. I was critical of Bruton's public and private stand, but we had to concentrate on moving forward.

That meant the Irish government using its influence to ensure that any meeting with British officials was not a replay of our previous experience. We needed to get the time-frame for talks sorted out and tackle the substantive issues.

The Irish officials expressed their desire to talk to their opposite numbers on the British side as part of the effort to resolve these problems. We also asked them to talk to John Hume and the US government, to bring them up to speed with developments. We had our own lines to both and were using them.

In between all of this private work around the peace process, the election campaign for the local councils in the North was taking place. As usual I was visiting all parts of the Six Counties, encouraging activists and meeting the voters, with occasional jaunts across the border to Dublin and other parts to participate in the general election campaign.

Martin and I, accompanied by Richard and Eamon, took the day off from all of this on 20 May to go to London and visit the House of Commons before we were barred. We insisted on getting our parliamentary passes and were duly photographed and processed by helpful and bemused parliament officials. But they were for one day only. The Right Honourable member from Derry's Bogside representing Mid-Ulster and I are probably the only MPs with such novel British parliamentary ID.

It was an interesting and entertaining visit. Martin and I met an affable Sergeant at Arms and Clerk of the House – the people who actually run the place. We expressed our opposition to the Speaker's arbitrary withdrawal of our facilities. She was denying us our rights and, more especially, denying our electorate their rights.

The British House of Commons is an exclusive club. Martin McGuinness and I and our like are rarely allowed to roam its historic precincts. Our visitation caused some little stir. Tory heads turned in alarm and distaste as they spotted us walking through their domain or sitting out on the terrace overlooking the Thames having lunch.

A succession of MPs from other parties like the Liberal Democrats and the Labour Party approached us to tell us of their disagreement with the new restrictions. We also met Tony Benn, Jeremy Corbyn, John McDonnell and others, who had for years spoken out against British policy in Ireland.

As we were leaving, I sought relief in a members' toilet. It also was a grand affair: all white tiles and large urinals, high cisterns and old-fashioned sinks replete with Victorian artefacts, stacks of towels and bottles of toiletries. After we had exercised our rights, Martin preened himself in front of one of the big old-fashioned mirrors.

"We might as well make use of all these facilities before our time runs out and they throw us out," he declared.

"Too right!" I said, and, lifting a long-handled brush, I began to brush the jacket of his dark suit. An ancient MP, vaguely familiar from some long-forgotten television appearance, emerged from a cubicle and looked at us in disbelief before leaving without saying a word. Or washing his hands.

"There you go," I told Martin as I gave his shoulders a last few brushes, "You're lovely."

"My coat is all shiny!" he exclaimed. He rubbed his sleeve. His hand blackened.

I looked at him in astonishment, then at the brush. The truth dawned.

"That's a polish brush!" he cried.

"Bloody Brits!" I chortled, fleeing before he could retaliate.

The next day was local government election day in the North. It was also the day that Martin (in an unpolished suit this time) and Gerry Kelly led a Sinn Féin delegation into a meeting with British officials at Stormont Castle, a few hundred metres from the talks venue at Castle Buildings.

The discussions between the two delegations lasted three hours. In Martin's view there was a change in the tone of engagement from previous meetings. The new government's stance was different from its predecessor's. We were told that both Tony Blair and Mo Mowlam were anxious, if not eager, to have Sinn Féin in the talks.

The timing of our entry into the negotiations clearly still posed a problem, with Quentin Thomas using what would become a favourite soundbite for the new Secretary of State: a decision would be taken "in the round". That is, when all matters had been taken into account.

The imminent Orange marches in July, particularly on the Garvaghy Road and the lower Ormeau Road, were again raising the political temperature. Thomas suggested that Sinn Féin could influence the mood on the ground.

Martin said, "The British government, the RUC, David Trimble and the Orange Order have greater influence."

"Don't lump all of these together," said Thomas.

Decommissioning was obviously a major difficulty, but again the officials emphasised the British government's desire to carry the talks forward. One official, dealing with the issue of unionist demands on weapons, reminded us all of the experience at the end of the IRA campaign in the 1950s, when after the IRA called a halt, the then unionist government had released all political prisoners with no mention of decommissioning.

The officials indicated a hope that the elections might have loosened up positions on the unionist side and that Trimble might now be in a more stable position. Martin and his colleagues were also told that "this government does not intend letting the process go beyond May 1998. If the process had failed to reach agreement by then, the governments would review their approach."

Gerry Kelly asked if it was possible to defer the 3 June start of the talks until after the general election in the South. He was told that that was really a matter for the Irish government.

After Quentin Thomas had a word with Mo Mowlam – who was in another room close by – it was agreed there would be another meeting at the beginning of June.

The next day was one of celebration. Sinn Féin made gains in twelve councils as the party vote surged to 16.9 per cent of the first preference votes, winning seventy-four seats. We made twenty-three net gains over our 1993 performance with more than half of these being taken from the SDLP; the remainder were from the UUP, the DUP and independent unionists.

In council areas throughout the Six Counties, the swell of support for the party paid off for nationalists who gained overall control of six councils west of the Bann and saw history made in Belfast where for the first time the main unionist parties lost control of Belfast City Council. With thirteen seats on Belfast City Council and again the highest vote share in Belfast at 27.7 per cent, Sinn Féin voters affirmed the party's number one status, even though the UUP still had the same number of seats achieved by a lower share of 20.7 per cent.

This was a remarkable turn around. Fourteen years earlier, Alex Maskey had been the first Sinn Féin councillor elected to Belfast. He was spat on, had perfume and air freshener sprayed in his face by unionists who wanted to make a point about the smell of republicans in their hallowed chamber, and he was physically attacked. Unionist councillors had refused to allow him to speak and had denied him membership of council committees. It had been a long, difficult battle – some of it through the courts – but here we were, now the largest party in Belfast.

Two days before our next planned meeting with British officials, Róisín McAliskey gave birth to a 5 lb 13 oz baby girl, but the conditions of her bail, which she got three days earlier, meant she had to stay in the hospital.

This meeting with the British government officials was less productive than the previous session. The discussions went round the houses again, touching on all of the main issues but not really moving them forward. In particular, the point at which Sinn Féin would enter negotiations after an IRA ceasefire continued to be conditional on meetings with one government, then both governments, with some parties having to meet Sinn Féin, ministers meeting Sinn Féin, the two governments consulting each other and other parties on the issue, and even George Mitchell would have to meet us in advance of inviting us in.

"How long will all of this take?" Martin asked.

We needed clarity and there was none. Perhaps they were awaiting the outcome of the general election in the South?

Whatever the reason for the prevarication, I was now more or less based full time in the Southern constituencies. An assessment by our election directorate had concluded that, while our vote would rise generally wherever we stood, winning seats against the established parties was going to be another proposition entirely. While Sean Crowe in Dublin was in with a chance, our best hope lay in Cavan-Monaghan, where Caoimhghín Ó Caoláin was our standard-bearer. So, we decided I should concentrate my effort there. Anyone who has ever fought in elections will know that they are never easy – away from home for long periods, travelling from dawn to dusk, doing interviews, pressing the flesh, and grabbing cups of tea or coffee, sandwiches or lukewarm soup on the run. Eamon, Richard and I clocked up a lot of miles.

At the start of June nine party delegations from the North headed off to South Africa for what Martin McGuinness later described as one of the most memorable experiences of his life. The purpose of the conference was to see if there were any lessons for us in South Africa's conflict-resolution process.

Sinn Féin already had a long and fruitful relationship with the ANC. But it was important that the other parties, especially the unionists, get a flavour of the potential for peace which a good conflict-resolution process can achieve. But, like the peace process, even this apparently straightforward trip and conference wasn't to be easy.

Peter Robinson, the deputy leader of the DUP, also journeying to South Africa, set the unionist tone a couple of weeks earlier when he remarked on the conditions the DUP had imposed on the organisers of the conference. He said: "The conditions are to ensure that we will be hermetically sealed off from Sinn Féin. We need to know that we will travel separately, lodge separately, socialise separately, meet people separately – apartheid in fact." The irony of unionists demanding an apartheid structure to the conference from a government, many of whose leaders, and whose president, had spent decades in prison fighting apartheid, was lost on Paisley's party.

Separate flights to and from the conference were arranged. Separate sleeping quarters; separate meetings with representatives of the South African parties. Separate facilities for relaxing. A separate bar. According to one report, there were separate ambulances, presumably in case of an emergency.

At the talks venue in Belfast, it was still all about exclusion. I arrived there on the day the talks recommenced, with many of our newly elected representatives, and was locked out again. So, too, were the delegates representing the UDA-linked Ulster Democratic Party. At least for a wee while. They arrived at Castle Buildings at the same time as us. They had to wait until we left before the gates were opened. The fact that they were allowed in, even though loyalist violence was by now a daily event, was not lost on many people.

And then it was time to celebrate another election victory. Caoimhghín Ó Caoláin topped the poll, easily winning his seat. And while we did well everywhere, Martin Ferris in North Kerry almost pulled off what would have been the coup of the election. As it was, the 574 per cent increase in his vote in that area sent a shudder through the other political parties.

However, the other implication of this election was that it now took three weeks for a new government to be formed by Fianna Fáil and the Progressive Democrats. In the meantime, Bruton remained as a caretaker Taoiseach.

During this time, discussions between officials from the two governments continued as they worked on proposals to tackle the decommissioning issue. At one off-the-record meeting, a senior Irish official told Rita that the two governments were close to finalising a paper. In essence, it would say that parallel decommissioning was an objective, not a pre-condition. But the fact that the officials were currently dealing with a caretaker government and a prospective incoming government was a problem for everyone.

In the North, attention was again being focused on contentious Orange marches, and there was much speculation about how the new Secretary of State would respond.

Then Paddy Kelly died from cancer. Had he received proper medical treatment when first diagnosed in jail in England, Paddy's life might have been saved. I travelled down to Killenard, County Laois, for the funeral: a sad, dignified affair. In the middle of the ceremony in the graveyard, adjacent to the Church of St John the Evangelist, several local republicans approached Richard about a stranger standing to the side under some trees. He wasn't a Special Branch officer – they knew all the local branch men. Mindful of recent loyalist attacks against Catholics and republicans, they were worried that he might pose a threat.

Richard told them not to worry. It was John F. Kennedy Jr, the son of the assassinated US president. Now editing *George* magazine in the US, he had asked for an interview with me. Richard and I had met him earlier and, when making arrangements for the interview, Richard had told John that I would be at Paddy's funeral. Later that day we met at our party head office in Dublin and did the interview. The day after, Richard and Chrissie spent seven hours showing him around Belfast.

John was curious about everything. As they left Central Station after his train journey from Dublin, they drove into a large number of British soldiers patrolling the streets. It quickly brought home to him the aberrant nature of the Northern state. He asked questions constantly, wanted the smallest detail explained. He was already knowledgeable about the issues, but on his first and tragically last visit to Belfast, he was seeing for himself what he had only read about or watched on television. Visiting the graves of the hunger strikers in Milltown Cemetery – Bobby Sands, Joe McDonnell and Kieran Doherty – he was struck by their youth and the human cost of the conflict.

I met John in the United States on several occasions after that. I was deeply shocked two years later when he and his wife Carolyn and sister-in-law Lauren Besette were killed in a plane crash off Martha's Vineyard, Massachusetts. His uncle, Senator Kennedy, and his aunt, Ambassador Jean Kennedy Smith, had contributed hugely to the development of our process. Their family was deeply committed to public service. It also suffered more hurt than seemed possible. The death of John Kennedy was another tragic example of this.

# Chapter Twenty-Seven

# *"Nothing But the Same Old Story"*

On 13 June 1997 the British government sent us an *aide-mémoire* that set out their position on the areas of contention between us. Quentin Thomas's accompanying letter suggested that we meet to clarify any concerns.

The shooting dead of two RUC members by the IRA in Lurgan three days later threw a dark cloud over all our efforts, creating a storm of protest and more demands for the exclusion of Sinn Féin. The British cancelled the next planned meeting between us, and John Bruton revived his "no contact" with Sinn Féin rule.

While this was inevitable given the governments' stance, it served no good purpose. When violence confronts us at a critical point, the imperative should be to keep on trying, to intensify dialogue, not end it.

With our meeting with officials cancelled, we had only a speech by Tony Blair in the British parliament to give us some explanation of British thinking around the *aide-mémoire*. His speech, however, didn't rule out the possibility that a demand might still be made for decommissioning as a pre-condition to further progress. This caused concern. Consequently, I wrote to him on 20 June; I received no reply.

Bruton and Blair met in New York for a twenty-minute session at which they agreed their joint paper on decommissioning. The paper, "Resolving the Address to Decommissioning", was then presented to the parties at Castle Buildings by George Mitchell. Both governments accepted that, while they would continue to pursue decommissioning alongside the negotiations, it would not block the progress of the talks. This was to be achieved through the establishment of an Independent International Commission on Decommissioning, and it was proposed that substantive negotiations commence in early September.

The proposals were along the lines of the Mitchell Report. However, there were differing interpretations of whether actual decommissioning of weapons would be required during talks. After meeting Blair, David Trimble said there would have to be evidence of a physical handover of weapons before Sinn Féin could enter substantive negotiations. In another speech in the Commons, Blair said that the British government would make its judgement on Sinn Féin's qualification for entry within six weeks of an IRA cessation; there was a one-paragraph summary of the paper on decommissioning; confidence-building measures were dealt with in general terms; and a target date of May 1998 was set for the conclusion of the negotiations.

The Blair government's position was an advance on Major's. The *aide-mémoire* addressed, in varying degrees, the four central issues to the creation of a meaningful and inclusive process of negotiations.

Unionist reaction was predictable. Paisley fumed, claiming that the two governments' proposals on weapons amounted to a surrender document.

I quietly met with the Taoiseach-in-waiting Bertie Ahern on 24 June. Having met the British Prime Minister, Ahern told me that he thought that this British government wanted the process to work. I pushed him on the need for British constitutional change out of any negotiation, and we had a wide-ranging discussion across all of the matters.

One of these was the Orange marching season, around which tension was now at fever pitch. The Orange Order wanted a repeat of the previous year when the RUC Chief Constable Hugh Annesley had forced a march down the Garvaghy Road. The residents objected strongly. They demanded that the Order talk to them. The Order was refusing.

Mo Mowlam met the residents' representatives on 2 July, four days before the march was scheduled to occur on the Sunday. Councillor Breandán Mac Cionnaith said he expected a decision within forty-eight hours and the residents were busy preparing a children's carnival on the road for Sunday. There was widespread speculation that the RUC was about to repeat their behaviour of the previous year. This was reinforced when they banned the children's carnival.

The same day that Mowlam met the Garvaghy Road residents, Martin McGuinness faxed a letter to Quentin Thomas asking specific questions and seeking clarification on diverse matters. We wanted to know, for example, would British ministers meet with Sinn Féin and on the basis of equality with all other parties?

The next day, Martin met Martin Mansergh who told him that Blair felt he had now gone as far as he could. The new Irish government also felt that it was the British government's intention not to break ranks with it as Major had done. Martin stressed the need for the British to respond positively and clearly to his letter. He also said that the Garvaghy Road residents needed assurances that this year would not be a repeat of last year.

Mansergh had an opportunity to follow up on this when officials from the two governments met on the margins of a meeting between the two Prime Ministers. I was told later that Martin Mansergh was asked for his view by the British on how they should interpret Martin McGuinness's letter. "Seriously," he told them. On 4 July, Martin McGuinness rang Quentin Thomas and had a useful conversation with him in which he indicated that we could expect a reply within a week.

It turned out to be one hell of a week.

While our efforts to restore the process went up another gear, so too did the situation on the streets. The sense of siege around Garvaghy Road was now so serious that I publicly called for calm, as well as for an agreement to defuse the potential for conflict. The Irish government also spoke out against forcing an Orange march down the Garvaghy Road.

Richard, Eamon and I travelled down to Kerry for a function to celebrate Martin Ferris's amazing performance in the recent elections. He might not have won the seat, but the Shinners celebrated as if he had, and there was an acute sense of optimism about "the next time". We had a great time and a great night, but around 11 p.m., and after I had made my speech, the three of us headed back to Belfast. It was a long drive, which would take about six hours. It was a beautiful night, and as we drove up the A1 from Newry to Belfast on the route we had taken with the Gibraltar funerals, it looked as if it would be a gorgeous summer dawn.

I had plenty of time to reflect on the overall state of the process on that long journey home. The objective reality we were now working in was that we had two new governments: one in London, no longer dependent on unionist votes, and another in Dublin, which had by instinct, if not policy, a more positive approach to the process. And we still had President Clinton and Irish America, President Mandela and the South African government, all willing to play a positive role.

The news on the car radio blasted all of my musing asunder. The Orange parade had been forced down Garvaghy Road. At 3.30 a.m., one grey RUC jeep after another sped on to the area. An iron fist of black-uniformed RUC, hiding behind balaclava masks, punched and batoned its way down the road. As residents tried to form up in peaceful protest, they were swept aside, batoned, kicked and punched as the RUC advanced. Some met this violence with bricks, bottles and other missiles. Plastic bullets were fired. People were injured. Others sat on the ground in peaceful protest. One by one, they were dragged and beaten through the RUC lines.

When I arrived home I turned on Sky News and watched the full horror unfold on my television screen. The decision to force the march down the road was a crazy one. Later, the RUC told the residents that they would not be allowed to go to Mass. The chapel was within the sealed off area. Five priests said Mass in the street.

I phoned colleagues and arranged an early meeting to discuss the events of the night. The anger was palpable. Crowds of young people were on the streets. Our objective was to prevent street confrontation and violence. We hurriedly sent out party activists in cars with loudhailers asking people to attend a march and rally that evening. Thousands marched to the RUC barracks in Andersonstown where I stressed the necessity of peaceful protests and the need to keep the focus on the appalling attitude of the British government. Similar protests were held across the Six Counties.

Later that evening Eamon, Richard and I were leaving Poleglass by the back road up toward Colin Mountain when we spotted a large construction lorry driving at speed down the road in our direction. There must have been fifty young people hanging on to it, and it was clearly destined for burning on one of the main roads. We stopped the car, jumped out and stood in the path of this twenty-tonne monster bearing down on us. The fifteen-year-old in the driving seat braked and with a screech of tyres he pulled up a few feet from us.

Most of the swarm of young people bailed out and headed across the fields. Some of the more determined stood their ground and demanded to know why we had stopped them. They then proceeded to sound off to me about the behaviour of the Brits, the RUC, the loyalists and the Orange Order. Now we were the ones trying to stop them striking back. It was hot and heavy stuff. But these were good young people infuriated by what was happening around them, and eventually our arguments won out. Meanwhile, Eamon got a contact number off the lorry and rang the owner to come and pick it up.

Other Sinn Féin activists were also out on the streets round the clock trying to persuade mainly young people from getting involved in fights with the heavily armed RUC. Mindful of the effect that drink can sometimes play in these situations, activists visited every off-licence in

West Belfast and asked them to close. To their credit, they all did. But the RUC were not as civic-minded. Within four days over 2500 plastic bullets were fired, leaving scores of people maimed, some in intensive care units fighting for their lives.

Two days later, the political fall–out deepened when someone within the British system decided to throw fuel on an already enflamed situation by leaking a confidential report, dated 20 June, in which "a controlled march" down the Garvaghy Road was accepted as the "least worst option". The implication was that while Mo Mowlam – even on the evening of the 6th – was telling the residents that no decision had been taken, the decision had been taken two weeks earlier.

This was hardly the way to encourage trust and confidence between republicans and nationalists and this new government – but then, that was the reason for leaking the report. This would not be the last time that people within the British system would deliberately leak material in the hope of derailing constructive efforts within the peace process.

Our project seemed to be in tatters. On the streets of Portadown young nationalist street fighters chanted "No ceasefire! No ceasefire!" as they fought the RUC. Their battle cry also echoed the attitude of most IRA activists. Emotions were high. Mo Mowlam's standing was low. The new British government was behaving as British governments usually behaved. It was nothing but the same old story.

# Chapter Twenty-Eight

# *A New Ceasefire*

The very next day Quentin Thomas replied to Martin McGuinness's letter. He addressed all the matters we had raised with him:

- Substantive political negotiations would commence in September . . . "the government believes its target at the end of May can be met".
- Both governments would "work to bring about due progress on decommissioning alongside progress in the substantive political negotiations . . ."
- A sub-committee on confidence-building measures would be established.
- On equality issues and on the Irish culture and identity, Thomas said that the government "will facilitate education through the medium of Irish where there is the demand for it . . ."
- "Ministers will meet Sinn Féin in the period immediately following a ceasefire and will also encourage the independent chair to hold early meetings with Sinn Féin in this period."
- And on prisoners, the British government committed to "ensuring that prisoners are treated with dignity and respect for their rights". Thomas also revealed that the British Home Office expected to announce decisions in the coming weeks on the transfer of republican political prisoners from England to prisons in Ireland close to their families.

The Irish government presented us with a five-page memorandum setting out its approach. In clear recognition of our concerns, the memorandum identified the need to develop "a more detailed working out of the spheres of operation of North/South institutions" . . . "the engagement of broader Constitutional negotiations, and an agreed new approach to Constitutional doctrines on both sides, including, in our view, change as regards the Government of Ireland Act 1920".

The Irish government agreed that it would expand its government resources to deal with the negotiations and make it its highest priority through its diplomatic mission. Ahern committed his government to accord Sinn Féin full equality of treatment.

Its position on decommissioning was governed by the "fundamental reality that decommissioning in the sense of the Mitchell Report has to be achieved with the co-operation of those holding such weapons. For that reason, we would consider that the test to be met was that of working in good faith to implement all aspects of the report of the international body. Provided we were satisfied that test was met, we would oppose any attempt to expel either Sinn Féin or the loyalist parties from the talks on the ground that they failed to meet some peremptory demand on this issue from other participants."

Our core group carefully analysed these two positions, and Martin McGuinness met Martin Mansergh to continue clarifying and, in effect, to negotiate the detail of what was on offer. Our objective was to secure a package that we could present to the IRA and republicans generally. That meant providing specific amendments to the memorandum, discussing with Mansergh how all of this would play out publicly and discussing the British government's position and the role of the USA.

Though we never conceded it, we were very conscious that we were allowing the issue of an IRA cessation to become a pre-condition for our involvement in talks. By so doing, we were working within the objective reality of the situation. In reality most of what we were negotiating about was not around our entry into dialogue but conditions, or a package for the IRA to consider calling a halt to military operations. It was a double-edged sword for us as well as London.

I spoke to the Taoiseach by phone on 12 July, stressing the constitutional element of the Irish government's memorandum. If the IRA was to be persuaded to opt for a cessation, especially on the back of recent events, it had to be persuaded that the Irish government was serious about securing British constitutional change, I said.

In the following days a variety of draft public and private positions were passed between Sinn Féin and the two governments. While the British government's Drumcree decision had damaged the efforts to put a package together, it did not mean that our peace strategy was finished. On the contrary, it was an incentive to promote that strategy. The arrival of

Quentin Thomas's letter was evidence that London also saw the need to move. The timing of his response was obviously influenced by events on the Garvaghy Road. It must have been clear to London that if the situation went into free fall, the window of opportunity, ajar at that time, would slam shut under the pressure of such events. Downing Street must have known that a process could not be developed or sustained against such a background. They were being handed a peace process on a plate. It was unlikely that they would reject this without exploring its potential.

The effort to get satisfactory positions from which this could be advanced involved only a small number of senior people in the two governments, the White House and our core group. Senior IRA people were briefed regularly on developments and the Sinn Féin leadership was up to speed, but few other people knew the detail of what was going on.

The attitude of the republican grassroots was badly affected by the Drumcree decision and its aftermath. The situation on the streets was tense. The Orange Order had been prevented from marching through the lower Ormeau Road when thousands of nationalists and republicans gathered there. Under immense pressure, the Orange Order agreed to reroute some of its more contentious parades.

Within the IRA, a backlash was also growing. The attitude of John Major's government had done tremendous damage to the Sinn Féin peace project. Before the 1994 cessation, it had been possible for some people to be hopeful that a British government might respond positively. Now, after the way the Tory government had handled the 1994 cessation and the volatile and highly charged situation on the streets, there was considerable cynicism – even though the Tories were gone.

As less involved elements within the broad nationalist constituency are educated and radicalised by developments, and as attitudes harden within the broad republican base, the vanguard leading the strategy and creating such developments can be tripped up and passed over by its own constituency. The last people to be surprised by British duplicity should be Irish nationalists, and our leadership certainly was not surprised or daunted by the way the British government behaved. But others were. Or they were reinforced or perhaps reassured in their assumption that politics didn't work.

The most important and crucial negotiation was with our own constituency, particularly with the activist core of this constituency. Here there were two organisations to be satisfied, as well as the wider circle in which these organisations functioned. Contrary to perceptions, the IRA and Sinn Féin are separate organisations. They cannot be expected always to respond in the same way to developments. For example, later in the process, while a minority dissented, the IRA generally came on board about Sinn Féin agreeing to the Mitchell Principles. They probably reasoned that this was a matter for the party. Within the party, however, there was a spirited reaction when one area in Cork repudiated this move and attempted to circulate a motion in this regard to all cumainn throughout the island.

Probably members of all organisations hate to receive news of upcoming events or developments through the media, especially in times of crisis or controversy. There was no way that our small, over-stretched national leadership could keep everyone up to speed, though we did our best and recognised that communications were a priority. We were dependent on middle leaderships to keep everyone informed and on board. Summoning our members to meetings was relatively easily done.

It was a different issue entirely for the army people. Sinn Féin is open and public. The IRA is secretive and covert. It functions in a quasi-military way with its operatives accustomed to giving or receiving orders. Sinn Féin could call big meetings. The IRA rarely did. At times, there were sensitivities if the membership of either organisation had information in advance of the other. The army was particularly sensitive about talk of cessations or ceasefires, and media speculation was a source of particular irritation. Speculative comment about this by even the best-regarded Sinn Féin spokespersons was a sure trigger for army irritation.

Some of this irritation and other concerns had been vented for some time, even before the 1994 cessation. The IRA's democratically elected General Army Convention is made up of delegates from all units who decide policy and elect the IRA leadership. The Convention directly elects a twelve-person Executive, which then goes on to secretly elect a seven-person Army Council. The Council appoints the Chief of Staff, who appoints the GHQ staff and command OCs. The CS runs the IRA, though he or she is responsible to the AC. The Army Executive is effectively the Army Convention's watchdog. One of its few powers is to recall an Army Convention if it is dissatisfied with the Army Council or with any other matter, though this would have to be a huge issue. The Army Council and the CS report to the Executive on a regular basis.

Martin McGuinness and I kept senior IRA people informed about ongoing developments informally. On a number of occasions we heard that there were some especially trenchant queries about what we were doing and the army's attitude to this. These were coming in particular from some members of the Army Executive, critical about the Army Council's benign attitude to the Sinn Féin peace strategy.

All of this was entirely legitimate, of course, though reports had it that Army Executive meetings were particularly gruelling and increasingly acrimonious affairs, especially those meetings attended by the CS or the Army Council representative. Although only a minority of the Executive was involved, after a while it appeared that there was almost a contest about the authority of the Army Executive versus the authority of the Army Council.

The Sinn Féin peace strategy had no chance if the IRA leadership was not prepared to tolerate it. If the broad leadership of the IRA was going to be sucked into an internal row over who had authority, any chance of progress would be dissipated. If our negotiations were successful, there was a better chance of winning IRA support if these internal IRA difficulties were sorted out. But there was no time for this. Martin had finished the negotiations with Dublin. It looked as though we had a package, a new context into which the IRA could step if it was so minded. We had no choice but to put all this before the IRA leadership.

If we were to succeed in persuading the IRA to call a cessation, this would be only the beginning of a difficult process of engagement with the unionists. In fact, a declaration of an IRA cessation was likely to have a destabilising impact on unionists. If the first cessation was any guide, they would see a new one as a threat.

For Sinn Féin, the imperative at this stage in the peace process was to construct a meaningful and credible negotiations process. We thought we had that now – if the governments could be kept to the commitments they were making. We were working on the basis that for a durable settlement to be reached there had to be a constructive context within which to resolve the conflict. That context could only be established by creating a level playing field as a means to guarantee the rights and the entitlements of all.

Equality meant civil, social, economic, cultural and political rights for unionists as well as for nationalists and republicans. Whether it was the right to a job or to vote, or to religious freedom, or the end of discrimination – these civil and religious rights and entitlements had to be guaranteed and protected.

Unionists saw the equality agenda as a nationalist issue rather than a question of rights for every citizen. Northern Protestants had fears, and there was a huge gulf of distrust and misunderstanding between republicans and unionists. Bridging that gulf was not going to be easy, but we wanted to try.

Our goals were clear. We were seeking conditions in which, for the first time, the people of this island could reach a democratic accommodation; in which the consent and agreement of both nationalists and unionists was achieved; and in which a process of national reconciliation and healing could begin. Unionist participation in this was essential.

The easy bit, relatively speaking, was the Sinn Féin engagement with the Army Council people. Essentially the same people who had authorised the 1994 cessation, they were fully briefed on our work with the two governments and others. But it was a tough discussion nonetheless. Martin and I were put through our paces. In the end, the decision was as we had hoped. The AC was in principle for restoring the cessation. It could easily have been otherwise. But first the AC was required to consult with the Army Executive. Depending on the outcome of that meeting, the GHQ people and the other IRA volunteers would be given their instructions. Then, if there were no insurmountable problems, there would be an IRA statement.

For our part, and in the expectation that the army was going to restore the cessation, other republicans and nationalists had to be given some sense that the Irish nationalist consensus was back on the agenda. I brought the Sagart up to date, and then, on 17 July, I met John Hume and briefed him on developments and my hopes for substantive progress. The next day, following a meeting of the Sinn Féin Ard Chomhairle, I told the media that Martin McGuinness and I had provided a detailed report and assessment to the IRA of our negotiations with the governments.

I had made it clear many times over the previous year and a half that Martin and I would only approach the IRA to restore their cessation if we felt that we had made sufficient progress to empower us to put a credible case. Without this, it would have been a waste of time simply asking the IRA to consider a new cessation. Most of the thinking media knew this, and our press briefing fuelled the sense that something might be happening. We were not that concerned about that at this stage. In any case, the IRA leadership had assured Martin and me that they would quickly respond in a public way.

We also set about informing a wide range of key US opinion makers of developments, including the White House, as well as the political leadership of South Africa, which had been so helpful to our project.

John Hume and I issued a joint statement saying we felt that if there was the political will, the peace process could now be restored.

Less than twenty-four hours later, on Saturday, 19 July, the IRA leadership announced that it had ordered the unequivocal restoration of the ceasefire of August 1994. The IRA said: "The Irish Republican Army is committed to ending British rule in Ireland. It is the root cause of division and conflict in our country. We want a permanent peace and therefore we are prepared to enhance the search for a democratic peace settlement through real and inclusive negotiations. So, having assessed the current political situation, the leadership of Óglaigh na hÉireann are announcing a complete cessation of military operations."

# Chapter Twenty-Nine

## *To Castle Buildings*

Not long after the IRA statement, a Sinn Féin delegation met officials at Castle Buildings to begin the process of taking up offices and preparing for our entry into the talks. Castle Buildings is an awful building. I am sure that would have been the first thing all the talks participants would have agreed on. No one liked the talks venue. Perhaps being stuck here for over a year before our arrival explained some of the problems between the other parties! An unwell structure, it was a 1960s style box building. The corridors were narrow, claustrophobic and sterile. Many of the rooms had no windows, and the rooms we were in, like their fellows, had little to look out at.

There were no nooks or crannies. We quickly learned that this meant no space for private, off-the-record, on-the-side meetings with other participants. This was not such a big deal for engagements with parties of a similar mind or for those who had no problems engaging together despite their differences. But some of our opponents were refusing to engage at all and others had hard and apparently irreconcilable positions. As some of this loosened up, and especially as some of the participants chilled out, we discovered that there was nowhere for private, outside-the-room conversations – essential to progress or even for initiating conversations.

Everyone was also mindful that the British intelligence service MI5 probably had the rooms, the phones and the computers bugged trying to pick up information that would be useful in the talks. Martin and I took to going for walks outside, both because it was good to get some fresh air, but also because it would be more difficult for the eavesdroppers. Later, it wasn't unusual for British ministers, including Secretaries of State, to take us outside for fear that our conversations would be picked up by their own system and used in a negative way.

George Mitchell, in his book on the negotiations, later gave an insight into this. Referring to one leak from within Mo Mowlam's office, he wrote: "Leaks were to be expected. But those from the Northern Ireland Office were different; they had the apparent intent to undermine the peace process, even though the government itself was an architect of that process."

The ground floor of Castle Buildings was occupied by the offices of the UUP, Alliance party, the PUP and the UDP parties, as well as administration offices for the British government's media people. The Irish government, the SDLP, the Women's Coalition, the locally based Labour Party and ourselves occupied rooms on the second floor.

Above our floor were the offices of the British government, including the Secretary of State, the offices for the independent chairs and a small bar. This top floor also contained the large room set aside for the negotiations. There were also small conference rooms on each floor.

Two offices were allocated to us. This was inadequate and the first negotiation when we went into the talks was about getting us decent space. Eventually, a wall was knocked down to extend one room and we were allocated a third office, originally allotted to the Irish government. The largest office became our administration and PR room. One of the others was for the negotiators, advisers and PR people to meet to discuss developments and plan responses. The third and smallest, the room given to us out of the Irish government's allocation, was where our papers for the negotiations were prepared. We used our own laptops and printers.

There was a row of air conditioning machines outside the windows of our two rooms at the front of the building. Consequently, when we opened the windows to let in some fresh air, the noise of the air conditioning machines made conversation difficult. The air conditioning was worse than on any plane I have ever travelled on. The air was constantly dry and the heat frequently uncomfortable.

To make the rooms a bit more comfortable and a bit more republican, we placed several framed posters, including one of Bobby Sands, on the walls. Cleaky also proudly unfurled the tricolour in one corner. We were set for business. We had walked the walk, now we were ready to talk the talk. But it was not as easy as that. Two days later, the DUP and UKUP voted against the two governments' paper on decommissioning. They walked out of the negotiations, pledging never to return.

We passed our time with a round of meetings with some of the smaller parties, as well as Irish Minister for Foreign Affairs Ray Burke. John Hume and I travelled to Dublin to meet the Taoiseach, but apart from this there was little happening politically. However, the harsh reality of conflict and the need to make this process work was driven home to us all by the brutal murder of a sixteen-year-old Catholic boy in County Down. His death was one of the most brutal of the conflict. Kidnapped by unionist paramilitaries, he was so badly mutilated that he could only be identified by his dental records. His body was thrown into a water-filled sinkhole used to bury animal carcasses. Other loyalist attacks against Catholics took place in North Belfast and the lower Ormeau Road.

The Castle Buildings process adjourned on 28 July for a six-week summer break. But behind the scenes NIO officials were privately trying to persuade the Irish government to shift their position on decommissioning. With the DUP and UKUP out of the talks, Trimble was feeling vulnerable and wanted some cover. The NIO was trying to provide this. It suited their agenda as well as the UUP's. For his part, Mr Trimble was expertly using his perceived weakness to extract concessions from the governments.

In the first week in August, Martin McGuinness, Caoimhghín Ó Caoláin, Martin Ferris, Lucilita Bhreatnach, Siobhán O'Hanlon and I met Mo Mowlam, her Political Affairs Minister Paul Murphy and their officials. We met at her office in the talks building. It was a good meeting – "businesslike" is the phrase which springs to mind. We were probably too formal, too keen to get our views across. She was content to let us.

We handed over a paper – "Peace in Ireland: An Agenda for Change" – and focused our discussions on the need to end British jurisdiction in Ireland, the equality agenda, demilitarisation, political prisoners, and the case for transferring prisoners from England to Ireland.

A few days after this, there was what many saw as a small breakthrough when the unionist MP Ken Maginnis went into a television studio for thirty minutes to discuss the peace process and the upcoming talks with Martin McGuinness. While Maginnis had joined me once before, three years earlier, on *The Larry King Show* on CNN, unionists had firmly resisted any requests to do joint interviews or discussions on panel programmes. It wasn't a great debate. Maginnis wasn't in good form. Its significance was that it had happened at all.

The same day, Martin launched a legal case against the decision by the Speaker of the British parliament to deny us facilities at Westminster. We weren't particularly hopeful of reversing the decision through the courts because Britain does not have a written constitution. Parliament is sovereign. And therefore parliament can change the rules or the laws as it sees fit. On that basis, it was unlikely that any British or European court would overturn the decision. But we were resolved to challenge the Speaker's ruling anyway.

Meanwhile, the UUP were debating whether they should participate in the talks when they reconvened on 9 September. Eventually, they decided to meet the weekend after 9 September to take that decision. By waiting until after the talks had recommenced, Trimble was exerting additional pressure on the two governments.

A deadlier battle was taking place between the UVF and its breakaway LVF faction. According to one of the PUP delegates to the talks, the UVF was going to kill off the LVF group led by Billy Wright. It was to be easier said than done.

Six weeks, almost to the day, after the IRA cessation was announced, I received a letter from Mo Mowlam inviting Sinn Féin to participate in the plenary sessions. But before then Martin, Caoimhghín and I headed off to the US. Our objectives were straightforward: to brief the White House and political leaders in Washington, and to fundraise and engage with Irish America. All of this was done with the help of "Friends of Sinn Féin", who successfully organised several major events right across the country. This engagement was important. We had made significant political gains. The peace process was back on track, but we were now entering probably the most difficult phase yet. Irish America needed to understand the crucial role they had played in getting us to this point and the importance of staying engaged if we were to achieve a United Ireland.

Back home, the core group was structuring our approach to the negotiations. This meant not just having a good front-line team of negotiators, but also ensuring that we had administrators, legal advisers, research, secretarial and PR resources to back this up. We knew from watching previous bouts of negotiations that a lot of effort was needed for the PR battle outside the room. Apart from influencing public opinion, this was an extension of the negotiations themselves.

Martin, Caoimhghín and I returned on 8 September from the US, the day before the first plenary – when all the parties with full delegations were to meet in round-table session. Although we already had had a presence at Castle Buildings, the next morning when we walked in, a sizeable media pack had gathered outside the building. This was to be the start of a negotiation that could see substantial movement towards a permanent end to 800 years of conflict in Ireland. Many people, and not just republicans, were hoping that a way could be found through what was assumed by many to be entirely contradictory and mutually exclusive positions. It was a heavy responsibility.

George Mitchell called the first plenary to order at 12.08 p.m. The room set aside for plenary sessions was a large square room with doors in each wall for access. Tables were placed together to form a rectangle. The independent chairs took up one side, flanked by representatives of the two governments. We sat opposite. The unionist places were to one side. The SDLP and others took up the remaining places.

There were vacant chairs. The UUP, the DUP, the UKUP, the PUP and UDP had all failed to turn up. The UUP were to meet at the weekend, and the two smaller loyalist parties were never going to stay in talks without one of the larger unionist parties present. They needed that safety net.

Stamina within a negotiation is almost as vital as the positions one articulates. Discussions could be intense. With different Sinn Féin negotiating teams talking with a variety of others, we could be in discussions round the clock. Rest was therefore essential.

We took every opportunity to stretch out on a floor or under a table. In addition, Siobhán spoke to the civil servants running the building and they gave us a camp bed, one of two they kept in the building. It saw great use over the following months.

The first order of business involved Senator Mitchell reading out the Mitchell Principles of democracy and non-violence and asking me to respond for Sinn Féin. I did so.

There was some anticipation that the unionists would soon return to the negotiating table. However, the initial optimism of 9 September evaporated when the IRA was brought back centre stage into a new crisis. In an interview for *An Phoblacht*, an IRA representative, commenting on developments since the 19 July ceasefire, was asked for the IRA's view of the Mitchell Principles and Sinn Féin, signing up to them. The spokesperson said that what Sinn Féin did was a matter for us. Significantly, he added that all republicans should understand and support the party as we did what was necessary to bring about a lasting peace. But in respect of the Mitchell Principles, the army representative said that the IRA would have problems with sections of them. He, or she, pointed out that the IRA was not a participant in these talks.

Sinn Féin had consistently said we were not the IRA and that we did not represent the IRA in the talks. We were there on the basis of our mandate. The reality was that the IRA had called its cessation to enhance

306

our collective efforts. But it was not a party to the negotiations. Its constructive decision to call a cessation and its repeated assurances of its support for a genuine peace process were all evidence of its commitment to peace.

The unionists stalled the negotiations. The DUP, refusing to attend the talks, wrote to Mitchell demanding our expulsion.

On Saturday, the 110-member Executive Committee of the UUP met in Belfast to decide whether it should participate or not. Two decisions were taken: Trimble would stay in the process and the approach to attendance at the actual talks would be left to him. He was given maximum room for manoeuvre by his party.

Monday morning, 15 September, dawned and we travelled to Castle Buildings for what was to be the actual start of substantive negotiations. Again, the unionists were not there when we arrived. But the DUP was present in word if not in spirit. Paisley's letter demanding our expulsion was the first order of business, and this led to a debate about whether a party, which had chosen not to take part, could nonetheless demand the expulsion of another party. Back to Monty Python.

Trimble had not shown up because the UUP leader, true to his tactical approach, was trying to extract more from the two governments on the decommissioning issue. The two smaller loyalist parties had no real choice. They stayed away also.

Blair and Ahern issued a joint statement in which they laid particular emphasis on the twin issues of consent and decommissioning. They said: "Consent will be a guiding principle . . . in the negotiations for which no outcome is of course excluded or pre-determined." To unionists this read like a reinforcement of the unionist veto. Of course, consent has a wider interpretation – nationalist and republican consent was also needed for any agreement – and the governments knew this.

The Taoiseach and the Prime Minister also acknowledged that the decommissioning issue was an indispensable part of the process of negotiation. They added that, while successful decommissioning would depend on the co-operation of the paramilitary organisations themselves and could not be imposed on them as a pre-condition for successful negotiations, they would both like to see the decommissioning of some paramilitary arms during the negotiations.

None of this persuaded David Trimble to enter the talks building.

The next morning the County Armagh town of Markethill was rocked by a huge explosion. The attack was on the RUC base, but also caused extensive damage to local businesses and homes. Now Trimble joined with Paisley in demanding Sinn Féin's expulsion. The talks looked as if they might be stillborn.

The IRA moved quickly to deny any involvement in the attack. Gerry Kelly, speaking for Sinn Féin, described the bomb attack as regrettable and disappointing. Responsibility for the bombing was later claimed by the Continuity IRA, a tiny republican faction that was set up in 1986.

Twenty-four hours later, David Trimble finally led his delegation into the talks building. As he strode through the car park and through the gates into Castle Buildings, he was flanked by the representatives of the two unionist parties representing the mainstream unionist paramilitary organisations. Despite his vitriolic objections to Sinn Féin, he saw no irony or hypocrisy in walking into the negotiations with the representatives of parties whose armed allies were daily involved in attacks and whose cessations were more often breached than honoured. Trimble told the media that he was not there to negotiate with Sinn Féin, but to confront us, and he would choose the time and the place to do it.

The UUP then demanded our expulsion because of the IRA comments on the Mitchell Principles and because of accusations that the IRA, and not the CIRA, was responsible for Markethill. The next few days were taken up by bilateral discussions between those parties which would talk to each other and with Senator Mitchell and his colleagues and the two governments.

Then on 23 September we all sat around the table in the large conference room given over to the negotiations. Well, at least the UUP, PUP and UDP and the rest of us were there. Paisley's DUP and the UKUP stayed away. Ken Maginnis for the UUP read out a paper which he described as a "Notice of Indictment". When he finished and before I could answer, he and David Trimble left the room. The "Notice of Indictment" was not a serious contribution. It was the unionists making propaganda and using the opportunity to explain how they planned to manage the process of negotiations and Sinn Féin's presence. Trimble said that the unionists would talk to everyone else, but not us.

The two governments deliberated, but in the end concluded that there was no basis for expelling us. Late the following evening, after another tortuous negotiation, a procedural motion was passed. This saw the formal establishment by the two governments of the Independent International Commission on Decommissioning; the appointment of General de Chastelain to chair it; the establishment of two sub-committees, one on decommissioning and one on confidence-building measures; agreement on a comprehensive agenda for the commencement of substantive talks; and acceptance that a business committee should meet as required to co-ordinate the progress and procedures of the negotiations. The date of 7 October was also set as the starting date for substantive negotiations.

It was an important stage in the negotiation process. For us, it was only a matter of a few weeks since we had joined the talks. The other participants had been here since June 1996, and now, for the first time, it looked as if there would be a chance to get down to the real business of making peace.

At this point we invited campaigning groups who wanted to raise their particular issues to come to Castle Buildings to lobby the parties and governments. The next months saw a succession of activists, representing justice, human rights and community groups, visit our rooms. The first was the Irish American campaigner Paul O'Dwyer from New York. Paul and his wife Pat dropped in for a short time. I was delighted to see them. From County Mayo, Paul had worked for many decades as a lawyer and elected official in New York, in support of the Irish cause. He and his friend Frank Durkan, another great justice campaigner, had also represented almost every republican arrested there in the previous thirty years.

Developments outside the talks continued to be a source of great concern. In London, efforts to extradite Róisín McAliskey to Germany were continuing. Since the birth of her daughter, Róisín had been held in the mother and baby unit of Maudsley Psychiatric Hospital. The magistrate had been told that it would be at least eighteen months before she would be fit to appear in court, but he was insisting she be brought before him in December. Further tension was introduced into the situation when three republican political prisoners in Whitemoor prison in England were stripped, assaulted and left naked as staff forcibly took DNA samples.

As we faced our opponents across the negotiating table, these problems pressed in on us. There was a need to make progress. We knew we didn't have sufficient strength at this time to get maximum gains from the negotiations but we could achieve much. It meant being tough and resilient and persuasive. It meant tackling the causes of conflict, establishing political processes and securing legislation and structures through which we could achieve the removal of inequality, discrimination, and division. It meant building support for Irish unity.

Equality is the most important aspect of republicanism. It is also a useful guide to life – or how life could or should be. The achievement of equality of treatment for nationalists and unionists, for everyone in the North will erode the very reason for the existence of this statelet. Unionists traditionally support the union because it enables them to be top of the heap here. A level playing field will make this impossible, and much of unionism will be left without any rational basis. Equality is good for everybody. The management of peace processes elsewhere has demonstrated the importance of creating a context in which the rights and the equality of all citizens can be guaranteed. But again, what did that mean for us sitting in the negotiations in Castle Buildings outside Belfast?

Mitchel McLaughlin put some possible meat on the bones when asked whether Sinn Féin could agree to anything short of a united Ireland. He remarked: "I believe that we can actually conceive, as they did in South Africa, of the possibility of a negotiated agreement that provides for transition from the present failed political entity to a democratic structure that all shades of opinion on this island can give allegiance and authority to."

It was this strategic approach that some of our opponents either ignored or failed to see. Others understood it perfectly and were trying to frustrate it. The Sinn Féin peace strategy is about transitional change, the transformation of political conditions on the island of Ireland. It is about getting a peace settlement and then building on that to continue the pursuit of our other goals and to persuade others – including and especially the unionists – of the efficacy of these. I argued then, and still do, that this requires building a political dynamic for change that is greater than the resistance and opposition to it.

What would it mean in terms of an agreement in these talks? In October 1997, there was a sense, evident too among some unionists, that there could be no going back to the failed policies of the past. That was the theme of our message on the first day of opening negotiations around the three strands. It had been agreed that 7 October would see initial meetings on each of the three, and then for the next two months or so one day each week would be given over to intense discussions. The rest of the week was devoted to bilaterals.

Strand One was chaired by the British Political Affairs Minister Paul Murphy. Its remit was to focus on political structures within the North. Strand Two was chaired by Senator Mitchell and had to tackle relations between the two parts of the island. Strand Three was Irish-British relations and was the responsibility of the two governments. There were also the two sub-committees on weapons and confidence-building measures. And a business committee to prepare for all of these. The agenda was essentially the same for all three strands. These came under the broad headings of: principles and requirements; constitutional issues; nature, form and extent of new arrangement; relationships with other arrangements; rights and safeguards. The only addition was in Strand One where justice issues had been added.

The first day was overshadowed by the resignation of Ray Burke, the Irish Minister for Foreign Affairs, who was at the centre of allegations of corruption in planning matters in the South. He was replaced by David Andrews. It also saw all the parties again setting out our respective stalls. This pattern replayed over and over again in the coming weeks as all of the participants approached each agenda item. David Trimble escaped most of this. He was nowhere to be seen. The unionists kept up their stance of not talking to us. Most of the time.

There were little cracks in their no-talk position. Every now and then some of us would bump into a unionist negotiator on their own. It could not have been otherwise. We were all under the one roof and at times in one room. That room was most often the canteen. Even though all the various factions ate in their own groups, sometimes we ended up in a non-segregated food line. I always said hello. The more rounded unionists would usually reply.

Other, more insecure fellows were downright rude. David Trimble was one of these. Red-faced and belligerent, he would exit stage left if a Shinner hove into view. Some unionists were obviously embarrassed by all this. But if they were in a group they generally ignored our greetings. On their own, some were pleasant. At this time most of my best conversations with unionists were in the toilets. It was generally just small talk.

But it was a beginning.

# Chapter Thirty

# *Meeting Tony Blair*

Tony Blair visited us all at Castle Buildings on 13 October. Under normal circumstances that would have been a good news story for the media, but with Shinners now about the place, it took on "historic" proportions. It would be the first meeting between leaders of Irish republicanism and a British Prime Minister in eighty years – a point repeated by the media ad nauseam.

Martin McGuinness, Pat Doherty, Siobhán O'Hanlon, Jim Gibney and I walked down the stairs from our rooms and along the corridors to the British admin room on the ground floor where the get-together was to take place. Jim was not part of the delegation so he waited in the corridor.

The room set aside for the meeting was a small one. All the blinds were closed. It was typical of the NIO, but it was for no good purpose because the windows faced blank walls. I opened the blinds and we rearranged the furniture to suit ourselves.

Outside the room, Jim made his own history by being the first republican to greet and shake hands with Blair. British officials accompanying the PM thought Jim was one of their own staff, until, that is, they spotted his green ribbon, worn in his lapel in support of the Saoirse campaign for the release of prisoners. But by then the handshake had occurred.

Mr Blair arrived just before ten past four, accompanied by Mo Mowlam, Paul Murphy and several officials. Hands were shaken all round – no one received a shock – smiles and greetings were exchanged, and I welcomed Blair to Ireland with a *céad míle fáilte*. I presented him with a small harp. It was made from turf and I told him it was the only bit of Ireland we wanted him to hold on to. Blair laughed and thanked me. The atmosphere was relaxed and friendly as we took our seats around a small table with a flower arrangement in the middle.

The Prime Minister opened the formal business by emphasising his government's recognition of the need for change and equality of treatment. He told us that he believed it was possible to get a settlement and he felt a deep responsibility to make this work. I acknowledged that he had moved speedily in restoring the process. I told him it was not my intention in the time available to us to give him a history lesson, but we did want him to be the last British Prime Minister with jurisdiction in Ireland.

"This is part of Ireland. In our view, the biggest cause of conflict is British government involvement. The British government has to be the engine for change. How you are going about that is of crucial importance," I said. "There is a need for constitutional change. That means getting rid of all the acts of your parliament which lay claim to Ireland. I heard you say you valued the union but the union for us and other people is of no great value. With all of the good will there is in Ireland and Britain, we could now have a new and better relationship."

Mr Blair told us that there were people who said that this conflict was intractable, impossible to resolve, but his instinctive belief, he said, was that "this is a moment in history" and he would do his bit to achieve it.

I stressed the importance of us talking again, of each of us trying to get into the other's head. "We want to reach out to the unionists. They are our neighbours," I told him. Republicans and nationalists needed to see progress on demilitarisation, on policing, on equality and other matters. "The security agenda has been running this place for thirty years. There has to be a sea change."

I outlined to him, as one example of the difficulties we faced, how Siobhán was stopped by the RUC on her way to see me with sensitive papers about the negotiations. They had searched and read all of the documents.

He asked if I thought the ceasefire would hold.

I told him that as far as I was concerned the last ceasefire was a good one. It had not been reciprocated.

"People have now stopped," I said. "We have to build upon that. It's a big challenge. We have to bring people with us."

Martin McGuinness warned him that there were those in British intelligence who saw all of this as an opportunity to split the IRA. "The British government," he said, "has to recognise that this is a political problem that needs a political resolution." He also pressed Blair for an inquiry into Bloody Sunday, and I told the Prime Minister that it was my intention to raise the Brian Nelson affair.

"Brian Nelson?" he asked.

"Brian Nelson is an agent of one of your government agencies. He brought guns into this country with the full knowledge of British army intelligence and put them into the hands of loyalists. Hundreds have died or been grievously wounded," I told him.

Tony Blair then concluded the meeting by saying that he, too, wanted a settlement which was lasting, and as he left he told us that we would meet again, the next time for a longer engagement. I liked Blair's relaxed style. It was the opposite of the stuffy, arms-length attitude of the Tories we had met. He was personable and informal, easy to talk to and obviously energised by the challenges of his job.

A short time later, while we were busy doing the rounds of the media outside Castle Buildings, the difficulties which this presented were driven home to the Prime Minister. He was surrounded at the Connswater Shopping Centre in East Belfast by scores of irate and angry loyalists. He had gone there to do a walkabout and to meet Peter Robinson, the DUP deputy leader. Someone in the Blair camp had obviously taken their eye off the ball. In the existing climate and on the back of a meeting with us, the more extreme unionists were bound to confront him. Especially when the DUP had been given advance notice of his visit by the NIO.

He was barracked loudly with shouts of "scum" and "traitor". Some of the Paisleyite crowd wore surgical gloves as protection from any contact with a prime ministerial handshake. At one point, it looked as if the Downing Street group would be over-run, and the British Prime Minister had to suffer the indignity of being hustled back into his car. It sped off to shouts of "Go on back to England."

Unionists weren't the only ones with an identity crisis. The presidential campaign in the South of Ireland was exposing the partitionist, anti-nationalist strain within the body politic there. There were five candidates in the field. Among them was Mary McAleese, a former lecturer in law at Queens University in Belfast. Nominated by Fianna Fáil to stand in the presidential election at the end of October, her support from the party leadership effectively shafted Albert Reynolds. He was understandably miffed: not at Mary McAleese, but at Bertie Ahern. Mrs McAleese was a good candidate, her nomination the brainchild of Martin Mansergh. She was from the North.

I met her a few times at Clonard when the Sagart introduced her into our conversations with John Hume some years before. She was a woman of considerable intellect, a strong but modernising Catholic and a funny,

314

engaging conversationalist. Her candidature brought out the worst in some sections of the political establishment in the South and among some in the SDLP. A leaked report of summaries of conversations she had had with an official from the Department of Foreign Affairs in Dublin about the North was run, as if she was supportive of, or sympathetic to, Sinn Féin. McAleese rejected the claims, but it didn't stop the whispering campaign against her.

Then I did an interview in which I pointed to the contradiction in an Irish citizen from the North being able to stand for the presidency but not able to vote for herself. No one in the North could vote in the election. Asked whom I would vote for, if I had a vote, I said that Sinn Féin had taken no formal position on supporting any particular candidate. Personally, I said, I would vote for Mary McAleese. It was all too much for Fine Gael leader John Bruton and others who thought Ireland stopped at the border. A new anti-nationalist crusade commenced with Mary McAleese, and to a lesser extent myself, as the target.

But for every negative there is a positive. The election contest sparked off a wider debate that touched on the issue of the nation and how we, the people of Ireland, see ourselves. Those who were now attacking McAleese were the same people who attacked John Hume and me when we first launched the peace process. They were the same people who condemned President Mary Robinson's visit to West Belfast in June 1993. In the past, censorship and the sound of bombs and guns and conflict had made their task relatively easy. Now they were being challenged!

The opinion polls in the South, as polling day drew closer, seemed to suggest that the result would be close. In the end, Mary McAleese won comfortably.

Back at the talks in Belfast, nothing much was happening. In fact, it is impossible to describe how boring they were at this point. It is impossible to take the reader through the tedium and the slowness of this aspect of the process. As each week passed, all of the parties made their submissions on the agenda points. There were no surprises as each party put up their respective positions. Sinn Féin submitted detailed papers.

I was now of a view that a Northern assembly would be part of any future political institutions. We couldn't expect the unionists to agree to anything else, and the two governments, the other parties and crucially the SDLP were on board for this. With the exception of Martin McGuinness, I kept this to myself.

One day as we drove through the Stormont estate and past the

Parliament Building, I said to him, "You know we are going to end up in there some day."

But even if we had the authority, and we didn't, this was not the point to concede on this issue as the SDLP had done. Our task had to be to ensure that an assembly, if there was to be one, would be ring-fenced and part of all-Ireland structures. This would be one of the crunch issues in the time ahead. In the meantime we pushed our position on decentralisation. The other parties, particularly the SDLP, were derisive about this. It wasn't a real negotiation yet.

On several occasions, the UUP delegates walked out over Articles 2 and 3 of the Irish constitution, which claimed sovereignty over the whole island. They also were working on their tactical approach and seeking to scare the governments with the possibility of a permanent withdrawal from the talks. They wanted Dublin to move. I also had a distinct impression that David Trimble thought that Sinn Féin's entire involvement in the process was tactical. He seemed intent on trying to force us to leave or to get us expelled from the talks.

October also saw a number of other events that were to have serious implications. There were deep divisions within the CLMC – the Combined Loyalist Military Command – the umbrella organisation for the unionist paramilitaries. Some reports spoke of a split. Others claimed that a loyalist death squad had tried to kill me in mid-October while I was launching a new book, *An Irish Voice: The Quest for Peace*, at the republican bookshop on the Falls Road.

Elements within the UDA were clearly unhappy with the process. Their instinct and desire was to go back to killing Catholics. There was also a territorial element as the UDA, UVF, and increasingly the LVF, fought over control of unionist working-class districts. By the end of October, the CLMC disbanded. Attacks on Catholic homes intensified, with Larne and East Antrim becoming a serious focus of petrol bomb attacks.

As a consequence, I met the British Security Minister Adam Ingram to discuss collusion and the presence of overt and covert British forces in nationalist areas. I specifically complained about the RUC refusal to provide information to people who had been told that their lives were at risk. In recent years, several thousand people had been told that personal details held by the British forces were now in the possession of unionist paramilitaries.

The other event in October which was to create problems was the resignation of a number of activists from within the IRA. The IRA had held a convention of the organisation that month. There was a small but vocal number of volunteers who disagreed with the decision to call a cessation in July. Apparently they put a motion to the Convention rejecting the cessation, opposing the Mitchell Principles and protesting about the manner in which the Army Council had dealt with the Army Executive. In essence, they were proposing a motion of no confidence in the outgoing army leadership and its strategy. The motion was rejected by the Convention. The dissidents then block-voted for places on the incoming Executive. They had some people elected, but failed to win any places on the Army Council. At a subsequent Executive meeting, they walked out.

Elements within the British and Irish intelligence systems learned of these developments and fed it to sections of the media. Some of the republicans who resigned also briefed journalists. Both exaggerated the numbers involved and the impact they had on the IRA. There were also some resignations from within Sinn Féin, mainly around the Dundalk area in County Louth on the border. A small number of Sinn Féin members joined an organisation titling itself the 32 County Sovereignty Movement. We informed them that this was incompatible with their Sinn Féin membership. If they wished to retain Sinn Féin membership, they needed to resign from the Sovereignty group. In this way we tackled head on, and within our own rules, the possibility of people exploiting their Sinn Féin membership to undermine the party or, more importantly, Sinn Féin's peace strategy.

One of our goals in the process was to keep republicans united. As the Irish writer and former IRA activist the late Brendan Behan once remarked, the first thing on any republican agenda is the split. Regrettably, too often in the past, this had been the outcome of divisions among republicans. And too often, republicans had killed other republicans over these differences. The worst of this had been the Civil War, but even in my own time in the 1970s there were several bloody feuds, mostly in Belfast. And in the 1970s, 1980s and 1990s, the INLA had fragmented into bitter and deadly factionalism.

When the dust settled on this a new armed group calling itself the "Real IRA" was to emerge. This assertion that it was the real thing meant that it was quickly nicknamed "the Coca-Colas" by young people in the North.

Despite the hype around these developments, the vast majority of republicans remained united. This was crucial if we were to build on the peace process. It was also essential if we were to advance the wider

317

republican goals of unity and independence. Divisions and schisms would only help our enemies.

Back at Government Buildings, rigor mortis had almost set into the proceedings. Outside in the real world, there was a tangible disappointment with the pace of the negotiations.

The lack of progress on demilitarisation and prisoners was putting us under pressure in the republican constituency. An announcement by Mo Mowlam on 25 November that daytime British army patrols were to stop in West Belfast caused outrage. It was a minimalist move, which showed a total ignorance of republican and nationalist attitudes to the British forces. For people in heavily militarised nationalist and republican areas, there had been little benefit on the ground to show for the cessation. This was compounded by an absence of progress in the negotiations. Most unionists were still refusing to even say hello, never mind enter into serious negotiations.

We therefore decided to do a series of activist meetings and talk to the base – to the grassroots activists who run the Sinn Féin party. These meetings provided us with an opportunity to give an update on the talks, reiterate the republican goals and persuade people to look to the future.

One of these meetings was in the Europa Hotel, once called the most bombed hotel in the world. Over a thousand republicans packed into its main conference room. I urged people to ensure that the struggle was not reduced to a negotiating room in Stormont. The future of the island was too important for that. I appealed to the audience not to be duped or hypnotised into spectatorism and not to leave the process to the negotiators.

There was thunderous applause when Des Murphy from Camlough in South Armagh declared that the people of that area were 110 per cent behind us. His intervention was a direct rejection of speculation in the media about serious divisions among republicans in that area.

A few days later, I spoke at a conference in Belfast organised by Saoirse, the campaign for prisoner release. In a blunt message to the two governments, I told them that there would be no deal without the release of prisoners.

We were also trying to focus attention on the need for demilitarisation. The South Armagh Farmers and Residents Committee visited Castle Buildings at our invitation to lobby the other parties and the two governments. This group had done sterling work in opposing and highlighting the intrusion into the life of this rural area. They did the round of whatever parties would meet them and then met with the Irish government.

The militarisation of South Armagh was highly offensive to the people of this tightly knit rural community. In this they were no different from other rural communities in Fermanagh or Tyrone, but the extent of the very visible spy posts and hilltop forts and other Checkpoint Charlie-type fortifications and the regional cohesion and sense of identity of the area brought a special passion to the rejection by its people of the British forces.

This was brought home forcefully to one unfortunate Irish official who tried to divert a vigorous engagement into less controversial topics. After failing a few times, he then seized on the fortunes of the Armagh Gaelic football team in a last effort to get some point of harmony.

"How far do you think Armagh will go in the championship?"

"We didn't come all this distance to discuss fucking football!" one irate lobbyist told him.

Tensions of a deadlier kind between the various unionist paramilitary organisations had increased since the collapse of the CLMC. November had seen a founding member of the UDA in Portadown and a notorious sectarian killer mysteriously killed in an explosion at Warrenpoint in County Down. Another man was beaten to death by the UDA in South-East Antrim. In Derry, feuding gangs were busy threatening each other. In Belfast, they went further and tried to kill one another. Sectarian attacks against Catholics increased.

The two governments circulated a paper seeking agreement by 17 December on the broad parameters of a settlement. This would comprise a succinct statement of the key constitutional, institutional, and rights, equality and confidence-building elements of an agreement which could prove widely acceptable.

The paper said: "A lot of further detailed negotiations would be necessary to fill out any such outline agreement, but once the key parameters had been set it would be easier to draw up a work plan to achieve that. Negotiations on specific individual issues or 'cross strand' issues would be easier to pursue once everyone had a reasonably clear general picture of the overall shape of the likely outcome."

At a plenary meeting on the same day it was agreed to change the format of the talks to try to get a better focus on the discussions. George Mitchell felt that a smaller format in a smaller room and without microphones might be more conducive to talks. The new format called for the party leader and deputy leader to represent the party.

This was an obvious and relatively straightforward move to bring the discussions into a more workable and productive format. It also reflected Senator Mitchell's style. He spent a great deal of his time in side meetings with the parties. I found him to be a good-natured, humorous and patient man.

When I asked him once why he was prepared to spend so much of his time in our process, he replied, "Because my President asked me." He reflected then for a minute and continued, "Also because I think it is a duty on me to help build a peace process."

He used his experience as Senate majority leader to good effect. During one plenary session of the talks when Ken Maginnis had attacked us in most unparliamentary language for the umpteenth time, I protested to the Senator. He called for a brief adjournment, presumably to settle things down. Then on his return he gave a little talk about protocol. The senate, parliaments and learned societies, he told us, used terms like honourable member or other such genteel titles so that business could be conducted in a good atmosphere. Ken Maginnis, like the rest of us, probably knew that. But the Senator's little reminder caused him to temper his tone. For a while anyway.

Meanwhile, back at the smaller meetings we were attempting to make progress. David Trimble was absent from the first meeting. The chairs circulated a paper identifying the key issues "as submitted by some of the participants". They were not listed in any priority and none were agreed.

Sinn Féin had already acknowledged the right of a participant to put any issue on the agenda, so no one on the republican side got upset at the presence of a proposal for an assembly in the North contained in Strand One. In anticipation of this, the Ard Chomhairle had agreed that, notwithstanding our own position, we could discuss this matter and seek to ensure that satisfactory safeguards were put in place to prevent unionist abuse. The new format was a significant little step forward, but securing a Heads of Agreement (or the outline of an acceptable peace agreement) was not going to be easy. Especially when the Irish government seemed intent on sending conflicting signals of its objectives in the talks. The new Minister for Foreign Affairs David Andrews had rashly said on taking up office that there wouldn't be a United Ireland in his lifetime. That angered republicans. Then he said he expected cross-border institutions with executive power would result from the talks. The unionists screamed foul and demanded an apology. Andrews obliged.

Gusty Spence, the former UVF leader and now part of the PUP team, remarked caustically: "Andrews is a nice man. But he doesn't know whether it is Pancake Tuesday or Easter Sunday."

The PUP and the UDP delegates were much more open for conversation with us than representatives of the larger parties. Gary McMichael, whose father, a paramilitary leader, was killed in a bomb attack by the IRA, had more reason than most to hate republicans. Yet he was among the first to shake hands, and though he fought his corner in a robust way he was always respectful towards us. Hughie Smith, a loyalist veteran from Belfast's Shankill Road, was always ready with a pithy and humorous put-down which lightened up the sometimes dour or boring sessions.

The other unionists continued to be stand-offish. According to media reports, they thought Sinn Féin was in a love blitz against them. We weren't, but that didn't stop them from complaining that smiling Shinners were always at hand to open doors and to greet them at every opportunity. We were behaving normally, and some of the more rounded unionists continued to respond in kind when they were on their own. But in a group, they returned to ignoring us again. The more decent ones still had the grace to look slightly embarrassed. With good cause. A genuine "Good Morning. How are you?" earlier was replaced by a sullen juvenile group stare later in the day, especially if the group included some of the ruder elements.

Progress was pitifully, painfully slow. I felt sorry for Senator Mitchell. He was flying back and forth across the Atlantic. And he was growing restless. Once, after a particularly frustrating day as he and I and Martin tried to pick a way through the negativity, he told us with a smile, "You have a life and this is it. I have a life and this isn't it."

Then at the beginning of December, Ahern told the London *Financial Times* that his government was willing to drop Articles 2 and 3 of the Irish constitution. We complained. And it took Ahern several days to qualify his remarks by placing them in the context of changes to the British Government of Ireland Act.

While this was going on, the LVF killed another Catholic member of the GAA. He was shot seven times at the entrance to St Enda's GAA Club.

The spectre of failure loomed large over the process. There was a simmering row going on inside the talks. Efforts to find a Heads of Agreement were getting nowhere. The UUP was trying to minimise and reduce the issues to be included under Heads of Agreement. Then the SDLP position collapsed. They and the unionists produced one list. It appeared that Seamus Mallon had done a side deal. Their list left out prisoners, the equality agenda and demilitarisation.

We and the Irish government rejected this because it was too vague. We insisted that any such list of issues had to include prisoners, equality and demilitarisation. We restated our willingness not to block any proposal by other participants. But the UUP refused to commit itself to this approach.

It was speculated that Trimble was loath to put his name to anything that would give Ian Paisley ammunition to use against him. But really, this was the unionists holding out for a better offer from the two governments.

On 8 December, Bertie Ahern paid the talks a visit and travelled into West Belfast where we brought him to the Meanscoil, the Irish language secondary school on the Falls Road, to meet teachers and pupils.

Three days later, Martin McGuinness, Michelle Gildernew, Siobhán O'Hanlon, Richard McAuley, Martin Ferris, Lucilita Bhreatnach and I travelled to London for the first meeting between a republican delegation and a British Prime Minister in Downing Street since the Treaty negotiations in 1921.

It was just before 2 p.m. when the seven of us walked into the inner hall of Number 10. I looked around at all the portraits on the walls of former Prime Ministers. A few seconds later we walked down the long hall to the Cabinet Room where Tony Blair, Mo Mowlam, Paul Murphy, Quentin Thomas, Alistair Campbell (Blair's press person), Jonathan Powell (Blair's Chief of Staff) and John Holmes (private secretary) stood in the doorway to shake hands and greet us.

Martin, always sensitive to the history of events, referred to the Treaty negotiations eighty years earlier and mused, "So this is the room where the damage was done in '21?"

"I think so," said Tony Blair.

"It also has the ghosts of the last government," remarked Martin.

The delegations faced each other across the Cabinet table.

I said, "It's a strange custom you English have of putting all your failures on the wall."

The Prime Minister understandably looked puzzled, so I explained.

"In the hall where we waited, you have portraits of Gladstone, Balfour, Lloyd George and others. All great statesmen in the eyes of the British people, but in the eyes of most Irish people they were all failures because they made a mess of Ireland. You have an opportunity to do what they didn't. To build a new relationship."

And then we got down to what turned out to be a good meeting. I acknowledged the risks that the Prime Minister and his government were taking and told him that we were absolutely committed to making this work.

"We want this to be the end game," I told the British delegation.

"I don't want this meeting to be one which gets into the nitty-gritty. We can do that with Mo," I said.

This was about persuading the British government to have a strategic view that went beyond containment or pacification. What was needed was a leap of imagination.

"Why should any British government be against Irish unity? Why can you not be agents of change? Every one of us in this room will be dead in fifty years. What legacy will we leave? This isn't about us; this is about our children."

I told the Prime Minister and his colleagues sitting across from me, "Your Irish policy will be your greatest challenge of your term or terms in office."

Blair told us that he didn't believe that people would vote for a united Ireland but he did want a new relationship that made sense of the history and of our situation. I pointed out that there was a time when people would not vote for his party. So, if we got 51 per cent opting for a united Ireland, then his government had to be prepared to legislate for that new situation. I told them that we wanted them to bring about the end of the union. As part of a process to achieve this, I raised the issue of the Government of Ireland Act and argued that there was a need for it to be dumped.

I told Mr Blair that changes in the relationship between these two islands would need to be reflected in a new act. We wanted to bring about an end to British rule in a way that was least disruptive and most beneficial to all the people who live on the island of Ireland.

The Prime Minister had obviously not been briefed on the Government of Ireland Act. He said that he was prepared to look positively at changing it, but then with a laugh he remarked, "I'd better watch I'm not going too far."

He looked to his officials for guidance, and after a brief consultation he told us he would come back on this issue.

Blair then asked about the ceasefire, and speculation in the media that it was to end.

"They have little enough to be writing about," I said.

I told him that if we achieved a level playing pitch on equality, on justice, on democratic rights, then I was quite convinced that through this unarmed alternative we could persuade people of the merits of a united Ireland. I pointed to the fact that already many business people in the North, mainly unionists, saw the benefits of Ireland being treated as a single economy.

There were two blocks to progress – British policy and the unionist veto. "What we want is that you and your government should end British rule in our country . . . let us begin to think outside the restrictions of British policy and the unionist veto."

The discussions slipped into some of the core issues – policing, demilitarisation, the need for an inquiry into Bloody Sunday and other matters. The way that Blair responded to the Bloody Sunday lobby was insightful. We knew he was being pressed by the Irish government, as well as ourselves and John Hume. Since Martin had raised it at our first meeting, Blair seemed more conscious of the issues involved. I had written before on behalf of the relatives, and there seemed to be a process of engagement on the issue by the Prime Minister. He was not dismissing our presentation; if anything, he seemed interested in hearing our views.

Martin McGuinness briefly brought our discussions back to the talks by urging Blair to realise that he needed to encourage David Trimble to engage.

Beyond this, it took a few minutes to wind the meeting up. I wished them all a Happy Christmas, and then Richard and Alistair Campbell on the side agreed our positions to the media going out. The meeting had lasted almost an hour.

It was a good beginning. There was a lot more to be done, but for the first time in my lifetime, we had a British Prime Minister listening directly to Irish republicans and hearing our concerns and our hopes. As we parted, I spoke to Blair on the side and encouraged him to keep going as he had started.

"You need to be the British Prime Minister to make the difference," I told him. "We can make this work if you make it work."

I found Blair to be an interesting and engaging personality. He seemed to have a genuine interest in what we were saying, and I dared to hope that there was a chance that we could actually do business with him. Of course, I knew that he was a highly skilled politician used to dealing with people and to winning their support.

Back in Belfast, there was an effort to conclude discussions around the Heads of Agreement. But it wasn't to be. David Trimble was not prepared to agree that matters of importance to us could be on the agenda for discussion. Before we were permitted into the talks, he had helped draw up the rules to allow for all parties to put issues forward for discussion. But now we were there to discuss these matters, David had changed his mind.

The negotiation teams met for the last time before Christmas on 16 December. It was not a good meeting. Our collective task was to conclude an agreed statement of the key issues to be resolved and an agreed format to achieve this. There was no agreement.

Senator Mitchell then set out the schedule of meetings for when the talks recommenced. Some were to be held in London in January, some in Dublin in February. Everyone had agreed to this previously, or so we thought. Now the Ulster Unionist Party objected.

The meeting got a bit hot and heavy. Everyone was tired. The end result was that there were no decisions taken. We adjourned for Christmas having met none of our targets. I suggested that it was important, notwithstanding the difficulties, that the message we give to the public should be positive. To do otherwise would be to encourage the death squads and others who were eager to derail the process. The fact was we were not giving up, the process was far from finished, and we would be back in January.

Before wishing us all a peaceful Christmas, George Mitchell reminded us that for most of the participants this was the fifth lengthy break in the process since it had begun in June 1996. It would be the last, he said.

But the Christmas and New Year period were to be far from peaceful. A few days before Christmas Day, loyalist prisoners warned that their support for the talks process would be reviewed over Christmas. Then Billy Wright – the man who had established the LVF – was shot dead in prison by an INLA prisoner. Wright had been sentenced to eight years in prison earlier in the year for threatening to kill a woman.

A few hours later, the LVF warned that, "Billy Wright will not have died in vain. The LVF will widen its theatre of operations in the coming weeks and months."

This meant killing Catholics. That night the LVF shot dead a Catholic doorman at a hotel in Dungannon. Four nights later, two loyalist gunmen walked into a pub in North Belfast and opened fire. One man was killed and five others wounded. The LVF claimed responsibility. However, most people believed that despite the use of an authentic LVF code word, it was more likely the work of the UDA. The RUC declared it was "keeping an open mind" on who was responsible. The reality, of course, was that if UDA involvement was proven, the presence of its political allies, the UDP, in the talks at Stormont would be in doubt.

The effort to build a peace process was proving to be difficult. Christmas that year was bleak, especially for the families of the dead.

# Chapter Thirty-One

# *Progress – and Setbacks*

Shortly after the New Year, the loyalist prisoners in Long Kesh said that they were withdrawing their support from the talks process. The PUP then threatened to pull out.

David Trimble and several of his colleagues visited the loyalist prisoners. They had a three-hour meeting. I was critical of their meeting. Not because I was against it – we had no difficulty with Trimble meeting the loyalists – but because he was refusing to speak to Sinn Féin.

Trimble's tactical approach was about minimising the potential for change. In an unprecedented move, Mowlam also met with loyalist prisoners in the H-Blocks at Long Kesh on 9 January. Her goal was to persuade them to continue their support for the talks process. She was widely criticised by unionist politicians. Some again demanded her resignation. But the loyalist prisoners opted to back the talks. Her unusual and widely publicised initiative was vindicated.

Two days later, and on the eve of the resumption of the final round of negotiations, I was asleep when my brother Paddy phoned me. I remember my sense of shock when he said, "Young Terry has been shot. He's dead. I'm up in the house now. Everybody is shattered."

Young Terry was Terry Enright, the twenty-eight-year-old husband of my niece Deirdre. He was shot and killed outside the Space Nightclub in Belfast's Cathedral Quarter. He was a community activist, particularly popular because of his work with young people. He was a big, athletic young guy, brash, open and friendly. Terry's wife Deirdre was my sister Margaret's oldest girl. She also was a confident and happy young person. She and Terry had two daughters: Aoife, almost two, and Ciara, aged four.

The Enright family and our clann were devastated by Terry's murder. So was the local community in the Upper Springfield area. During Terry's wake, I continued with meetings in Government Buildings. On the evening before his funeral, some of the senior Irish government officals travelled across town with me to pay their respects. They were visibly shocked by the unrestrained sound of keening and wailing as we walked up the street to the wake-house. It was the young people. A sense of mass hysteria seemed to have overcome the hundreds of youngsters who were gathered outside.

It was the same at the funeral, which took place on a bitterly cold January afternoon. Thousands lined the route and thousands more followed the cortège, led by a lone piper from Terry's home to Holy Trinity Church in Turf Lodge. A huge number of young people attended. Many carried homemade banners and placards, some representing local youth groups; others had made their own personal tributes.

Terry was a keen hurler and footballer for Gort na Móna, the local GAA club. His coffin was draped in the club's colours, and the funeral procession was stewarded by his clubmates and preceded by members of Gort na Móna camogie team. They carried a floral tribute to "a true Gael".

After the Mass, as we made our way down the Springfield Road towards the Whiterock Road, I was walking close to Deirdre and gently joking with her in an effort to keep her spirits up. She was being tremendously brave. We were talking about Terry and about the crowds who came to mourn him.

"If only I had got talking to him. Even just to say goodbye," Deirdre said. "Even if he would send me some signal."

Almost as soon as she spoke, a rainbow appeared in the sky above us. Then as we got to the top of the Whiterock another rainbow criss-crossed the first one, making a huge multi-coloured cross in the blue heavens. It stretched above us, from the heights where our sad procession meandered, across and over the city of Belfast. There was an excited little ripple of exclamations through our family group, particularly among the younger ones. Someone declared, "That's Terry."

I know it sounds daft. But Deirdre and I and the rest of the clan thought it was him.

\* \* \* \* \*

The two governments had put together a Heads of Agreement paper. Tabled on their behalf by Senator Mitchell, it included proposals on changes to the Irish and British constitutions; a new British-Irish agreement to replace the Anglo-Irish Agreement; an intergovernmental council drawn from the two governments and the various assemblies within Britain; a North-South Ministerial Council to bring together those with executive responsibilities in both parts of Ireland in specific areas; implementation bodies; an assembly in the North elected by proportional representation; and a bill of rights. There was also a cursory nod in the direction of prisoners, policing and other matters.

Most of the parties generally welcomed the proposals. We didn't. They failed to address properly some crucial issues. There was no equality of approach across the three strands. For example, the issue of an assembly was elevated above the North-South institutions. It needed to be an integral part of them. There could be no Six County internal solution. When unionists had a parliament at Stormont they abused their powers. There could be no return to this system. The assembly was dealt with in quite specific language, whereas the North-South bodies were outlined in more ambiguous terms.

The unionists publicly claimed that the Heads of Agreement paper was a victory for them.

The killings went on at a frightening rate. On 18 January, a young Catholic was killed in Maghera. The following day, the INLA killed a UDA man in South Belfast, and within hours another Catholic – a taxi driver – was shot dead on the Ormeau Road. The next three days saw three more Catholics shot and killed. Belfast was a dangerous town. I was conscious of this as I moved around. While life appeared to go on as normal, there was an increased tension and brittleness about the place. Nationalists in the city were particularly aggrieved because all the recent killings were happening in the context of the IRA cessation. It seemed that nothing would satisfy the unionists. The random nature of the attacks also meant that any Catholic was a potential target. History was being repeated. Little wonder Belfast Catholics felt particularly vulnerable during times of change or potential change.

I wrote to Mo Mowlam and David Andrews asking specific questions about the North-South institutions. I also travelled with senior colleagues to London to meet Tony Blair again. This time we raised our concerns about the Heads of Agreement paper. I gave Mr Blair another potted history of the Brian Nelson affair and British involvement with the UDA. I put the ongoing UDA campaign in that context. I also pressed him about the killing of Pat Finucane and other state-sponsored killings.

While he had no direct responsibility for these actions which had occurred in the past, he did have a duty to lift the lid on this practice if he was serious about building peace. And he had a responsibility about what was happening now. These killings were continuing with the indulgence, direction or approval of elements of British government agencies – particularly the RUC Special Branch and British military intelligence. Again we raised the need for a Bloody Sunday inquiry, and again I noticed a marked difference in his approach. He was more informed than in our earlier discussions. As I listened to him and Martin discussing in a fairly detailed way the events of that day, I knew progress was being made.

The IRA was also watching events unfold. On 21 January a statement from the army rejected the Heads of Agreement paper as a basis for a peace settlement. It accused Tony Blair of succumbing to the Orange card.

The next day the RUC Chief Constable Ronnie Flanagan acknowledged what everyone already knew. He blamed some, although not all, of the recent killings of Catholics on the UDA. Twenty-four hours later, the UDA admitted that it had killed a number of people in "a measured military response" to the INLA. According to the statement, the UDA was now back on ceasefire. A few hours later a thirty-nine-year-old Catholic was shot dead in North Belfast. His death was followed twenty-four hours later by that of another Catholic taxi driver. Their deaths made a mockery of the UDA statement.

But what to do about the UDP, the UDA's political representatives in the talks? That was the question that now faced the governments. They and the other parties had agreed the rules during the period when Sinn Féin was excluded from the talks. We wanted no one excluded, and I said it was a matter for the two governments.

The talks were to move to Lancaster House in London on 26 January, and it was expected that the presence of the UDP would be the first item on the agenda. Meanwhile, in private meetings with senior Irish government officials, we were focusing in on the need for a North-South paper, which would bring any envisaged institutions into line at least with the Framework Document. We were also making it clear, in a without-prejudice way, that there would have to be major checks and balances and safeguards against unionist abuses if an assembly was established, despite our opposition to it.

Constitutional changes were also discussed, including the need for changes to Article 29 of the Irish constitution to allow for the new North-South structures. We were assured there would be no constitutional changes to the Irish constitution without a wider agreement, and we were given draft words that Dublin had written up on Article 1 of any new agreement. This would deal with the issues of self-determination and consent. We agreed to look at it and come back to them.

At another meeting with senior officials, I was told that the two governments were beginning to put down their thoughts on an endgame paper and that this would be ready in a few weeks. The North-South paper was unlikely to be ready for the start of talks in London, and anyway the issue of the UDP would take up the first day.

A large Sinn Féin delegation flew to London on Sunday. That night some of us spoke at a packed public meeting. Back at the hotel, the lights burned late in my room as fourteen of us jammed together to plot a course for the Lancaster House meetings. Pat Doherty had grabbed the one chair. Everyone else either stood or sat on the floor or the edge of the bed. We had twenty-four or perhaps thirty-six hours in which to influence the North-South paper by the two governments.

Our meeting decided on a straightforward approach. It was to establish if the North-South institutions would exercise executive, harmonising and consultative functions; would they be responsible for policy and implementation; what areas would be covered? There was also a brief discussion about the participation of the UDP. We agreed that there would be no definitive public position by us on whether the UDP should be in or out.

The next morning we were all up bright and early. It was chilly but nice. We walked to Lancaster House, a short distance across Piccadilly to the end of Green Park. This is part of the Royal Parks complex including St James's Park. With my Walkman plugged in and Christy Moore singing in my ear, I was glad to stretch my legs along the avenue of mature trees, many of them very old and gnarled. En route a number of people greeted us pleasantly and wished us well. A dander down Queens Walk, alongside Lancaster House and we were on The Mall, across from Buckingham Palace. And not a peeler in sight.

Lancaster House was originally built in 1825 as York House. It is now owned by the British government and used for major conferences. It sits in the grounds of St James's Palace, the London home of the Prince of Wales. After we cleared the security at the entrance, we walked into a huge hall dominated by a central staircase that is 80 foot square and 120 feet high. We left our coats and walked up the staircase to the stately rooms on the first floor, which had been allocated for our discussions. These had witnessed many historic events over the years. Perhaps most famously it was the venue in 1979 for the negotiations which led to the end of Rhodesia and the creation of Zimbabwe. Almost two decades earlier, this is where the Commonwealth decided to kick out the apartheid regime of

South Africa. And in another century, the cause to end slavery was debated within these walls.

It was here – amid the grandeur and the Louis XIV interiors and the other fine furnishings, undoubtedly stolen from around the world or purchased with ill-gotten imperial gains – that we were trying to make our own history. The first order of business was the UDP. Senator Mitchell was asked by the two governments to speak to its delegation. He gently suggested to them that rather than wait until they were expelled, they should voluntarily leave. They agreed and left quietly soon after. The governments announced if there was a complete restoration of the UDA ceasefire, the UDP would be allowed back into the talks. They returned four weeks later.

That evening Martin and I went for a walk. We were taken by Phil – a supporter who looked after us in London – to Speakers' Corner at Marble Arch. It was late evening and there weren't many people around. Phil explained to us the tradition behind Speakers' Corner. I invited Martin to say a few words and loudly introduced him. For a few minutes, to the amazement of our friends and the few people hurrying to their homes, Martin McGuinness stood in oratorical pose and spoke loudly about Irish republicanism and the need for the British to leave Ireland. Our small group applauded him with enthusiasm. That Speakers' Corner speech was one of his best orations. It was certainly one of his shortest.

More seriously, back at Lancaster House, I tried to focus the media on the refusal of the UUP to speak to Sinn Féin. This wasn't about having a go at David Trimble. I believed then, and still do, that we needed a good engagement with a section of unionism to get an agreement and to make it work. Getting David Trimble into dialogue with us was central to this.

Chances of that continued to be remote. At one point I tried to speak to Ken Maginnis. He was on his own and by now he had done several television interviews with Sinn Féin representatives, including me. So in a tiny little effort to build a conversation, I said hello and tried to engage him in conversation. He wasn't having any of it.

"I don't talk to fucking murderers," he said and stormed off.

I also tried to speak to Trimble on the margins of the conference room but he reddened, snapped his heels together and took off with an angry gasp of annoyance and nary a backward glance. Or an expletive.

Tuesday afternoon saw the eventual delivery of the two governments' long-awaited paper – "Strand Two – North/South Structures". In it they restated their firm commitment to the positions set out in the Framework Document. The paper then posed fourteen questions to the delegations, ranging from what the purpose of such bodies should be to the nature and basis of the Ministerial Council. I welcomed the paper and stressed the importance of the equality agenda and the need to deal with justice, policing, cultural matters and much more.

That evening there was a reception in the front hall of Lancaster House attended by Tony Blair. He said a few words of encouragement to the assembled talks participants. It was a low-key event, though I could see how the venue, with its plentiful supply of nooks and crannies, the move away from Government Buildings and the absence of Belfast tension could encourage progress. That is, if there was a political will.

The following morning I wrote a private note to David Trimble and asked for a meeting. I got his response through *The Irish Times*. They received my note and a claim from Trimble that I wasn't serious and that the invite was just a PR stunt. That told a lot about Mr Trimble's mindset. He probably thought he was getting one up on me by breaking this wee initiative to the media. But if he really thought it was a PR stunt then why, I asked myself, was he acting as my press officer?

The last day of the Lancaster House talks saw the parties respond to the governments' questions. Senator Mitchell agreed that written answers could be submitted. The unionists were dismissive of the Strand Two paper. To underline this point, the UUP MP Jeffrey Donaldson tore up a copy of the Framework Document at a packed press conference, proclaiming, "We as a party will not put our hand to any agreement based on the Framework Document."

Rumour had it that he couldn't possibly have torn up the document without first having it already partially cut and sections of it removed. This provided light relief to talks insiders, but it did not detract from the serious message of intransigence he was delivering.

We gave our views to the Senator. We also put it to him that he needed to be serious about setting a deadline for the talks. He was amused by our insistence.

"You think I like flying back and forth across the Atlantic? I've told you before: you have a life and this is it. I have a life and . . ."

". . . this isn't it!" Martin and I chorused back at him.

Near the end of that month, Tony Blair took the courageous step of announcing in the British House of Commons that there would be a fresh inquiry into the events on Bloody Sunday twenty-six years earlier. I considered this a brave decision. I believe the big breakthrough was achieved when Blair read a book of evidence prepared by the families of the dead and wounded of Bloody Sunday and presented by the Irish government. He read it over a weekend at Chequers. That made up his mind. Whatever emerges from that inquiry, it was a huge vindication of the decades of campaigning by the Bloody Sunday families.

We moved into February with a paper from the talks secretariat posing another list of questions for delegations in respect of an Assembly. Behind the scenes we were engaged in extensive discussions with the Irish government across all of the major issues which this involved.

It was our view that it was tactically too early to even consider changing the Sinn Féin position on a Northern Assembly. We continued hardballing. If this was now a real negotiation, and it was, we wanted strong North-South bodies, and if there was to be an Assembly, we wanted the strongest possible safeguards and as much power as possible.

The UUP seemed to be after a non-legislative assembly with minimal powers. Their logic appeared to that the fewer powers the assembly had, the less powers any all-Ireland structures would have; the less influence and power nationalists and republicans would have; the safer would be the union.

The SDLP had already conceded on the assembly, but in fairness to them they were arguing for an assembly with more power and authority than the UUP wanted. For our part we knew that this negotiation had some time to run, and, on the basis of what government officials were telling us privately, it would conclude with a paper prepared in the main by the governments, along with Senator Mitchell and his team.

An agreement needed Sinn Féin, so this gave us some leverage in the negotiations. We intended to play it for all it was worth. I also knew that republicans would not countenance any involvement which resembled the old unionist status quo at Stormont. I would not countenance it myself, though I thought, as I have said before, that we would have to give on the assembly if we got proper terms and an acceptable agreement across all the other issues. The trick was not to tell any of our opponents this while trying to get the best assembly possible, firmly locked into and interdependent on the all-Ireland institutions. Without the all-Ireland architecture, there could be no Northern assembly.

Some within the SDLP accused us of being obstructive over the issue of an assembly. The reality was that we wanted more than the SDLP. Our strategy was an all-Ireland strategy, not one focused on structures within the North, and with little attention being paid to the rest. This negotiation was going to go to the wire.

On 9 February a known drug dealer was shot dead in South Belfast.

Almost immediately the RUC started briefing the media that it was the IRA who had shot him. The next day a senior UDA figure was killed in Dunmurry, on the outskirts of West Belfast. It was alleged that he had been involved in recent sectarian attacks on Catholics, including at least one murder. Again, the RUC pointed the finger at the IRA. A short time later three men were arrested in the nearby nationalist Twinbrook estate.

Unlike his procrastination over naming the UDA, within days the Chief Constable was telling Mowlam that the IRA was responsible for the attacks. The IRA said that its cessation of military operations remained intact. But the unionists had the bit between their teeth, and as the talks prepared to move to Dublin for three days of discussions on Strand Two, the demand was for Sinn Féin to be expelled.

Sinn Féin was not involved in either killing. We were opposed to these actions. We had not dishonoured the Mitchell Principles, and there was no evidence to suggest otherwise. In addition, double standards were being applied by the British, both in respect of the killings by unionist paramilitaries and also by the ongoing actions of its own forces. We decided to fight any effort to expel us.

I made this clear to Mo Mowlam when I met her in Dublin Castle early on the Monday morning. It was not a good meeting. I challenged her to present evidence of Sinn Féin involvement in these attacks. How could we respond to an indictment if we couldn't see the evidence?

The media, and probably the other parties, thought it was cut and dried and would be over by mid-afternoon. That was certainly the impression the British briefers – spin-doctors – were giving. The penny finally dropped around 3 p.m. when Martin McGuinness told a bunch of astounded journalists that we intended fighting this every step of the way. Our mandate came from the people, not from the RUC.

Mowlam didn't make a formal indictment of Sinn Féin. Her position was set out in remarks she made to the plenary from a speaking note. Privately, on the side of the plenary, in the plenary session itself and in the media, our delegates and press people argued, debated, objected and challenged. Later that night, a thousand people packed into Liberty Hall. There was an overflow of several hundred outside. Gerry Kelly addressed the crowd outside. I told the audience inside that if the British government thought they could bring us into Dublin Castle, kick us in the arse and send us home again, then they were wrong.

Defiance was in the air, and we brought it with us the next morning when we walked back into Dublin Castle.

The British remained reluctant to formally indict us. The Alliance Party came to the rescue. With no information to substantiate the British accusation, they indicted us.

As the arguments raged inside Dublin Castle, we initiated a legal challenge in the courts. It was all very bizarre. Thus far there had been little or no substantive progress on the core issues. The unionists were barely talking to anyone and not at all to us. Now the entire focus was on expelling us. All of our efforts and the risks we had taken for peace, all the years of hard, quiet, mind-numbing work were being thrown back in our faces. And we were fighting a rearguard action for our rights and the rights of our voters against unsubstantiated allegations. To cap it all, the unionists accused us of having an exit strategy from the talks.

By Tuesday evening, the anger and frustration that had been building up within me exploded at a media doorstep. I told a surprised media pack that I was absolutely pissed off at republicans having to stretch ourselves all the time to save this process. It was not one of my more considered expressions, but it caused some amusement back in Belfast where someone produced T-shirts with "I'm pissed off too" across their chests.

By the time the talks ended on Wednesday, no other business had been done. The governments told us they would give their verdict to us on Friday. This was done at a ten-minute meeting at Castle Buildings where I was informed by some sheepish Irish government representatives and their British counterparts that provided nothing else happened we could be back by 9 March. I warned that we might not turn up on 9 March and asked for early meetings with the Taoiseach and the British Prime Minister. An interesting and important postscript to this crisis came with the release several months later of the three men whose arrest and alleged links to the IRA had been used to justify our expulsion. The releases did not get the same coverage as the arrests.

The same day we were expelled, a huge bomb exploded at Moira, and two days later there was another one in Portadown. Both caused extensive damage, but thankfully no one was hurt. Once again, the unionists jumped to blame the IRA. It denied any involvement. Responsibility for the explosions was claimed by the CIRA.

The meeting I had requested with Taoiseach Bertie Ahern took place on 24 February. He was relaxed but worried. We were out of the negotiations and the unionists were still setting out their impossibly inflexible position while refusing to engage properly with anyone. I told Bertie that the governments needed to build confidence into the talks. In the meantime, we would continue to meet with officials. After I met the British Prime Minister, Sinn Féin would decide what we would do.

Other Sinn Féin demands were piling up. There were by-elections in Limerick and Dublin, as well as the normal work of running a party and representing a constituency. In the midst of this, and before we met Mr Blair and headed off for the usual St Patrick's Day events in the USA, Richard, Eamon and I travelled to Wexford for the 200th anniversary of the 1798 Rising. It was a wonderful journey through some of the most scenic parts of Ireland. The weather was bright but cold. Wexford is a county replete with the history of struggle against the British. It was also the setting for some of the bloodiest fighting during the 1798 Rising.

Cnoc Fíodh na gCaor, or Vinegar Hill, overlooks the town of Enniscorthy, through which runs the River Slaney. Its rocky terrain and steep sides must have seemed a perfect place in late June 1798 for the 20,000 rebels to make a stand. Now here we were two centuries later, thousands of us standing and remembering and celebrating the ideals for which they had died.

Terror was also never far away from the streets of the North. The uncertainty created by our expulsion from the talks, the refusal of the unionists to engage, the bomb attacks, the ongoing attacks by unionist paramilitaries and the behaviour of the RUC and British army, all fed into a deteriorating atmosphere. This was made worse on 3 March by the murder of two friends – Damien Trainor, a Catholic, and Philip Allen, a Protestant – as they sat in a pub in Poyntzpass in County Armagh.

That same day we were working our way through proposals on the political institutions and continuing with our lobby of the Irish government on constitutional issues. We had submitted advanced propositions on rights, equality and justice, prisoners, security measures, decommissioning and victims, and we were considering how an agreement would be implemented, validated and reviewed. We had also identified almost two dozen specific safeguards, which we felt would be necessary to prevent unionists abusing any assembly.

Our core group was now a cohesive and effective unit, and our approach in these private discussions was to seek to extend the powers and scope of the all-Ireland institutions, to immunise them against unionist obstruction and subversion, and to ensure that there was both the dynamic and freedom for them to grow and develop further. We also took the opportunity to put to the Irish government the potentially far-reaching proposal that MPs from the Six Counties could sit in the Irish parliament.

These issues needed to be aired publicly. We needed to give people some sense of where Sinn Féin was trying to take the negotiations. I therefore wrote an article for the Dublin-based *Ireland on Sunday* on 8 March and followed this up the next morning with a press conference in Belfast to formally launch a short document entitled *A Bridge into the Future*.

I felt that it was important to ensure that republicans especially understood that we did not expect these negotiations to produce a united Ireland by May that year. But any agreement had to provide a context in which we could continue to effectively pursue unity. Such a process also had to have an equality agenda with teeth, a process of demilitarisation, justice and an end to the RUC, as well as the release of prisoners.

We now had a detailed view of all these matters, influenced by our private negotiations with the two governments and proofed by a number of legal advisers. The first rustling of ideas – the need for an alternative way forward – that marked the beginning of this journey with Fr Des and the Sagart had become a detailed programme for change.

The following Thursday I was in London again for a 9 a.m. meeting with Tony Blair. He told me that, despite speculation, some people felt the British were trying to force us out of the talks, he wanted a deal with Sinn Féin. I told him that we appreciated his decision on Bloody Sunday and I spelt out the difficulties created for us by our expulsion from the talks. But I repeated: we were committed to playing our part in sorting out relationships between our two islands and we would be back into the talks, probably by 23 March.

I had copies of *A Bridge into the Future* for Blair but he had already read it. Once again, I raised the crux issue of sovereignty and the need for the British government to start unravelling the Act of Union by ending the Government of Ireland Act and the Northern Ireland Constitution Act, by which Britain claimed jurisdiction over the Six Counties. We also ran through the other issues of demilitarisation, prisoners, equality and human rights.

The Irish government was to hold a referendum on 22 May to ratify the Amsterdam Treaty, which dealt with the proposed reform and enlargement of the European Union. Blair told us that the governments were looking at that date to also hold the referendum on any agreement. Mo Mowlam, who was present, acknowledged that the Orange marching season would create problems if the date was later.

A large part of our conversation was taken up with discussing the assembly and its implications, and the North–South bodies. Whatever chance there might be of Sinn Féin signing up to any agreement which included an assembly would be dependent on how much power was vested in the all-Ireland institutions and how Blair tackled the constitutional issue. Sinn Féin could not and would not be part of any Northern assembly without the support of two-thirds of an Ard Fheis.

Immediately after this meeting Richard and I were off to New York. As usual, I arrived there tired, and this time there was no opportunity to catch my breath. A helicopter was waiting to bring us to Seton Hall University in New Jersey. Five of us crammed into the small chopper. I doubted it could lift off with the weight. Slowly we whirred upwards and then, gathering height and speed, away we flew over Brooklyn, flitting between the skyscrapers and across the Manhattan skyline, directly over the Statue of Liberty and on to a playing field at Seton Hall. It was a magical journey, providing a view of New York unlike any I had seen before.

Seton Hall was packed and the reception was great. But it was a late night, and by the time we drove back into New York to our hotel, our body clocks were screaming. The next few days were spent travelling, talking and lobbying. We eventually arrived in Washington where, on a bright and beautiful Sunday morning, we drove out past the Pentagon to a little Baptist Church in Virginia. Colleen, one of our support staff, is an African American with Irish and Native American ancestors. She was a member of the congregation and she invited us to join them for Sunday service. It was a wonderful experience. Our group, including Irish journalist Eamonn Mallie, were the only white people in the church. We were warmly welcomed. The music and the *craic* were mighty and the service was communal and uplifting.

The following evening we spent an hour – minus Eamonn – in the Oval Office meeting President Clinton and Secretary of State Madeleine Albright. As ever, his knowledge of the detail and complexities of the conflict and of the personalities involved in the peace process was impressive. At this time, he was going through a difficult time in his personal life and looked a little drawn. But he was still focused on our issues.

He knew that we were particularly irked that the unionists were still refusing to talk to us. He was trying to encourage David Trimble to engage with me and expressed some frustration that so far he had not done so. While most of our discussions were about Ireland, I also raised the Middle East situation with him, as well as the question of Cuba and the huge problems suffered by Third World countries crippled by debt. I urged him to cancel Third World debt and to use his influence to get other countries to do the same.

Madeleine Albright was heavily engaged in the Balkans situation at that time and she volunteered a little update on what was happening there. As always, the discussions with President Clinton went over time. He was an instinctive communicator, thirsty for information, soaking up opinions and eager to swap ideas and reduce issues to digestible concepts.

At the Speaker's lunch on Capitol Hill and at the reception in the White House, President Clinton told and retold the story of how the Israeli and Palestinian leaders had eventually got round to talking to each other and how necessary that was if there was to be any hope of peace anywhere in the world. In a pointed reference to Trimble, the President quoted President Kennedy, who once famously remarked, "Civility is not a sign of weakness." It made no difference. Despite White House efforts to have Trimble speak to me, he refused.

First Lady Hillary Clinton was also an avid supporter of the peace process. On a number of occasions she sat in for discussions between us and the President. Her political instincts on issues of equality meant that she had a natural affinity with the struggle for justice and equity. I also think that she understood the dynamics of the peace process and of the need for it to have both forward momentum and a capacity to deliver on issues which affected disadvantaged people in their daily lives. She was to bring a singular contribution to the process on the issue of empowerment of women, but in my engagements with her it was obvious that her mind was busy on all the issues that required attention.

George Mitchell had also been busy. On 25 March he set a deadline of midnight 9 April for the talks to end.

This phase of talks was to start on 30 March. The aim was to get final comments from the governments and the parties, and to produce a first draft of an agreement by Friday, 3 April. After weekend consultations the plan then would be to produce a penultimate draft on the Monday and then have four days in which to come up with a deal.

It was an ambitious plan. But a lot of drafting had already been done by the governments and the talks officials. The key would be political will on the part of the participants.

One piece of good news to emerge around this time was the release of Róisín McAliskey. British Home Secretary Jack Straw refused Germany's extradition case on the grounds that it would be unjust and oppressive.

The day Mitchell announced his timetable for agreement, our

negotiatiors met with Irish government officials for five hours. On the back of this our own drafters prepared a range of detailed papers with specific proposals for the coming negotiations around all of the core issues. This included a draft publicity campaign for the next twelve weeks, working on the assumption that a deal was done. Our calendar included, at the very least, the Easter weekend, with its hundreds of republican commemorations across the island; our Ard Fheis in April; the referendum battle and an election.

The unionists were also preparing for the coming phase of intense talks. Trimble used a party conference to try and hook the SDLP into a separate deal. He said it was time the SDLP had the "courage to move forward with us. I say to them, the days of relying on the Irish government to do your negotiating are over."

This was, at best, a naïve proposal, with no real chance of the SDLP biting. At worst it was just plain stupid. The unionist position was well stated. They wanted an assembly with limited powers and a firm unionist majority to veto everything; limited cross-border bodies; no prisoner releases; no reforms of the RUC; and they were still denying that structural inequality or discrimination ever existed! Hardly a good deal for any party looking for nationalist votes.

As for the British, we feared that they would go down to the wire on some key issues and force the Irish government to negotiate back from what were the promising positions we had been working on with them. We were also concerned that the officials at the British end – mostly the same ones who handled this issue during John Major's term – would once again take up a unionist line.

There was nothing new about any of this. If we had concerns, so did our opponents. It was a matter of doing our best and keeping our nerve. We had to play to our strengths.

On the eve of the start of the intense talks, I pulled on a hooded anorak and slipped away on my own with our two dogs, Cara and Osgur, in tow through the streets of West Belfast. It was a good evening for a quiet walk. My thoughts were sombre. We didn't know what would come out of the talks. The reality was that they could go on for ever in this form, and that was doing our cause no good. I had argued that negotiations were now a part of our struggle. But negotiations had to advance the struggle. Our strategic aim was to secure an acceptable peace deal.

For four years we had been arguing for intensive, concentrated and focused talks. We had first asked for and consistently pressed for a time-frame in the negotiations. In the absence of any other dynamic, a tight time-frame could act as a catalyst.

Now we had two weeks. We knew the general outlines of an agreement and the detail of the substance, but God alone knew how it would end up, or if there would be an agreement at all.

Our dogs enjoyed the walk. So did I. No one disturbed our contemplative dander. As we turned for home, the canines nuzzled close to me.

"Down," I snapped at them. "If you two mutts had my problems, you wouldn't be so giddy." Then I ruefully reminded myself that no one had asked me to be an Irish republican.

# Chapter Thirty-Two

# *The Good Friday Agreement*

Monday morning started with a headache, a sore throat and a blocked nose. I grabbed the vitamin C and the echinacea, but the flu was not to be denied. It gradually settled into my system over the next few days.

As we gathered in our rooms at Castle Buildings, I told the negotiations team to be prepared for a lot of hard work and probably some sleepless nights. Our job was to do the best we could. We were a good team who had learned to work together efficiently over the preceding years, but in particular the last few months. There were a few new faces: additional admin staff and several lawyers. All in all, we had a team of over two dozen. But with the exception of our core group, they were rarely all there at the same time.

Castle Buildings was fronted by a sizeable car parking area and surrounded by a chain-link fence. I, and mostly Martin McGuinness, used to walk regularly in the car park. Just beyond the perimeter fence, the British had erected a marquee for the press. There were also a couple of small portacabins and the type of portable toilets you get on building sites or at big outdoor events. The marquee had tables and chairs and, most important of all, phone lines. There was hot food for the hungry hacks. Between the fence and the marquee, the various media broadcast outlets had erected their own little tents, which provided some shelter. But, generally, facilities for the media were atrocious. The BBC eventually went so far as to construct a small studio twenty feet up on top of a steel framework. This allowed the presenter to stand or sit with his or her back to Castle Buildings and talk solemnly about events inside. Occasionally, they would focus in on movement in our office or next door in the SDLP office. It was like being in a fish bowl.

As more and more international media crews arrived and the days passed, the media's tent city grew. Our press people would take me, Mitchel

McLaughlin, Martin McGuinness, Bairbre de Brún or another of our spokespersons outside to do press conferences and interviews. Sometimes we would be ushered along the line of cameras. The next ten days saw the efficiency of this operation increase enormously. I would occasionally sit at the window watching this slow-motion version of *Riverdance* as either Sinn Féin or the other parties waltzed up and down the chorus line.

There was a copse of trees behind the media swamp. When I first arrived at Stormont I had asked for, as I do in all new places I visit, and received a little booklet about the Stormont estate. To my delight, I discovered that there was a badger sett beyond the trees. I never saw Broc, though I wandered around there a few times and kept watch regularly from our window. Maybe they were still hibernating. I wondered what they thought of the media invasion. Another time when Martin and I were walking in the car park, I noticed a strange looking bird walking along the top of the air conditioning below the first-storey windows. It was a chunky bird with a long, heavy, dark pink, straight beak, short legs, large dark eyes and grey and brown plumage. I was standing almost opposite it, and although it saw me it was not perturbed as it made its way along the front of the building, while I ambled alongside it on the tarmac. Martin joined me as the woodcock – for that was what it was – turned the corner of the complex. It obviously knew we were following it, but it proceeded into a little cul-de-sac where it nestled in some loose gravel. As Martin McGuinness watched, I stepped forward cautiously and made little clucking noises. The bird cocked its head and looked beady-eyed at me. I inched forward again and it flew off up on to the edge of the flat roof above us and gazed down at the two of us from this lofty perch.

"You couldn't get a bird in the Canary Islands! That poor thing probably thinks you want it for the cooking pot," Martin remarked.

In between watching for birds and badgers, the first couple of days were given over to a succession of meetings with Senator Mitchell, the two governments and the other parties – or at least those parties that would talk to us. There were so many meetings that it proved difficult to keep track of them all.

Castle Buildings was now a second home. Some of the discussions were intense and protracted. In between meetings we took every opportunity to stretch out on a floor or under a table. The concentrated bouts of negotiating and the preparations were exhausting. Unlike the governments, we could not fall back on the serried ranks of civil servants who resourced their every negotiating need.

344

Instead, we worked in a compact way. For example, our negotiators, and the small number of drafters – those who had the job of parsing documents and writing our draft responses – and the PR people, would come together around the core group to review the work to date. We had a position paper that set out our goals, and this was the template for all our discussions.

These talks saw the first of a series of formal negotiations with the two governments on constitutional matters. They had their experts, we had ours. The British agreed that all the main provisions of the agreement and the all-Ireland bodies would be established through legislation at Westminster. This was important because it removed the possibility that the unionists might repeal, through legislation in the assembly, what we were trying to put in place through these negotiations.

Our first meeting with the SDLP was good. Martin and I and several others met a delegation led by John Hume and Seamus Mallon. We wanted to secure common positions with them on key issues. In that way we believed we could counter unionist efforts to minimise any propositions while pushing the two governments – in particular the British – to maximum positions. In our view policing and criminal justice were not problems that we could resolve in this negotiation. A mechanism was needed, which would have its own dynamic, to push ahead on these matters. Commissions were the obvious answer and we plumped for two commissions rather than one. But the detail, the terms of reference and the time-frames had to be negotiated.

It was Senator Mitchell's stated goal to produce a first draft of an agreement by the end of the first week. This meant that negotiations were also taking place between the Taoiseach and the British Prime Minister. Much of their efforts were concentrated on the role and extent of the all-Ireland bodies in the Strand Two negotiations. They also had to make any final decisions on how far either government would go in respect of constitutional change. On the Tuesday I had a fifteen-minute telephone conversation with Mr Blair. I told him that if the governments pushed hard it was possible to get a deal. That would mean Blair taking tough decisions on constitutional matters. We were prepared to accept commissions on policing and criminal justice provided that the British were serious about creating a new policing service. The RUC had to go. The issue of an assembly was also raised and, in the context of transitional arrangements, I told the Prime Minister that we were prepared to look seriously at this, but it meant the equality and human rights agenda being faithfully implemented and the all-Ireland bodies having real powers.

Blair felt that he had moved the unionists a long way and that they now accepted the need for North-South bodies. He seemed confident that they could be persuaded to sign on for an agreement. We both acknowledged that dealing with the weapons issue was going to be, as he put it, "tortuously difficult".

Ahern and Blair were scheduled to meet in London on Wednesday evening. Instead of travelling up to Castle Buildings on the Wednesday morning, I left West Belfast before 6 a.m. for a meeting with the Taoiseach. As I drove to Dublin, the scale of the problem to be resolved – just around the policing issue – was brought home to me with the news on the car radio. The United Nations was publishing a report that day calling for an independent inquiry into the murder of lawyer Pat Finucane and a second inquiry into allegations of intimidation and harassment of defence lawyers by the RUC. The report had been produced by a special UN Rapporteur, who also cited the fact that of 2,540 complaints lodged against the RUC in 1986 only one officer had been found guilty of an abuse of authority.

My meeting with the Taoiseach lasted several hours. He was flying to London later in the day, and this was a last opportunity to directly emphasise to him the goals – as Sinn Féin saw it – nationalists needed to achieve in this negotiation. I met him in his office in Government Buildings. We had tea and scones below a portrait of Patrick Pearse, the 1916 leader. On another wall, Eamon de Valera looked down at us. Bertie was affable as always. His genuinely positive outlook on life has been incorporated into his political persona. He is a natural conciliator, not the perfect disposition for dealing with the Brits I would have thought. Not to say that he is not tough. He could not be the leader of Fianna Fáil without being tough and shrewd. Especially coming as he did from the Haughey era, with its corruption and sleaze. To survive all that and become Taoiseach was no mean achievement.

I told him that we believed the unionists were playing a tactical game designed to minimise the potential of the talks, and to force nationalists and republicans to accept less than we were entitled to. This process had to be about righting wrongs – not entrenching them further. It couldn't be about producing a replay of the Treaty of 1921, but had to involve fundamental British constitutional change.

I also gave Bertie a copy of a paper we were giving to Senator Mitchell that day. For the first time we were outlining the safeguards necessary for Sinn Féin support for an assembly in the North. This was a major step for us and included the need for key decisions to be taken by sufficient consensus, that is, a majority on the unionist and nationalist sides had to support a particular position.

After a thorough discussion on all these matters and proposed changes in the Irish constitution, I left for Belfast again. The Taoiseach departed later that day for London. Before he left for his meeting with Blair, he told the media that there were large disagreements "that could not be cloaked". Their meeting lasted three hours. We were subsequently briefed that the British had agreed that the North-South Ministerial Council would have a legislative basis; that the number of areas to be designated to the council would be detailed in any agreement; and that a number of implementation bodies would be established. But there were still big problems to be sorted out, including the demand of unionists to have the North-South structures incorporated in a structure covering relations between Britain and Ireland. We wanted a stand-alone, all-Ireland body. As a result, Ahern and Blair were to meet again the following day.

I went directly from Government Buildings in Dublin to Castle Buildings in Belfast. Relations between Sinn Féin and the SDLP were deteriorating once again. Some SDLP spokespersons maliciously briefed the media that Sinn Féin had taken up observer status in the negotiations. The PR battle over who was best representing nationalist interests was unsettling them, and we were also finding difficulty in getting bilaterals. This was a serious problem, which could only work to the advantage of the British and the unionists. I raised it with the Irish government representatives and asked them to convene trilateral meetings.

The Irish government gave us its proposed amendments to Articles 2 and 3 of the Irish constitution. These give constitutional expression to the Irish nation and its territory, and we sought expert legal and constitutional advice on these amendments and on our required changes to the British constitution. The coming days also saw extensive papers produced and argued over on issues as diverse as a mechanism for policy appraisal and fair treatment; policing and the administration of justice; rights and equality; and the Irish language.

Human rights was an issue that was exciting a lot of debate. The British record in the North was lamentable. The Standing Advisory Commission on Human Rights (SACHR) had been in existence for some years, but it had no teeth to tackle human rights abuses by the state. Now we were discussing the creation of two human rights commissions, one in the North and one in the South. As well as a review role and the public promotion of human rights, the human rights commissions needed to have

347

the powers to go to court or to help individuals to take court cases. In keeping with our all-Ireland view, there had to be a mechanism to bring together the new commissions. The British government also appeared to be accepting that the European Convention on Human Rights would be incorporated into law in the North.

A stranger walking the corridors of Castle Buildings would not know that these discussions were going on. The corridors were like a sanitised zone. All the work was being done behind closed doors. Every so often we would get reports back from the Irish government on their discussions with the British. Following their negotiations on the North-South issues, Dublin was upbeat. But whether these discussions would conclude in time for Senator Mitchell to produce his first draft of an agreement by Friday was unclear.

The Irish government had been assured by the British that any new constitutional legislation would supersede anything written before it. Their legal experts were working on this. In a phone conversation with the Taoiseach on the Thursday, I expressed caution. I also raised with him again the issue of Northern representatives being able to attend the parliament in Dublin.

Meanwhile, Martin McGuinness was talking to British minister Paul Murphy. He was hopeful that Senator Mitchell would have a paper to put before the parties by 3 p.m. the following day. But there were still serious issues to be resolved. Foremost among these was whether there should be an executive or cabinet or simply committees to run any government.

Friday, 3 April, dawned, and my flu was no better. The dry heat of Castle Buildings was not helping. More importantly, we didn't yet know for certain when we would get a paper from Senator Mitchell. In Dublin, Rita was talking to senior Irish government officials. In London, Bertie Ahern and Tony Blair met twice that day. In Castle Buildings we continued with focused discussions with both governments and some of the smaller parties.

We received two papers that day on the issue of prisoners, and while the governments appeared to have accepted in principle that prisoners had to be released, there was no time-frame. There were also intensive talks about the status and the resourcing of the Irish language. Irish had no official status in the North. We were determined to change this and for months had been putting pressure on the British government to sign up to the European Charter for Regional and Minority Languages.

That day we also received an agreed text from the two governments for

348

a section in the agreement covering the decommissioning issue. The terms were not acceptable. No party could have delivered on them. We were determined to do our best to take the gun out of Irish politics, but this needed a collective effort. It was back to the template which had emerged from the discussions all those years ago with the Sagart and later with John Hume. We had to provide an alternative, so that those with guns could be persuaded that they were no longer needed. All the parties and the two governments needed to commit to that while, at the same time, doing our collective best to bring about disarmament or, as some put it, a demilitarisation of society. We told the governments this. In our view, all the participants should commit to those objectives and to working to achieve them.

Later that day, in an effort to maximise the ability of the Irish side to make gains, and to re-engage in a more positive atmosphere with the SDLP, I suggested to the Irish government that the three of us meet. We eventually got together for over an hour and ranged across all of the issues relating to the commissions now being considered for policing and criminal justice. The details of an assembly and the safeguards required for nationalist approval were also discussed, as well as a code of practice for ministers.

At around 6.30 p.m., Senator Mitchell received a call from the two Prime Ministers closeted in Downing Street. They hadn't finished their work on the Strand Two paper, and they asked the Senator to go ahead and produce his paper on all of the other matters, leaving Strand Two to the side for the moment. The Senator was reluctant to do this.

A series of meetings was held with government officials and the parties; the consensus position was to wait until the Strand Two paper would be included. The delay in producing this first paper and the speculation of problems between Ahern and Blair excited the media and led to a general pessimism about the likely outcome. The Senator was told by the two governments that he would have his Strand Two paper on the Sunday.

On Sunday a team of us went back to Dublin to see the Taoiseach. Meeting with him and his officials helped put some meat on the bones of what was emerging. It was a good-natured meeting, uplifted by the Irish government's sense that Tony Blair had agreed to a substantial Strand Two document, and that he was committed to persuading David Trimble to come on board.

I asked how the governments were going to define consent for Irish unity. There was no doubt – no equivocation – "a majority is always 50 per cent plus one", I was told. We had already raised objections to the possibility that any commissions would be titled "royal" commissions, and at this meeting we were assured that this would not be the case. Our paper on the Irish language came in for some unexpected praise, with one official remarking that the SDLP had been astounded when they saw it. "That's why they don't negotiate for us," one of our team said.

Flags and emblems, equality and of course North–South arrangements were all discussed. I left Government Buildings for the North, reassured that we were making progress. But I was mindful that the unionists and the British system were going to do their best to undermine the potential for agreement that now existed.

Later that evening officials from the two governments finally brought the long-awaited Strand Two paper to George Mitchell. He said later that as he read it he knew that David Trimble would not accept it. It was, he felt, too specific. For unionists, this translated into cross-border bodies having too much independence and power. A series of annexes (or appendices) listing the possible areas of co-operation between the North and South was still being worked on by the governments. They weren't ready until nearly midnight the following Monday evening.

It is difficult to translate the complexity and interwoven nature of this phase of the negotiations. For example, while some of us were trying, as we saw it, to keep Dublin right, Pat Doherty and Bairbre de Brún were having yet another run at British officials on the prisoners issue. That engagement ended in a row.

The Brits "hoped" that a body, not a commission, would review each prisoner's case so that most prisoners would be out in three years, but some would still be expected to do much longer than that. Prisoners serving less than five years would not be eligible at all. When Pat remarked that this was a mechanism to keep people in prison, not to get them out, the officials said they were restricted in what they could do, especially with lifers.

Pat reminded them of the case of Lee Clegg, the British soldier released within three years of a life sentence for murder. When Bairbre de Brún asked how many prisoners were serving less than five years, one official remarked, "We don't think there were many terrorist prisoners who fell into that category."

Bairbre retorted: "And we didn't know we had any terrorist prisoners." The curtain fell on that meeting.

Generally speaking, meetings with officials yielded little progress, particularly with NIO people. The more senior officials could be expected to absorb positive or progressive ideas, but they did not move unless politically directed to do so. That direction had to come from their political bosses. But these bosses were subject to the demands of their own system, their own politics and the fierce lobbying of the unionists and the other parties. It was no secret that Sinn Féin was the party which wanted the most advanced positions from the governments. For their part, both governments were quite prepared to get the best deal possible with the other parties and then to try and cajole, coax or shoehorn us into this. They – that is, both Dublin and London – watched where the unionists were on every issue. We could understand this. An agreement – if it was to be made at all, never mind delivered on – needed the unionists. The unionists knew this also. They appeared to believe that their safest position was not to budge.

Another huge problem was that the Six County state was entirely unionist in its ethos, agencies and symbols. This meant that there had to be a huge amount of change at every level to bring about a level playing field. It also meant that no one within the state had any notion of the depth of republican or nationalist alienation or the determination on our part to change all this. So they put a lot of wasted effort into trying to wear us down – either as a negotiating tactic or because they just did not know where we were coming from. This was one of the products of decades of refusing to countenance genuine grievances or to dialogue with us, or people like us. They just didn't know, never mind accept, our point of view. The ignorance of the system about so many issues was palpable. There was no democratic culture and little experience of accountability mechanisms or transparency in what passed for government in this part of Ireland. There was a deep resentment that we were threatening this, not least because there was little real sense of why we would want to do this, except, of course, because we were subversives, or, as it was suggested once, because we were uppity fenians. That attitude left little room for pragmatism.

At Blair's level and with one or two of his senior advisers, there seemed at least to be a sense of why there had to be change and of what motivated us to struggle for this. This did not mean that they were up for this. They had their own constraints, including the desire on their part to uphold the union, to keep their own system on board and to keep the unionists engaged. I was also conscious that we lacked sufficient political strength to get everything we wanted at this stage. But we negotiated as if we were as strong as Mr Blair.

Notwithstanding any of this, negotiations went through well-worn processes. For example, after the run-in by Pat and Bairbre on the issue of political prisoners, we sought meetings with the Irish government and the British Secretary of State. We told them their position was totally unacceptable. If not resolved, it could jeopardise the process. I later spoke to Tony Blair twice on the phone, and by 10.30 that night we had a paper on prisoners that accepted the need for an accelerated programme for release. But there was no timetable – obviously an issue we would have to return to. And so, in this way, all the issues were processed.

Despite the intensity of the engagements, the atmosphere in Castle Buildings remained impassive and suffocating. As a matter of course, unless we were actually in discussion, we kept the doors to our rooms open. John Hume would wander in for a chat from time to time. Mo Mowlam was another regular visitor. She would amble in, sit down and put her feet up on a chair. She wore a wig because of hair loss following medical treatment for a brain tumour. Occasionally, she pulled the wig off and put it on the table. Then she would launch into conversation with whoever was in the room. I liked her style. Sometimes, she was deliberately provocative. Other times, she was funny. At times, I got the impression that she was just bored and wanted a bit of *craic*.

On one occasion as she got up to leave, Mowlam spotted an Easter lily lying on the table. The lily, made of paper, is a small green, white and orange emblem, worn at Easter time in memory of Ireland's patriot dead. Mowlam lifted the lily off the table and, remarking that it looked nice, she asked what it was. When she was told, she pinned it to her blouse and left. Martin McGuinness returned just then and, when he was told that Mo was away off wearing an Easter lily, he ran after her. He caught her just as she was heading for the unionist offices and gently persuaded her to remove the lily. Some of our group thought Martin should have let Mo go ahead.

"Have a heart," he said. "She is in enough trouble without that."

Later, when Blair came into the talks, Mowlam was sidelined completely. Whatever role she may have played on her own side, she was not at any of the meetings I attended with the Prime Minister. This was strictly a Downing Street operation. There was a small group of officials around Mr Blair, led by his Chief of Staff Jonathon Powell, and they dealt with everything. Maybe Mowlam attended to the smaller parties. I don't know if she resented her exclusion. Later, as I got to know her better, she would give off about the style of the Downing Street operation, but during the Castle Building talks she appeared to accept that her role was secondary to Downing Street.

Another caller to our office was Pádraig Wilson, the OC of the republican prisoners in Long Kesh. He did not call in person, of course, but Gerry Kelly rang the prison one day, as well as Portlaoise in the South, and asked for access to the respective prison OCs. We needed specific information on life-sentenced prisoners: how many, how long had they been in and so on. The OCs asked for our telephone number in the talks building and that was the start of it. From then on, we received two or three or four phone calls each day, and sometimes in the middle of the night as the talks went on round the clock. By the end of the week, the prisoners knew more about what was going on in the negotiations than most people in the building.

By the middle of the second week, the walls in our administration office were covered with messages of support from outside. Local community groups and party structures were faxing in, posting or delivering messages of solidarity. Competition developed between Belfast and Derry comrades in our offices, led respectively by Sue Ramsay and Bríd Curran, over which area sent the most messages. Belfast won.

As we waited on Senator Mitchell's paper, I received a letter from Mo Mowlam setting out the British government's response to our demands for constitutional change covering the Act of Union of 1800, the Government of Ireland Act 1920, and nine other separate acts of the British parliament.

The British Secretary of State explained that the new constitutional legislation contained in the agreement would repeal the Government of Ireland Act. It would reflect the principle of consent, "that if there were majority consent for a united Ireland that wish should be given effect". She explained that under British constitutional law, it is a convention that the new legislation replaces the old. However, because of the many concerns we had raised on this, the British now planned to put this issue beyond doubt by stating expressly that it was to have effect notwithstanding any other previous enactment.

I considered this to be a little victory. When I had first raised the issue with Dublin some time before, in an effort to get them to tackle the Brits on it, they resisted my entreaties. Then I raised it with Blair myself the first time we met, and at every subsequent meeting. I knew he wouldn't dump the Act of Union at this time, though we pressed that also, but it was crucial to get new constitutional arrangements which moved in that direction. In fairness to Ahern, after my failure to get his closest adviser on board, I asked him to tackle Blair on the Government of Ireland Act, and when I explained why, he readily agreed.

Sinn Féin had long argued that the unionist veto had to end; consent had to apply both ways. It is not just unionist consent but nationalist and republican consent as well. Any new agreement had to be built on a working partnership of equality. Tackling the unionist veto constitutionally also had other longer-term consequences. At its heart, it was about sovereignty, and the British acts we were challenging gave expression to that sovereignty. As Tony Benn explained to me in a paper – which he sent during the talks – absolute British sovereignty can be regarded as having been absorbed and consolidated in the Act of Union of 1800, which united Scotland, Ireland and England and Wales as one kingdom. It remained absolute in 1920, when Ireland was partitioned, even though the majority of Irish people had voted for independence. Now, according to Tony, absolute sovereignty was being vested instead in the people of the North "to be quantified or assessed by a referendum requiring a simple majority".

As one of our team observed, what other state in the world has written into its legislation, and hopefully as part of an international treaty which we wanted to underpin the agreement, the right of a part of that state to secede if a majority within a specific geographical area wished to? States fought wars over secession. This was an important development, which highlighted the fact that everyone, including the British government, saw the North as different from other parts of the United Kingdom. We were the semi-detached part, the optional bit.

Just before midnight on 6 April the governments delivered the Strand Two paper including three annexes. These listed the areas of implementation in which the North–South Ministerial Council would take decisions on an all-island basis. It also listed areas where the council should try to reach common agreements on policy.

Senator Mitchell called us all into the conference room where we were given a sixty-five-page document with the words "draft paper for discussions" at the top of each page. At this wee small hours of the morning meeting, the Senator appealed to the parties not to leak the paper. He underpinned this by telling us all that subtle changes in each text would allow the chairs to identify which party leaked the paper, if any appeared in the press. Whatever the truth of this, the document did not leak.

I pulled all of our team together to parse the Senator's document. I advised everyone to expect to be here round the clock until an agreement was reached or the process collapsed.

The next morning, the unionists went into overdrive. Trimble's deputy leader John Taylor told the media that he wouldn't touch the paper with a forty-foot barge pole. Trimble spoke to the Irish government, the British government, on three occasions to Tony Blair who was in Downing Street, to the White House and Senator Mitchell. He threatened to walk if they did not renegotiate the Strand Two document.

Senator Mitchell urged the Irish government to renegotiate. By this time Trimble had released the text of a series of points he had put to Blair two hours earlier. He had warned the Prime Minister that the UUP couldn't recommend the Mitchell paper. He was prepared to contemplate alternative proposals, but wanted to know first if the two governments were prepared to do likewise. At an acrimonious meeting mid-afternoon involving the Irish government and a unionist delegation, led by Jeffrey Donaldson, the unionists said they were opposed to the establishment of the North-South Ministerial Council and its implementation bodies by legislation in Westminster and the Dáil. They wanted the bodies established by the assembly. They also argued for "working bodies" as opposed to "implementation bodies"; and a reduction in the number of areas of co-operation contained in the annexes. They also opposed the terms of reference for the policing commission, and not unexpectedly decommissioning was a problem.

The Taoiseach's mother had died the previous morning. He was in Dublin to attend her church service. I spoke to him by phone just before 4 p.m. At that point, he seemed prepared to hold fast against Trimble's efforts. But with the unionists talking about alternative proposals, I wondered whether there was any point in us working on amendments to Mitchell's paper. The Taoiseach's view was that if these amendments were more than presentational it would mean going back to the start again. He assured me that the Irish government had agreed positions with the British government and intended sticking to them.

Irish officials later recalled that Ahern was concerned that the Irish government should not be blamed if the unionists walked away and the talks collapsed. Some had urged him to hold firm; others wanted him to agree to renegotiate Strand Two.

Later that evening, Tony Blair arrived at Hillsborough Castle just outside Belfast. He was joined a short time later by David Trimble.

In our offices at Castle Buildings, we were working away on a response to Mitchell's draft paper, as well as continuing to network with the government ministers and officials based there. Other colleagues, including Joe Cahill, Martin Ferris and Caoimhghín Ó Caoláin, had joined us. Our little suite of offices was becoming seriously overcrowded. The camp bed was in constant use, and occasionally one of our wordsmiths, working away on a laptop, would have to turn or prod a loudly snoring colleague.

The final phase of negotiations began early on the Wednesday morning. Bertie Ahern had flown up for a breakfast meeting with Tony Blair. He travelled then to Stormont House, a short distance from Castle Buildings, where Martin, Richard and I met him and a sizeable party of officials. We were told that there was no movement on policing or prisoners. The unionists had put forward a list of eleven or more items, including issues relating to Strand Two. The Taoiseach wasn't for the Senator producing a second draft. He was prepared to put everything on the table and go through all of this one item at a time.

I told him that the Brits could be moved on prisoners and policing. It might be at the last minute, but we didn't intend to move unless they did. We also made it clear that any dilution in Strand Two would be disastrous. We had seventy-six separate observations, including amendments to Senator Mitchell's paper, and we briefed the Taoiseach on these before we met Tony Blair. At Stormont House as well, I gave him a copy of a document we had prepared covering our main issues of concern. I talked him through it.

In between meetings, I made my way into the back of the fine old building and wandered about for a while in the garden. I was joined by a gang of sleek and well-groomed cats. They seemed to be living in Stormont House. The place was full of surprises.

When Martin, Richard and I arrived back into our offices in Castle Buildings, cats were also a big issue. Aidan's cat had become a mammy, and when Gerry Kelly called early that morning, about 6 a.m., to pick up Aidan, one newly born kitten was stranded in a small gap behind the fireplace. The rest were in the hot press with their mother. Gerry arrived as Aidan was trying to rescue the kitten. They had to leave it and head for Castle Buildings leaving Aidan's partner, Teresa, to sort out the problem. There was a loud cheer in the admin office when the word came through that afternoon that Teresa had got some builders to remove the fireplace. The kitten had been reunited with its mother. Both were doing fine. A notice to this effect went up on the notice board. I was beginning to get concerned that our group were stir crazy. When other parties enquired about the kitten, I knew we had all been together too long.

Senator Mitchell, Martin and I met to discuss his draft paper. He was genuinely frustrated by the unionists' refusal to talk to us. He was also perplexed at the gap between their position and ours and somewhat daunted by the paper we had given him. Martin once again outlined how far we had moved even to contemplate some of the concepts involved. For example, the notion of an assembly. I don't know if the Senator thought we had put a lot of negotiating fat into our position – that is, elements that we would be prepared to cut out later in return for more important bits. He told us he had a sense that if no one walked out beforehand, that would be the kind of necessary trade-off in order to get agreement. He thought the big challenges were for the unionists. If we had the persistence, we would eventually get where we wanted. The unionists were in a mess, rejecting everything out of hand because they were afraid to give anything. We, he felt, saw the need to do business with the unionists.

At one point, I told him that his paper was OK if presented in a different context. But we were dealing with a conflict-resolution process. There was a need to get an alternative way, a process to bring about justice and people's entitlements. His job had to be about righting wrongs.

He looked at me directly and said quietly: "My job is about facilitating agreement. The agreement itself is up to the two governments and the parties involved. But you are right. If my job was about righting wrongs then I would have provided a different paper."

I met with the Taoiseach again later that day. He had gone back to Dublin for his mother's funeral and then returned to Stormont. Along with the British Prime Minister, he held a meeting with the Ulster unionists. We were told that it was his intention to look at the issues raised by David Trimble. Blair put it to the unionists that if the Taoiseach was prepared to do this, they needed to approach other aspects of this negotiation more positively than they had done so far. In particular, this should mean the UUP talking to the SDLP about the assembly and the issues related to it. The game was clearly on. The two governments needed closure on Strand One matters, and that meant getting the unionists to move on key areas of disagreement there. The unionists wanted something on Strand Two matters. The Taoiseach and I talked about this at some length. I understood that in the negotiations he needed to play Sinn Féin demands off against the demands of unionists.

Thursday, 9 April, was supposed to be our last day. George Mitchell's schedule called for a deal to be concluded by midnight. But as the meetings began, it became clear that the unionists were as yet not prepared to agree on an executive or cabinet structure or to the safeguards nationalists demanded. Battle had also been joined over Strand Two. Discussions around the Strand Two paper continued all day, and drafts were going back and forth between the governments and the main parties, sometimes only thirty minutes apart. We had abandoned even the thought of going to the canteen for our food. Sue Ramsay and Siobhán had developed a relationship with the staff there. Sue and others helped clean up and wash dishes. Consequently, every so often they would arrive with trays of food and copious amounts of coffee.

In the early hours of the following morning, the unionists got some of what they wanted on Strand Two. The list of areas of possible co-operation was reduced, but the twelve that remained covered key areas like tourism, relevant EU programmes, urban and rural development, strategic transport planning and aspects of agriculture, education, health and other matters. We succeeded in ensuring that the North–South Ministerial Council would be established through legislation in Westminster and the Dáil, with executive powers, and participation in the council as an essential responsibility of relevant ministers in any new administration.

We also succeeded in ensuring that the assembly, the North–South Ministerial Council and the British–Irish Council, which was being proposed, would all come into effect at the same time in order to reduce any possibility that unionists might succeed in frustrating the birth of any one of the institutions. All of these structures would be interlocked and interdependent to minimise the possibility that the unionists might try to collapse those aspects they didn't like and keep those bits they did.

Progress on Strand Two appeared to free the unionists up on their discussions on an assembly. By 3 a.m. they had agreed to the establishment of an executive with many of the safeguards we and the SDLP had argued for. John Hume kept us posted on their discussions with the UUP. Next door in the SDLP offices there were sounds of celebration, prematurely we thought. Nothing was agreed until everything was agreed, and there was some way to go. Bits of the jigsaw were being put together, but the unionists still had to sign off on the complete board. So had we. The issue of prisoners – as well as the equality agenda, demilitarisation and decommissioning – were still unresolved. These separate and parallel negotiations had intensified as Thursday evening drew to a close and Good

Friday beckoned. This meant more meetings right through the night between us – that is, mostly Martin and myself, the Taoiseach and the Prime Minister.

The prisoners issue was complicated by a number of factors, including outstanding warrants against individuals, the case of people facing extradition, prisoners transferred from Britain, and cases which were known as the "forty-year men" – that is, prisoners in the South serving a minimum forty-year term. And then there was the case of people who were then facing trial and who might be convicted of the killing of Garda Jerry McCabe. Most of these issues, we were told, could be resolved, but we needed more than that. Like all other aspects of the agreement, these matters needed to be tied down.

Gerry Kelly and several others had held a meeting with British Secretary of State Mo Mowlam and officials from the prisons department of the NIO late on Thursday evening. We had a sense that the Brits would probably settle for three years for the release of prisoners. We wanted to move them to a year, but our fallback position was two years. Up to this point, we had refused to give any time-frame. So had they. They now presented our representatives with a new paper, but refused to allow them to leave the room with it. Gerry Kelly told them that that wasn't acceptable. If we were being given a new position, our full negotiating team had to know what it was. Mowlam looked to the officials. The officials were adamant. Gerry brusquely told them that that was not the way to do business and left. A few minutes later, as he was relaying an account of all of this to us in our room, a breathless Mo Mowlam arrived at the door with a copy of the document. She asked Gerry when we wanted the prisoners out. He said immediately. She said that wasn't possible. Gerry then remarked that it needed to be within a year. Mowlam went off to reflect on that.

A few hours later, around 1 a.m., President Clinton's first call came through. Blair had been talking to him, so he knew that we were stuck on the prisoners issue. I explained to the President that enormous progress had been made so far, but that bringing people on board required early releases. This was important to bolster republican confidence that this agreement was real and was bringing change. I asked the President to use his influence to make the British realise the importance of this. Mr Clinton said that Blair needed us to endorse the agreement. He explained that the Prime Minister's worst nightmare was Sinn Féin not accepting the agreement. His worry was that we wouldn't oppose, but we wouldn't endorse. He had told Blair that there had never been a time when I hadn't been straight with him. He felt that we could figure out a way to resolve the prisoners issue. Blair had a political problem. We had a political necessity. We ended the call by agreeing to stay in touch.

Blair was being advised by those around him that the release of prisoners was one issue on which he was very vulnerable within British public opinion. One aide warned him that it could be presented as him being soft on terrorism. They were obviously discussing the issue back and forth. In a tight session with Blair and Ahern, the Prime Minister made an offer that covered all prisoners belonging to organisations on cessation, without exception, and which would see all prisoners out in three years. I told him we needed to get it done within a year. We left it at that.

We still believed it would be possible to persuade Blair to reduce the release dates further. I asked Gerry Kelly to meet with the smaller loyalist parties, the UDP and the PUP, to see if they would come on board in a joint effort to get the prisoners out earlier. Gerry went down to their party rooms. He rapped on the door and put his head in. The large crowd of men sitting around on chairs and tables were surprised to see him. Gary McMichael and David Ervine came out into the corridor. Gerry explained the current situation on the prisoners issue and urged them to join us in lobbying the two governments. With both of us pressing on this issue, we were confident we could reduce the time-frame further. McMichael and Ervine said they would think about it and get back to him. A short time later, Ervine told Gerry that they had already agreed with David Trimble a three-year period for the prisoners to be released. He said that they didn't want to upset Trimble at such a delicate point in the process.

We were all dead tired. Surrounded by sleeping comrades, Martin, Gerry Kelly and I and a few others discussed all this. I decided to have another go at Blair.

I was padding about the place in my socks. I had discarded my shoes hours before for comfort's sake. When I went in to see Blair, he and Bertie were sitting quietly talking together. Blair told me that Bertie was concerned, if we got agreement, about winning any future referendum on the Irish constitutional matters. Bertie himself said that Articles 2 and 3 could be a difficult issue for Fianna Fáil. I agreed with him. I asked Blair where he was on the prisoner releases. I put it to him that if we came on board with an agreement the prisoners should be released within a year. After a brief but intense discussion, he said he would do it in two years. I pressed again for one year. He said he would publicly commit for two years. If it was possible to do it before, he would try and expedite matters.

360

If we campaigned for a change in the Irish constitution, he said he would definitely try to do it within a year. I asked if he would publicly commit to that. He said that he was taking a big step and upsetting his own system by publicly committing to two years. He could go no further. I told him that the question of what Sinn Féin would do in any future referendum would be for our Ard Fheis to decide. Of course, if there was an agreement we could accept, we would promote it wholeheartedly. I made my sock-soled way back to our offices.

Later I had to talk to the Taoiseach. Again, the issue was prisoners. This time it was the prisoners on remand and facing charges arising from the killing of Garda Jerry McCabe. Pat Doherty had conducted our engagement with the Irish government on a number of issues in its jurisdiction. When he asked for assurance that these prisoners, if sentenced, would be included in the early release scheme, he was advised that it would be better if one of us saw the Taoiseach. That someone was me. I saw the Taoiseach on his own. I explained how important it was that we had clarity on this issue. It would only arise if the prisoners involved were sentenced. I told him I was raising the issue because I realised that this might be an unpopular decision for him and that I was sure the Garda Representative Association would use all its influence to prevent the men being released. I understood exactly how they felt and, more importantly, how Garda McCabe's wife and family would feel, but the reality was that these prisoners, by virtue of their involvement with the IRA, would be qualifying prisoners for the release scheme we were negotiating. It would be impossible, I told him, to keep the IRA on board if a few prisoners were to be excluded from any agreement. He understood this. Part of the problem was that according to the reports he had received, some of these men had not been fully under IRA control, but he could see that the organisation would not abandon them. If we got an agreement, the Taoiseach told me, I would have nothing to worry about on that score. Fair enough. We shook hands on it.

At the same time as this negotiation on prisoners was taking place, another negotiation – potentially more perilous to the outcome of the whole process – was going on. The unionists were trying to secure a procedural linkage within the agreement between actual decommissioning and holding office in an executive. We had consistently warned the governments that any pre-conditions on our participation in an executive would undermine all of our efforts. Martin and I had three meetings with Blair and Ahern in the wee hours of Friday morning. They both knew that we weren't negotiating for the IRA, and that there was no possibility of us signing up to something we couldn't deliver.

It was obvious that the British had listened to us when we challenged the first draft on the decommissioning issue. They had opted for a good conflict resolution answer to this vexed question. This called on all parties to use their influence to achieve decommissioning in the context of the implementation of the overall agreement. After our initial discussions we did not have to do any heavy lifting to get the British government to adopt this position. Our effort was to prevent them from moving from it at the behest of the unionists.

Around 2.30 a.m. President Clinton had a long call with Senator Mitchell, who briefed him on where he thought the talks were and how close a deal was. After this, President Clinton rang me again. It was a call I almost didn't get. Sue Ramsay was tired. The phone rang and a voice said, "This is the White House. I have a call for Mr Adams from the President." Sue almost dismissed the call as the work of another republican having a joke at her expense. Fortunately, she quickly realised it was the real thing and passed it to me. I gave the President an update of where the negotiations were. I asked him to keep an eye to the issues which were of concern to us. He told me that he would do everything he could to work through the remaining issues. He also said that he felt we were making the best we could of the negotiations.

We still needed some aspects of the agreement to be sorted out, as well as other issues like Northern representation in Southern institutions. We were assured by the Taoiseach and the Prime Minister that these could be addressed in the course of further meetings between us after Easter. We had also received a detailed paper from Dublin dealing with the concerns we had listed on receipt of Senator Mitchell's paper. The Senator and the two governments knew that our negotiating team was not mandated to close on a draft agreement. That decision had to be taken by the party. But we had to make up our minds on whether we had enough to justify going to the party with the positions that were now in place. It was a difficult call to make. There was clarity and a definitive quality to some aspects of the agreement. Other aspects were more aspirational. Some were ambiguous. Others were kicked back into touch to be dealt with by commissions or other mechanisms. We had a commitment from the British government and from the Taoiseach to meet us after Easter on all these matters. We had an Ard Fheis in ten days time.

It was past dawn. The canteen was bare. There was no breakfast. The catering staff had been working to Senator Mitchell's schedule and were not expecting us still to be here on Friday morning. But a loaf of bread had been put aside for the Sinn Féin dishwashers. When one of the other delegations saw republicans with bread there was a row! Later, when the negotiations were over, I received a very nice letter from the management thanking our people for all their help during that time.

I phoned President Clinton. The situation room in Washington put me through to him. It was only when he came on the phone that I realised the time. It was 4.45 a.m. in Washington. He had obviously been wakened from his sleep. He was in bed and when I apologised for this he told me not to worry. I told him that I thought we had the basis of an agreement, but a lot depended on how the British delivered on its commitments. I pointed out some of the weaknesses in the agreement in terms of delivery, time-frames and mechanisms. I told the President that if we were to see this agreement delivered, then he had to ensure that the British didn't pull out of their commitments. I also pointed up the hard reality that the unionists had yet to engage with us. I told him my fear was that once the negotiations were over, pressure would be off the Brits and the UUP. Regardless of Tony Blair's intentions, his focus would be elsewhere and the unionists and the securocrats and the Brits' permanent government would come into the ascendancy again.

Bill Clinton understood this. He was prepared to do all he could to guarantee any agreement.

Martin and I went up to see Senator Mitchell. His colleagues were now busy pulling together all the bits and pieces of paper that were to make up the agreement. We told him we were prepared to go to our party with a draft agreement, but only if there were no further changes. We told the two governments the same thing.

David Trimble, who had left in the early hours of the morning, returned to learn that a final copy of the agreement would be ready for 11 a.m.

A plenary was scheduled for noon. Each party was to receive four copies of the agreement. That wasn't nearly enough for the large number of people we had in the building. Apart from our usual team, we had been joined by Alex Maskey, Mick Murphy, Jim Gibney and Dawn Doyle. Siobhán and Sue went up to the photocopier room close to the Senator's office. They began to slowly photocopy old documents, blank sheets of paper – anything, in fact, that kept them in possession of the copier. Several delegates from other parties, who obviously had the same idea, arrived too late and stood frustrated for a short time, perhaps hoping that

Siobhán and Sue might give up. They didn't know Siobhán and Sue. When the document was delivered, our intrepid duo still had control of the photocopier and our full delegation quickly received copies to examine.

As Siobhán and Sue were holding the copier against all comers, I had several quiet conversations with Senator Mitchell who, by this stage, was exhibiting all the classic signs of what republicans call "gate fever". For those thousands who were held in Long Kesh prison in the 1970s and 1980s, with its wire fences and gates, the closer one got to release the greater the personal stress. Internees who never knew when they might be released would slag each other off about "watching the gate". Sentenced prisoners who knew their release dates would also become the butt of jokes from others as their date for walking through the gates to freedom drew closer. "Gate fever" is a human condition, and Senator Mitchell now had it, in a big way. He had promised his wife Heather to be home to spend Easter with her and newly born baby Andrew.

In the UUP offices, a much-enlarged unionist delegation was now going through the agreement clause-by-clause, line-by-line. It wasn't going down well. It was, probably for the first time, dawning on some of them that they had before them a document that would see them in a power-sharing executive with Sinn Féin ministers.

The 12 o'clock plenary didn't happen. Instead, shortly after lunch, a unionist delegation led by Trimble and Donaldson went up to see Tony Blair. They set out their concerns to him. Blair told them that he would not change the agreement. But it transpired later that he provided Trimble with a side letter outlining his attitude to two of the issues the unionists had raised. Although it had no status, the letter clearly breached the terms of the agreement. Blair wrote that it was his view that the effect of the decommissioning section of the agreement meant that the process of decommissioning should begin straightaway. Trimble was looking for a mechanism to exclude Sinn Féin ministers from the executive. While refusing to concede this, Blair said that he would keep it under review. This was no part of the agreement. It ran in the face of all our discussions.

For some in Trimble's party this letter was not enough. Some wanted to walk away. Others knew that this would project the UUP internationally as wreckers of the hopes for peace. The pressure on David Trimble must have been enormous. Blair was phoning every few minutes wanting to know what the UUP had decided. The Irish government and the other parties were also demanding to know what was going on. President Clinton phoned Trimble.

All this time we, like everyone else, were sitting around waiting to learn the outcome of the unionists' deliberations. Periodically, John Hume would drift in or some of us would wander into the Irish government's rooms to get an update. The minutes and the hours slowly slipped past. We were unwashed, unslept, unfed. There was also by now a fairly big crowd slumped together in our little office, half-awake, half-asleep. Someone discovered the bar was open. Siobhán went off for supplies of Coke, bottled water and orange juice.

"The only bar in Ireland open for drink on Good Friday, and we're not in it," Ted growled.

"Mother Ireland, get off my back!" someone retorted.

By mid-afternoon, there was a sense of stupor about the talks building. I spoke to Senator Mitchell. "The problem for David Trimble is that he didn't think you were serious," the Senator told me. "He expected Sinn Féin to blink first. He expected you to walk out. You haven't. And he is running out of time."

Not long after four o'clock, I called our core group together. By now Jeffrey Donaldson, the leading UUP member, and several others – nicknamed the "baby barristers" because of their youth and professional standing – had stormed out of the meeting and the building.

Apart from our people who were doing the press work, and Mitchell McLaughlin was carrying a lot of this for us – the media scrum was now huge – most of the group, like almost everyone else, was doing nothing. We had taken the negotiations as far as our political strength and our ability could take them. It might yet all come to nothing if the UUP did not come on board. As we contemplated the options, I gloomily reminded myself that even if Trimble did signal assent, he had not even uttered one word to us.

I tell a lie. He actually had said two words to me. We met in the toilet one day. There was no one else there.

"We can't keep meeting like this," I said to him in an effort to break the ice.

"Grow up," he said.

I suggested to our group that we should press the Irish government to bring matters to a head. When I joined the senior officials they were as tired as everyone else. They told me the Taoiseach and Blair were together.

"Tell them we are going home soon if things don't shape up," I said.

One of them was alarmed.

"Ask them to call the plenary. Otherwise, the unionists will dither for ever," I suggested to him. "They have kept everyone waiting . . ."

"Someone needs to put testicles on David Trimble," another official agreed. He encouraged his colleagues to go to Ahern and Blair. The most senior person agreed to go. When he left I waited. Minutes later, the messenger returned.

"Message delivered," he told us.

"Good," he was told by his colleagues. "Someone had to do it."

Shortly afterwards, we were told that a plenary was set for five. Apparently David Trimble had phoned the Senator at 4.45 p.m. to tell him the UUP was ready to sign up.

I went up to see the Senator with Martin and we thanked him and Martha Pope, who had been a consistent and positive influence through the deliberations. We also thanked all the staffers. Siobhán and Sue had managed to get a small present for the Senator. Actually, it wasn't for him. It was a small Aran sweater and an Easter egg for the Senator's son Andrew.

When we returned to our office, I pulled our people together. I congratulated them all. As I looked around at the tired, drawn faces, I couldn't help but think of all the hard times we had been through together over the years. In prison and out. Some of our group had been combatants. Some had injuries. We had all lost loved ones. A lot of people depended on us in these negotiations. I felt proud to be part of our effort. Everyone had done their best, including the security section and the drivers, the comrades who brought us back and forth every day and hung about for hours on end waiting for us.

Our team had matched the larger, more experienced negotiating teams of our opponents. We had tried to be mindful of the concerns of the unionists while defending our own position. The work begun with the Sagart many years before had culminated in this agreement. Would it provide an alternative way forward to peace with justice? We were too close to the process to make that judgement.

By the time we got to the conference room, it was packed. Additional members of all the parties stood together behind their delegations. There was an air of quiet excitement. Television cameras were allowed in and the plenary was broadcast live. Senator Mitchell invited each of the parties to say whether they supported the agreement. When it was my turn, I explained that we would have to bring it back to our party. But I said that our delegation would be urging support for the agreement and that Sinn Féin would democratically debate its content. I said that while everyone had difficulties with the document, we hoped it signified a new beginning.

I was flanked by Martin McGuinness, Lucilita and others from our leadership. Joe Cahill was standing behind me. He was seventy-seven years old and had spent his life fighting the British presence. Since the 1970s he had been a key member of our party leadership, helping to develop and promote our peace strategy.

When it came to David Trimble's turn, he seemed to hesitate for a split second when Senator Mitchell invited him to speak. He reddened slightly as he used a pencil to stab the microphone button on the table before him.

"Yes," he said.

There were smiles all round. Even some of the unionists were smiling. When all the leaders had said their piece, the Senator closed the proceedings and there was sustained applause. For a few minutes everyone milled around shaking hands. Some people hugged each other. It took a long time to get from the conference room to the front porch. For a while, we were all packed together in the entrance hall waiting to go outside to do the obligatory press conference. Tiredness had really kicked in by this time. I felt slightly deflated by the size of the task that lay before us. George Mitchell had observed that making the agreement work would test us all as much as getting the agreement. Even now, the unionists would still not talk to any of the Shinners, let alone shake hands.

The next few hours were spent on a conveyor belt of media interviews. By the time we had finished, it was dark. At one point, I slipped into the trees for a leak. A prominent Ulster Unionist, Dermott Nesbitt, was there before me. I stood shoulder to shoulder with him as we watered the shrubs. He studiously ignored me as the steam rose round our ankles.

"This is the pee process," I slagged him. He had the grace to smile as he zipped up and left me.

In my remarks to the media, I said that while there was much in the agreement, much more still had to be done. The equality agenda was paramount. The agreement had to be a vehicle to bring about parity of esteem, equality of treatment and equality of opportunity for all citizens in all aspects of society. It was now time to draw breath, to reflect and to face the future in hope. Sinn Féin's task was to assess all that had been agreed and to determine, in consultation with our party and supporters, whether the agreement had the potential to really transform society. Our view was that it was transitional. We were seeking fundamental, political and constitutional change. We knew from the parameters of the talks laid down by the two governments that Irish unity would not come out of this phase of the negotiations, but we set ourselves the task of weakening the British link while defending Irish national rights.

We had dealt the union a severe blow. The inclusion of a clause limiting the life of the union to the will of a majority in the Northern state was a bit like a partner in a relationship saying that the relationship is over, but that she or he had to wait until the children have grown up. There was now no absolute commitment, no raft of parliamentary acts to back up an absolute claim, only an agreement to stay until the majority decided otherwise. This was still not good enough for us, but it was a long way from being, as Thatcher had once remarked, "as British as Finchley".

Our first big test of public and especially republican reaction to the agreement came two days later on Easter Sunday. I was speaking in Carrickmore in County Tyrone. It was a cold but beautifully clear day as we walked through the town to the republican memorial. It is an impressive monument set in its own grounds. Several broadcast companies had sent satellite trucks to carry my remarks live, probably the first time ever that this was done at an Easter commemoration. The crowd was larger than usual, and indeed, this was true of the commemorations everywhere that year. As I looked around the crowd, at many of the faces I recognised, I knew I was talking to Sinn Féin activists, republicans who had struggled over the decades, relatives of our patriot dead and undoubtedly IRA volunteers as well.

I paid tribute to the IRA for providing the opportunity for peace. I appealed to everyone to read and study the agreement carefully. The conclusion of the talks had ended one phase of struggle, but the one opening up would present many new challenges. I believed the impetus we had generated would move us towards unity and independence.

When the ceremony was over, I was surrounded by many well-wishers. Among them were the mothers of some young IRA men who had been killed in Tyrone not long before at Loughgall and Cappagh. I particularly remember Mrs Arthurs, mother of volunteer Paul Arthurs, and Mrs Quinn, mother of John Quinn. They both hugged me. I felt a huge sense of relief. We had taken the republican struggle and republicans generally on a huge roller-coaster of emotions. That Easter Sunday in Carrickmore, when these two fine women demonstrated that they supported what we were doing, I felt validated.

# Chapter Thirty-Three

## *Unfinished Business*

We had one week to prepare for our Ard Fheis. The Ard Chomhairle met on Easter Tuesday, and it was clear that there was a lot of concern within republican ranks. We spent the rest of that week in contact with both governments getting clarification on elements of the commitments they had given, taking possession of bits and pieces of paperwork outstanding from the negotiations. For example, the Taoiseach sent me a copy of a letter he wrote to the Joint Oireachtas Committee on the Constitution in which he asked the committee to examine how citizens in the North could play a more active part in national life. He specifically asked it to consider our proposals that Northern MPs would sit in the Dáil and that Irish citizens in the North would vote in presidential elections and referendums.

I had a long session with the Sagart. He thought the Holy Ghost had played a blinder. I agreed, but the game was not over yet. That week most of the efforts of our leadership were focused on the upcoming engagement with our own party. The 92nd Sinn Féin Ard Fheis began on 18 April. We had proposed an adjournment at the end of its business and a reconvened one-day session on 10 May to take a formal decision on the agreement. We needed that time for party activists and republicans generally to discuss and debate the many issues raised by the agreement. I was determined that we would not be rushed. We had to maintain internal unity and cohesion. That could best be accomplished if people had ownership of the process of agreeing a position on the agreement. My hope was that we would endorse the agreement, but do so in a way that even those opposed to it would not walk away from the struggle.

It was a good Ard Fheis. One of the highlights was the speech by Thenjiwe Mtintso, the Deputy Secretary General of the ANC. She arrived with a prepared speech. As she rose to speak after listening for a few hours to the debate, she discarded her text.

Thenjiwe then delivered an enthralling and riveting speech from the heart. She told the packed RDS hall in Dublin of her experience of struggle as a soldier in Umkhonto we Sizwe (MK) – the military organisation that led the fight against apartheid. She also dealt at length on her experiences of negotiations. It was a powerful contribution which caught the mood of the moment and touched on many of the fears evident among republicans.

Despite the fact that everyone knew we would be back a few weeks later, scores of people indicated that they wished to speak on the agreement. The debate went through Saturday and into Sunday. While many raised concerns about the agreement, the overwhelming majority expressed confidence in the party leadership and in the party strategy. The UUP was holding a meeting of its ruling Council that day also. A few days earlier the Orange Order had come out against the agreement. About mid-afternoon on the Saturday, news came through that the Ulster Unionist Council had endorsed by 540 votes to 210 support for David Trimble and the agreement. When this news came into the Ard Fheis I was speaking, and I departed from my script to say, "Well done, David." The initial response from the Ard Fheis was uncertain. They didn't know whether I was serious or not. But then, probably for the first time in the history of our party, the conference spontaneously applauded a unionist leader.

The party president normally gives the keynote address at the Ard Fheis. This time, however, we decided that Martin would join me. Between us we gave delegates a lengthy, blow-by-blow account of the negotiations. Our aim was to give delegates as much information as possible. I told them I wasn't going to prejudge the outcome of the vote we would have in a few weeks' time. But united, I said, we could achieve what we desired.

After the Ard Fheis our delegates returned to their areas armed with reams of information and with instructions to hold strategic discussions at all levels of our party. We also decided to conduct a leadership-led nationwide series of meetings. It was a brutal schedule, but our leaders travelled around the country. Having negotiated with the other parties and the governments, we were now negotiating with our activists and our supporters.

Two days after our Ard Fheis, the LVF killed a young Catholic man in Portadown, and four days later another young Catholic was shot and killed in Crumlin. The reactionaries weren't defeated, and the innocent were paying the price for progress.

The big historical failing of republicanism was the failure to build ideological unity. We needed to achieve an ability at all levels of struggle to differentiate between principles and tactics, objectives and strategies. Now we had strategies which were inclusive and aimed at empowering people. The primacy of politics and the need to build political support for our objectives was at the core of all our strategies. But we were also making huge changes in how republicans worked. We were changing the nature of our struggle. It was all very high risk. It wasn't enough only to get activists to vote the way we wanted. We needed them to have ownership of the changes and to think ahead to see how this would affect the ongoing evolution of our struggle.

So, as part of our internal debate, we asked President Mandela if he would send a senior ANC delegation to Ireland to speak to republicans about their process of negotiations, the management of change and the challenges this presents. The effect of Thenjiwe's contribution to our Ard Fheis was the trigger for this request. If activists could learn from the experience and question those who had been through a similar experience, then what we were attempting wouldn't be such a leap into the unknown. They could take this experience and fit it to our own conditions. We were surprised but deeply honoured when Cyril Ramaphosa, Mac Maharaj, South African Minister for Transport, Matthew Phosa, the Prime Minister of the Eastern Transvaal, and Valli Moosa, ANC executive member and Minister for Provincial and Constitutional Affairs, arrived to offer their opinions. They had all been key participants in the process of negotiations in South Africa.

These comrades travelled widely throughout republican Ireland, speaking to audiences eager to hear their thoughts on struggle. In Crossmaglen in South Armagh, Mac Maharaj, who spent twelve years on Robben Island, spoke of change as a permanent condition, in which we had to reconcile our strategy, tactics and principles. He remarked, "You can make a wrong choice in your strategy, but if you do it as a united force you can later change your course." In making judgements about the agreement, he pointed out that like everyone else, "When change looms there is doubt and hesitation." Cyril Ramaphosa, speaking to a crowded Ulster Hall in Belfast, said, "Negotiations are about give and take. Had we wanted everything or nothing, we would have ended up with nothing." Ramaphosa and Matthew Phosa also visited the men and women in Long Kesh and Maghaberry prisons. In Portlaoise prison, there was a stand-off between the ANC delegation and the prison warders. Old habits die hard, and government ministers from South Africa, statesmen all, refused to be dictated to by overzealous screws.

We weren't expecting these experienced revolutionaries to come to Ireland to tell us what to do next. There were differences as well as similarities in our struggles. We had to make our own choices. But their contribution was pivotal. I also have to say that they themselves all hugely enjoyed the experience.

At the end of April, the IRA gave its verdict on the agreement. It restated its belief that a durable peace required national self-determination. Whether the agreement heralded a transformation of the situation was, the IRA said, entirely dependent on the will of the British government. The IRA would monitor developments. Its statement also emphatically ruled out decommissioning. It concluded by commending the efforts of Sinn Féin.

Others had a different perspective. In Dublin, posters appeared featuring photos of Martin and me with the legend "Wanted for Treachery" on them.

The feeling now among republicans was for unity. Whatever differences we might have or doubts we might hold, the call for unity was overwhelming. No one wanted a split; we had had too many of those over the years. We had been lobbying for months for the British to transfer republican prisoners from jails in Britain. I put it to Mo Mowlam that this was crucial in the build-up to the second part of the Ard Fheis. And in a move clearly calculated to influence republican thinking, six republican prisoners were eventually transferred. Among them were four IRA volunteers – Hugh Doherty, Harry Duggan, Joe O'Connell and Eddie Butler – who were known as the Balcombe Street Four. They had been in prison twenty-three years, much of it in solitary confinement.

The Ard Chomhairle met again, and we agreed two emergency motions to be put to the delegates at the reconvened special Ard Fheis. There were many in the media who saw this as a foregone conclusion. They were convinced we would win any vote. But for Sinn Féin to take seats in the assembly in the North, we had to change the party's constitution and rules. That required a two-thirds majority. I knew that to carry the party and remove any risk of a serious schism we needed a massive endorsement. The Ard Chomhairle also agreed to ask the Ard Fheis to pass a motion to call for a "Yes" vote in the referendum in the Twenty-six Counties. Many colleagues in the South were especially unhappy with the proposed changes to the Irish constitution. I knew there was bound to be resistance, but I couldn't judge how extensive it might be. All of the feedback from our internal meetings pointed to almost all the Southern delegates being against changes to Articles 2 and 3 of the Irish constitution. Some of our key activists, including leadership people, felt strongly about this. Most of the Northerners were much more pragmatic. They saw these clauses as being meaningless in a practical sense. The constitutional amendments conceded none of the principles and actually had a practical effect because Dublin was now devolving and would exercise practical sovereignty in the North.

On Sunday, 10 May, we returned to the RDS for our one-day Ard Fheis. As before, the hall was packed. Unbeknownst to the delegates and visitors, we had persuaded the Irish government to release the recently transferred Balcombe Street prisoners for their first parole in twenty-three years. Other prisoners were also released on parole from prisons in the North, including Pádraig Wilson, the OC of Long Kesh, and Geraldine Ferrity, the OC of the women republican prisoners in Maghaberry.

When the Balcombe Street men entered the hall, there was sustained and wild applause and cheering lasting over ten minutes. There were some who accused us of triumphalism in bringing the four to the Ard Fheis. In truth, the intention was to show that the agreement was making a difference. Still, all of us underestimated the reception these men would receive. That shows how busy we were on other issues. The Balcombe Street Four were iconic figures. There is a great affinity with prisoners within republicanism, and prisoners incarcerated in Britain itself are held in special regard. Some years before, we had launched a publicity campaign around the Balcombe Street Four. The huge spontaneous outpouring of welcome when they entered the Ard Fheis was a measure of the love and respect in which they were held. Tears flowed freely down many faces. They came on to the stage, and the RDS shook with the sound of clapping and the rhythmic stamping of feet.

In the end, after five hours of debate, 331 of the 350 delegates voted to alter the party's constitution and allow successful candidates to sit in a Northern assembly. Of all the moments that have been described as historic, this truly deserved that description. The Ard Fheis really did make history.

I again had the job of summing up, of giving people some sense of how far we had come, but also of how much we still had to do. British rule was not ended. Neither was partition. Our struggle had to continue. But that brought us back to the development of strategies and tactics that were needed to build and increase our political strength.

"The struggle is where the activist is," I told them. It was about ending poverty, building political and economic democracy, as well as equality and ending British rule.

Coincidentally, 10 May was also the day, eighty-two years previously, when James Connolly, one of the leaders of the 1916 rebellion, was shot dead by a British firing squad in Dublin's Kilmainham jail. I reminded a hushed hall of that fateful day and of his words: "Sinn Féin. That is a good name for the new Irish movement of which we hear so much nowadays. Sinn Féin, or in English, 'Ourselves'. It is a good name and a good motto."

Now the challenge was about winning the referendum on 22 May. It was obvious that the nationalist vote, North and South, would be overwhelmingly "Yes". Within unionism, there was enormous uncertainty. For hundreds of years, nationalist and republicans had been the enemy. Now there was an agreement which promised equality and other changes. Now there was the prospect that republicans and nationalists would share equal responsibility with unionists in a new executive, answerable to an assembly which was part of all-island political structures and institutions.

Unionist misgivings about the agreement were deep-rooted. An *Irish Times* opinion poll one week before the vote suggested that 55 per cent of unionists were against the agreement. David Trimble was failing to sell it to his people. There were times when his stance seemed to echo that of the "No" camp who were running a vigorous campaign.

The British Prime Minister made three high-profile visits to the North in two weeks. He took part in numerous interviews and, in almost every instance, his words were directed at reassuring unionists. Behind the scenes Labour Party people from Britain were trying to focus the UUP on how to fight and win the battle for the hearts and minds of unionism. The turnaround came at the beginning of the last week of the campaign when Trimble and Paisley went head to head on television. Trimble won.

He won because he took up a positive position, putting clear blue water between the pro- and anti-agreement unionist camps. For once he sold the agreement like a leader who believed in it. When the votes were counted on 23 May, the day after the referendum, the result was clear-cut. In the South, 94.39 per cent of voters voted "Yes". In the North, 71.1 per cent voted "Yes" and 28.9 per cent voted "No".

The unionists were still refusing to talk to Sinn Féin. On the day of the count at the King's Hall in Belfast, I sat in a temporary television studio on the first floor overlooking the count. John Hume was on one side and

David Trimble was sitting across from me. David still wouldn't talk. He wouldn't even be interviewed with me.

Within four weeks, we were to fight elections to the assembly. Sinn Féin and UUP representatives, with others, were then supposed to go into an executive in government together. How could this work if David Trimble wasn't prepared even now to talk? We were also getting dangerously close to the Orange marching season. The referendum was barely over when the decommissioning issue was dragged back centre stage by Trimble, demanding of the British that no decommissioning should mean no Sinn Féin in government. It was obvious that the election campaign was going to be difficult and messy. If the UUP was truly for the agreement, regardless of its misgivings, the sensible thing for Mr Trimble to do was to rally the pro-agreement majority within unionism who had voted Yes in the referendum. In theory at least, there was a new majority in the North. It was neither exclusively unionist, nationalist nor republican. It was all of these. But it wanted an end to conflict and had endorsed the changes to bring this about. Not surprisingly, with Paisley's DUP in high gear, the UUP leadership was turned in on itself. The rest of us could only watch as pro- and anti-agreement elements of the party clashed in television studios and on radio programmes.

We had work to do ourselves. We, too, wanted to increase our electoral strength, and days which had until recently been filled with negotiations were now occupied with the preparations for the upcoming contest. I had little time to reflect on what had been achieved, but I knew that thirty years on we were into the endgame. Maybe it was only the beginning of the endgame, but we had to see our way through the next few decades if we were to bed down a peace process and to build a new Ireland. There was so much to do. Building a political party right across the island. Delivering on the outcome of the negotiations and getting the agreement implemented. It was truly going to be a battle a day. And somewhere in the midst of it all there was a need to find space for the pleasures and joys and normality of everyday living with Colette and our family and friends.

I was buoyed up by the example of my friends and comrades and gratified by the increasing confidence of ordinary nationalists whom I met every day. People were uplifted by the potential for real progress. On many occasions I was stopped in the street by women who thanked me for giving their children the chance of a future. It was the same for all of our public figures. "Keep up the good work," was almost a daily salutation. It was good to be an Irish republican. It was good to feel that you could bring about positive changes in the lives of ordinary people. It was good to have a sense that the killing could be put behind us and that the healing could start.

It wasn't going to be easy. When the euphoria died down, when the elections were over, it would be back to the tedious, mind-numbing effort to make the rhetoric of the agreement a reality. I didn't underestimate how difficult all of this was going to be. Particularly in meeting the needs and removing the fears, or at least helping unionists to remove the fears and concerns they had about the future. Senator Mitchell's words came back to me. Implementing the agreement was going to be harder than negotiating it. And that was saying something. Negotiations were now a part of struggle.

We launched our election campaign in the middle of June. Martin McGuinness and all the rest of our leadership figures, from right across Ireland, came together for a press conference. When we were finished, Martin and I parted outside the venue.

"Don't you know that we have a huge amount of work to do?" he said. "There's no guarantee that the Brits or the unionists are going to stick to their commitments."

"I know," I replied. "It's going to be trench warfare every day. You could be seventy before we get freedom," I joked.

"Seventy would be a good age to be free," he replied seriously. "Ask Joe Cahill."

Martin went off to canvas in Derry. The rest of our leadership team were leaving to do exactly the same thing in their own areas. Bairbre and Mitchel waved as they and Pat Doherty and Michelle Gildernew and Dodie McGuinness went off about their business.

Martin Ferris left for the long journey back to Kerry. Caoimhghín headed for Monaghan. Joan and Dawn and Mairéad headed into the constituencies. Lucilita had a carload of comrades going back to Dublin.

It was a nice day for making hope and history rhyme.

I got into Big Eamon's car and Richard and I headed off to the next meeting.

We had a life and this was it.

# *Epilogue*

The Good Friday Agreement, endorsed in referendums by the people of Ireland, is the most important political development in recent Irish history. It was accompanied by a sense of great hope from those who wanted or were prepared to tolerate change, and outright rejection and hysteria from those who were against it. Unionism split, the agitation over contentious Orange parades, especially on Garvaghy Road and the lower Ormeau, intensified, and there was a sustained campaign of bomb and firebomb attacks on Catholic homes, schools, churches and businesses.

The majority of political prisoners were released. Those convicted over the killing of Garda Gerry McCabe were kept in prison in breach of the agreement. There was very little progress on demilitarisation. An Independent International Commission on Decommissioning was established, headed by John de Chastelain. Other commissions were established in line with the agreement, including one on policing headed by former British Conservative minister and Hong Kong governor Chris Patten.

In the elections to the new assembly Sinn Féin won eighteen seats. The UUP won twenty-eight, the SDLP twenty-four, and the DUP twenty; the Women's Coalition got two; independent or small unionist parties secured fourteen seats, and the PUP, which had represented the UVF in the talks, won two; the UDA representatives failed to win any seats. The elections led to the selection of David Trimble and Seamus Mallon, representing the largest parties, as First and Deputy First Minister, but the unionists prevented the establishment of the executive and the other political institutions.

The small factions who had left the IRA continued with a sporadic campaign of bomb attacks. The most disastrous of these was on 15 August 1998. The centre of Omagh, a busy County Tyrone market town, was devastated; twenty-nine people were killed, including one woman who was expecting twins, and over 200 were injured, some seriously.

The period after the agreement was marked by intense diplomatic activity by the two governments and most of the pro-agreement parties. There were numerous summits at Castle Buildings and at Stormont as we tried to get the political institutions up and running. President Clinton remained engaged, as did President Mandela. The unionists persisted with their refusal to talk with Sinn Féin. Eighteen months later, after many false starts and an initiative on the arms issue by the IRA, the executive was eventually established.

Martin McGuinness became the Minister of Education. Bairbre de Brún was the Minister of Health, Social Services and Public Safety in an executive which included the UUP and the SDLP. Paisley's DUP accepted its electoral entitlement to two ministries but refused to attend the executive.

Over five years have now passed since Good Friday 1998, and many aspects of the agreement are still in abeyance. Soon after its establishment, the executive was suspended on threat of resignation by the UUP. This became a repeated pattern, and the institutions have been in place for only twenty-one months out of a possible five years. Downing Street has suspended the institutions a total of four times at the behest of the unionists, and has stepped outside the terms of the agreement to bring in legislation unilaterally.

The five years have been filled with negotiations, setbacks, and breakthroughs, followed by more negotiations, breakthroughs and setbacks. Senator George Mitchell got it exactly right when he told us all after the agreement had been put together that the hard bit would be implementing it.

The agreement is a charter for change across a range of social, economic, political, cultural, institutional and constitutional matters. It is about rights and entitlements. In its essence the Good Friday Agreement is about creating a new political dispensation based on equality and parity of esteem. It is all still very much work in progress – or at times, work not in progress.

Many republicans and others will contend that the main problem with implementing the agreement lies in the unwillingness of unionism to embrace the type of process that this entails. Unionists will point to republicans, and particularly the IRA, as being the main problem. For my part I think the central faultline in the agreement, and every crisis in it, can be traced back to Number 10 Downing Street. Of course unionists have problems with change, but the British government should not have pandered to this.

378

Even as the Good Friday Agreement was being proclaimed to the world, Prime Minister Tony Blair had already provided a get-out for them, in the form of a side letter to UUP leader David Trimble. The letter was outside the scope and terms of the agreement, and it effectively subverted the political imperative and the conflict resolution ethos which underpinned the decommissioning section.

The British government has told us since that this was for good tactical reasons in order to keep the unionists engaged. I have no doubt that Mr Blair thought his letter would encourage unionist engagement. In fact, it created a space for Mr Trimble to target the agreement; that he should have such intent is understandable from his perspective. He has not thus far risen above a narrow unionist perspective into the wider vision required of a First Minister. So he can only be expected to manage change if there is an actual process of change in progress. If he can delay or dilute the change he will do so.

The process has been one of almost continuous negotiations. These have taken us back scores of times to Downing Street, to the White House and to other big houses in Ireland and Britain where the details were worked and reworked and efforts to cajole, shoe-horn or fabricate progress have been tried again and again. In the course of these perambulations the unionists commenced talking to Sinn Féin, though David Trimble shook my hand only in July this year.

We have got to know each other: Brits and Shinners, unionists and nationalists and everyone in between. Some have also moved on: John Hume retired as SDLP leader and Seamus Mallon followed. Seamus deserves credit for his efforts as Deputy First Minister. He and Trimble were an odd couple, but he did his best in very difficult circumstances. Mo Mowlam has gone also; the unionists succeeded in getting her moved, and she has now retired from the British parliament. There have been three British Secretaries of State since then, and I have learned to work with all of them.

David Trimble has survived. So far. Ken Maginnis and John Taylor are now in the British House of Lords. Ken eventually chilled out with us, and in fairness to the Lord Taylor, he never took himself too seriously anyway. Neither did I. Most of his jousting was tongue-in-cheek. I think he knew sooner than most of his colleagues that the old agenda could not prevail and that the new agenda cannot be delayed indefinitely.

President Clinton has gone from the White House, but he maintains a deep interest in the Irish peace process and I talk to him regularly about it. Hillary Clinton is now a Senator and she remains engaged. So do other champions of the process like Teddy Kennedy and Chris Dodd and their colleagues in the Congress. The Committee on Irish Affairs and the Ad Hoc Committee on Ireland do sterling work. These committees draw support from both Democrats and Republicans. President Bush and his administration continue to support our process. And the role of Irish America as always remains crucial.

Concerns and cover-ups about the British state's involvement in killing citizens persist. The death of Brian Nelson, one man at the centre of some of this, was reported in the media earlier this year.

Nelson Mandela remains a source of encouragement to struggling people everywhere and to us in particular. The ANC's consistent advice and assistance goes on. Mandela's successor, President Thabo Mbeki, has continued to be an ally of our process. Canadian Prime Minister Jean Chretien is also an ally.

The Sagart and Fr Des are still spreading the gospel.

There have been other stresses and strains. The general, if shaky, consensus between Dublin, the SDLP and Sinn Féin has been shattered, particularly on the issue of policing. The Patten Commission made a number of quite radical recommendations to create a new beginning to policing. But its recommendations were rejected by the unionists and then systematically emasculated by the securocrats who were ably supported by Peter Mandelson, Mo Mowlam's successor as Secretary of State.

Despite this, the Irish government and the SDLP acquiesced on the policing issue, and the SDLP joined the Policing Board on the promise that the Patten recommendations would be fully implemented. At the time of writing, this has still not been done. Democratically centred and politically accountable civic policing has yet to be achieved.

Sinn Féin has pressed for powers on policing and justice to be transferred from London to the political institutions in Ireland and to be subject to the same institutional structures as other matters in the Good Friday Agreement. The British government has agreed to this in principle, but the unionists have not agreed the time-frame or mechanisms.

Other issues remain to be implemented. In April 2003, after weeks of negotiations with Sinn Féin, the British and the Irish governments eventually came forward with a Joint Declaration, which addressed the unfinished elements of the Good Friday Agreement. These negotiations were longer and even tougher than the negotiations for the Good Friday Agreement. The length and the detail of the Joint Declaration is graphic testimony to the two governments' failure to fulfil their obligations. The issues include equality and human rights, demilitarisation, the political institutions, policing, victims, Irish language rights, prisoners and those people who are described as "on-the-run", sectarianism and the issue of arms.

The intensive discussions which led to the production of the Joint Declaration followed considerable political turbulence in the summer of 2002. Since the agreement there has been unionist paramilitary activity, particularly against vulnerable nationalist communities in Belfast, including a protracted blockade of schoolgirls of the Holy Cross school and gun and bomb attacks on isolated families in the rural north-east.

There were claims that the IRA was procuring weapons and gathering intelligence. There was controversy over the arrests of three Irish men in Colombia. Whatever I think about the unionist willingness to embrace the process of change, the unrelenting concentration on these allegations was grist to the mill of those who are opposed to change. Wall-to-wall daily coverage in the media – fed by stories planted from within the British system – destabilised those who countenance change. On the republican and nationalist side, the lack of focus on the killing campaign by unionist paramilitaries and the actions of the British forces has caused anger, frustration and annoyance.

In October 2002, Mr Blair made a speech in which he called for an act of completion by the IRA. Although he did not define this, his remarks, understandably, were portrayed in the media as a demand for the IRA to disband. Mr Blair also recognised that Catholics had been treated in the North as second-class citizens. He said that the overwhelming majority of people wanted the institutions to remain in place. The time for transition had come to an end. There was a need for acts of completion, and the British government thought the Good Friday Agreement should be implemented in one fell swoop, instead of a concession to one side here and a concession to the other there.

Sinn Féin has long called for the agreement to be implemented in full. Above all, this means dealing with the matters involved as modest rights and entitlements, instead of security problems. It means embarking on a process of irreversible change. For that reason, just before Christmas 2002, Sinn Féin submitted a fifty-seven-page document to the two governments. It was from this template that the Joint Declaration emerged.

Following the negotiations on the Joint Declaration and discussions also with the UUP, Martin McGuinness and I engaged with the IRA leadership. We had advised both governments and the unionists that we would try and get a statement of advanced commitments from the IRA setting out the status of its cessation, the IRA's present disposition, its future intentions, and the issue of weapons.

Draft elements and concepts of an IRA statement were shared with the two governments and the unionist leadership. In response, the two governments engaged in an outrageous propaganda offensive around the suggested IRA words; they cancelled publication of the Joint Declaration and pulled out of an all-party meeting.

Despite republican annoyance at this behaviour, the IRA finalised its statement, presenting a declaration of entirely peaceful intent, setting out the status of the cessation, the IRA's future intentions and its attitude to the issue of arms, including a process to put arms beyond use. Even though the governments and the unionists acknowledged that it was unprecedented, and that it showed a desire to make the process work, they publicly rejected it.

On 23 April, the British Prime Minister stepped outside of protocol when in the course of private negotiations dealing with these very issues he publicly asked whether activities inconsistent with the Good Friday Agreement were at an end; secondly, whether the IRA's commitment was to put all arms beyond use; and thirdly, whether the implementation of the Good Friday Agreement and commitments in the Joint Declaration would bring complete and final closure of the conflict.

Following a suggestion from the Irish government and President Bush's special ambassador Richard Haass, I answered the questions put by Mr Blair. I said that the IRA statement dealt definitively with these concerns about alleged IRA activity, and any such activities which in any way undermine the peace process and the Good Friday Agreement should not be happening.

"The IRA statement is a statement of completely peaceful intent. Its logic is that there should be no activities inconsistent with this. Secondly, the IRA has clearly stated its willingness to proceed with the implementation of a process to put arms beyond use at the earliest opportunity. Obviously this is not about putting some arms beyond use. It is about all arms. And thirdly, if the two governments and all the parties fulfil their commitments, this will provide the basis for the complete and final closure of the conflict."

Within the republican constituency there was deep scepticism because there was no indication that the UUP would reciprocate even if the IRA moved on the arms issue. Nevertheless, the IRA leadership authorised a third act of putting arms beyond use, timed to facilitate the UUP holding an Ulster Unionist Council meeting. Mr Trimble was to respond to this with a public recommendation that his party actively support the sustained working of the political institutions and other elements of the Good Friday Agreement.

The governments responded that two of my answers were clear. The problem was that I had used the word "should" instead of "will" in my answer to the first question. So, in the interests of eliminating any doubt I said: "The IRA leadership makes clear in its statement that it is determined that its activities *will* [emphasis added] be consistent with its resolve to see the complete and final closure of the conflict. The IRA leadership is determined that there *will* [emphasis added] be no activities which will undermine in any way the peace process and the Good Friday Agreement."

When a further five questions were posed by Downing Street, Martin McGuinness and I declared that the game of scrabble was over. By intervening to explain the IRA statement, I had broken my long-standing practice of not interpreting or explaining the IRA's position. I did so because the governments were prepared to accept this and because I did not want the process to lose what we had achieved. Nationalists and republicans were now angry, not only because the IRA initiative was rejected, not only because my efforts were dismissed, but because they thought I had gone too far. The British government added offence to injury by stopping the assembly elections despite entreaties by the Taoiseach.

The progress that we have all collectively made in recent years has been remarkable. Why then did a British government and an Irish government reject what was a hugely significant contribution by republicans? Was it solely because Mr Trimble was calling the tune? Was it really all about the IRA? Were there other factors?

I believe that the growth of Sinn Féin has been a critical factor. All other things to one side, that is what brought about this latest crisis in the peace process. The British and Irish establishments' version of the peace process had a different script from the one that has been written in recent years. The growth of Sinn Féin was not part of their script, according to which the SDLP and the UUP were to coalesce to form the so-called centre ground. In essence, British policy was about modernising the union so that a section of Protestants and Catholics in the North could be persuaded to support the union. Sinn Féin was to be perhaps a significant but nonetheless small element in an anaemic political system in the North.

It hasn't turned out like that. The Good Friday Agreement has been correctly seen as an instrument of real change in people's lives. For that reason, nationalists and republicans support it. For that reason, rejectionist unionists oppose it. For that reason, the British government has minimised or diluted or delayed many of the changes it involves. The Good Friday Agreement, despite their protestations to the contrary, has so far been too big a challenge for the British government – perhaps more accurately it is a bridge too far for its agencies.

It was never going to be accepted by rejectionist unionists, by Ian Paisley and others, and apart from the latent sectarianism of their position, their opposition has a political basis. They understand that the Good Friday Agreement is about establishing a level playing field. Ulster unionist leaders know this. So do British unionists, those in the British establishment and the London government. That is why it is so difficult to get them to implement the changes that constitute the Good Friday Agreement.

The British government is a pro-union government, and its strategy – or to be more accurate its tactical day-to-day management of the process – has exacerbated the crisis within unionism and encouraged the rejectionists. But regardless of the difficulties, all citizens have the right to equality of treatment. British government strategy has offered more modest objectives, but even this has failed to satisfy the rejectionists within political unionism or British government agencies.

Sinn Féin is now the largest nationalist party in the North. Far from being outshone by others, our ministers in the executive were efficient, modernising and reforming. Our assembly team was effective, not only in the chamber but also across all the committees, and in their constituencies. The growth of Sinn Féin hasn't been confined to the Six Counties. In the last elections to the Irish parliament, five Sinn Féin TDs were elected and other seats were lost by only handfuls of votes. Sinn Féin is seen by an increasing section of the electorate right across Ireland to be a party which is the engine of the peace process. And the peace process has become a cherished and important process for most sensible people.

When the Sagart started his work it was all very different. There was no peace process. Sinn Féin was a demonised organisation in transition sowing the seeds of our peace strategy on the barren ground of a censored and sceptical media, pioneering delicate and difficult talks in a society which was polarised by the relentless cycle of injustice and violence. We were told that peace was impossible in Ireland and that Irish unity was a pipe dream. We have seen what is possible. There have been many ups and downs, but there has been real change. More importantly than the fate of Sinn Féin across this island, life is better for the vast majority of our people. Great progress has been made. It must not be squandered. There may be set-backs along the road, but there can no be giving up. Peace is possible – real, lasting, permanent – and a united, independent Ireland is ours if we want it badly enough, if we win support for that objective and if we are prepared to work hard to achieve it.

The British government's decision to stop the elections made many people despondent. They think that the British government believes that the survival of David Trimble and the ascendancy of the UUP within unionism is more important than anything else.

And where stands the Irish government in all of this? The Good Friday Agreement is an international treaty between the Irish and British governments, which share joint responsibility for its implementation. The British government has no right to act unilaterally on these matters, and it needs to be told this again and again. In particular, Irish citizens, victimised and targeted by sectarian violence, have a right to expect effective political protection from our government in Dublin. The Irish government needs to keep its commitments on other issues also. At the time of writing, it has not provided, as it has agreed to, for Northern representatives to participate in the Dáil.

The Stevens Report into the killing of Pat Finucane concluded in April 2003. It found that there was collusion. But the report has not been published. It is another instalment in the effort to dodge the truth of the RUC Special Branch and MI5's involvement in the killings of citizens on behalf of the British state.

The IRA has been blamed for the difficulties in the process. I believe that the maintenance of its cessations and various initiatives by the IRA demonstrate that organisation's commitment. The IRA also created the space for all the opportunities that have been developed since. My view is that the IRA cessations effectively allowed the rest of us to begin an entirely new process.

Sinn Féin strategy is about bringing an end to physical force republicanism, by creating an alternative way to achieve democratic and republican objectives. The development of that strategy created conditions which enabled the IRA to do the unthinkable. It not only engaged with the Independent International Commission on Decommissioning (IICD) but also put arms beyond use under its auspices at a time when unionist

385

paramilitaries were on a killing spree, when Orange marches were being forced into Catholic neighbourhoods and when the British army was remilitarising.

The IRA leadership's initiatives on arms should not be undervalued. To engage with the IICD in the first instance was a huge step. The IRA leadership also invited independent arms inspectors to inspect its arms dumps on a number of occasions to vouch that they were unused. This was unprecedented. Later the IRA permitted the IICD to verify that it had put weapons beyond use. These initiatives and the army leadership's response to the Joint Declaration are proof of the IRA's intentions.

As an Irish republican, as a citizen of Ireland, I want to see an end to British rule in this country. I believe this will happen. And I will continue to work towards this until it is a reality. It will be achieved through a process, not by way of ultimatums. Similarly, the IRA is never going to disband in response to ultimatums from the British government, or from David Trimble.

I believe the logic of the peace process puts all of us in a different place. All of us have to make politics work, have to strive to bring closure to these issues in ways which are realistic and achievable.

While I believe that the majority of unionists want to embrace change, it is clear that their political leaders do not want the Good Friday Agreement to be implemented. Dr Paisley has always been clear about this. So, too, is the UUP's current position. Most of the Joint Declaration was too much for the unionists, even though the commitments are on a conditional and protracted basis.

The declaration also contains other difficulties, some of which, as we have made clear, are wholly unacceptable to Sinn Féin. The two governments, for example, intend to introduce sanctions aimed at Sinn Féin and the Sinn Féin electorate, which are outside the terms of the Good Friday Agreement. These sanctions would contravene the safeguards built into the agreement. The Joint Declaration is not an act of completion. It is, at best, a commitment to a process towards completion. There is no act of completion from the unionist paramilitaries or from the British securocrats.

It appears that the demands of unionism are insatiable. They are also not deliverable. Not unless the two governments tear up the Good Friday Agreement. Not unless nationalists and republicans in the North decide to accept less than our very basic entitlements.

Part of the problem for those of us who have to manage this process is that Irish republicanism is seen by the British establishment and its system, quite correctly, as being against its long-term interests. It sees unionism as an ally, even with all its imperfections. So the challenge for Mr Blair is quite profound. He has made a singular and exceptional contribution to this process. He understands as well as I do that it is a process and that all of us need to apply ourselves and see beyond the difficulties of the moment. Mr Blair should see Britain's strategic interest being best served by the democratic resolution of the long-standing quarrel between the people of these two islands. His task in the short term has to be to continue the process of peace-making.

At this time there is little sign that unionism is contemplating a more positive approach to the Agreement. On the contrary, the cancellation of the elections has encouraged rejectionist unionism and Mr Trimble is the target of yet another leadership heave. Will he survive? Who knows? And if he does will he embrace the Agreement more fully?

Whatever emerges from the unionist debates – or indeed whoever emerges as leader – the two governments need to make it clear that for unionism the Good Friday Agreement is as good as it gets. The British government has pandered to unionism. There can be no doubt about that. But the cancellation of the elections was motivated also by London's agenda. Mr Blair needs to commit to a date certain for the election as soon as possible, and without any preconditions or qualifications.

This is a matter of political principle. It is the democratic imperative. It is also the right tactical and strategic thing for Mr Blair to do. An election is required to set a new context and to reinvigorate the process.

There can be no renegotiation of the Agreement. The price unionism has to pay for a return to devolved structures, a northern Assembly, is that these are in an all-Ireland context with all-Ireland institutions and interlocking and interdependent political structures. And if unionism refuses to play a partnership role with the rest of us, then pottering along with direct rule is not an option.

If there cannot be political institutions of the kind envisaged by the Good Friday Agreement at this time then the two governments need to proceed along an all-Ireland path to implement all other elements of the Agreement, and with a democratic mechanism in which London and Dublin are both held accountable by the rest of us. Such an arrangement needs to be put in place until the unionists are prepared to engage properly and on the basis of equality.

The Irish peace process is not perfect. Many may argue that we have an imperfect peace. But despite the failure to implement the agreement, the situation in the North of Ireland is better for the vast majority of people. Of course, for some people things are worse; particularly for the victims of sectarianism or those families which have been bereaved as reactionaries try to prevent progress. But things haven't all been bad. In fact, in comparison to other conflicts worldwide, the progress made in Ireland has been remarkable. So the challenge for a British government is to shape its own system, its agencies, to make this process work, and in so doing to accept that the leaderships of political unionism will not journey along the Good Friday Agreement process if they can avoid that. But like people everywhere, they will respond to the conditions in which they live. I therefore retain a confidence that if unionism is liberated, like the rest of us, from the conditions of the past, they will rise to the challenge. There can be no escape from the reality that the conditions in which we will all have to live are those contained in the Good Friday Agreement.

Until the unionists know that for a certainty they will resist that agreement. This is a hugely traumatic process for unionism. In their hearts many of them know that the game is up. It isn't over. But it is up. And whether the majority of unionists ever had any real advantage from the old agenda depends on how you define the word "advantage".

Never again can any of us accept that anyone on this island will be treated except on the basis of equality. The days of second–class citizens are over. Let me make it clear also that Irish republicans will never treat unionists the way the British government and the old unionist regime treated us.

There will undoubtedly be more talks. By Mr Blair's own admission, his government, thus far, has not implemented what it is obliged to implement. In the last few years, on a number of occasions, when it faced the hard choice of offending unionism it backed down. It knows this. It is the government with the largest majority in the history of the British Labour Party. How on earth can it expect us to persuade others of its good intentions if it fails to do what Mr Blair has said is the right thing? So further talks must not be about renegotiating the Good Friday Agreement; they must be about implementing it. We must aim for a just peace. No one ever said that this was going to be easy. But it is the single most important thing that any of us can do at this time in our history.

Gerry Adams,
Belfast, Ireland
August 2003

# Glossary

**Abstentionism** After the 1922–23 Civil War the defeated republican side refused to accept the legitimacy of the institutions in the two states established by the Treaty. Consequently, successful Sinn Féin candidates in elections to the parliaments North and South and to Westminster refused to take their seats. Sinn Féin candidates also refused to take seats won in the elections to the Westminster parliament.

**Alliance Party** Moderate unionist party in the North, set up in 1970, led by David Ford.

**Anglo-Irish Agreement** Document agreed by the Irish government led by Garret FitzGerald and Margaret Thatcher's Conservative government in 1985.

**Ard Chomhairle** National executive.

**Ard Fheis** National conference.

**Ard Rúnaí** General secretary.

**Bilaterals** Meetings involving two participants, usually political parties or governments.

**Blanketmen** Republican political prisoners who refused to wear prison uniforms.

**Bloody Sunday** 30 January 1972, when fourteen people on a demonstration in Derry against internment were killed by British soldiers.

**B-Specials** Controversial unionist state militia formed in 1920 as a back-up force for the police. Disbanded and reformed as the Ulster Defence Regiment (UDR) in 1970, then disbanded and replaced by the Royal Irish Regiment (RIR) in July 1992.

**Connolly House group** Senior Irish American businessmen and trade union leaders who played a pivotal role in the development of the peace process.

**Continuity Army Council/Continuity IRA** Small breakaway armed republican group.

**Craic** fun, conversation, banter, a good time.

**Dáil** Irish parliament.

**Democratic Unionist Party (DUP)** Right-wing unionist party, formed in 1971 and led by Revd Ian Paisley.

**Downing Street Declaration** Statement issued December 1993 by British and Irish governments, setting out principles towards a settlement for the North of Ireland.

**Fianna Fáil** Founded in 1926 by Eamon de Valera; the largest of the Irish political parties; led by Bertie Ahern.

**Fine Gael** Formed 1933, second largest political party in the South; led by Enda Kenny.

**Forum for Peace and Reconciliation** A consultative body set up in Dublin in October 1994 to examine ways in which a lasting peace could be established by agreement among all the people of Ireland; its final report was published in February 1996.

**Framework Document** Published in February 1995 by the British and Irish governments, it outlined agreed parameters for a talks process.

**GAA** Gaelic Athletic Association.

**Gaeltacht** Irish-speaking area.

**Government of Ireland Act** Act of the British parliament passed in 1920 that claimed British jurisdiction in Ireland.

389

**H-Blocks** Maze prison, so called because the prison blocks are shaped like the letter H with four prison wings and a connecting administrative building.

**Irish National Liberation Army (INLA)** Small republican armed group.

**Internment** Imprisonment of political dissidents – principally republicans – without trial, in both states in Ireland; used in the North in 1922, 1939, 1956 and 1971–75.

**Irish Republican Army (IRA)** Original Irish republican armed group which has fought the British since the proclamation of the Irish republic in 1916 until the present day.

**Loyalists** Unionists who use violence to achieve their ends are often described as loyalists, although not all those who would call themselves loyalists support political violence.

**Northern Ireland Office (NIO)** The British government's colonial and administrative office in the North of Ireland.

**Orange Order (Orangemen)** Sectarian organisation characterised by ritualistic pageantry and supremacist celebrations; its name derives from the victory of Protestant William of Orange over Catholic King James II.

**Progressive Unionist Party (PUP)** Unionist party linked to the paramilitary Ulster Volunteer Force (UVF).

**Radio Telifis Éireann (RTÉ)** Irish state radio and television network.

**Real IRA** Small splinter republican group; responsible for Omagh bomb, August 1998.

**Republicanism** Political ideology born out of the French and American revolutions; believes in the right of Irish people as a whole to determine the future of Ireland; seeks a democratic, non-sectarian, pluralist society – a thirty-two county Irish republic.

**Royal Ulster Constabulary (RUC)** Paramilitary state police force in North of Ireland.

**Social Democratic and Labour Party (SDLP)** Northern Ireland party, founded in 1970; currently led by Mark Durkan.

*Seisiún* Music session.

**Sinn Féin** "We Ourselves", commonly translated as "Ourselves Alone"; republican party founded 1905, organised throughout the thirty-two counties; and currently led by Gerry Adams.

**Shinner** Name given to members and supporters of Sinn Féin.

**Six Counties** "The North"; the six counties (Antrim, Armagh, Derry, Down, Fermanagh, Tyrone) under British jurisdiction, out of the nine counties which make up the province of Ulster.

**Stormont** Seat of the unionist government and parliament from 1932 to 1972.

**Tánaiste** Irish Deputy Prime Minister.

**Taoiseach** Irish Prime Minister.

**Teachta Dála (TD)** Elected member of Irish parliament (Dáil).

**Trilaterals** Meetings involving three participants.

**Twelfth of July** Annual commemoration of the Battle of the Boyne by the Orange Order, part of the "marching season". More than parades and pageants, this is a time when unionist fervour is at its height and clashes occur regularly with Catholic areas.

**Twenty-six Counties** The Republic of Ireland; the South.

**Ulster Defence Association (UDA)** Major loyalist paramilitary group, founded 1971.

**Ulster Defence Regiment (UDR)** See "B-Specials".

**Ulster Unionist Party (UUP)** Largest unionist party, led by David Trimble, also known as the Official Unionist Party.

**Ulster Volunteer Force (UVF)** Originally formed in 1912 to oppose Home Rule, it is now a loyalist paramilitary group.

**Unionism** Belief in maintaining political union between North of Ireland and Britain.

# Biographies

**Ahern, Bertie** Taoiseach 1997– and leader of Fianna Fáil.

**Ahtisaari, Martti** Former Finnish President and one of two international statesmen who acted as arms inspectors.

**Blair, Tony** British Prime Minister 1997– and leader of the British Labour Party 1994–.

**Bhreatnach, Lucilita** Ard Rúnaí (general secretary) of Sinn Féin 1987–2003. Member of the party's negotiating team and Ard Chomhairle member.

**Brooke, Peter** British Secretary of State 1989–92. He authorised the secret talks with Sinn Féin which began in October 1990.

**Brown, Ron** US Commerce Secretary. The first of President Clinton's Cabinet to officially meet Gerry Adams, in 1994, he was tragically killed in a plane crash in April 1996.

**Bruton, John** Taoiseach 1994–97 and leader of Fine Gael 1990–2001.

**Cahill, Joe** Honourary Vice-President of Sinn Féin, he was an IRA activist during the 1930s, 1940s, 1950s, 1960s and 1970s.

**Clarke, Terence "Cleaky"** Head of Sinn Féin's security team and former political prisoner and close friend of Gerry Adams; he died in June 2000.

**Clinton, Bill** President of the USA 1992–2000, he played a crucial role in supporting the efforts to build a peace process.

**Clinton, Hillary** Former First Lady, now a US Senator and a consistent supporter of the peace process.

**Daly, Cahal Dr** Bishop of Down and Connor and Cardinal and Primate of Ireland, now retired.

**de Brún, Bairbre** Sinn Féin member of the assembly and former Minister for Health, Social Services and Public Safety, a member of Sinn Féin's negotiating team and Ard Chomhairle.

**de Chastelain, General John** Canadian chair of the International Independent Commission on Decommissioning.

**Dodd, Chris** US Senator who helped persuade President Bill Clinton to give Gerry Adams a visa in February 1994.

**Doherty, Pat** Vice-President of Sinn Féin, MP and assembly representative for West Tyrone and a member of Sinn Féin's negotiating team.

**Doyle, Dawn** Sinn Féin's director of publicity.

**Feeney, Chuck** US businessman and member of the Connolly House group.

**Ferguson, Colin** British government's representative in the secret dialogue with Sinn Féin 1991–93.

**Finucane, Pat** Human rights lawyer shot dead in 1989 by the UDA.

**Flynn, Bill** US businessman and member of the Connolly House group.

**Gibney, Jim** Member of the Sinn Féin Ard Chomhairle and former political prisoner.

**Gildernew, Michelle** MP for Fermanagh South Tyrone and a member of the Sinn Féin negotiating team.

**Gilman, Ben** Retired congressman, as chair of the House International Relations Committee played a key role in keeping Ireland on the political agenda in Washington DC.

**Green, Leo** Former republican hunger striker, now a member of Sinn Féin's negotiating team.

**Hamill, Robert** Nationalist man kicked to death by a loyalist mob in May 1997.

**Hartley, Tom** Leader of the Sinn Féin group on Belfast City Council and Ard Runaí of Sinn Féin 1983–87.

**Haughey, Charlie** Taoiseach 1979–81, 1982 and again 1987–92; leader of Fianna Fáil 1979–92.

**Howell, Ted** Member of Sinn Féin's Ard Chomhairle and of the party's negotiating team; former political prisoner.

**Hume, John** Leader of the SDLP 1979–2001. MP for Foyle 1983– and MEP 1979–.

**Keane, Mairéad** Member of the Sinn Féin Ard Chomhairle and Sinn Féin's first representative to the US.

**Kelly, Gerry** Sinn Féin assembly member and one of the party's senior negotiators, he spent sixteen years in British prisons.

**Kennedy, Ted** Senator and influential voice on Ireland in the US for over three decades.

**King, Peter** Stalwart, longstanding supporter of the peace process and Sinn Féin within the US Congress.

**Lake, Tony** National Security Advisor to President Bill Clinton 1993–98.

**McAteer, Aidan** Member of the Sinn Féin negotiating team, a former political prisoner and advisor to Martin McGuinness.

**McAuley, Richard** Sinn Féin press secretary to Gerry Adams, a member of the party's negotiating team and former political prisoner.

**McAuley, Chrissie** Sinn Féin councillor in Belfast, political advisor on equality and human rights to the party's negotiating team and former political prisoner.

**McGrory, P.J.** Gerry Adams's lawyer who also represented the families of the Gibraltar victims.

**McGuinness, Martin** Sinn Féin's chief negotiator, MP for mid-Ulster, a former political prisoner and Minister for Education in the executive.

**McLaughlin, Mitchel** Sinn Féin party chairperson and assembly representative, a member of the party's negotiating team.

**Major, John** British Prime Minister 1990–97.

**Mallon, Seamus** Deputy leader of the SDLP 1979–2001, MP for Newry and Armagh 1986– and Deputy First Minister in the executive following the Good Friday Agreement.

**Mandela, Nelson** Former political prisoner, President of South Africa and leader of the African National Congress.

**Mansergh, Martin** Senior advisor on the North to successive Fianna Fáil leaders.

**Mbeki, Thabo** President of South Africa 1999 – and leader of the ANC from 1997.

**Mitchell, George** Former US Senator and Senate Majority Leader, he chaired the negotiations leading to the Good Friday Agreement.

**Molyneaux, Jim** Leader of the Ulster Unionist Party 1975–95 and MP for South Antrim, then Lagan Valley, from 1970–97; he now sits in the British House of Lords.

**Morrison, Danny** Former Sinn Féin director of publicity and political prisoner, now a writer and media commentator.

**Morrison, Bruce** Former US Congressman and member of the Connolly House group, a longstanding activist on Irish issues.

**Moran, Tom** US businessman and colleague of Bill Flynn, a consistent supporter of the peace process.

**Mowlam, Majorie (Mo)** British Secretary of State 1997–99 during negotiations leading to the Good Friday Agreement.

**Neal, Richard** US Congressman with keen interest in Ireland who lobbies for support for the peace process.

**Nelson, Brian** Senior figure in the UDA who was also a British agent.

**Oatley, Michael** British intelligence figure, the British government's secret representative in contacts with republicans.

**Ó Brádaigh, Ruairí** President of Sinn Féin 1970–83, former political prisoner; President of Republican Sinn Féin 1986–.

**Ó Caoláin, Caoimhghín** Leader of the Sinn Féin group of representatives in the Dáil, he is TD for Cavan Monaghan.

**Ó Conaill, Dáithí** Republican leader in the 1970s; a former political prisoner, he became Vice-President of Sinn Féin but left the party in 1986 and helped found Republican Sinn Féin.

**O'Dowd, Niall** Publisher of the *Irish Voice* in New York, he played an important role in the Connolly House group and as a link between Sinn Féin and the US government.

**Ó Fiaich, Cardinal Tomás** Primate of all Ireland and a strong nationalist, he encouraged Fr Reid and Gerry Adams in their efforts to develop an alternative to armed struggle; he died in 1990.

**O'Hanlon, Siobhán** Member of Sinn Féin's negotiating team and former political prisoner.

**O'Hare, Rita** Former director of publicity for Sinn Féin and editor of *An Phoblacht*; a former political prisoner, she is now the party's representative in the US.

**Paisley, Revd Ian** Established the Free Presbyterian Church in 1951; founder and leader of the right-wing DUP; MP for North Antrim.

**Ramaphosa, Cyril** Former General Secretary of the ANC who was its chief negotiator during discussions to end apartheid; one of two international statesmen who acted as arms inspectors.

**Reid, Fr Alec** Redemptorist priest who played a pivotal role in the development of the peace process.

**Reynolds, Albert** Former Taoiseach and leader of Fianna Fáil 1992–94.

**Robinson, Mary** First woman President of Ireland 1990–97.

**Sands, Bobby** First of the ten republican hunger strikers to die in 1981; the others were Francis Hughes, Raymond McCreesh, Patsy O'Hara, Joe McDonnell, Martin Hurson, Kevin Lynch, Kieran Doherty, Thomas McElwee and Michael Devine.

**Smith, Jean Kennedy** US Ambassador to Ireland 1993–98.

**Staunton, Ciaran** Irish American from Mayo who played an important role in building support for Sinn Féin's peace strategy in the US.

**Thatcher, Margaret** British Tory Prime Minister 1979–90.

**Trimble, David** Leader of the UUP 1995–, he was first minister in the executive established after the agreement.

# Index

abstentionism, 45–7, 153, 272
Act of Union (1800), 338, 353–4
Adams, Annie (mother), 103, 113–14
Adams, Colette, 4, 9, 22–3, 24, 26, 47, 90, 104, 119, 161, 185, 375
   grenade attack on, 91
Adams, Davy, 211
Adams, Gearóid, 4, 22–3, 24, 26, 90, 91, 214, 219
Adams, President John, 206
Adams, Paddy (brother), 23, 72, 327
Adams, Paddy (uncle), 23
Adams, Sean, 23, 114
Ad Hoc Committee on Ireland, 193, 380
Ad Hoc Committee on Irish Affairs, 157, 204, 380
African National Congress (ANC), 97–8, 169, 214–20, 256, 287, 369, 380
   send senior delegation to Ireland, 371–2
   women's delegation meet Sinn Féin women, 217
Agnew, Paddy, 12
Ahern, Bertie, 197, 222, 235, 274, 281, 291, 296, 304, 307, 314, 322, 336–7, 369
   appeals to British not to stop assembly elections, 383
   and constitutional change, 321, 354
   death of mother, 355, 357
   general election campaign, 275–6
   negotiations on Agreement, 345, 346–7, 348, 349–50, 356, 357, 359, 360–2, 365–6
Ahern, Dermot, 81
Albright, Madeleine, 339–40
Alderdice, John, 159
Allen, Philip, 337
Alliance Party, 102, 159, 162, 251, 265, 273, 280, 303
   indicts Sinn Féin, 336
all-party talks, 257, 262–3, 265–6, 269, 270, 274, 302–4, 305–11, 315–16, 318–26, 330–42
   date announced, 239
   exclusion of Sinn Féin from, 254–6, 265–7, 276, 285, 287
   deadline set for end of, 340–1
   Good Friday Agreement drafted, 343–68
   "Ground Rules for Substantive All-Party Negotiations", 244
   Heads of Agreement negotiations, 320, 321–2, 324–5, 328–9
   in Lancaster House, 330, 331–3
   negotiations for holding, 241–53
     Sinn Féin excluded from, 210–11, 220, 239, 241, 244, 251–2, 253
   rules of procedure agreed, 263
   Sinn Féin expelled from, 336, 337, 338
   Strand One, 310–11, 320, 329, 357
   Strand Two, 310–11, 329, 332, 333, 335, 345, 349–50, 354, 355–6, 357–8
   Strand Three, 310–11, 329
   substantive talks begin, 309
   *see also* Mitchell, George

Ambrosio, Aniello, 157
"Americans for a New Irish Agenda", 154–6
   Sheraton Hotel meeting, 160
Amnesty International, 163
   *Political Killings in Northern Ireland*, 89–90
   on shoot-to-kill policy, 76, 83
   "urgent action" notice on Damien Austin, 103
   "urgent action" notice on Róisín McAliskey, 273
Amsterdam Treaty referendum, 338
Ancram, Michael, 207, 208, 209, 222–3, 226–7, 236, 238, 241, 245
Andrews, David, 311, 320, 329
Anglo-Irish Agreement (1985), 38–40, 42, 43, 44, 48, 76, 81, 92–3, 106, 118, 122, 129, 165, 328
   inter-governmental element suspended, 102
Annesley, Hugh, 259, 260, 291
*An Phoblacht*, 45, 93, 134, 223, 306
Anti-Apartheid Movement in Ireland, 103
Apprentice Boys, 220, 263
Armagh women's prison, 7, 9–12, 18, 59, 69, 115
   *see also* hunger strikes
arms crisis, 47–8
Arthurs, Paul, 368
Articles 2 and 3 of the Irish constitution, 48, 282, 316, 330, 360–1
   proposed amendments to, 347, 372–3
Asmal, Kadar, 103–4
Assembly elections (1982), 15, 18, 28, 30–1, 251
Atkins, Humphrey, 8
Austin, Damien, 103
Austin, Janice, 103
Austin, Joe, 50, 61, 63, 103, 163

Baird, Michelle, 138
Balcombe Street Four, 372, 373
Balkans crisis, 340
Ball, Jonathan, 118
Ballyfermot Residents Association community centre, 107–8
Ballykinlar (County Down) landmine, 276
Ballymurphy Seven, 102–3
Barnard, Niel, 216
Barrett, Ken, 88
Barry, Bill, 156
Basset, Ray, 187
*Before the Dawn*, 267
Begley, Thomas, 138–9
Behan, Brendan, 317
Belfast, 3, 4, 230–4, 282, 288–9
   Bodenstown commemoration, 9
   "A Celebration of Culture and Creativity", 129
   Connswater Shopping Centre, 314
   Conway Mill, 254
   Culturlann, 231
   demolition of slums, 18
   economic conference (1994), 198–9, 199, 208
   inter-republican feuds (1977), 5, 6

McErlean's bakery, 230, 231, 232
Mackies engineering plant, 230, 231
Meanscoil Feirste, 231
New Lodge Road, 11
Ormeau Road betting shop attack, 109–10
Saint Dominic's High School, 231
St Malachy's College, 5
Shankill Road fish shop bombed, 138, 139
Sinn Féin election results in, 251
Space Nightclub, 327
Springfield Road barracks attacked, 53
taxi driver shot on Ormeau Road, 329
unionists lose control of City Council, 286
see also Milltown Cemetery
Belfast Institute of Further and Higher Education, 129, 130
Belleek (County Fermanagh) killing, 71
Benn, Tony, 17, 284, 354
Besette, Lauren, 289
Bessbrook, County Armagh, 16
Bhreatnach, Lucilita, 27, 107–8, 200, 209, 234–5, 304, 322, 367, 376
Biko, Steve, 51
Birmingham Six, 70–1, 152
    released, 101–2
Blair, Tony, 271, 275, 282, 285, 290, 307, 330, 382, 387–8
    announces inquiry into Blood Sunday, 333–4
    calls for IRA act of completion, 381
    comes to power (1997), 278, 279–80
    demands changes to Irish constitution, 282
    meetings with Sinn Féin at, 312–14, 336, 338–9
        at Downing Street, 322–4, 329–30
    negotiates for Sinn Féin to enter talks, 291–2
    negotiations with talks on Agreement, 333, 345–6, 347, 348, 349–50, 351–2, 355–6, 357, 359–62, 363, 365–6
    provides Trimble with a side letter, 364, 379
    response to pressure for constitutional change, 353–4
    visits Belfast, 282
Blasket Islands, 189
Bloody Sunday (1972), 129
    Blair announces new inquiry into, 333–4, 338
    inquiry pressed for, 313, 324, 330
Boal, Desmond, 36–7
Boothroyd, Betty, 282
border between North and South, 187–8, 200
    cross-border roads opened, 196
    see also partition
Bradley, Denis, 97, 104, 118, 144–5
Bradwell, James, 268
Brady, Paddy, 70
Breslin, Eileen, 243
Bridge into the Future, A, 338
Brighton bombing, 31–2, 34
British army, 1, 2, 44, 50, 91, 93, 102, 162, 165, 170, 208, 270, 281, 316, 337, 381
    attack republican funerals, 52–5
    extent of military garrison in Ireland, 187, 214
    ill-treatment of IRA suspects, 5
    leak hints about reintroducing internment, 107

Lisburn HQ attacked, 267–9
Osnabrück base attacked by IRA mortar bomb, 258
    see also Bloody Sunday; collusion issue; plastic and rubber bullets
British Broadcasting Corporation (BBC), 15, 252
    at Castle Buildings, 343
    programme on Gibraltar killings, 73–4
    radio debate between Hume and Adams (1985), 42
British government, 8, 32, 50, 82–3, 92, 109, 123, 130, 151, 152, 153, 154, 164, 172, 176, 185, 186, 188–9, 199, 203–4, 206–12, 282–3
    briefings through Derry group, 104–5
    building blocks paper, 227–9
    criminalisation of IRA prisoners, 7, 11–12, 13–14, 59, 279
    decontamination period for Sinn Féin, 207, 212
    derogate on European Court of Human Rights decision, 83, 84
    dialogue with Sinn Féin, 93–9, 115–17, 120–4
    and Downing Street Declaration, 147–50, 165, 168
        and clarification of, 162, 163, 167, 169, 171
    Fair Employment Commission, 102
    IRA mortar-bombs 10 Downing Street, 101
    and joint declaration negotiations, 105–7, 110, 112, 124, 127–8, 132–4, 135, 140–5
    leak of confidential report on Garvaghy Road march, 294
    lifting of exclusion orders, 196, 198
    meet with Sinn Féin
        in Derry, 222
        at Stormont, 200–1
    negotiations on hunger strike, 9–10
    relationship with USA, 151, 152, 155, 160, 161
    and "Select Committee on Northern Ireland", 140
    and Spring's "principles", 139–40
    strategy of attacking funerals, 52–5
    and visa issue, 158, 159, 178, 180, 203
    see also all-party talks; Blair, Tony;
        demilitarisation; Major, John; Thatcher, Margaret
British–Irish Council, 358
British Irish Watch, 89
Broadcasting Act (Section 31), 64, 83, 132, 150, 164
Brooke, Peter, 92, 93–4, 101–2, 104, 109, 110, 112, 117, 128, 144
    on British strategy in Ireland, 97–8
Brophy, Susan, 204
Brown, Revd Godfrey, 126
Brown, Jerry, 153
Brown, Ron, 199, 209
    lunch at Springvale Training Centre for, 233
Brown, Sean, 281, 282
Bruton, John, 197–8, 200–1, 205, 213, 214, 222, 223, 224, 225, 226, 228, 240, 242, 246, 250, 252, 254, 257–8, 259, 266, 269, 270, 283, 315
    announces date for all-party talks, 239
    caretaker Taoiseach, 288
    "no contact edict" with Sinn Féin, 271, 274, 280, 281, 290

Bruton, John (*cont.*)
    reaction to Canary Wharf bombing, 238–9
    reassures nationalists in North, 247–8
Buncrana, County Donegal, 104, 119, 146
Bundred, Kathy, 17
Bundred, Steve, 17
Burch, Revd Sam, 50
Burke, Ray, 303, 311
Bush, George, 380, 382
Butler, Eddie, 372
Byrne, Gabriel, 194

Cahill, Joe, 63–4, 356, 367, 376
    negotiations for visa for, 178–9, 180
Cahill, Tom, 50
Campbell, Alistair, 322, 324
Canada, 380
    Adams visits, 194–5, 196
    Sinn Féin party political broadcast by Ulster
        Television, 251
Canary Wharf bombing, 238
Carey, Hugh, 152
Carolus, Cheryl, 215
Carrickmore (County Tyrone) Easter
    commemoration, 368
Carron, Owen, 14, 15
Castro, Rene, 194
Catholic Church, 6–7, 14, 27, 29–30, 34–8, 39–40,
    41, 52, 57, 98, 105
    Bishops' Conference (1985), 35, 36
    public debate with Adams, 34
    *see also* Reid, Fr Alec
censorship of Sinn Féin in media, 64, 83, 123–4,
    132, 134, 135, 150, 159, 161, 185, 186, 315
    lifted in Britain, 188
    lifted in Ireland, 164
Chilcot, John, 110, 117
Chrétien, Jean, 380
Christopher, Warren, 158, 159, 203
Church of Ireland, 126
civil rights struggle, 6, 20, 83, 152
Civil War, 151–2, 317
Clann na Gael, 152
Clarke, "Cleaky" Terence, 65, 69, 82, 136–7, 170,
    187, 201, 254, 255, 303
Clarke, Kenneth, 122
Clarke, Paddy, 65
Clegg, Lee, 220–1, 240, 350
Clifford, Kieran, 206
Clinton, Bill, 153–5, 157, 158, 159, 174, 178, 179,
    180, 185, 189, 191, 198, 199, 208, 209, 211,
    228, 237, 243, 246, 247, 257, 270, 292, 378,
    379–80
    and Agreement negotiations, 359–60, 362, 363,
        364
    first visit to Ireland, 224, 225, 226, 229, 230–4
    public handshake with Adams, 230, 232
    manifesto position on Ireland, 154
    and Patrick's Day meetings with Adams, 204–6,
        339–40
Clinton, Hillary, 205, 340, 380
Clinton, Jim, 168

Clinton, Theresa, 168
Clonard Church Ministry, 13, 41, 50–1, 126, 156,
    314
Coachman's Inn, Dublin Road, 63
Coagh, County Tyrone, 102
Coalisland (County Tyrone) barracks ambush, 110
Cochrane, Thomas, 16
Collins, Gerry, 56
collusion issue, 24, 25, 70, 84–91, 104, 112, 137, 154,
    169–70, 235, 276, 314, 316, 329–30, 380, 385
Combined Loyalist Military Command
    1991 ceasefire, 102
    1994 ceasefire, 195, 259, 265, 308
    disbanded, 316, 319
    issues death threat against Billy Wright, 265
Concannon, Don, 279
Conlon, Mick, 210
Connolly, James, 196, 374
Connolly House group, 155–7, 174, 178, 179–80,
    190, 242–3
    "Policy Statement by Irish American Leaders",
        176
Conservative Party conference, 31–2
Continuity IRA, 308
    bomb Moira and Portadown, 336
Coogan, Tim Pat, 48
Corbyn, Jeremy, 17, 284
Cork, 298
Corrigan, Paul, 55
Cran, James, 210
Crowe, Sean, 286
Cruise O'Brien, Conor, 131–2, 185–6
Cuba, 339
    missile crisis, 191
Curran, Bríd, 353
Currie, Austin, 75, 79
Cyprus, 92

*Daily Mail*, 270
*Daily Star*, 160
*Daily Telegraph*, 61, 161
Dalton, Tim, 187, 225
Daly, Cardinal Cahal, 14, 30, 34–5, 150
Darragh, Síle, 143
Davey, John, 88, 105
Davis, Angela, 194
Davitt, Michael, 151
Dearie, John, 153
de Brún, Bairbre, 185, 344, 350, 352, 376
    on executive, 378
de Chastelain, John, 234–5, 236, 248, 308, 377
decommissioning issue, 196, 200–1, 203–4, 205, 211,
    213–14, 223, 225–9, 235, 236, 243, 249, 250,
    252, 259, 265, 266, 285, 288, 296, 304, 311,
    337, 346, 349, 355, 358, 361, 362, 364, 375, 381
    IRA statement on arms, 381–3
    parallel, 236, 247–8, 307
    "Resolving the Address to Decommissioning",
        290–1, 303
    *see also* Independent International Commission
        on Decommissioning; international body
        on decommissioning

de Klerk, F.W., 216
DeLay, Thomas, 204
demilitarisation issue, 181, 206, 240, 246, 313,
    318–19, 322, 324, 338, 349, 358, 377, 381
Democratic Unionist Party (DUP), 44, 93, 130, 133,
    141, 159, 162, 241, 251, 265, 266, 270, 273,
    274, 276, 278, 280, 314, 375
  in all-party talks
    refuse to attend, 257, 303, 304, 306, 307, 308
  assembly elections, 377
  blockade Catholic Masses, 266, 269
  local government elections, 285
  refuse to take seats on executive, 378
  in South Africa, 287
Derrane, Joe, 206
Derry, 20, 44, 206, 222, 262, 263, 376
  1992 peace conference ("Beyond Hate"), 156
  1993 peace conference, 129
  Clinton visit to, 233
  secret link group, 93, 94–5, 96, 97, 104, 116–17,
    122, 143, 144–5
de Valera, Eamon, 47
Devenney, Danny, 108
Deverell, John, 93, 94
Devine, Micky, 10
Devlin, Fay, 189
Dicks, Terry, 163
Dodd, Chris, 158, 199, 204, 380
Doherty, Hugh, 372
Doherty, Kieran, 10, 12, 68, 289
Doherty, Pat, 27, 46, 110, 117, 143, 185, 266–7, 274,
    277, 312, 331, 350, 352, 361, 376
Doherty, Peter, 11
Donaldson, Denis, 49
Donaldson, Jeffrey, 333, 355, 364, 365
Donegan, Joseph, 16
Donlon, Sean, 225
Doris, Tony, 102
Downes, Larry, 189
Downes, Sean, 189
Downing Street Declaration (1993), 147–50, 157,
    162, 163, 164, 165, 167, 169, 171, 172, 186, 197
Doyle, Dawn, 363, 376
Dropping Well bombing, 17
Drumboe (County Donegal) executions, 119
Dublin, 171–2, 376
  Clinton visit to, 234
  Iveagh House, 262
  Joxer Daly's bar, 187
  Killanarden Community Centre, 163
  Kilmainham jail, 374
  Waterstones, 267
Duffy, Henry, 11
Duggan, Harry, 241, 372
Dunfey, Bob, 211
Dunfey, Jack, 211
Dunfey, Jerry, 211
Durkan, Frank, 309
Duty Free Shoppers Ltd, 156

Easter Rising (1916), 47, 151, 187, 196, 234, 374
Eaton, Shannon, 189, 206, 209, 211

Eksund, 56, 57
emigration, 151, 189–90
Enniskillen (County Fermanagh) bombing, 55–6, 57,
    118
Enright, Deirdre, 327, 328
Enright, Fr Seamus, 42
Enright, Terry, 327–8
equality issue, 150, 157, 165, 201, 211, 299, 309–10,
    313, 319, 322, 323, 333, 337, 338, 340, 345,
    347, 350, 354, 358, 367, 374, 381, 388
  republican march to City Hall, 136
Ervine, David, 211, 360
European Charter for Regional and Minority
    Languages, 348
European Convention on Human Rights, 348
European Court of Human Rights, 83, 84
European Union, 50, 127, 153
Evening Press, 133

Famous Original Ray's Pizza (Manhattan), 157
Farrell, Mairéad, 12, 58–60, 61, 62–9, 71, 74, 185
Farren, Sean, 75, 79
FBI (Federal Bureau of Investigation), 158
Feeney, Chuck, 156–7
Féile an Phobail, 129, 264
Fenian Movement, 151
Ferguson, Colin ("Fred", or Robert McLaren),
    118–19, 121, 122, 128, 200
Ferris, Martin, 288, 292, 304, 322, 356, 376
Ferrity, Geraldine, 373
Ferry, Jim, 26
Finucane, Geraldine, 87
Finucane, Pat, 87–8, 90, 329, 385
  UN calls for independent inquiry into murder
    of, 346
Fitt, Gerry, 17–18
Fitzgerald, Garret, 34, 43, 76
Fitzroy Presbyterian Church, 50
Flanagan, Fionnuala, 194, 209
Flanagan, Ronnie, 330, 335
Flynn, Bill, 156, 157, 233
Flynn, Raymond, 154
Foley, Tom, 158
Foot, Michael, 279
Force Research Unit (FRU), 85–6, 87, 89
Forman, Sadie, 217
Forum for Peace and Reconciliation, 118, 148, 176,
    186–7, 200, 221–2, 222
  inaugural meeting of, 196
Framework Document, 202, 203, 330, 333
Frankfurt, 267
Freeh, Louis, 158
Friends of Ireland, 193
Friends of Sinn Féin, 305
  first annual dinner, 209
Fullerton, Eddie, 26, 104

Gallagher, Dermot, 187
Gallagher, Marguerite, 232
Galvin, Martin, 154
Galway Arts Festival, 132
Garda Representative Association, 361

397

*George* magazine, 288
Germany re-united, 2, 97
Gibney, Jim, 1, 27, 71–2, 126, 186, 312, 363
Gibraltar killings of IRA volunteers in, 1, 58–74, 75, 82, 83, 264, 292
Gildernew, Michelle, 322, 376
Gilman, Ben, 152, 157, 199, 204
Gingrich, Newt, 204–5
Global Citizens Circle, 211
Good Friday Agreement (1998), 369, 370, 377, 378–9, 380, 381, 383–4, 385, 386–8
    negotiations for first draft, 343–68
    referendum on, 374–5, 377
Gore, Al, 161, 191, 192, 203, 209, 224, 234
Government of Ireland Act (1920), 43, 51, 118, 296, 323, 338, 353–4
Gracey, Harold, 259
Grand Hotel, Brighton, 31
Great Hunger, 151
Groves, Emma, 131
*Guardian*, 137, 161
Guildford Four, 192
Guiney, Desmond, 11
Guiney, Eric, 11
Gulf War, 101

Haass, Richard, 382
Hackett, Dermot, 70
Hailsham, Lord, 151
Hall, Blair, 231, 232
Hamill, Catherine, 230–1
Hamill, Patrick, 231
Hamill, Robert, 281
Hamilton, Paul, 260
Hanna, Eamon, 78
Hannaway, Kevin, 5, 8, 27, 67
Harryville (County Antrim) blockade, 269
Hartley, Allison, 231, 232
Hartley, Liz, 231, 232
Hartley, Tom, 10, 27, 67, 75, 126, 245
Haughey, Charles, 40, 47–8, 80–1, 82, 102, 106, 110, 346
Havel, Vaclav, 97
Hayden, Tom, 194
H-Blocks *see* Long Kesh
Heaney, Seamus, 130, 184
Heffer, Eric, 63
Helsinki Watch, 103
Hendron, Joe, 111, 112
Hershey, Barbara, 194
Hevesi, Alan, 190
Higgins, Gerald, 85–6
Higgins, Michael D., 132
Hill, Paul, 192
Hoban, James, 206
Ho Chi Minh, 99
Holkeri, Harri, 234–5, 236
Holmes, John, 273, 322
Holy Cross school blockade, 381
Houston, Angelica, 194
Howard, Michael, 135
Howe, Sir Geoffrey, 62

Howell, Ted, 117, 143, 155
Howes, David, 6, 73
Hughes, Brendan, 9
Hughes, Francis, 10, 279
Hughes, Mary, 49
Hughes, Sean, 137
human rights issue, 347–8, 381
Hume, John, 37, 40, 41–5, 101, 110, 117, 125, 152, 159, 178, 178, 182, 198, 206, 237, 283, 300, 304
    and Adams meet with Irish government, 186–7, 188
    and Adams release joint statements, 120, 180
    in all-party talks, 345, 352, 358, 365
    efforts to overcome talks impasse, 222, 226, 227, 228
    endorses visa application, 158
    introduces Adams to Clinton, 205
    internal SDLP tensions, 175
    media leaks Adams visit to, 119
    meets with IRA leadership, 239
    negotiations to restore ceasefire, 258–9, 264, 266, 267, 268–9, 271–2, 273, 274
    pushes for Bloody Sunday inquiry, 324
    response to Greysteel attack, 145–6
    retires, 379
    vilified by Dublin media, 122, 146
    visits USA, 134–5
Hume, Pat, 80
Hume/Adams initiative, 43–5, 48, 51, 57–8, 75–6, 79, 80, 93, 94, 95, 96, 97, 105, 106–7, 111, 112, 118, 119–20, 123, 124, 127, 128, 132–5, 137, 138, 140–7, 149, 164, 174, 177, 181, 197, 257, 314, 315, 349
    rejected by both governments, 140–5
Hungary, 97
hunger strikes, 9–12, 13, 14, 18, 28, 31, 32, 36, 48, 49, 53, 59, 68, 93, 94, 128, 215, 267, 279, 289
Hurd, Douglas, 83, 119, 122, 149, 160, 161
Hurson, Martin, 10
Hutchinson, Billy, 211
Hutton, Brian, 89
Hyland, Chris, 154

*Independent*, 62, 161
Independent Broadcasting Authority programme on Gibraltar killings, 73–4
Independent International Commission on Decommissioning (IICD), 290, 308, 377, 385–6
Independent Newspaper group, 122
Ingram, Adam, 316
Inis Eoghain, County Donegal, 26, 27
international body on decommissioning, 234–5, 236–7, 244, 247, 265, 296
    negotiations for, 214, 223, 224, 225–9
International Book Fair, 267
internment, 5, 186
    end of (1975), 4
    hints about reintroducing internment leaked, 107, 149
    unionists demand, 258

*Ireland on Sunday*, 338
*Irish America*, 155
   America's Top 100 Irish-Americans, 275
Irish Americans *see* United States of America
Irish government, 28, 35, 94, 98, 118, 125, 163,
   164–5, 171, 174, 181, 182, 186–7, 207, 213–14,
   291–2, 303, 348
   and Anglo-Irish Agreement negotiations, 36–40
   arms raids on republicans (1987), 56
   bans Sinn Féin from New Ireland Forum, 31
   and Brendan Smyth crisis, 196–8
   change of government in 1993, 116
   and Forum for Peace and Reconciliation, 31,
     175–6, 186–7
   and Irish national interests in USA, 152, 153
   and joint declaration negotiations, 105–7, 110,
     112, 117, 120, 122–4, 127, 128, 133–5,
     140–7
   negotiations for restoring ceasefire, 245–7, 257,
     262, 265, 266–7, 270–1, 283, 295–6
   non-paper on proposed all-party talks, 248–51
   Offences against the State Act, 29
   and President Robinson's visit, 130
   secret meetings with Sinn Féin, 80–2
   and visa issue, 178
   *see also* Ahern, Bertie; Bruton, John; Reynolds,
     Albert
Irish language issue, 200, 231, 268, 347, 348, 381
   Sinn Féin paper on, 350
Irish National Liberation Army (INLA), 17, 317, 330
   kill UDA man, 329
   prisoner shoots Wright, 325
*Irish News*, 252, 274
Irish Northern Aid (Noraid), 152, 153, 154, 155
*Irish Press*, 146
Irish Republican Army (IRA), 2, 14, 16, 33, 36, 38–9,
   44, 50, 51, 92, 94, 119, 125–6, 128, 142, 144,
   148, 162, 166–7, 178, 226, 228, 285, 294, 308,
   321, 361, 362, 368, 378, 381
   accused by RUC of shooting drug dealer, 335, 336
   Army Council meet with Sinn Féin, 95–7
   attack Coalisland barracks, 110
   attack Lisburn HQ, 267–8
   attack Loughgall barracks, 54–5
   attacks on British forces when ceasefire ends, 270
   Ballykinlar landmine, 276
   bomb commercial centre of London, 112
   bomb royal Marines Music School, 93
   bomb Shankill Road fish shop, 138, 139
   Canary Wharf bombing, 238
   ceasefires, 29, 143, 385–6
     of 1994, 183, 184–6, 187, 192, 195, 197, 207,
       208, 211, 213, 221, 222, 223–4, 235,
       241
     at Christmas, 100–1, 107, 167
     at Easter, 167–8
     negotiations to restore cessation (1996), 238,
       239, 240–1, 242, 246, 247, 249–50,
       251–2, 257–8, 259, 265–76, 282–3,
       286, 291–2, 295–301
     pre-condition for talks, 116–17, 120–2,
       140–1, 145, 175, 176, 177, 179, 180–3

   restored 1994 ceasefire, 301, 302, 305, 306–7,
     313, 318, 323, 329, 335, 382
   rumours of, 78, 165, 166–7, 171
   truce of 1974, 9, 28, 94, 142
     for US delegation, 155, 156
   Columbian arrests, 381
   decommissioning initiative, 378
   discuss end of cessation with Hume and Adams,
     239, 240–1
   divisions within movement, 317
   Drumboe executions, 119
   end abstentionism in South, 46
   and Enniskillen bombing, 55–6
   failed Hammersmith Bridge bomb, 247
   give verdict on Agreement, 372
   injure Pat Treanor, 172
   intensify war against British forces, 102
   internal tensions, 299
   invites Hume to talks, 42–3
   kill Catholic building contractor, 37
   kill senior UDA members, 171
   landmine attack on RUC barracks (1992), 109
   Lisburn and Tyrone killings of British soldiers, 83
   London to Glasgow rail-line bombs, 276
   Manchester bombing, 257, 258
   meet with Gordon Wilson, 118
   meet with Protestant Church at Feakle, 126
   mortar attack on army base at Osnabrück, 258
   mortar attacks on Heathrow, 165–6
   mortar-bomb 10 Downing Street, 101
   negotiate with Adams and McGuinness, 117–18,
     166, 171, 174–7, 180–3
   oppose Mitchell Principles, 306, 308, 317
   premature explosion on Covent Garden bus, 239
   put arms beyond use, 383, 385–6
   and republican funerals, 52
   refuse to surrender arms, 234
   reject Heads of Agreement paper, 330
   resignations over cessation, 316–17
   response to Gibraltar killings, 60–1
   shooting of RUC officers in Lurgan, 290
   shooting of Wood and Howes, 1, 6, 72–3, 82
   statement on arms, 381–3
   support Hume/Adams initiative, 123, 124, 127,
     132, 134, 144, 147
   Trafalgar Square bomb defused, 239
   unauthorised killing of Garda Jerry McCabe,
     253, 258
   and Warrington bombing, 118
   *see also* decommissioning issue; Gibraltar
     killings; prisoners issue
*Irish Times*, 131, 151, 157, 158
   article by Major in, 249
   Trimble's response to Adams note, 333
*Irish Voice*, 154, 155
*Irish Voice, An*, 316
Irvine, Charlie, 162
Ivers, Eileen, 206

Jameson, Joe, 157
John Paul II, Pope, 13
   visit to Ireland, 30

Joint Declaration *see* Downing Street Declaration
Joint Declaration (April 2003), 380–2, 386–7

Kavanagh, Dr James, 36
Keane, Mairéad, 150, 179, 189, 193, 199, 205, 206, 210, 223, 243, 376
Keenan, Joe, 20–2
Keenan, Sean, 20–2
Kelly, Basil, 89
Kelly, Carol Anne, 11
Kelly, Gerry, 98, 117, 118, 121, 143, 200, 209, 245, 256, 270, 284, 285, 308, 335, 353, 356–7, 359–60
Kelly, Paddy, 241–2, 250, 288
Kennedy, Carolyn, 289
Kennedy, Courtney, 191, 192
Kennedy, Edward, 151, 152, 154, 155, 158, 189, 191, 199, 204, 275, 289, 380
Kennedy, Ethel, 192
Kennedy, John F., 152, 191, 192, 340
Kennedy, John F. Jr, 288–9
Kennedy, Robert, 191
Kennedy Smith, Jean, 155, 179, 180, 204, 247, 289
    endorses visa application, 157–8
Kennedy, Vicky, 191
Kerry, John, 158
King, Larry, 159, 193
King, Peter, 152, 157, 193, 199, 204–5
King, Tom, 57, 89
Kitson, Frank, 84–5, 103
    *Low Intensity Operations*, 84
Knight, Torrens, 264

Labour Committee on Ireland, 17
Lake, Tony, 157, 174, 191, 192, 198, 199, 224–5, 232, 237, 243, 247, 249
La Mon Hotel bombing (Comber), 7
Land League, 151
Largey, Eamonn, 90
Lavery, Bobby, 136–7
Lavery, Martin, 136
Lavery, Sean, 137
Lenihan, Bill, 157
Lennon, Dr James, 36, 37–8, 40
Letterkenny, County Donegal, 171, 174
Lewis, Ed, 243
Libyan arms shipments, 56, 57, 179
Lillis, Michael, 118
Livingstone, Julie, 11
Livingstone, Ken, 17
London
    Adams visits, 198
    bomb explodes prematurely on bus near Covent Garden, 239
    bombs on rail-line to Glasgow, 276
    Canary Wharf bombing, 238
    failed Hammersmith Bridge bomb, 247
    Trafalgar Square bomb defused, 239
Long Kesh H-Blocks, 4, 5, 18, 82, 94, 108, 115, 215, 267, 279, 373
    ANC delegates visit prisoners, 371
    blanket protest, 7–8

escape from H-Blocks, 52
    "gate fever", 364
    loyalist prisoners withdraw support from talks, 327
    Operation Tollan, 276
    prisoners maintain contact with all-party talks, 353
    *see also* hunger strikes
Loughgall barracks, County Tyrone, 54–5, 67
Loughinisland County Down) killings, 172
Loughran, Paddy, 109, 233
Lower Ormeau Residents Action Group (LORAG), 261
Loyal Black Preceptory, 263
loyalist arms factories uncovered, 222
Loyalist Volunteer Force (UVF), 259, 281, 305, 316
    kill Catholic in Portadown, 370
    kill member of GAA, 321
    shoot hotel doorman in Dungannon, 325
Lurgan, County Armagh, 16, 17
    two RUC officers shot dead in, 290
Lynagh, Jim, 54, 67
Lynch, Jack, 47, 48
Lynch, Kevin, 10
Lyne, Roderic, 168, 198
Lyttle, Tommy, 87, 88

Maastricht Treaty, 127, 137
McAleese, Mary, 314–15
McAliskey, Bernadette Devlin, 273
McAliskey, Róisín, 273, 281
    Germany's extradition case, 309, 340
    gives birth to baby girl, 286
    released, 340
McAllister, Jim, 15, 49
McAllister, Ciaran, 103
McAteer, Aidan, 111, 113, 117, 118, 143, 169, 194
McAuley, Chrissie, 115–16, 214, 217, 218–19, 232, 288
McAuley, Richard, 49, 115–16, 143, 172, 189, 190, 193, 199, 205, 206, 209, 210–11, 214, 220, 231, 232, 238, 242, 243, 255, 256, 267, 277, 283, 287, 288, 292, 293, 324, 337, 339, 356, 376
    and Orange march stand-off, 260–1
    visit to Downing Street, 322
MacBradaigh, Bríd, 72–3
MacBradaigh, Caoimhín, 6, 70, 71, 72, 73, 75, 82
McBride, Pat, 109, 233
McBride, Robert, 215, 219
MacBride, Sean, 125
MacBride Principles, 154
McCabe, Brian, 160, 190, 225
McCabe, Garda Jerry, 253, 258, 359, 361, 377
McCabe, Nora, 11, 233
McCann, Dan, 58–9, 60, 61, 62–9, 71, 74
McCann, Fra, 111
McCann, Gerry, 65
McCann, Margaret, 60
McCartney, Bob, 251, 273
McCaughley, Big Eamon, 231, 232, 260, 283, 287, 292, 293, 337, 376
Mac Cionnaith, Breandán, 291

McCracken, Kevin, 67, 70
McCrea, Revd William, 141, 265, 274
McCreesh, Raymond, 10
McCulloch, Maureen and Billy, 91
McDaid, Terence, 89
McDermott, Sean, 59
McDonnell, Arthur, 162
McDonnell, Joe, 10, 12, 23, 68, 72, 289
McDonnell, John, 284
MacDonogh, Steve, 131–2, 267
McElwee, Thomas, 10
McErlean, Thomas, 70, 71
McGeever, Jenny, 64
McGeown, Pat "Beag", 267
McGeown, Pauline, 267
McGirl, John Joe, 46
McGivern, Pat, 232
McGoldrick, Michael, 259
McGrady, Eddie, 78, 83, 246
McGrillen, Charles, 67
McGrory, P.J., 7, 21, 61
    approaches Hume, 43
    and failed compensation claim, 24–5
McGrory, Phyllis, 61
McGuigan, Gerard, 194
McGuinness, Catherine, 196
McGuinness, Dodie, 69–70, 376
McGuinness, Martin, 15, 17, 20, 26, 27, 33, 44, 54,
    63, 64, 67, 71, 104, 139, 142, 143, 144, 156,
    167, 168, 184, 185, 202, 206, 207, 208, 209,
    213, 220, 222–3, 248, 250, 259, 262, 274, 277,
    315–16, 372, 376
    and Adams are refused entry to Stormont talks,
        254–6
    and Adams negotiate with IRA, 117–18, 166,
        171, 174–7, 180–3
    in all-party talks, 302, 304, 312–13, 333, 335,
        343, 344, 345, 348, 352, 356, 357, 359, 360,
        361, 363, 366, 367
    banned from Westminster, 282, 283–4
    challenges Speaker's ruling in court, 304–5
    dialogue with British government, 94–7, 98, 117,
        121
    discusses decommissioning body with Ancram,
        226–7
    on executive, 378
    and IRA statement on arms, 381–3
    leads Sinn Féin delegation for talks at Stormont,
        200–1
    meets with Connolly House group, 179–80
    meets with international body on
        decommissioning, 234–5
    meets with Martin Mansergh, 113, 169
    meets with third Stevens Inquiry, 90
    negotiations to restore cessation, 291–2, 295,
        296, 298–9, 300
    rapport with Reynolds, 197
    on reinstatement of IRA cessation, 249–50
    shares keynote address at Ard Fheis, 370
    in South Africa, 287
    Speakers Corner speech, 332
    in USA, 305
    visits to Downing Street, 322–4, 330
    visit to Westminster before ban takes effect,
        283–4
McKee, Wilma, 138
McKenna, Finbar, 53
McKenna, Sean, 9, 10
Mackin, Sean, 189
McKnight, Sean, 18
McLaren, Robert see Ferguson, Colin
McLaughlin, Mary, 26
McLaughlin, Mitchel, 27, 44, 49, 51, 75, 98, 117,
    126, 148, 211, 245, 310, 343–4, 365, 376
McLaughlin, Raymond, 26
McLaverty, Michael, 130
McManus, Sean, 200, 209
McMichael, Gary, 211, 321, 360
McNally, Lawrence, 102
McPeake family, 131
McPolin, Kevin, 70
Magennis, Peter, 11
Maghaberry prison, 371, 373
Maghera killing, 329
Maginn, Loughlin, 88, 89
Maginnis, Ken, 133, 160, 193, 268, 320, 332, 379
    on Larry King Show, 304
    reads "Notice of Indictment", 308
Maguire, Sean, 131
Maharaj, Mac, 371
Mahoney, Fr Stephen, 41
Major, John, 89, 104, 110, 112, 113, 117, 119, 122,
    124, 128, 130, 161, 162, 168, 169, 186, 188–9,
    196, 197, 198, 201–2, 203, 208, 214, 242, 243,
    250, 252, 254, 264, 266, 267, 282, 291, 297,
    341
    Adams writes to, 99, 167–8
    announces date for all-party talks, 239
    and Downing Street Declaration, 147–50, 157,
        163
    and Framework Document, 202
    general election (1997), 276, 278
    and Hume/Adams initiative, 127–8, 133, 135,
        137, 140–5, 146
    lifts broadcasting restrictions, 188
    on Mitchell Report, 236–7
    negotiations to restore ceasefire, 266, 268–9, 270,
        271–2, 273, 274, 276
    parliamentary majority reduced, 235–6
    publishes article clarifying the Declaration for
        unionists, 148–9
    publishes proposals for Forum elections, 244
    reaction to Canary Wharf bombing, 238–9
    stalls on negotiations for all-party talks, 222,
        223–4, 226, 228, 237
Makem, Tommy, 209
Mallie, Eamonn, 141, 339
Mallon, Seamus, 36, 37, 39–40, 45, 73, 75, 76, 79,
    186, 322, 345
    Deputy First Minister, 377, 379
Manchester bombing (Arndale Centre), 257, 258
Mandela, Nelson, 97, 185, 189, 215, 216, 218, 223,
    292, 371, 378, 380
    Adams meets with, 219–20

Mansergh, Martin, 81, 105, 106, 113, 118, 187, 242, 275–6, 291–2, 296, 314
Manton, Tom, 152, 157, 204
Manuel, Virginia, 199
Markethill (County Armagh) explosion, 307–8
Marley, Kathleen, 53
Marley, Larry, 52, 53
Martinez, Val, 158
Maskey, Alex, 18, 286, 363
Mason, Roy, 279
Mates, Michael, 193, 245
Maudsley Psychiatric Hospital, 309
Mayer, Roelf, 216
Mayhew, Sir Patrick, 89, 112, 117, 118–19, 122, 134, 140, 141, 142–3, 144, 163, 196, 202, 203–4, 207, 208, 220, 222–3, 235, 237–8, 241, 245, 251, 252, 253, 255, 263, 268, 270
    Coleraine speech, 115–16, 128
    meeting with Adams at Washington conference, 208, 209–12, 213
    "Washington 3", 225, 227
    replies to Adams' five questions, 274
Mbeki, Thabo, 215, 380
Meagher, Fr Brendan, 9–10
Meaney, Colm, 194
Meissner, Chuck, 199, 209
Methodist Church, 126
Meyer, Pedro, 194
MI5, 17, 93, 302, 385
Middle East peace process, 2, 50
Military Reconnaissance (or Reaction) Force (MRF), 85
Milltown Cemetery, 192, 289
    massacre, 1, 68–73, 88
Mitchell, George, 199, 209, 224, 229, 234–5, 236, 245–6, 247, 252, 256–7, 376, 378
    chairs all-party talks, 257, 258, 266, 270, 290, 303, 306, 307, 308, 319–20, 321, 325, 328, 332, 333, 334, 340–1, 344, 345, 346, 348, 349, 350, 362–7
    draft paper, 353, 354, 355, 356, 357, 362
    death of brother, Robbie, 263
Mitchell Report, 236–7, 243, 244, 248, 290, 296
    Principles, 236, 243, 244, 248, 249, 257, 265, 269, 317, 335
        endorsed by Sinn Féin, 250, 298, 306
        flouted by unionists, 263
Molloy, Francie, 50
Molyneaux, James, 44, 92, 93, 143, 148, 159, 185, 263
Moore, Marie, 49, 126
Moosa, Valli, 371
Moran, Tom, 156
Morrison, Bruce, 154, 157, 160, 179, 233
Morrison, Danny, 8, 15, 17, 24, 27, 54, 60, 61, 71, 75
"Mountain Climber", 9–10
Mowlam, Mo, 275, 276, 279, 280, 283, 285, 291, 294, 303, 304, 312, 318, 322, 323, 329, 335–6, 338, 359
    invites Sinn Féin to participate in plenary sessions, 305
    persuades loyalist prisoners to back talks, 327

    retires from British parliament, 379
    role in all-party talks, 352–3
    transfers six republican prisoners, 372
Moynihan, Daniel, 152, 158
Mtintso, Thenjiwe, 369–70, 371
Mulligan, Kevin, 67
Mulvenna, Paddy, 184
Mulvenna, Patrick, 113, 184
Murphy, Des, 318
Murphy, Lenny, 16
Murphy, Mick, 363
Murphy, Paul, 304, 322, 348
Murray, Bob, 20–2
Murray, John, 70, 71
Murray, Leanne, 138
Murray, Fr Raymond, 69
Murray, Sean, 65
Mutual of America Life Insurance Company, 156

Nally, Dermot, 106
National Committee on American Foreign Policy, 156
    Waldorf Astoria conference, 159
Nationalist Party, 75, 82
Neal, Richard, 152, 157, 189, 204
Nelson, Brian, 85–7, 88, 112, 231, 313–14, 329
    death of, 380
    released from prison, 264
    ships arms from South Africa, 86–7
    talks to Stevens Inquiry, 88–9
    trial of, 89–90
Nesbitt, Dermott, 367
Newell, Ken, 50
New Ireland Forum, 31
    report, 34, 36, 57
News of the World, 186
New York Times, 158
Nicholson, Jim, 40
Noraid see Irish Northern Aid
Northern Ireland Office (NIO), 24, 25, 110, 117, 141, 193, 198, 207, 223, 245, 255, 256, 280, 304, 312, 314, 350–1, 359
North–South institutions, 316, 329, 330–1, 332–3, 334, 337, 338–9, 341, 345–6, 347, 348, 350, 355, 358, 377, 381, 383
Nugent, Kieran, 11–12

Oatley, Michael, 93, 94, 95, 97, 104
Ó Brádaigh, Ruairí, 9, 19, 20
    and abstentionism issue, 45
O'Brien, Edward, 239
Observer, 133, 207
Ó Caoláin, Caoimhghín, 211, 286, 287, 304, 305, 356, 376
O'Clery, Conor, 151, 157
Ó Conaill, Dáithí, 47
O'Connell, Joe, 372
O'Connor, Garrett, 194
O'Connor, Tim, 187
Odling-Smee, William, 26–7
O'Dowd, Niall, 154, 155–7, 158–9, 191, 233, 275
O'Duill, Piaras, 64

O'Dwyer, Ella, 264
O'Dwyer, Michael, 109, 233
O'Dwyer, Paul, 152, 154, 160, 309
Ó Fiaich, Cardinal Tomas, 8, 29, 34, 35, 36, 41
O'Hagan, Bernard, 105
O'Hanlon, John, 187
O'Hanlon, Siobhán, 111, 112, 117, 143, 200, 202,
    206, 207, 209, 256, 283, 304, 312, 322, 358,
    363–4, 365, 366
    exchange with Quentin Thomas, 280–1
    stopped and searched by RUC, 313
O'Hara, Patsy, 10
O'Hare, Rita, 27, 186, 214, 217, 218, 235, 262, 269,
    271, 275, 288, 348
Ó hEara, Gerry, 49
Ó hUiginn, Seán, 106, 187, 225
Omagh bombing, 377
O'Malley, Des, 258
O'Neill, Diarmuid, 266
O'Neill, Tip, 152
Orange Order marches, 196, 220, 246, 259–62,
    263–4, 285, 288, 291, 292–4, 338, 375, 377,
    386
    Drumcree, 222, 296, 297
        stand-off, 259–60
    Garvaghy Road, Portadown, 222, 240, 259, 260,
        263, 285, 291, 292–3, 294, 297, 377
    lower Ormeau Road, 222, 259, 260–2, 285, 297,
        377
    rerouting of some contentious parades, 297
Osnabrück army base attacked, 258, 273

Paisley, Ian, 44, 93, 159, 185, 244, 254, 256, 257,
    263, 270, 278, 287, 291, 308, 322, 375, 378,
    384, 386
    demands Sinn Féin's expulsion from talks, 307,
        308
    "Save Ulster Campaign", 150
    triumphalist dance after Garvaghy Road march,
        222, 224, 259
Parks, Rosa, 190, 199
Parry, Timothy, 118
partition, 27, 30, 32, 82, 84, 123, 151, 175, 354
Pataki, George, 243
Patten, Chris, 377
Patten Commission, 380
peace convention proposal, 123–4
Peace People, 156
Peake, Martin, 221
Penn, Sean, 194
"Persuading the British – a Joint Call", 77
Peters, Maryann, 243
Philippines, 41
Phosa, Matthew, 371
plastic and rubber bullets, 11, 53, 72, 93, 131, 233,
    260, 294
pogroms of 1969, 6, 60
Poland, 97
policing issue, 268, 313, 324, 329, 333, 345, 346, 347,
    349, 355, 356, 377, 380, 381
Pope, Martha, 199, 235, 270, 366
Portlaoise prison, 94, 353

ANC delegates visit prisoners, 371–2
Powell, Enoch, 92
Powell, Jonathan, 322, 352
power-sharing executive, 315–16, 329, 330, 334, 337,
    338–9, 341, 345, 346–7, 349, 357, 358, 372,
    380, 387
    1996 elections, 244, 251, 254, 255
        as pre-condition, 236–7, 243, 245
    British government stop elections, 383, 385, 387
    elections for, 375–6, 377
    repeated suspensions, 378
    Sinn Féin agrees to enter, 246
    Sinn Féin boycotts first meeting, 257
Poyntzpass (County Armagh) killings, 337
Presbyterian Church, 126
Prevention of Terrorism Act (PTA), 17, 83, 135
prisoners
    early release issue, 123, 150, 200, 201, 221, 222,
        318, 322, 329, 337, 338, 341, 348, 350, 356,
        359–61, 377, 381
    ill-treatment of, 240, 241–2, 276, 279, 281, 309
    released on parole for Ard Fheis, 373
    Saoirse campaign, 312, 318
    Sinn Féin campaign for, 8–9, 10
    strip-searching, 60, 152, 273
    transferral from Britain to Ireland, 281, 372
    see also Armagh women's prison; hunger strikes;
        Long Kesh H Blocks
Progressive Unionist Party (PUP), 211, 251, 265,
    266, 303, 305, 306, 320–1, 360
    assembly elections, 377
    threaten to pull out of talks, 327

Queen's University, Belfast, 63
Quinn, John, 368

Radio Telefís Éireann (RTÉ), 43, 64, 164
Ramaphosa, Cyril, 215, 371
Ramsay, Sue, 353, 358, 362, 363–4, 366
Real IRA, 317
Redemptorist Order, 5, 75, 81, 113
Rees, Merlyn, 279
Reid, Fr Alec ("the Sagart"), 5–6, 7, 8, 9, 13–15, 16,
    17, 27, 29–30, 33, 34, 35–7, 39–40, 41, 51, 53,
    57, 69, 73, 80, 94, 95, 96, 97, 101, 106, 110,
    112, 113, 118, 120, 125, 134–5, 142, 156, 176,
    187, 234, 300, 314, 338, 349, 366, 369, 380
    arranges meeting between Sinn Féin and SDLP,
        75–6
    letter to Irish Times, 98
    negotiates with Haughey, 47–8
    negotiates with Hume, 42, 43
    negotiates for visa for Joe Cahill, 178–9
    "Proposal for a Democratic Over All Political
        and Diplomatic Strategy for Justice, Peace
        and Reconciliation", 105
    sends his proposals to the IRA, 36
Reilly, Karen, 221
Reilly, Thomas "Kidso", 76
Relatives' Action Committees, 8, 115
Reno, Janet, 158, 159
Renwick, Robin, 160, 210

403

Republican Sinn Féin, 47
Reynolds, Albert, 110, 111, 112–13, 116, 124, 128,
    130, 134, 135, 137, 146, 155, 169, 175, 178,
    179, 180, 183, 207
  Brussels statement (1993), 140
  and Downing Street Declaration, 147–50
    provides clarification of, 163
  endorses visa application, 157–8
  meeting with Hume and Adams (1994), 186–7,
    188
  and presidential election, 314
  resigns, 196–7, 198
  "Steps Envisaged", 123–4
Reynolds, Fr Gerry, 15, 35, 42, 50
Reynolds, Kathleen, 197
Rice, Angela, 250
Rising of 1798, 337
Rising Sun bar (Greysteel) attack, 139, 145, 264
Riverdance, 244
Robertson, George, 62
Robinson, Mary
  visits the North, 128–31, 230, 315
Robinson, Peter, 133, 287, 314
Romero, Fr Rudy, 41
Rooney, Kevin, 21–2
Royal Black Institution, 220
Royal Marines Music School (Deal), 93
Royal Ulster Constabulary (RUC), 11, 20, 84, 89, 91,
    93, 101, 102, 104, 113, 137, 158, 163, 165,
    169–70, 188, 214, 221, 232, 233, 255, 259, 279,
    281, 285, 313, 325, 330, 335, 337, 338, 341,
    345, 385
  accuses IRA of shooting drug dealer, 335
  Anderstown barracks, 293
  attack civil rights demonstration, 83
  attack republican funerals, 52–5, 72
  ban the children's carnival, 291
  baton nationalist children in protest march, 196
  Coalisland barracks ambush, 110
  escalate harassment after IRA cessation, 208
  and Gibraltar funerals, 63–70, 71
  infiltrate loyalist paramilitary groups, 85
  invasion of Derry repulsed, 20
  Markethill explosion, 307–8
  and murder of Pat Finucane, 87–8, 90
  officer kills Sinn Féin workers, 109
  and Orange Order marches, 222, 260–2, 291,
    292–4
  raids on Catholics, 269–70
  role in Adams murder bid, 20–3, 24, 84
  "shoot-to-kill" policy, 16–17, 76, 83, 235
  treatment of IRA suspects at Castlereagh, 102–3
  UN demands inquiry into harassment of defence
    lawyers by, 346
  workers killed while refurbishing barracks, 109
RTÉ see Radio Telefís Éireann
Ryan, Pete, 102

St Agnes' Choral Society, 131
Saloojee, Yusof, 215
Sands, Bobby, 9, 10, 11, 12, 14, 55, 68, 215, 279, 289
SAS (Special Air Service), 72, 166, 170, 279

and Adams murder bid, 24
and Loughgall barracks attack, 54, 55
Savage, Sean, 59, 60, 61, 62–9, 71, 74
Scenario for Peace, 51, 52, 53, 92
SDLP see Social Democratic and Labour Party
Shankill Butchers, 16
Sheen, Martin, 194
Simpson, Alistair, 263
Simpson, Charles, 86
Sinn Féin, 17, 37, 39, 45–7, 49–50, 120, 133, 135,
    138, 148, 149, 150, 152–3, 272
  accept Agreement, 366–7
  Adams elected president of, 20
  alter constitution for entry to assembly, 372–3
  Ard Fheis of 1994, 163–5
  Ard Fheis at Ambassador Cinema (1996), 244–5
  Ard Fheis in Monaghan (1997), 277
  Ard Fheis in RDS (1998), 369–70, 371, 372–4
  "Building a Permanent Peace in Ireland", 235
  car bomb left outside Sinn Féin office, 276
  Connolly House rally, 184–5
  draft statement to restore peace process, 264,
    265
  election campaign of 1997, 272–3, 274, 275,
    276–8, 283, 384
  electoral strategy, 15–16, 17–19, 38, 57
  Foreign Affairs Bureau, 153
  growth of, 383, 384–5
  holds demonstrations to save the peace process,
    226
  Letterkenny conference, 171–2, 174
  local elections (1985), 35
  local elections (1997), 283, 284, 285–6
  loyalists attack march into Belfast City, 170
  loyalists attempt to bomb advice centre, 136
  meeting at Stormont Castle, 284–5
  meetings with grassroots activists, 318
  need to reach out to unionists, 299–300, 313, 332
  New Ireland policy, 19, 28
  office workers killed by RUC officer, 109
  Peace Commission report, 172
  "Peace in Ireland: An Agenda for Change", 304
  peace strategy, 14–15, 31, 32–3, 51, 75, 79, 94,
    107, 167, 238, 245, 296, 299, 310, 317
  prisoners' campaign, 8–9, 10
  proposal that Northern MPs can sit in Dáil, 337,
    369
  radical overhaul, 9
  releases record of exchanges with British, 143–4
  resignations over peace process, 317
  submits document to two governments (2002),
    381
  talks with British, 115–17, 140–5
  talks with unionists, 125–7, 245
Sisulu, Walter, 215, 218
Sky Television, 185, 186, 293
Slane, John, 276
Sloan, Gerard, 89
Slovo, Joe, 218
Smith, Hughie, 321
Smyth, Fr Brendan, 197
Smyth, Revd Martin, 246, 263

Social Democratic and Labour Party (SDLP), 17,
    31, 35, 36–8, 39–40, 41–5, 55, 57, 73, 75–80,
    82, 83, 82, 83, 102, 110, 127, 162, 164, 186,
    236, 245, 246, 251, 280, 281, 341, 379, 383
    in all-party talks, 303, 306, 321–2, 343, 345, 347,
        349, 350, 357, 358
    assembly issue, 315–16, 334
    claim British neutrality, 76–7
    election campaign of 1997, 272–3, 274, 277
    on executive, 377, 378
    internal difficulties, 174–5
    join Policing Board, 380
    local government elections, 285
    loyalist attacks on homes of members, 168
    meetings with Sinn Féin, 75–9, 80, 93, 105, 120
    policy, 77–8, 80
    and presidential campaign, 315
    tactical voting strategy in 1992 election, 111
    withdraw from Forum, 257
    see also Hume, John
Soderberg, Nancy, 154, 157, 158–9, 174, 191, 192,
    199, 224, 243
    visits Ireland, 226
South Africa, 2, 50, 51, 86, 97–8, 103, 105, 135, 152,
    169, 185, 211, 256, 292, 300, 310, 332, 370,
    371
    Adams visits, 214–20
    arms shipments from, 86–7, 91, 139, 162
    conference on conflict resolution, 287
    Major visits, 188–9
    and Rugby World Cup, 217
    see also ANC
South Armagh Farmers and Residents Committee,
    318–19
"Southern California IRA" bomb threats, 158–9
Spence, Gusty, 320–1
Spring, Dick, 116, 130, 134, 135, 197, 222, 235, 237,
    241, 252, 253, 259
    "principles", 139–40
    proposes George Mitchell to chair the all-party
        talks, 245–6
    suggests Dayton-style talks, 237–8
    suggests an international commission on arms,
        214
Springhill Community House Education
    Development Project, 5
Stalker-Sampson report, 76
Standing Advisory Commission on Human Rights
    (SACHR), 347
Staunton, Ciaran, 155, 157, 189, 199, 206
Staunton, Orlaith, 155
Sterrit, David, 230
Stevens, Jonathan, 207
Stevens (John) Inquiry, 88–9, 90, 91
    Report (April 2003), 385
Stobie, William, 88
Stone, Michael, 69–70, 71, 88
Strabane, County Tyrone, 53
Straw, Jack, 340
*Street and Other Stories, The*, 128, 232
    RTE court case over ad, 131–2
*Sunday Independent*, 131, 146

*Sunday Observer*, 141
*Sunday Times*, 160, 194
*Sunday World*, 270

Tambo, Adelaide, 217
Tambo, Oliver, 217
Taylor, John, 133, 137, 162, 236, 256, 355, 379
Teahon, Paddy, 187, 225
Thain, Ian, 76
Thatcher, Margaret, 10, 31–2, 34, 36, 38, 44, 73, 82,
    93, 97, 128, 143, 189, 279, 368
    forced to resign, 98–9
    introduces media ban on Sinn Féin, 83
Third World debt, 339–40
32 County Sovereignty Movement, 317
Thomas, Quentin, 117, 198, 200, 201, 207, 280–1,
    285, 290, 291, 292, 295, 297, 322
Thompson, Harry, 90
Thompson, Kathleen, 90
*Times, The*, 61
Tomlinson, Mike, 188
*Towards a Lasting Peace in Ireland*, 108–9
*Towards a Strategy for Peace*, 77
Trainor, Damien, 337
Treanor, Pat, 172, 178, 180
Treaty (1921), 322, 346
Trimble, David, 228, 244, 256, 263, 268, 278, 280,
    285, 291, 304, 305, 327, 332, 339, 340, 355,
    379, 385, 386
    all-party talks, 307, 311, 320, 322, 324–5, 327,
        349, 350, 360, 363, 364–6
    accepts Agreement, 367, 370, 383
    demands Sinn Féin's expulsion, 308, 316,
        335
    elected First Minister, 377
    elected leader of UUP, 224
    meets with Billy Wright, 259
    offers a deal to SDLP, 341
    proposes elections for an assembly, 236, 246
    responds to Adams note through *Irish Times*, 333
    shakes Adams' hand, 379
    triumphalist dance after Garvaghy Road march,
        222, 224, 259
    wants verification committee, 266
Tutu, Desmond, 105, 185
twin track process, 226, 227, 228, 229, 231, 233, 235,
    237
Tyrie, Andy, 86

UK Unionist Party (UKUP), 251, 270, 273
    refuse to attend all-party talks, 257, 303, 304,
        306, 308
Ulster Defence Association (UDA), 24, 65, 67, 70,
    85, 86, 87–8, 89, 137, 138, 211, 251, 276, 287,
    316, 319, 325–6, 335
    assembly elections, 377
    attack on Lavery home, 136–7
    attack on Rising Sun bar, 139, 145
    breaches of ceasefire, 329, 330
    Connolly House attacks, 162–3, 179
    doomsday scenario, 150
    Ormeau Road betting shop killings, 109–10, 171

Ulster Defence Association (*cont.*)
  restoration of ceasefire, 332
  senior members killed by IRA, 171
Ulster Defence Regiment (UDR), 16, 55, 76, 89
Ulster Democratic Party (UDP), 211, 251, 265, 266,
    287, 303, 306, 308, 321, 360
  expulsion issue, 330, 331, 332
Ulster Freedom Fighters (UFF), 86
Ulster Resistance, 86
Ulster Television, 251
Ulster Unionist Party (UUP), 40, 44, 58, 92, 93,
    127, 133, 143, 148, 159, 160, 162, 193, 202,
    224, 236, 237, 241, 246, 251, 263, 266, 273,
    276, 278, 280, 286, 375, 381, 385, 386
  and all-party talks, 303, 304, 305, 306, 307, 308,
    316, 321–2, 325, 326, 332, 333, 334, 355,
    357, 358, 363, 364, 365–6
  on executive, 377, 378
  support Trimble on Agreement, 370, 382–3
  *see also* Trimble, David
Ulster Volunteer Force (UVF), 16, 84, 85, 86, 87,
    211, 222, 251, 259, 320, 377
  blockade Catholic Masses, 266, 269
  Drumbeg mobile shop killing, 102
  kill Roseanne Mallon, 169–70
  tensions with LVF, 305, 316
unionists
  campaign of intimidation by paramilitaries,
    259–60, 263, 276, 304, 319, 329, 377, 386
  commence talking to Sinn Féin, 379
  lose control of Belfast City Council, 285–6
  prevent establishment of executive, 377
  protest against Anglo-Irish Agreement, 40, 92,
    93
  refuse to talk to Sinn Féin, 125–7, 311, 318, 321,
    327, 332, 336, 337, 339, 340, 357, 363, 365,
    367, 374–5
  reject joint paper on decommissioning, 266
  response to Hume–Adams talks, 57–8
  tensions between paramilitary organisations,
    305, 316, 319
United Nations, 346
United States of America (USA), 50, 106, 107, 118,
    120, 125, 134, 151–61, 176, 177, 178–9, 182,
    223, 224, 245, 257, 283, 292, 296, 300, 305,
    380
  Arlington, 192
  Civil Rights Movement, 190, 199
  Foreign Agents Act, 200
  forum on Irish issues in Sheraton Hotel, 153
  Hickory Hill, 191–2
  immigration reform movement, 155
  lifts ban on contact with Sinn Féin, 192
  Oklahoma bombing, 208–9
  peace envoy idea, 155
  response to end of IRA cessation, 242–3

Sinn Féin and fundraising in, 189, 199–200, 203,
    204, 209, 305
  Sinn Féin party political broadcast by Ulster
    Television to, 251
  visits by Adams to, 159–60, 189–94, 196, 198,
    199–200, 203–6, 209–11, 213, 224–5, 237,
    242–4, 289, 339–40
    St Patrick's Day celebrations, 242, 243–4,
      337
    speaking tour, 208–11
  Washington office for Sinn Féin, 179, 189, 193,
    200, 204, 206
  White House Conference on Trade and
    Investment in Ireland, 208–12
  *see also* Clinton, Bill; Connolly House group;
    visa issue
USSR, 2, 97, 135

Vargo, Trina, 158
Very Special Arts programme, 155
Vietnam war, 192
Viljoen, Constand, 215–16
Vinegar Hill, County Wexford, 337
visa issue, 150, 153, 154, 157, 159, 176, 178, 179,
    180, 189, 203, 204

Walesa, Lech, 97
Warrenpoint (County Down) explosion, 319
Warrington bombing, 118
Washington "principles", 203–4
Waterstones Bookshop, 198, 267
Webb, Jack, 194
Weir, Revd Jack, 126
Westmacott, Peter, 210
Whitelaw, William, 17
Whitemoor prison, 309
Whitters, Paul, 11
Williams, Tom, 113, 179
Wilson, Fr Des, 5, 6, 7, 8, 15, 30, 35, 125, 338, 380
Wilson, Gordon, 118
Wilson, Marie, 118
Wilson, Pádraig, 353, 373
Wolfe Tone, Theobald, 9
Women's Coalition, 251, 303
  assembly elections, 377
Wood, Derek, 6, 73
Woods, Donald, 51
Wright, Billy ("King Rat"), 169–70, 259, 305
  death threat against, 265
  shot by INLA, 325
Wright, Dick, 86
Wright, Margaret, 168

Ziff, Trisha, 194
Zimbabwe, 331
Zuma, Jacob, 215